Corruption, Integrity and Law Enforcement

Corruption, Integrity and Law Enforcement

Edited by

Cyrille Fijnaut

and

Leo Huberts

KLUWER LAW INTERNATIONAL
THE HAGUE / LONDON / NEW YORK

Published by:
Kluwer Law International
P.O. Box 85889, 2508 CN The Hague, The Netherlands
sales@kli.wkap.nl
http://www.kluwerlaw.com

Sold and Distributed in North, Central and South America by:
Kluwer Law International
101 Philip Drive, Norwell, MA 02061, USA
kluwerlaw@wkap.com

Sold and Distributed in all other countries by:
Kluwer Law International
Distribution Centre, P.O. Box 322, 3300 AH Dordrecht, The Netherlands

A CIP Catalogue record for this book is available from the Library of Congress

Printed on acid-free paper.

Typeset by *Steve Lambley Information Design*, The Hague.

ISBN 90-411-1866-7
© 2002 Kluwer Law International

Kluwer Law International incorporates the imprint of Martinus Nijhoff Publishers

Foreword

"A Global Forum on Corruption", hosted by United States Vice President Al Gore, took place in Washington between 24 and 26 February 1999. The conference stemmed from the security policy that the Clinton administration had outlined in its International Crime Control Strategy. This strategy plan embraced the notion that the integrity of public officials, particularly in the police and the judiciary, forms the foundation for maintaining the rule of law and democracy, and ensuring free markets. The main purpose of the forum was therefore to convince governments around the world of the need to fight corruption amongst officials and to give them ideas on how to tackle the problem. The conference was attended by delegations from many countries, representatives from a wide range of international and regional institutions and a few individual academics. The conclusion of the forum was a series of Guiding Principles for Fighting Corruption and Safeguarding Integrity among Justice and Security Officials.

During the conference the Dutch Government gave an undertaking to organise a second Global Forum on Fighting Corruption and Safeguarding Integrity. It kept its word and on 28–31 May 2001 the second forum was held in The Hague. This time the starting point was:

> "The fight against corruption and the promotion of integrity are themes of relevance to all of us. Corruption is a phenomenon that not only undermines economic growth and trade, but it also tends to hit hardest the most vulnerable groups in our societies, since they lack the means to obtain the necessary goods and services in a corrupt environment. In this regard, preventive measures promoting integrity are just as relevant as aspects of criminal law and law enforcement."

In keeping with this statement the papers and discussions at the forum centred around five themes: "integrity and governance", "law enforcement", "customs", "corruption, transition and development" and "government and the business sector". This second conference was also attended by delegations from nearly every country

Cyrille Fijnaut, Leo Huberts (eds.), *Corruption, Integrity and Law Enforcement*, v-vi
©2002 Kluwer Law International, The Hague. Printed in The Netherlands.

in the world and by representatives of all major international and regional institutions. Many individual experts also took part in the five workshops organised on the themes mentioned. The third conference will be held in Seoul, Korea, in 2003.

This book contains most of the papers presented during the workshop on law enforcement. We felt it was necessary to publish these papers because together they clearly illustrate the way in which the problems of corruption and integrity in the field of law enforcement are of importance worldwide. Not just in the West, as might be expected, but also in eastern, northern and southern parts of the globe. Not just at international and regional institution level, but also at individual country level. And not just in academic research, but also in everyday life. Precisely because of this versatility we feel that this book enriches the literature available on the subject; it was therefore an extremely worthwhile exercise asking the speakers to prepare the text of their papers for publication. We are very grateful to them for doing it so well and within such a short time. Our general introduction includes the full text of the conclusions of the discussions during this workshop.

We would like to take this opportunity to thank Stan Dessens, Jan van de Heuvel and Bernard Oosterop of the Dutch Ministry of Justice for their help in preparing this book for publication. We are also grateful to Iris Van den Hauten-Hinnen and Carla Maas, both from this same ministry, for providing secretarial assistance in the organisation of the workshop.

Steve Lambley took on much of the editing work. We consider ourselves fortunate that we did not hesitate to go along with the suggestion of Lindy Melman, publisher at Kluwer Law International, to join forces with this talented designer. We would also like to thank her for the effective and pleasant way in which she oversaw publication of this book.

Cyrille Fijnaut and Leo Huberts
Tilburg – Amsterdam, January 2002

Table of Contents

Part IV Legal Instruments and Institutions

Part V Independent Institutions

PART I

INTRODUCTION

CHAPTER 1

Corruption, Integrity and Law Enforcement

Cyrille Fijnaut and Leo Huberts

1. Introduction

Corruption, ethics and integrity have become more important issues in the practice and theory of politics, public administration, law, economics and society. As a consequence, corruption and integrity nowadays are significant topics for law enforcement organisations. Two aspects can be distinguished. First, the role law enforcement organisations play in the struggle against corruption in society; and secondly, the corruption and integrity problem in police, public prosecution and judicial organisations themselves. Both aspects of "corruption, integrity and law enforcement" are discussed in this volume.

This introductory chapter puts the different contributions in context.

First, we will briefly discuss the meaning of concepts such as corruption, ethics and integrity (§ 2), the extent of the problem (§ 3), the causes and levels of corruption in different nations, and the solutions proposed to curb corruption and to safeguard integrity (§ 4). The description illustrates the broadness of the problem and it presents a framework in which law enforcement efforts have to be seen.

Secondly, we focus on the law enforcement sector which is relevant for the struggle against corruption (§ 5). Integrity of the law enforcement system appears to be a crucial element in anti-corruption strategies in developing countries as well as developed countries.

Thirdly, we point at the results of the Second Global Forum against Corruption and Safeguarding Integrity, held in The Hague in May 2001 (§ 6). The outcome of various workshop sessions on corruption and law enforcement were summarised in a specific report. Its definitive text is published in full in this introduction. This report offers a sketch of the main issues signalled at that Conference.

Finally, § 7 of this chapter introduces the rest of the book. Each part of the book consists of papers from academics and practitioners and its content can be seen as a state of the art on the different subjects. Part II presents brief descriptions of the

Cyrille Fijnaut, Leo Huberts (eds.), *Corruption, Integrity and Law Enforcement*, 3-34
©2002 Kluwer Law International, The Hague. Printed in The Netherlands.

corruption problem in three countries, which is followed by chapters in which special attention is being paid to available corruption and integrity in the law enforcement system (Part III), chapters about the legal instruments and institutions (Part IV) and more specifically the independent institutions and commissions (Part V) that are operating in several countries. Reflections on anti-corruption strategies can be found in Part VI. Part VII focuses on the international organisations and institutions involved in the struggle against corruption. Finally, Part VIII looks at some of the global initiatives taken to combat corruption.

2. Corruption, ethics and integrity

Clarity about concepts like corruption, ethics and integrity is important, certainly when it concerns public debate, policy-making and theory development on an international level. At the same time it is clear that we are discussing phenomena whose content will always be contested. Let us summarise a number of aspects.

Public corruption is often defined as involving behaviour on the part of officials in the public sector, whether politicians or civil servants, in which they improperly and unlawfully enrich themselves, or those associated with them, by the misuse of the public power entrusted to them. A briefer definition is the abuse of public office for private gain. In this more narrow definition, corruption is a specific type of violation against the moral norms and values for political and administrative behaviour. Broader interpretations focus on corruption as synonym for all violations of the moral norms and values. Then it is identical to the concept of "integrity", a concept which has become more prominent in the discussion in many (developed) countries.

Public integrity denotes the quality of acting in accordance with the moral values, norms and rules accepted by the body politic and the public. A number of integrity violations or forms of public misconduct can be distinguished: corruption including bribery, nepotism, cronyism, patronage; fraud and theft; conflict of interest through assets, jobs, gifts; manipulation of information; discrimination and sexual harassment; improper methods for noble causes (using immoral means to achieve moral ends); the waste and abuse of resources; and private time misconduct.

It is important to realise that both conceptions of corruption are present in the international discussion: corruption as the umbrella concept, covering all or most types of integrity violation or unethical behaviour and corruption as a type of integrity violation (misuse of public power for private benefit). In both interpretations, a point for debate is what are relevant "morals" or "ethics"?

Public ethics might be defined as the collection of values and norms in the public sector, functioning as standards or yardsticks for assessing the integrity of one's conduct. The *moral* nature of these principles refers to what is judged as right, just, or good conduct. *Values* are principles or standards of behaviour that should have a certain weight in choice of action (what is good to do, or bad to refrain from doing). *Norms* state what is morally correct behaviour in a certain situation. Values and norms guide the choice of action and provide a moral basis for justifying or evaluating what we do.

In the international community there are clear differences of opinion about the content of public ethics. Although organisations like Transparency International argue that cultural relativism concerning corruption should be out of the question, it is undeniable that cultures, religions and ideologies differ in their appreciation of values and norms. It will be inevitable and necessary to continue the discussion about the "Standards in Public Life" with values as selflessness, integrity, objectivity, accountability, openness and transparency, honesty and leadership.[1] This public life is national as well as international, and the development of international anti-bribery conventions and laws shows a development in the direction of common standards. These are criticised by some as morally imperialistic and dangerous intrusions into the affairs of other nations, but this contradicts the dominant perspective on corruption: "Anti-bribery laws are legally and ethically unremark-able, and no evidence supports a claim they are considered intrusive or generate hostility" (Nichols, 2000, p. 655).

3. Extent of the problem

Empirical research by social scientists on the extent of public corruption and fraud is by definition complicated. Corruption is crime without a (recognisable) victim and the corruptor and the corrupted both benefit from secrecy. Most empirical data therefore concern:

    a. Rough estimations of the damage caused by corruption (each year many billions of US dollars);

---

[1] Part of the well-known ethical framework for public officials that was developed in the United Kingdom by the Committee on Standards in Public Life chaired by Lord Nolan. The Nolan Committee sketched out Seven Principles of Public Life, based on the mentioned values. See e.g. Sampford and Preston, 1998; Huberts, 2002.

b. Statistics on criminal cases involving corruption: what has been discovered, investigated, prosecuted and convicted can most easily be counted;

c. Results of opinion surveys on the extent, causes and solutions among different populations (the general public, politicians, civil servants, business people, experts in the field).

The most famous research has been done by Göttingen University and Transparency International. Since 1995 a Corruption Perceptions Index (CPI) has been published, based on the perceptions of the degree of corruption as seen by business people, risk analysts and the general public. Some countries have the reputation of being very corrupt and, as might be expected, most of these are developing countries like Nigeria and Indonesia or transitional (Eastern European) states like the Ukraine. Northern European countries are perceived as being among the less corrupt. The image of countries appears to be rather stable. Once a reputation for corruptness is established, it takes time and effort to change.

Expert panel research additionally showed that corruption experts in higher income countries differ from their colleagues in poorer countries concerning the prominence of corruption in the public and private sector. Respondents from the lower income countries think corruption is much more prominent in the public sector, while experts from higher income countries find the opposite to be the case (Huberts, 2000).

Table 1: *Corruption Perceptions Index, Transparency International 2001*

(10 highly clean – 0 highly corrupt)

Least corrupt countries

Country	*2001 CPI score*
Finland	9.9
Denmark	9.5
New Zealand	9.4
Iceland	9.2
Singapore	9.2
Sweden	9.4
Canada	8.9
Netherlands	8.8
Luxembourg	8.7
Norway	8.6

Most corrupt countries

Country	*2001 CPI score*
Bangladesh	0.4*
Nigeria	1.0
Uganda	1.9
Indonesia	1.9
Kenya	2.0
Cameroon	2.0
Bolivia	2.0
Azerbaijan	2.0
Ukraine	2.1
Tanzania	2.2

Other countries

Country	*2001 CPI score*
United Kingdom	8.3
United States	7.6
Japan	7.1
South Africa	4.8
Brazil	4.0
China	3.5
India	2.7

(* TI adds that the Bangladesh data should be viewed with extra caution)

Source: Transparency International and Göttingen University, http://www.gwdg.de/ ~uwvw (August 2001); also: http://www.transparency.org/documents/cpi/2001 (June 2001)

Another index is worth mentioning. The Transparency International Bribe Payers Survey concerns the willingness of companies from leading exporting states to pay bribes to public officials to win or retain business. It shows that companies from countries like China, South Korea, Taiwan, Italy and Malaysia are most likely to pay bribes. Additionally, the survey shows that the scores for countries like the United Kingdom, the United States and Japan are lower than the corruption scores for the countries themselves. Bribing a foreign official seems more acceptable than bribing an official in the country itself.

Indexes, we explicitly add, are of only limited importance to get an idea of the extent of the corruption phenomenon and the damage it causes. They do indicate however that the corruption problem is omnipresent and they illustrate the importance of continued efforts to investigate the phenomenon with a variety of research methods in order to get a clearer and more precise picture.

Among these efforts are country studies that offer a more comprehensive description of corruption. Several transitional states in Eastern Europe have been investigated, using population surveys and other research methods (The World Bank, 2000), case studies of developing and developed countries offer more in-depth insight in the extent and the forms of corruption in every day life as well as in government and administration.[2]

4. Causes and solutions

4.1. Causes

Research shows that a conglomerate of social, economic, political, organisational and individual causal factors are important to explain cases of public corruption and fraud in a country (Heidenheimer, Johnston & Levine, 1989; Heywood, 1997; Klitgaard, 1988; Cooper, 2001).

Among the more important political causes are the values and norms of politicians and civil servants and their commitment to public integrity, the organisational quality of the public sector (working conditions, control and auditing), the relationship between the state and the business sector and a number of social factors (e.g. the presence of organised crime and the content of social norms and values).

These factors are important in explaining the corruption in higher and lower income countries but a full explanation also has to take into account the differences between these countries. A number of factors which are related to developmental problems are of crucial importance to lower income countries (UNDP, 1998). Economic failure and poverty, poor conditions for human development (schooling, health) and corruption are interrelated. For example, it is clear that low salaries and bad working conditions in the public sector can be disastrous for the possibility and the willingness to behave ethically.

---

[2] See in this book, for example, the work of Queloz on Switzerland (for Germany, see the report by Vahlenkamp and Knauss in 1995). The chapters by Doig and Moran on independent institutions and by Langseth and Stolpe on the United Nations' initiatives against corruption contain many references to country studies on corruption.

For countries going through a process of privatisation, liberalisation and democratisation, the period of transition offers extra possibilities for corruption (Heywood, 1997; UNDP, 1998; The World Bank, 2000). It takes time to establish a more stable political and economic system which is able to curb corruption.

4.2. Solutions

It is always necessary to relate anti-corruption strategies to characteristics of the actors involved (and the environment they operate in).[3] There is no single concept and program of good governance for all countries and organisations, there is no "one right way" (Pope, 2000; Transparency International, 2001; Huberts, 2000). There are many initiatives and most are tailored to specific contexts; societies and organisations will have to seek their own solutions.

Concepts and programs like National Integrity Systems (Transparency International), The Ethics Infrastructure (OECD) and A Framework for Integrity (World Bank) offer numerous methods and institutions to curb corruption and promote integrity (Transparency International, 2001; Pope, 2000; OECD, 2000; Pieth & Eigen, 1999). The main elements are summarised here.

The overall *goals* should include development strategies which yield benefits to the nation as a whole, including its poorest and most vulnerable members, and not just to well-placed elites. Additionally it is important that public services are both efficient and effective and that government is functioning under law, with citizens protected from arbitrariness (including abuses of human rights).

Many *institutions and activities* are important in the struggle against corruption.

Leadership counts – the research is unanimous on this. Embodying the political will to fight corruption, leaders set the tone through their policies and the example they present. In the political system, parliament as representative of the people and watchdog of political power is at the centre of the struggle to attain and sustain

---

[3] The internet is a rich source for information about anti-corruption initiatives: Council of Europe (http://www.coe.int) and its Group of States against Corruption (http://greco.coe.int), Independent Commission against Corruption of Hong Kong (http://www.icac.org.hk) and New South Wales, Australia (http://www.icac.nsw.gov.au), Organisation of American States (http://www.oas.org), Organisation for Economic Co-operation and Development (http://www.oecd.org), Transparency International (http://www.transparency.org), Programme for Accountability and Transparency of the United Nations Development Programme (http://www.unpan.org) and The World Bank's public sector program (http://www1.worldbank.org/publicsector/anticorrupt).

good governance and to fight corruption. An independent, impartial and informed judiciary holds a central place in the realisation of just, honest, open and accountable government. The public service is important for its services as well as for the protection of the public decision-making process (including the system of public procurement, often vulnerable because of its opportunities for corruption). Integrity is a crucial element of professionalism. People should be given a feeling of pride in their work and that deviance undermines the core of the profession.

A powerful anti-corruption device is also simply the establishment of sound financial management practices, including a timely and efficient accounting system combined with punctual, professional review by internal and independent auditors. Important institutions include an effective auditor-general as a watchdog over financial integrity and the credibility of reported information, an ombudsman who can recommend improvements to procedures and practices and act as an incentive for public officials to keep their files in order, and independent anti-corruption agencies to raise awareness among the public, to stimulate prevention and to detect and investigate corruption cases. The availability of resources, their independence from management and the availability of mechanisms of transparency and accountability are important factors for the success of these institutions.

Of importance is a judicious balance between positive and negative social control. An extreme accent on control can be highly counter-productive. An anti-corruption campaign in New York City fostered its own pathology of excessive rules and procedures, paralysis of decision-making, and the undermining of quality (Anechiarico & Jacobs, 1996). To safeguard integrity presupposes that attention is being paid to group and organisational culture (norms, values and perceptions), including training and education in ethical dilemmas and the development of codes of conduct.

Additionally, it is important that the media and civil society play a role. Information and public awareness, (the "right to know") are linked inextricably to accountability, the central goal of any democratic system of government. The principal vehicle for taking information to the public is an independent and free media. The role for civil society must be to claim and defend its own values, and not leave this integral function to those in power.

4.3. Doubt

The involvement of many international and national organisations in the struggle against corruption might suggest more consensus than actually exists. Two types of critique should be borne in mind.

First, there is the criticism already mentioned – although it is often stated that there is no "one right way", the multitude of comparable initiatives leaves little room for other strategies than those favoured by institutions like the World Bank and the OECD.

Secondly, fundamental questions have been raised about the driving forces behind the anti-corruption policies. It is argued that the concern is not attributable to any substantive increase in corrupt practices, but rather to the "re-framing of corruption in light of broad shifts and transformations within the global economy" (Williams & Beare, 1999, p. 115). Is it moral to ultimately favour the poor and powerless, or is the self-interest of companies and Western states the driving force, because of their interest in greater market penetration and transparency (Windsor & Getz, 2000)?

5. Law enforcement and anti-corruption strategies

The sketch of the general framework of institutions to fight corruption shows that law enforcement and law enforcement organisations play an important role, but that the role must not be overestimated. The National Integrity System (NIS) approach illustrates this. An NIS contains a number of crucial institutions, sectors or activities – the pillars. Among them, there are several institutions that belong to the law enforcement system (Transparency International, 2001):

- an auditor-general, acting as a watchdog over financial integrity and the credibility of reported information;

- the attorney-general as chief law officer of the state, "guardian of the public interest";

- the public service, erecting a system designed to protect the public decision-making process;

- the rule of law, to adjudicate whether or not a particular action taken by, or on behalf of, the state is in accordance with the law;

- the judiciary which should be independent, impartial and informed; it holds "a central place in the realisation of just, honest, open and accountable government";

- an ombudsman, who "acts to prevent corruption and maladministration; it can recommend improvements to procedures and practices and act as an incentive for public officials to keep their files in order";

- independent anti-corruption agencies, "as the corrupt grow more sophisticated, conventional law enforcement agencies are becoming less able to detect and prosecute complex corruption cases".

5.1. Law enforcement system

The National Integrity System has been described and analysed by 19 countries (Transparency International, 2001). The studies present examples of the importance as well as the vulnerability of the law enforcement system. This is also well understood by the public itself. The Ghana report states:

"Are there any cases of corruption within the prosecuting agencies?
    Yes. 67% of household respondents to the Ghana Governance and Corruption Survey ranked the regular police (who prosecute most crimes) among the institutions perceived to be most corrupt. Though its personnel are hardly ever arrested, it is common public knowledge that the criminal justice system is corrupt. Court staff and prosecutors have sometimes tampered with or stolen exhibits. Judges are also widely perceived to be corrupt.

How many cases of prosecution have been undertaken in the past years? How many have been successful?
    No cases of corruption have been prosecuted in the past 10 years through the criminal justice mechanism. The Commission on Human Rights and Administrative Justice and the Serious Fraud Office have handled such matters more than the traditional police" (Ghana country report, p. 14).

Elements of the law enforcement system are more often identified as the pillar most susceptible to corruption. As is noted for Brazil:

"The judiciary is probably the weakest link in the control chain, since it is unable to convey to society the message that crimes of corruption are actually punished. The individual institutions charged with mounting cases – police, public prosecutors and courts – don't work in an integrated fashion. The police suffers from political interference and is vulnerable to organised crime take-over; furthermore, is ill-prepared to conduct investigations. Public prosecutors, whose powers were significantly enhanced under the 1988 Constitution, are yet finding their new identity and run the risk of becoming entangled in political considerations. The latter comes from what is perceived by some as a hyper-militant attitude from some young prosecutors. The courts are affected by opacity and slowness and can't adequately respond to the growing number of cases that reaches the Judiciary. Reforms of the penal process and in administrative procedures could change the image that, in Brazil, corruption crimes remain unpunished" (Brazil country report, p. 23).

More often, a lack of enforcement capabilities is mentioned as a primary concern. The Fiji country report states (p. 6):

"The public sector has not carried out sufficient necessary institutional strengthening programs to enhance their enforcement roles. The shortage of qualified people in the enforcement arm of the government has been an ongoing concern. The Director of Public Prosecution's (DPP) office for instance is staffed with some of the most junior legal practitioners in the country but is expected to deliver tasks and responsibilities of high standards."

One of the reasons argued for such incapability in the office is the low salary level in the civil service.

On the other hand, where there appears to be appropriate capacity, it may be limited by the lack of transparency in the selection of judges, the dependence of the judiciary on the Executive and the political and economic pressures obstructing investigations. The anti-corruption agency (BAC) in Bangladesh exemplifies the issues:

The BAC is controlled and administered by the executive organ of the government, the officers of the higher grade such as the director general or the director are transferable in an ordinary manner. Its activities are not at all transparent nor is it accountable to the representatives of the people. It is mandatory to obtain prior clearance ... for deciding the course of action to be followed after investigations are complete since initiation of anti-corruption cases against government servants from mid to the highest level and against political office holders needs prior permission of the Prime Minister there is no instance of filing any corruption case against a political office holder belonging to or supporting the party in power" (Bangladesh country report, pp. 7-8).

For all countries, it is clear that the integrity of the law enforcement system is a crucial element in all anti-corruption strategies. This is true for developing countries, as mentioned in the previous examples, as well as for developed countries (Fijnaut, 2000).

5.2. One side of the shield

Although the importance of a law enforcement system characterised by effectiveness and integrity can hardly be overstated, it must also be stressed that investigation and prosecution are just one side of the shield. A broad, "holistic" approach is necessary. We should not focus on the controllable components of compliance with agencies, procedures and laws. As Jacobs and Anechiarico argued: "in searching for solutions to the corruption problem, we must look beyond the traditional strategies of monitoring, control and punishment laws, rules, and threats will never result in a public administration to be proud of; to the contrary, the danger is that such an approach will create a self-fulfilling prophecy: having been placed continuously under suspicion, treated like quasi-criminals or probationers, public employees will behave accordingly" (Anechiarico & Jacobs, 1996, p. 207).

Both repression and prevention, both changes in structure and in culture are necessary. As Pope and Transparency International stated:

"Monitoring corruption cannot be left only to public prosecutors and to the forces of law and order. Action cannot depend solely on detection and criminal prosecution. Rather, action must also include a combination of interlocking arrangements. In part, this approach includes improving the transparency of relationships, and to the extent possible, preventing the development of relationships which can lead to corruption. It includes transparency in the financial affairs of key players and the prospect of reviews being conducted by independent institutions which are likely to be outside any particular network. Although corruption can never be completely monitored, it can be controlled through a combination of ethical codes, decisive legal prosecutions against offenders, organisational change, and institutional reform" (Pope, 1997, p. 19).

6. Results of Global Forum II

6.1. Final declaration

At the Second Global Forum on Fighting Corruption and Safeguarding Integrity in May 2001 in The Hague, representatives from many countries talked about preventing and combating corruption and promoting integrity in government and in society.[4] Representatives reaffirmed their determination to prevent and combat corruption, "a virus capable of crippling government, discrediting public institutions and private corporations and having a devastating impact on the human rights of populations, and thus undermining society and its development, affecting in particular the poor". Workshops on "integrity and governance", on "law enforcement", on "customs", on "corruption, transition and development" and on "government and the business sector" were held.

The workshop sessions on "law enforcement" contributed to the incorporation of recommendations on law enforcement in the final declaration of the Global Forum. The text shows what kind of recommendations were politically acceptable for the broad range of nations presents at the conference:

- Participants stress the need for including in national criminal law clear definitions of conduct that is to be considered to constitute corruption offence, as well as a precise description of a public official. They expect the comprehensive report of the Secretary General of the United Nations on "Existing international legal instruments, recommendations and other documents addressing corruption" (E/CN.15/2001/3) to be an inspiration for national legislators and others.

- Furthermore, participants deem it essential to provide for a broad scope of corruption offence in national legislation, including, as necessary, foreign and international corruption.

- Participants recognise the need for governments to make available adequate resources for investigation and prosecution of corruption offence as well as for international co-operation in corruption cases.

- Participants consider improvement of law enforcement co-operation and mutual legal assistance necessary. Possible avenues are intensifying existing

---

4   See http://www.gfcorruption.org for the final declaration and the reports of the workshop sessions.

exchange of operational information and rendering technical and other types of assistance, identifying lacunae and developing new methods and techniques. Where necessary, creating an adequate legal basis for new activities should be considered. Consideration could be given also to ways and means to facilitate the matching of requests for and offers of expertise.

- They are deeply conscious of the need to improve co-operation relating to the returning of funds derived from acts of corruption. They welcome the relevant recommendations forwarded by the United Nations Commission on Crime Prevention and Criminal Justice.

Additionally, a brief report of the workshop sessions was added to the final declaration. This report summarises the reflections and recommendations that were expressed by the participants in these workshop sessions. The following paragraph contains the definitive text of this report.

6.2. Results of the workshop on law enforcement

6.2.1. Introductory remarks

Any anti-corruption strategy depends on the willingness of the political leadership to take corruption problems seriously, to make anti-corruption policy a priority and to assign sufficient resources to the relevant institutions.

The relationship between corruption and law enforcement is a challenging one. On the one hand, law enforcement institutions are crucial for the struggle against corruption; on the other hand, the integrity and perceived integrity of these institutions is essential for the credibility of that struggle.

6.2.2. International co-operation

International instruments are important for bridging the gaps between various national legal systems. They create the conditions for improving co-operation between national law enforcement institutions. Their importance is nowadays increasing because of the internationalisation of corruption problems. This development stimulates the integration of police co-operation and mutual legal assistance.

A new United Nations Convention against Corruption could become a useful instrument for the struggle against corruption if it succeeds in complementing existing instruments like the United Nations Convention against Transnational Organised Crime, if it takes into account the difficulties experienced with investigations in the past (e.g. bank secrecy should no longer be a ground for refusal to reply to requests for mutual assistance and provisions on the return of the proceeds of corruption should be included), and if it urges the requesting and requested parties to play an active role in investigations.

An important issue with respect to a new convention is the support for countries in order to enact legislation and build up the institutions and the expertise needed for its implementation and enforcement.

In conjunction with existing and new instruments, there is a need for leadership in organising the use of these instruments at an international level in specific cases. Interpol and regional institutions like Europol could function as linking organisations in international investigations. To further international co-operation, the exchange of investigators among anti-corruption entities could be stimulated.

A next step could be the establishment of multinational investigative anti-corruption units at a regional level. Along with other innovative measures, such an initiative must be embedded in regional agreements. There is a need for active promotion of speedy exchange of information between states concerning their anti-corruption efforts.

6.2.3. National integrity systems

The international and national struggle against corruption is dependent on the quality of the national integrity system of countries (the rules, laws, organisations to curb corruption and safeguard integrity). The system should contain institutions for information, for prevention and advice and for investigation and prosecution.

There is no system that is applicable in all countries because its effectiveness is related to the societal (political, economic, cultural and social) circumstances within which it has to function. Multinational institutions should have an open eye for these circumstances when giving advice to governments on the containment of corruption.

The success of any anti-corruption system depends upon the availability of sufficient resources. This condition covers budget and personnel as well as legal powers and public support. In conjunction with this, the publication of cases of corruption might be very helpful.

An anti-corruption system should be capable of handling "big" cases but should also deal with the corruption problems with which ordinary citizens are confronted. The establishment of independent institutions can contribute to curbing corruption. It will depend on the circumstances which type of institution is most suitable.

Protecting integrity in society is also the responsibility of the private sector. Undertakings should enhance corporate governance and install compliance systems. External accountants should be obliged to report cases of corruption to public authorities. The notion of civil society certainly is of great importance in this context. It is however necessary to define and to clarify this concept in order to make the relationship between governmental bodies and social institutions more effective from an operational point of view.

6.2.4. Law and law enforcement

Police forces, prosecution services and courts are mutually dependent in realising an effective anti-corruption strategy. At the same time they should co-operate with regulatory bodies, administrative authorities, Customs etc. Corruption problems are often too complicated to be solved by the law enforcement system alone.

The criminalisation of corruption in the public and private domain at the national level should be as much as possible consistent with the developing international standards. The same should apply to the powers of investigation. In addition to credible penal sanctions, disciplinary, administrative and civil law sanctions might equally be very effective.

Among the powers of investigation to be considered in serious cases are electronic surveillance and undercover operations. It is important to be aware of the risks of corruption in connection with the use of such intrusive powers, however.

Whistle-blowing can be of great help when it is part of a comprehensive strategy against corruption. The protection of the whistle-blower needs to be carefully designed.

In order to investigate serious cases of corruption special police units are usually required. The success of these units depends not only upon their powers and resources but also on their capability to define targets and priorities within the framework of a governmental anti-corruption policy. A close working relationship between such units and the prosecution service is a *conditio sine qua non*.

An independent judiciary is an absolute requirement for any effective and legitimate anti-corruption strategy. Its independence should be enshrined in the Constitution as well as safeguarded in the working conditions of the judges. The judiciary has the responsibility to create an internal control system that guarantees its integrity.

In order to prevent investigations into corruption from being abused as an instrument of power politics, measures should be taken to avoid any political interference in the handling of individual cases.

To raise awareness on the risks of corruption, the issue of integrity should be included in the training for public officers. Selective integrity testing can be an effective instrument to check rumours and indications of a serious corruption problem.

6.2.5. Assessment of anti-corruption policies

More research on the effectiveness of anti-corruption strategies and instruments at the national level is needed. This presupposes research on the nature, the extent and the impact of corruption.

International comparative research can increase our knowledge of the role significant elements of national integrity systems play in the containment of corruption problems in widely diverging societal circumstances.

Monitoring systems are necessary to evaluate the extent to which the law enforcement systems of countries meet their obligations under international law.

7. The structure and content of this book

This volume presents the papers that contributed to discussions in the workshops at the Second Global Forum. Each part of the book addresses a subject of the broad area of law enforcement, corruption and integrity.

Although corruption is an international phenomenon, which makes it hard to distinguish between the national and international aspects of the problem and the strategies to fight it, we start with the papers that focus on the national level. Part II presents a description of corruption in three countries, offering information about the content of corruption and about anti-corruption strategies used in Switzerland, Germany and Indonesia. Part III then deals with "Corruption and Integrity in the Law Enforcement System" itself. Part IV sketches the legal instruments and institutions that are available in the fight against corruption. Of course, this portrait is embedded in a description of corruption and corruption cases. An exhaustive and detailed description and analysis of the independent institutions against corruption can be found in Part V, "Independent Institutions". Part VI offers reflections on these institutions and more in general on the possibilities of a law enforcement strategy to contain corruption and to protect integrity.

The last two parts of the book reflect the truly international character of the *Global* Forum. Participants from many countries paid special attention to international initiatives against corruption. Several organisations and institutions are involved in that struggle. Part VII illustrates this, with chapters on initiatives by the United Nations, the Organisation for Economic Co-Operation and Development (OECD), the Council of Europe, the European Union (EU) and the Organisation of American States (OAS). In Part VIII, attention is paid to the problem of the repatriation of corruption money or embezzled state funds. All chapters in this part are on probably the most difficult aspect of the fight against corruption: the necessity to increase international co-operation in law enforcement in order to make the international and national battles against corruption more effective.

7.1. Corruption and its containment: three case studies

Nicolas Queloz, in "Processes of Corruption in Switzerland: Where is the Problem?", analyses the attention being paid to corruption in that country. The subject did not cause much concern before the 1990s. The first alarm bells went off in 1991 with the arrest of a government official in charge of authorisations to open cafes, restaurants, pubs, night-clubs, etc. Since then, much more attention has been paid to the problem. Queloz reports on an extensive research project on corruption (corruption being *an abuse (misuse) of a representative power*, whether the interests represented are private or public). The project contains an analysis of statistical data and the contents of criminal and disciplinary files relating to actual events of corruption; interviews with "privileged informers" (politicians, judges, policemen, businessmen, journalists); a study of procurement contracts in the construction sector; and cases studies on the "grey areas" of corruption processes, namely trading in influence, clientelism, and cronyism. The research showed that between 6 (in 1990) and 20 (in 1997) people are condemned each year and 8 out of 10 of the people convicted are private actors (private individuals and businessmen found guilty of so-called "active" corruption). However, these data show merely the tip of the iceberg of corruption. Other research shows that many companies suffer losses because of corruption. In particular the building industry seems to be affected. This includes understandings on prices reached between awarders and bidders; cartel agreements between entrepreneurs; favouring of firms that are local and close to the majority political party; cheating on the definition, estimate and final award of services; inflated invoices, etc. The recommendations resulting from the project included policies with regard to companies, aimed at organisations, professional practices and the legal framework.

Manfred Nötzel, the head of the Anti-Corruption Department of the Public Prosecutor's Office in Munich, Germany, shows in "Investigation Strategies and Tactics in the Prosecution of Corruption Offences: Experiences from Germany" that the field of "corruption in economic life" was not seen as a problem in Germany until the beginning of the 1990s. Then, examples of fraudulent price-fixing arrangements and bribery attracted an extraordinary amount of public attention. A lot of cases were discovered in Frankfurt (airport) and – briefly afterwards – also in Munich. These experiences, and the realisation that it did not concern isolated cases by any means but that – in any event in some areas – orders by the public authority could over years exclusively be obtained by bribery payments, fraudulent price fixing arrangements and cartels, led to the deep concern and indignation of the public. As a reaction to this, the political forces decided that the fight against this type of criminality should receive increased priority. One of the first measures in Bavaria was the establishment of the Special Department of the Public Prosecutor's Office, Munich. Nötzel describes the experiences of this department, its successes and problems. For intensive and effective investigations, it appears to be very important to have open and early co-operation with and between the other authorities such as the police and revenue offices. A key question is how to break open the "cartel of silence" of everybody involved in the corruption (investigations nearly always rely on the confession statements of the perpetrator, which never is "for free"). New laws open new possibilities in this respect. For the future, this is important, but this is even truer for the intensified international co-operation.

Adi Andojo Soetjipto, former Chairman of the Joint Investigation Team for Fighting Corruption in Indonesia, presents in "The Battle against Corruption in the Context of a Developing Country: the Case of Indonesia" an impressive map of corruption in that country. In all fields, especially in bureaucracy, from the lowest level to the highest level, people practice corruption whenever there is a chance to do so. It is not wrong to say that corruption has become a common practice in Indonesia – he states that it is part of every day life in Indonesia. There is also mega-corruption, with the money kept overseas (estimated funds: US$ 200 to 300 billion). The development of corruption in Indonesia cannot be separated from the social form which in the beginning was based on paternalism, the obligation to provide "*upeti*" (gift) to please the boss and the influence of feudalistic authoritarian lifestyle under Soeharto's 32-year nepotic and autocratic administration. Efforts to combat corruption all ended in failure. In the end, it comes down to the government's will to seriously combat corruption (with the declaration of the state of emergency against corruption, for example). If the combat of corruption is only used as political commodity, as is happening in Indonesia, the problem of corruption will remain serious, if not worsen.

7.2. Corruption and integrity in the law enforcement system

Robert Mischkowitz reports on his research in "Corruption in Law Enforcement Agencies – Views from within the Criminal Justice System: Results of a German Corruption Study". This important study was conducted by the Bundeskriminalamt (Federal Criminal Police Office) in the latter half of the 1990s on corruption among the police, the judiciary and customs officials. Several methods were used in the study: questionnaires, interviews and case analyses. One key feature of the study is that people were asked about corruption within their own institution and also within the other institutions – with surprising results. The results also constitute an important source of critical considerations about the picture of corruption that emerges in official criminal statistics. Another important aspect is that the interviewees were asked what they thought were the causes of corruption and about their views on the best ways to combat corruption. On this latter point, the study revealed that many interviewees attached a great deal of importance to heightening officials' awareness of the problem (for example during their training period), improving administrative and professional supervision and strengthening the role behaviour of managers and trainers.

Willy Bruggeman sees "Corruption from a Police Perspective". Corruption is a broad term that subsumes many different forms of wrongdoing, he states, although common elements can be distinguished: the conduct is prohibited by law, it involves the misuse of position and it involves personal gain for the officer. Aspects of police work such as discretion, low visibility and peer group secrecy make corruption more likely than in other sectors of society. Variable factors include leadership integrity, a reduction in regimented work group solidarity and a code of conduct. Among the corruption control strategies, Bruggeman mentions investigations by external, specialised, highly professional police units, a proactive internal affairs unit (monitoring and analysing data) and the use of vigorous media. Studies reveal a cyclic pattern of corruption which makes it necessary to protect successful methods of investigation for continued use.

Michael Taylor's chapter on "Combating Corruption within the Metropolitan Police Service" outlines how the police force in London views the problems of corruption in police circles. The phenomenon is a kind of "durable and flexible" virus that constantly adapts to changing circumstances and hence also to the methods used to combat it. He then describes the major campaigns waged in the past few years to combat corruption in the Metropolitan Police in London and the strategies and methods that have been and are being adopted. He concludes by summarising the lessons that the Metropolitan Police have learned from real-life corruption cases in recent years.

Jan d'Oliveira focuses on the "Corruption within the Judicial System: Some Remarks on Law and Practice in South Africa". He confronts us not so much with the problem of corruption in South Africa's judiciary, but rather with the measures that have been implemented in the past few years to both prevent and combat this problem, ranging from provisions in the Constitution right through to regulations relating to the legal status of judges. In the second part of the chapter he explores the shortcomings of current anti-corruption legislation, particularly in the light of international developments. He concludes by pointing out some recent amendments of the law, which go some way towards meeting the wishes of the public prosecution service.

7.3. Legal instruments and institutions

Barbara Huber discusses the "Sanctions against Bribery Offences in Criminal Law". She analyses sanctions in supranational instruments – devised within the OECD, the Council of Europe and the European Union – as well as sanctions in several countries such as the United States, China, Turkey, Germany, the United Kingdom, Belgium and The Netherlands. The study on which this comparative survey is based was carried out by the Max Planck Institute for Foreign and International Criminal Law in Freiburg im Breisgau in Germany. The purpose of this research was to find out whether a more integrated approach to the issue of criminal sanctions might be possible. She comes to the conclusion that there are still significant differences between the sanctions used in response to the various different forms of corruption and that harmonisation in this area will not be possible in the short term. However, she makes no secret of her doubts about the benefit of prosecuting corruption offences, raising the question of whether other means besides criminal law are not more effective.

Keonjee Lee from the Korean Ministry of Justice raises the same question as Barbara Huber to some extent, albeit in relation to the powers and instruments needed to be able to adequately deal with problems of corruption by legal means: "Criminal Procedure: What Powers, Instruments and Safeguards are Necessary for Adequate Law Enforcement?" He bases this question primarily on the fact that in international instruments little or no attention is generally paid to the ways in which corruption can or should be prosecuted. In contrast, in his view, this issue is attracting more and more attention at regional and national level. By way of an example he talks about the powers of the police and the public prosecution service in Korea, including the power to arrest suspects and conduct a search of premises, gain access to financial information and intercept electronic communications. Over the next few years there are plans to extend money-laundering legislation, to introduce witness protection schemes and to tighten up control of financial transactions. He concludes by calling for more discussion in regional and international fora on prosecution issues in the fight against corruption.

Benoît Dejemeppe examines "Corruption Cases and their Consequences for Legislation and Judiciary". He examines several cases of corruption that have come to light in recent years in Belgium and also looks at the measures successively taken to combat corruption more effectively. In particular he discusses the Law of 10 February 1999, in which the entire spectrum of anti-corruption legislation was reviewed in a few key areas. In his view Belgium leads the way in Europe in this respect. He also discusses the initiatives that have been taken in the past few years not only to ensure that this legislation can be enforced more effectively, but also to prevent corruption as much as possible. He concludes with a long list of recommendations to help organise international co-operation in the fight against corruption more effectively and efficiently.

Peter Alldridge's chapter on "The Sentencing of Corruption" addresses two issues that are of key importance in the global community: first, the determination of the scale of corruption in relation to the appropriateness of sanctions under a rational punishment model and, secondly, the link between the conviction for corruption and the seizure of the assets derived from this practice. On the basis of legislation and real-life cases in the United Kingdom, he clearly explains the problems associated with establishing the seriousness of corruption and hence determining an appropriate punishment and seizing the proceeds. His analysis culminates in a number of proposals for a possible response, both internationally and nationally, to cases of corruption in terms of criminal prosecution. For instance, the scale of the corruption within government circles should be irrelevant when it comes to sentencing. He also feels that when confiscating the proceeds of corruption the costs incurred and the tax already deducted must be taken into account. In his view, British legislation is not exactly an example for the rest of the world.

7.4. Independent institutions

Grant Poulton discusses in "Independence in Investigation and Prevention: The Role of the New South Wales Government's Independent Commission against Corruption" the role and work of this commission in order to assess the value of independence in undertaking anti-corruption work. The ICAC is an example of an anti-corruption institution that is independent and combines investigative, preventative and educative functions. He outlines the history of the ICAC, specifically how and why it was set up. The way in which the Commission is independent, particularly in its investigation functions, is then described. The chapter then examines the ways in which the Commission's independence is tempered by accountability mechanisms and describes some of the costs and benefits of combining investigation and corruption prevention functions within one organisation. The chapter is positive about ICAC's successes. It has shown that for New South Wales there is an on-going need for the prevention and investigation of corruption, and the ICAC serves the public interest by this work. This does not mean that the ICAC is a suitable model for export. This will depend on the political and legal institutions and the corruption problems being faced by the importer.

Amy Comstock, in "Maintaining Government Integrity: The Perspective of the United States Office of Government Ethics", stresses the importance of ethics programs and ethics institutions for the creation of a democratic culture, the avoidance of cynicism and public confidence in government. Institutions are needed that ensure that public officials are held accountable and that government operations are open to public scrutiny. The ethics program in the United States is only one model, she stresses, for achieving the challenging task of integrating accountability with democratic governance. It is designed to provide alternatives to relying strictly on law enforcement efforts to address wrongdoing by emphasising prevention approaches that both complement and enhance law enforcement efforts. It has proven effective in accounting for the size, extent, and diversity of the executive branch, while implementing systems of prevention, such as a code of conduct and – most important in this respect – financial disclosure. These elements are important pieces of the larger mission to prevent conflicts of interest and provide the public with the access and information it needs to hold government accountable to the highest standards of integrity and honesty.

Alan Doig and *Jon Moran* are sceptical in "Anti-Corruption Agencies: The Importance of Independence for the Effectiveness of National Integrity Systems" about the simplicity with which both individual countries and donors continue their enthusiasm for independent anti-corruption agencies (ACA) as the lead institution to combat corruption. Such agencies are also often seen as the lynchpin of the development of a country's National Integrity System (NIS). Much attention is given to the need to allow both ACAs and the NIS the freedom and independence of relevant agencies to work unimpeded, individually and collectively. The chapter suggests that the issue of independence both for ACAs and the NIS are neither certain nor embedded, despite the rhetoric of reform, because of operational, resourcing and political issues. Effective ACAs are based a complex set of structural and organisational factors which condition their establishment and operation. Overall, Doig and Moran conclude, ACAs can be effective but they need an effective application for proven business planning techniques. Without that, they might add another layer of (ineffective) bureaucracy to the law enforcement sector, divert resources from existing organisations involved in anti-corruption work, function inefficiently if they are unable to target high level corruption cases and function as a "shield" to satisfy donors and governments not wholly committed to reform. Ineffective or weak, ACAs not only damage their own role, they undermine the overall impact and success of the National Integrity System.

Michael Johnston stresses in "Independent Anti-Corruption Commissions: Success Stories and Cautionary Tales" that there is no single "ICAC strategy". What differs is the jurisdiction (the public or private sector), its prevention capabilities (including training) versus investigation and prosecution, the power to reverse burdens of proof and access to private as well as public financial records, and the strength of the research capabilities. The essentials of an ICAC strategy are nevertheless clear: most obvious – and most critical – is real independence. But independence in turn requires permanence, coherence, and credibility. Even when all are in place, they do not guarantee success: other factors, ranging from international and regional dynamics, through the skill and dedication of managers and agents, to pure good luck are also in the mix. Additionally there are dangers and risks stemming from lack of civil support and accountability, isolation from other normative institutions and the neglect of the necessity of an adaption of strategies and institutions to social, political and economic settings.

7.5. Reflections on law enforcement strategies

Because we tend to think favourably about everything that is done to curb corruption, we tend to underestimate possible disadvantages of anti-corruption policies. Three papers offer a critical evaluation of some of law enforcement strategies.

Tom vander Beken advocates "A Multidisciplinary Approach for Detection and Investigation". His plea is mainly based on academic research that he and a few colleagues conducted into corruption in the meat industry for the Belgian Ministry of Justice. The results of their study revealed the complexity of this form of corruption and lead to proposals being formulated for an integrated policy to combat these corrupt practices more effectively. The Belgian government subsequently commissioned them to translate these proposals into concrete strategies to tackle corruption. Vander Beken stresses the advantages of a multidisciplinary approach. Such an approach is preferable to a repressive and hence reactive approach to corruption problems.

James Jacobs is critical about the present state of the art of our knowledge of corruption control. There has, for example, been hardly any evaluation of the United States anti-corruption project. It makes it difficult to reach confident conclusions about what works and what does not. Doubts are nevertheless justified, he argues in "Dilemmas of Corruption Control". Since the Watergate scandal, corruption became a more salient political issue in the United States. The normative expectations for official conduct increased dramatically and perhaps unrealistically. It included the use of an ever-expanding definition of corruption (including private, even sexual, behaviour). The implications for American democracy of the much more scandal-sensitive politics are not clear. Another consequence is that government has become less effective and less efficient because many anti-corruption controls tend to reinforce the pathologies of bureaucracy. Corruption controls entail costs, and, in some cases, these costs outweigh any benefits as measured by reduced corruption. The challenge, of course, is to find the optimal type and amount of corruption control (and, odd as it may at first sound, an *optimal amount of corruption*). The goal must be to identify: 1) the most costly types of corruption (such as judicial corruption, election fraud); and 2) the most cost-effective anti-corruption strategies. Practically all corruption controls involve costs and trade-offs. Therefore, they should carry the label "use with caution".

Frank Anechiarico's arguments are in line with Jacobs chapter (as might be expected since they published *The Pursuit of Absolute Integrity* together). Nevertheless, Anechiarico is optimistic about the possibility to control corruption without further burdening public administration. In "Law Enforcement or a Community Oriented Strategy Toward Corruption Control" it is argued that lessons learned by the civil society movement can be applied to the prevention of corruption. Scepticism is justified concerning the law enforcement paradigm. When no attention is paid to democracy and to (civic and administrative) culture, strategies such as the Independent Commission Model might bring the worst of both worlds: administrative inefficiency and no appreciable reduction in corruption in the most problematic agencies. Those concerned with the procedures by which ethical government is maintained should also be concerned with the manner in which administrative culture and civic culture interrelate, as an aspect of democratic development. If bureaucracy develops without citizen involvement, even with the best of intentions regarding the reduction of temptation, administrative culture will remain isolated and pathologies will become more evident. If civic culture is not engaged in governance, it will atrophy and encourage either counter-agendas or cynicism.

7.6. International organisations and corruption

Nowadays, a lot of attention is being paid to corruption and ethics in international fora. Anti-corruption congresses and conferences with thousands of participants are unexceptional, as the Global Forum in The Hague and the 10th Anti-Corruption Conference in Prague proved. Conventions and treaties have been prepared, signed and implemented, and in international relations conditions of good governance have become an important topic. In Part VII, the efforts of international organisations to create a framework for fighting corruption are discussed, and the last section, Part VIII, deals with a number of international initiatives to curb corruption (Interpol's work, regional co-operation in Southern Africa, the repatriation of corruption funds and the involvement of private policing).

Peter Langseth and *Oliver Stolpe* describe "United Nations' Approach to Help Countries Strengthen Judicial Integrity". A case study form Nigeria illustrates what can be done. The United Nations Office for Drug Control and Crime Prevention established a Global Programme against Corruption in March 1999. The Programme employs a process of "action learning" intended to identify best practices and lessons learned through pilot country projects, programme execution and monitoring, periodic country assessments and by conducting a global study on corruption trends. Within the Programme, attention is also given to institution building, prevention, raising awareness, education, enforcement, anti-corruption legislation, judicial integrity, repatriation of foreign assets derived from corruption, as well as the monitoring and evaluation of these things. It also includes initiatives as for example a *United Nations Manual for Anti-Corruption Policy* and a *United Nations Anti-Corruption Tool Kit* and co-operation with the United Nations Program against Money Laundering, conferences and workshops and a Judicial Leadership Group to strengthen the judiciary against corruption and to effect judicial reform across legal systems. An integrated approach seems to yield positive results. Extra attention for judicial integrity is crucial, Langseth and Stolpe stress. Any effort to eradicate corruption within a society is useless if the very institutions that are designed and expected to protect the individual's rights and to ensure adequate sanctioning of the perpetrators of these rights are either too corrupt and/or inefficient to carry out their institutional mandates. Among the criminal justice institutions it is the judiciary that needs to be addressed first.

Manfred Möhrenschlager's chapter is about substantive criminal law issues in the anti-corruption convention of the Organisation for Economic Co-Operation and Development (OECD). The OECD with 29 member states representing the industrialised world, has made anti-corruption initiatives and ethics and integrity policies an important aspect of its work. The OECD convention – a form taken in preference to a mere recommendation – was adopted at the end of 1997 and entered into force on 15 February 1999. Underlying this was the conviction that only a co-ordinated approach on the basis of a binding international agreement can guarantee effective suppression of corruption at international level. The negotiations in the Working Group and, ultimately, at an international diplomatic conference, included not only the 29 OECD members but also five non-members from South America and Central and Eastern Europe. The new convention has become a great success. Over thirty of the advanced industrialised countries have bound themselves to criminalise and prosecute foreign and international bribery through a new anti-bribery convention. It made the OECD an important actor in the battle against international bribery. Full implementation is not an easy task as, for example, the introduction of the liability of legal persons reveals. Nevertheless a Working Group has noted that there was overall compliance with the convention's obligations in the great majority of countries. Active monitoring has been important to achieve results.

Gemma Aiolfi and *Mark Pieth* show optimism about OECD initiatives as their chapter's title illustrates: "How to Make a Convention Work: The OECD Recommendation and Convention on Bribery as an Example of a New Horizon in International Law". They argue that the recent fight against the deleterious effects of corruption have taken on a dynamism hardly credible a decade ago. This accomplishment is particularly apparent in the OECD initiative against bribery in international business transactions which culminated in the Recommendation and Convention of 1997. The path leading to these instruments became something of a high-speed process during its evolution with several interesting – and unique – features en route to the final instruments. The first part of this chapter describes the journey to instrument and examines how this convention has developed bite. The second part outlines the latest developments that complement international law with a review of recent initiatives taken by key industries in their efforts to take a proactive stance on the issue of bribery and corruption within their particular spheres of influence. The focal point here, Aiolfi and Pieth argue, must be on companies. Whilst the convention criminalises bribery when committed by a natural person it leaves the issue of criminal liability as it pertains to companies open and only requires that monetary sanctions be "effective, proportionate and dissuasive". Whether the profits of a company can be forfeited is an unresolved question. Nevertheless, it seems apparent that change is possible and entrenched behaviour in this area can be altered, political and economic factors as well as risks to reputation all combine to create a climate of change.

Guy de Vel and *Peter Csonka* of the Council of Europe summarise the activities of the Council against corruption, carried out on the basis of a Programme of Action adopted by the Committee of Ministers in 1996. It has become a priority for the organisation and its 43 member states. This chapter presents overview of the specific results obtained in the implementation of a Programme of Action against Corruption. A framework was adopted with 20 Guiding Principles for the fight against corruption, followed by the establishment of the Group of States against Corruption (GRECO). It aims at improving the capacity of its members to fight corruption by following up, through a process of mutual evaluation and peer pressure, compliance with in particular the Guiding Principles and the implementation of the Criminal Law Convention (adopted in 1998). This convention concerns active and passive bribery of domestic and foreign public officials, bribery in the private sector and officials in international organisations as well as money laundering of proceeds form corruption offences and "trading in influence". Attention has also been paid to the use of civil law remedies. A last initiative to be mentioned is the Octopus Programme against organised crime and corruption in countries in transition (of the European Commission and the Council of Europe, launched in 1996).

Michael Grotz describes what the European Union has done since the European Parliament adopted a Resolution on Combating Corruption in Europe in December 1995. The picture is an ambivalent one. On the one hand many Resolutions, Conventions, Protocols, Joint Actions and Inspections are mentioned. On the other hand there are the serious doubts concerning the instruments: a multitude of legal instruments, hardly ratified by member states and therefore not entered into force. This is very much the case when practical application contains provisions for judicial co-operation in penal matters. International co-operation in penal matters is cumbersome, time-consuming and complicated and often leads to the decision not to request mutual assistance in criminal matters, hoping to solve a case without any help from outside.

Jorge Garcia-González of the Organisation of American States (OAS) presents the main developments that the Countries of the Americas have made for consolidating co-operation among them for combating corruption. The OAS consists of 35 member states, constituting the only regional setting in which all the countries of the Americas (with the exception of Cuba) can come together and debate issues of common interest and reach an accord on them. Many of these conclude in legal instruments like Conventions or Resolutions agreed upon by the OAS General Assembly. The Inter-American Convention against Corruption has been the most important step that has been taken on a hemispherical level in combating this phenomenon. Two major purposes of the convention are: to promote and strengthen the development by each of the states of the mechanisms needed to prevent, detect, punish and eradicate corruption; and to promote, facilitate and regulate co-operation among the states to ensure the effectiveness of anti-corruption measures and actions. It constitutes the most important inter-American legal instrument for extraditing those who commit crimes of corruption; in co-operation and assistance among the states in obtaining evidence and facilitating necessary procedural acts regarding the investigation or trials of corruption; and for the identification, search, immobilisation, confiscation, and seizure of goods obtained or derived from the commission of the crime of corruption.

7.7 International initiatives to combat corruption

Willy Deridder, the Executive Director of the International Criminal Police Organisation, better known as Interpol, stresses the importance of the corruption issue for the law enforcement community. As he emphasises in "Interpol's Approach to Combating Corruption" it can diminish and even destroy the ability of law enforcement to accomplish its mission. Interpol, the only truly global police organisation with a current membership of 178 countries, therefore is very involved in the fight against corruption. Its main objective is to facilitate the flow and exchange of information between these members, and Interpol has also accepted the responsibility for setting international standards and sharing best practices in priority, serious transnational crime areas. For corruption in 1998 a Group of Experts was created with a mission statement, code of conduct, best practices guide and early warning system. The group will also develop a set of standards or norms for the investigation and management of corruption investigations.

Peter Gastrow's chapter is called "Combating Corruption in South Africa: Towards more Effective Regional and International Law Enforcement Co-operation". It describes the attempt being made in Southern Africa to improve co-operation between 14 countries in their efforts to combat corruption. Not only has a separate agreement been entered into; this agreement has also been incorporated into a framework agreement for mutual co-operation on crime prevention in general. Now it is a question of putting these positive policy developments into practice. Two things that must be borne in mind here are support – and that includes financial assistance – for the governments concerned in implementing the policy, and the need to reinforce the operational capability of the police to actively track down corruption in this region. In the long term, however, co-operation between the states concerned could be expanded and intensified, for example by organising training, exchanging experts and equipment and setting up a permanent liaison system.

Hairat Balogun's chapter "The Repatriation of Embezzled State Funds" concerns one of the most sensitive issues in contemporary international co-operation in the fight against corruption. It is discussed using the example of Nigeria. Mrs. Balogun first briefly talks about the history of anti-corruption legislation in relation to the development of actual corruption problems. She then explains why the problem of the "repatriation" of corruption funds is so important in practice and mentions the limited scope that international treaties have in this area. Yet the situation is by no means completely hopeless, as negotiations with Switzerland, Brazil and Liechtenstein have shown. Nevertheless, there is a need for international legislation that makes it very unattractive for countries to provide a safe haven for the financial proceeds of corruption perpetrated in other countries.

Pascal Gossin offers another perspective on the same problem in "Restitution of Assets and Corruption". He addresses the issue of international co-operation in tracking down and returning funds derived from corruption from the point of view of Switzerland. He first examines current Swiss legislation in this area and then considers a number of cases in terms of the amount of money seized and in how many cases funds have been returned to the country of origin. He devotes particular attention to the problems that arise when politically sensitive issues are involved.

Michael Levi is concerned with "Private Policing and Corruption". What is, and what will be the role of the public police and of private sector involvement? He sketches the considerable area of private policing in the economic and white-collar crime area (forensic services arms of accountancy firms, specialist security firms). International companies use private trouble-shooters and investigators in fraud and corruption cases because of their expertise and because companies want the to stay in control over the investigation and want to avoid bad publicity. This development has been accompanied by – and is partly the cause as well as the result of – a decline in public policing of fraud (public police having other priorities, the drain on skilled public police personnel). Levi concludes the public police will have to improve their motivation, their skills and confidence substantially before they are able to re-appropriate this arena of crime control.

References

Anechiarico, F. & J. Jacobs, *The Pursuit of Absolute Integrity. How Corruption Control Makes Government Ineffective,* University of Chicago Press, Chicago, 1996.

Cooper, T. (ed.), *Handbook of Administrative Ethics,* Marcel Dekker, New York, 2001.

Fijnaut, C., "De integriteit van de politie in Europees perspectief", *Delikt en Delinkwent*, 30, 2000, pp. 478-508.

Heidenheimer, A., M. Johnston & V. Levine (eds.), *Political Corruption. A Handbook*, Transaction Publishers, New Brunswick, NJ, 1989.

Heywood, P. (ed.), *Political Corruption*, Blackwell, Oxford, 1997.

Huberts, L., "Anticorruption Strategies: The Hong Kong Model in International Context", *Public Integrity*, 2, 2000, pp. 211-228.

Huberts, L., "Global Ethics and Corruption", in J. Rabin (ed.), *Encyclopedia of Public Administration and Public Policy*, Marcel Dekker, New York, 2002 (to be published).

Klitgaard, R., *Controlling Corruption*, University of California Press, Berkeley, 1988.

UNDP United Nations Development Programme, *Corruption & Integrity Improvement Initiatives in Developing Countries*, UNDP, New York, 1998.

Langseth, P., R. Stapenhurst & J. Pope, *The Role of A National Integrity System in Fighting Corruption*, The World Bank, Washington, DC, 1997.

Nichols, P., "The Myth of Anti-Bribery Laws as Transnational Intrusion", *Cornell International Law Journal*, 33, 2000, pp. 627-655.

OECD, *No Longer Business as Usual. Fighting Bribery and Corruption*, OECD, Paris, 2000.

OECD, *Trust in Government. Ethics Measures in OECD Countries*, OECD, Paris, 2000.

Pieth, M. & P. Eigen (eds.), *Korruption im internationalen Geschäftsverkehr. Bestandsaufnahme. Bekämpfung. Prävention*, Luchterhand, Neuwied, 1999.

Pope, J., *Confronting Corruption. The Elements of a National Integrity System (TI Source book 2000)*, Transparency International, Berlin, 2000 (also at http://www.transparency.org).

Punch, M., E. Kolthoff, K. van der Vijver & B. van Vliet (eds.), *Coping with Corruption in a Borderless World. Proceedings of the Fifth International Anti-Corruption Conference*, Kluwer Law and Taxation Publishers, Deventer, 1993.

Sampford, C., N. Preston (with C.-A. Bois) (eds.), *Public Sector Ethics. Finding and Implementing Values*, The Federation Press, Annandale and Routledge, London, 1998.

Transparency International, *The National Integrity System. Concept and Practice. A Report by Transparency International (TI) for the Global Forum II on Fighting Corruption and Safeguarding Integrity* (A Report Prepared by A. Doig and S. McIvor), Transparency International, Berlin, 2001.

Vahlenkamp, W. & I. Knauss, *Korruption. Hinnehmen oder Handeln?* Bundeskriminalamt, Wiesbaden, 1995.

Williams, J. & M. Beare, "The Business of Bribery. Globalisaton, Economic Liberalisation, and the 'Problem' of Corruption", *Crime, Law & Social Change*, 32, 1999, pp. 115-146.

Windsor, D. & K. Getz, "Multilateral Co-operation to Combat Corruption: Normative Regimes Despite Mixed Motives and Diverse Values", *Cornell International Law Journal*, 33, 2000, pp. 731-772.

The World Bank, *Anticorruption in Transition. A Contribution to the Policy Debate*, The World Bank, Washington, DC, 2000.

PART II

CORRUPTION AND ITS CONTAINMENT: THREE CASE STUDIES

CHAPTER 2

Processes of Corruption in Switzerland: Where is the Problem?

Nicolas Queloz

1. Introduction

Is corruption, such an apparently colourful and exotic topic, in any sense a cause for concern in Switzerland, a country notorious for its earnest and law-abiding disposition? We know of no scientific research carried out on corruption in Switzerland before the 1990s. However, by then the odd alarm bell was beginning to ring.

The first rang out in the summer of 1991, when Raphaël Huber was arrested in Zurich. He was a government official in charge of authorisations to open cafés, restaurants, pubs, night-clubs, etc. In 1995, he was found guilty of repeated and aggravated passive corruption, having pocketed "commissions" amounting to at least SFr. 2.4 million for granting such permits: a serious case of corruption of a Swiss public officer which became known as the "Wirte Connection", or the hotelkeepers' network.

Another important signal is that the number of Swiss Press Agency despatches about corruption events in Switzerland shot up from 11 in 1986 to 114 in 1996. If nothing else, this goes to show that the media no longer sees it as taboo to ask questions about the existence of corruption in Switzerland. At the Federal Parliament level, corruption was the subject of no fewer than 38 interventions (interpellations, motions, questions to the Government) submitted between 1990 and 1996.

On the international front, Switzerland, which in 1995 ranked 8th on the Transparency International integrity of public servants scale, dropped to number 12 in 2001.[1] This is clearly significant, and this country's reputation for being immune to corruption has become tarnished in the minds of international economic and financial analysts.

---

[1] Transparency International Corruption Perceptions Index; *cf.* www.transparency.org.

Cyrille Fijnaut, Leo Huberts (eds.), *Corruption, Integrity and Law Enforcement*, 37-48
©2002 Kluwer Law International, The Hague. Printed in The Netherlands.

To take a final, though not exhaustive, example, a Swiss court judge, Franco Verda, a member of the Supreme Criminal Court of the Canton Ticino, was arrested in June 2000, much to everybody's dismay. In June 2001, he was found guilty of aggravated passive corruption and repeated violations of professional secrecy on account of the benefits he sought and because of the guilty relations he had with Italian cigarette smugglers. This story sparked off a violent political and legal storm, which in no time came to be known as "Ticinogate".[2]

2. Description of our research project

From 1997 to 1999, we directed a research project on the processes of corruption in Switzerland (Queloz *et al.*, 2000) as part of a National Research Programme entitled "Everyday Violence and Organised Crime".[3] This interdisciplinary study (including law, criminology, sociology and political sciences) involved the Universities of Fribourg and Geneva working jointly to achieve three main objectives:

1. To fill in part the deficiencies in scientific and empirical knowledge on the subject of corruption in Switzerland;

2. To identify the branches of industry and the inter-relations between the political, administrative and economic spheres, which are the most vulnerable to corruption in Switzerland;

3. To draw up adequate action proposals to prevent and to respond as effectively as possible to corruption processes in Switzerland.

The successive steps and research methods used were:

1. An analysis of statistical data available (figures for both the economy and crime) and of the news stories logged in the Swiss Press Agency database;

2. An analysis of the contents of 330 criminal and disciplinary files relating to

---

2 However, whereas in 1995, R. Huber in Zurich was sentenced to five years' detention, fined SFr. 200,000 and obliged to pay back to the state SFr. 1.4 million, in 2001, in Lugano former Court Judge Franco Verda was sentenced to 18 months' detention, which he was in fact spared, as it was, generously, a suspended sentence.

3 This programme (NRP 40) has been approved by the Federal Government and financed by the Swiss National Science Foundation.

actual events of corruption involving public administration officials in the Cantons of Geneva, Ticino, and Valais;

3. A first series of more than 60 interviews with "privileged informers' (politicians, judges, policemen, businessmen, journalists) in the Cantons of Geneva, Ticino, and Valais, in an attempt to identify those areas of public and economic activity that are perceived as being the most sensitive to processes of corruption;

4. A thorough study of procurement contracts in the construction sector, a sector which from the evidence gathered in 2. and 3. has turned out to be the most vulnerable to corrupt practices; an analysis of laws and regulations, of economic conditions, plus 98 in-depth interviews (51 with entrepreneurs and with construction professionals; and 47 with politicians and with government officials in charge of procurement contracts, in the Cantons of Geneva, Ticino, and Valais);

5. A study of the "grey area" of corruption processes, namely trading in influence, clientelism, and cronyism, in particular; in Ticino, an analysis of the (seemingly) inevitable intermediary role played by political parties between public officials and company executives; in Geneva, the allocation procedure for work permits and residence permits (especially to multinational corporations); in Valais, surveillance (administrative supervision) and sanction procedures against corruption, and especially the much criticised role of justice;

6. Finally, a collation and summary of these numerous data, which we have also compared with the lessons drawn from other empirical studies conducted on corruption in our neighbouring countries (in Germany: Claussen, 1995; Vahlenkamp & Knauss, 1995; Poerting & Vahlenkamp, 1998; in France: Becquart-Leclercq, 1995; Cartier-Bresson, 1995 and 1999; Delmas-Marty & Manacorda, 1997; in Italy: Della Porta & Vannucci, 1994; Vannucci, 1997).

3. Processes of corruption

Switzerland has neither an act nor a global policy with which to confront corruption. If we wish to encompass the notion of corruption, therefore, we need to plough through quite a number of sections of our federal, cantonal and local legislation.

Despite this lack of transparency, we can attempt a simple, straightforward definition of corruption as being *an abuse (misuse) of a representative power*, whether the interests represented are private or public. Take the example of a local authority which, bypassing all public bid procedures, awards a school hardware and software equipment contract to a councillor who is both a member of the majority party and the director of a computer company. This is where the members of the executive abuse their official power of representation of public interests. As far as he is concerned, the entrepreneur-politician who has scooped up the contract abuses the power his electors entrusted to him to do his best to make public interest prevail over and above his own private interest. Another example: the architect or the engineer overseeing the building site for a new shopping centre, who, in collusion with other tradesmen, approves falsified work reports (excavation work, painting and decorating, electricity, etc.), misuses his power of representation and of safeguarding the proprietary interests of his elector (the owner).

Under public law, several scattered norms are supposed to prevent corruption, namely, the legislation on fair trading, on the home market, or on procurement contracts, various norms on the granting of authorisations and of permits of any sort, as well as administrative procedure regulations designed to prevent all conflicts of interest or to make it binding for anyone whose decision may be biased by self-interest to step down.

Company law, which includes regulations for book-keeping practices as well as for external auditors' responsibilities, also adds its contribution to the building of prevention of corruption.

It is no doubt criminal law that draws most sharply the contours of the dark face of corruption – its forbidden, repressed face. However, criminal law has a major drawback, for its task is to react after the event, only when an episode – one of many – has suddenly burst onto the public scene, and when the (long-diverted) funds can often no longer be recovered. Let us bear in mind that criminal law forbids both *public corruption* (where one of the protagonists is a public official, Swiss or otherwise)[4] and *private corruption*, between economic actors, against other economic actors (acts of unfair management and unfair competition).[5]

---

[4] Articles 322*ter* to 322*octies* of the Swiss Criminal Code, amended in 1999 (in force since May 2000) with a view to enabling Switzerland to sign the December 1997 OECD Convention on Combating Bribery of Foreign Public Officials in International Business Transactions.

[5] Articles 158 of the Swiss Criminal Code, and 4b and 23 of the Federal Act against unfair competition.

Reality is even more reductive in that a rather small part of public corruption (less than 25% of known cases) ends up being punished by the courts. As to private corruption, it goes virtually unpunished altogether.

Finally, influence peddling is not (yet) forbidden in Switzerland, whereas it is so in France and in Spain. The 1999 Council of Europe Criminal Law Convention on Corruption recommends that member states – and Switzerland is one – consider trading in influence as a punishable crime. Trading in influence is a subtler form of cronyism and favouritism that is definitely more widespread than corruption pure-and-simple. Thanks to trading in influence, one may obtain benefits, services, authorisations or employment on the basis of a network of acquaintances and "friendships" in exchange for returning the favour later. Trading in influence is an integral part of the Swiss social fabric. It has pride of place in what is customarily known as *processes of corruption*, in other words that whole set of corrupt trading practices, because it makes a mockery of the fundamental principle of equal opportunity of individuals and of non-discrimination between social groups.

4. Different facets of corruption in Switzerland

Reading first through the figures for *convictions* delivered on cases of corruption in Switzerland, we are struck by the following facts:

- Between six (in 1990) and 20 people (in 1997) are condemned each year;

- Eight out of ten people convicted are private actors (private individuals and businessmen: found guilty of so-called "active" corruption), whereas "passive" corruption imputed to public agents has remained at a fairly stable level and lower than "active" corruption: in 1997, for example, 16 private actors were convicted of corruption in Switzerland, as opposed to a mere four public ones.

Table 1: *Persons convicted of corruption in Switzerland*

1987-1997	*Switzerland as a whole*	*Evolution 1987-1997*
In all	133 (100%)	+ 18.5%
Public actors	26 (19.5%)	+ 22.5%
Private actors	107 (80.5%)	0%

In terms of quality, we may describe the following *typology* for acts of corruption condemned by a court:

1. Cases of petty corruption, be they out of misery or distress (e.g. relating to illegal immigrants), or out of trifling matters of which the "prototypes" are, on the one hand, the car driver who has been caught red-handed in a traffic offence, who tries to get away with not paying a fine, or, on the other hand, a civil servant who pockets small profits and who violates his duties;

2. Cases of corruption on public procurement contracts, the majority of which relate to the construction industry;

3. Cases of corruption connected with the issuing of authorisations, permits and other such documents;

4. Cases of corruption mixed up with economic and corporate crime, generally with forged documents, swindling, tax evasion, etc.;

5. A few cases of corruption connected with organised crime, in particular with human beings, arms, and narcotics trafficking, or cigarette smuggling;

6. Finally, several requests for international co-operation are established (mostly in Geneva and Ticino) regarding corruption cases abroad for which the money involved is deposited in Switzerland (money laundering investigations). In Ticino, for instance, approximately 4,000 requests for legal co-operation were received from Italy between 1992 and 1999 following the *Mani pulite* operation; 80% of these requests were linked to corruption episodes.

Nevertheless, what all these data show us is merely the tip of the iceberg of corruption. A survey conducted on Swiss companies has pointed out that at least 35% of the losses they admit to having suffered because of economic crime have something to do with corruption (ReviSuisse, 1997). While companies declare that corruption is costing them some SFr. 5.5 million a year, ReviSuisse reckons that this amount must be multiplied by at least 25 to get a more realistic notion of the costs of corruption inside the Swiss domestic economy!

What industry sectors are the most exposed and vulnerable to corruption practices? In-depth interviews with several professionals have enabled us to answer this question in a way that confirms the analysis of the court files. The building industry has been by far the most affected of all private procurement contract sectors, followed closely by property and tourism infrastructure. Next to these we find the supply of motor cars, computer hard- and software, health care equipment, furniture, etc. Between 1977 and 1997, for example, half of the people convicted in the

Cantons of Geneva, Ticino and Valais were professionals of the building industry (mostly private – entrepreneurs; less frequently public – civil servants).

Offences and abuses in the public contracts sector in Switzerland also include understandings on prices reached between awarders and bidders; cartel agreements between entrepreneurs; favouring of firms that are local and close to the majority political party; cheating on the definition, estimate and final award of services; inflated invoices, etc. Table 2 below not only shows up the various vulnerable sectors, but also highlights the interaction and unavoidable connections between the services of public administration and the private firms.

Table 2: *Sectors sensitive to corruption in Switzerland*

In public administration	*At the business end*
• Public works (roads, buildings)	• The entire building industry
• Regional planning and development	• Surveyors offices
	• Property, tourism infrastructures
	• Solicitors, accountancy firms, portfolio managers
• All services requiring equipment	• Garages
	• Computer firms
	• Various equipment: medical and sanitary, commercial, office furniture, etc.
• All services issuing licences, permits, expertise	• All submitting companies
• Tax, insolvency and receivership	• Several companies, including those in financial difficulties
• Police, customs and excise	• Companies under surveillance

5. Free competition in Switzerland: is it truly so?

Political philosophy and the philosophy of law tend to see the process of corruption as an offence against the basic democratic principle of the equality of all citizens and social actors before the law. In terms of philosophy of economics, however, the process of corruption is considered as an obstacle to free competition and, accordingly, its concrete effect as an expensive price to pay for the consumer, the taxpayer, and the entire economic and social system. Because procurement contracts are not subject to public tender under a given expense threshold (which varies according to the sort of service provided, but may reach as high as SFr. 750,000 for the building industry), the result is that those public bodies whose customary policy is to assign jobs in these protected sectors to their "old chums" make these happy in the short term, but in the medium and long term, this strategy can only be detrimental to the community as a whole.

Even in those cases where public contracts may be expected to be transparent, as for example in the building of motorways – abuse, fraud, and corruption are present. Total costs for Switzerland's motorway network were estimated at SFr. 5.7 billion in 1960; the final bill actually worked out at SFr. 60 billion in 1997 – an increase of 950%! Such an explosion of costs can hardly be put down to a simple rise in the cost of living, since the rate of growth of the latter between 1960 and 1997 was 273%.

It is quite striking to notice to what degree our findings match the figures produced by economic competition analyses. Thus, the latest (2000) Organisation for Economic Co-operation and Development (OECD) summary concludes that Switzerland remains swamped by cartels and that the malfunctioning of contracts results in price levels that are 30% higher than in the European Union member countries. According to the OECD, the consumer ends up footing the bill for these forms of anti-competitive behaviour, which also harm technological innovation.

As part of its recommendations, the OECD emphasises the importance of strengthening the effectiveness of Swiss legislation (on cartels and the domestic market) by providing the Federal Monopolies and Mergers Commission with much stronger resources and, as is the case in other European countries, with direct sanctioning powers that are a better deterrent. The Monopolies and Mergers Commission's annual reports illustrate the stunning variety of industry sectors in which Swiss companies regularly sign illegitimate agreements or regularly abuse their powers. As a matter of fact, everyday practices are therefore diametrically opposed to the tenets and to the ceaseless talk on the merits of economic liberalism!

6. Prevention and response strategies

To counter these processes of corruption, we firmly believe that a global strategy must be launched, which integrates in the first place measures of *prevention* (to this end we have formulated 35 proposals (Queloz & Borghi, 2001)) and, secondly, measures for sanctioning corruption (see our 15 proposals more directly connected with justice and the criminal code).

With regard to companies, our recommendations are aimed at organisation, professional practices and the legal framework. It must be pointed out that the values at stake do not regard merely the safeguarding of perfect competition in the economy. More fundamentally, it is a matter of respecting the principle of equal opportunity and of making sure that all decisions of general interest are based on objective – never venal – criteria. As to organisation, it should be possible, without becoming over-bureaucratic, to strengthen the supervision of people and procedures as well as to set up a regular rotation of staff (both private and public) that are the most exposed to reports on corruption.

As to procurement contracts, we put forward a set of measures designed to spread and reach further afield with publicity, transparency and the oversight of the smooth running of its agencies. Having ascertained how much the relations between companies, the administration, and the political class inevitably depend on the intermediary of political parties, there seems to us to be no choice for Switzerland but to pass a law regulating political party funding, including provisions setting a ceiling for election campaign expenses (Balmelli, 2001). In fact, it makes no sense regulating party funding unless one also sets an upper limit to their out-goings. Having omitted to do so, France and Germany find themselves tangled up in countless cases of secret financing and corruption.

Concomitantly, it is important that all contracts and deals tainted with corruption be rendered void (*ab initio*), that private corruption (i.e. between economic partners) be paid as much attention as public corruption, and that influence peddling be made a criminal offence. In this respect, from the interviews we have conducted for the purposes of this research we can infer that public opinion in Switzerland is inclined, on the whole, to regard trading in influence as a crime (*cf.* Table 3). This is bound to encourage the Federal Government in its determination to have Parliament ratify the Council of Europe Civil and Criminal Law Conventions on Corruption, for which trading in influence is part and parcel of the process of corruption.

Table 3: *Social perception of trading in influence in Switzerland*

(Questionnaire used in the Canton of Valais)

	Yes
Is cronyism, clientelism or trading in influence a component of corruption? (People answering = 64)	76.5%
According to you, the practice of cronyism, clientelism or trading in influence is: (People answering = 64)	*Yes*
• Ethically and juridically unacceptable, hence to be punished?	54%
• Public actors:	60%
• Private actors:	45%
• Ethically unacceptable, but juridically acceptable (hence not punishable)?	43%
• Public actors:	40%
• Private actors:	46%
• Ethically and juridically acceptable (hence not punishable)?	3%
• Public actors:	0%
• Private actors:	9%

Finally, Switzerland must introduce into its legislation – which is far from being the case yet! – the principle of criminal responsibility for legal entities, companies and firms. This criminal liability must be matched by effective sanctions such as suspension, or even final exclusion, for firms that do not abide by the rules of fair-trading and public contracts. We expect most company executives to be honest people, hence they, too, may be expected to mobilise and lend a hand in putting the house in order by throwing out the black sheep who give the economy a bad name

(Elliott, 1997). On the other hand, self-regulation and codes of good practice are not enough. They need to join forces with the public mechanisms of this global strategy to withstand the attacks of the corruption process. There is no denying that such a strategy will require radical changes in political and economic outlook and behaviour (Alvazzi del Frate & Pasqua, 2000). Let us hope that Switzerland and the other rich countries of the world act with determination and implement these changes without hypocrisy.

References

Alvazzi del Frate, A. & G. Pasqua (eds.), *Responding to the Challenges of Corruption*, Unicri, Rome, 2000.

Balmelli, T., *Le financement des partis politiques et des campagnes électorales; entre exigences démocratiques et corruption*, Éditions Universitaires, Fribourg, 2001.

Becquart-Leclercq, J., "Réseaux politiques: gagnants et victimes de l'échange corrompu", in P. Claeys & A. Frognier (eds.), *L'échange politique*, Editions de l'Université de Bruxelles, Bruxelles, 1995, pp. 247-270.

Cartier-Bresson, J., "Les réseaux de la corruption et la stratégie des 3 S: Sleep – Silence – Smile", in M. Borghi & P. Meyer-Bisch (eds.), *La corruption, l'envers des droits de l'homme*, Éditions Universitaires, Fribourg, 1995, pp. 81-106.

Cartier-Bresson, J., "Causes et conséquences de la délinquance financière 'grise': le cas de la corruption", *Les cahiers de la sécurité intérieure*, 36, 1999, pp. 63-89.

Claussen, H., *Korruption im öffentlichen Dienst,* Carl Heymanns Verlag, Köln, 1995.

Della Porta, D. & A. Vannucci, *Corruzione politica ed amministrazione pubblica,* Il Mulino, Bologna, 1994.

Delmas-Marty, M. & S. Manacorda, "La corruption: un défi pour l'état de droit et la société démocratique", *Revue de science criminelle et de droit pénal comparé,* 1997, 3, pp. 696-706.

Elliott, K., *Corruption and the Global Economy*, Institute for International Economics, Washington, DC, 1997.

OECD (Organisation for Economic Co-operation and Development), *Economic Study of Switzerland*, Paris, 2000.

Poerting, P. & W. Vahlenkamp, "Internal Strategies against Corruption. Guidelines for Preventing and Combating Corruption in Police Authorities", *Crime, Law and Social Change*, 29, 1998, pp. 225-249.

Queloz, N., "Criminalité économique et criminalité organisée: comment les différencier?" in S. Bauhofer, N. Queloz & E. Wyss (eds.), *Wirtschaftskriminalität – Criminalité économique*, Verlag Rüegger, Chur, 1999, pp. 17-50.

Queloz, N., M. Borghi & M. Cesoni, *Processus de corruption en Suisse*, Helbing & Lichtenhahn, Basle, 2000.

Queloz, N. & M. Borghi, "50 proposals towards an integrated strategy to prevent and counter corruption", *AGON* (Review of the Associations of lawyers for the protection of the financial interests of the European Communities) 30, 2001, pp. 1-4. In French, see *AGON*, 27, 2000, pp. 6-15. In German, see *AGON*, 31, 2001, pp. 15-18.

ReviSuisse, *Wirtschaftskriminalität*, ReviSuisse PriceWaterhouse, Zürich, 1997.

Vahlenkamp, W. & I. Knauss, *Korruption. Hinnehmen oder Handeln?* Bundeskriminalamt, Wiesbaden, 1995.

Vannucci, A., *Il mercato della corruzione*, Società aperta, Milano, 1997.

CHAPTER 3

Investigation Strategies and Tactics in the Prosecution of Corruption Offences: Experiences from Germany

Manfred Nötzel

1. Introduction

The field of "corruption in economic life" was not seen as a problem in Germany until the beginning of the 1990s. Only a few isolated cases were known.

The first relevant examples of fraudulent price-fixing arrangements and briberies attracted an extraordinary amount of public attention. Many cases were discovered in Frankfurt (at the airport) and, briefly afterwards, also in Munich. These experiences and the realisation that it did not concern isolated cases by any means, but that – in any event in certain areas – contracts from public authorities could, over the years, exclusively be obtained by bribery payments, fraudulent price-fixing arrangements and cartels, led to the deep concern and indignation of the public. As a reaction to this all, the political forces decided that the fight against this type of criminality should receive increased priority.

2. Department XII

One of the first measures in Bavaria was the establishment of the Economic Department XII of the Public Prosecutor's Office Munich I. It has the task of dedicating itself exclusively to the fight against corruption. The Public Prosecutor's Office Munich I is within the jurisdiction of the Regional Court Munich I. This court is essentially responsible for the area of the Bavarian capital together with some surrounding municipalities. It therefore covers approximately 1.5 million inhabitants. The city accommodates a number of very large firms known throughout the world and it is a very strong economic centre in southern Germany. In particular the Bavarian capital, with the establishment of fair and congress centres, a large airport, sewage purification plants and road as well as tunnel constructions, is an

Cyrille Fijnaut, Leo Huberts (eds.), *Corruption, Integrity and Law Enforcement*, 49-58
©2002 Kluwer Law International, The Hague. Printed in The Netherlands.

extremely powerful client for firms in the construction industry. From one of these projects, the sewage purification plant "Munich II", developed the first large preliminary investigation in Munich, which had far-reaching consequences.

In the case of this large building project somewhere outside Munich, an electrical industrialist had in 1991 claimed in his tax declaration an extraordinarily high (DM 400,000) alleged commission payment as an operating expenditure. This sum, in relation to the extent of the orders and the unknown invoicing parties from the Middle East for the project, raised strong doubts as to the correctness of this document on the part of the auditor from the tax office. He contacted the Public Prosecutor's Office, which affirmed the special public interest in the prosecution of this type of tax evasion. Investigations were opened and took a course which nobody in Bavaria could have foreseen. The industrialist was held on remand and his firm was investigated. Within a short time, one of the accused confessed his participation in an area-wide electricity cartel, which had for years divided up among itself *all* the main electricity orders from the public authority. The data required extensive investigation in a vast number and wide range of acts before individual cases could be investigated in depth. Beyond the area of the electricity cartels, the investigations had to be quickly extended to cover engineering in the area of canal and road construction, Munich II airport, painting and sanitary work, gas and water pipe laying and many other fields.

2.1. Results

Up to the end of October 2001 some results are to be recorded from the activity of Department XII, which was set up in 1994 and comprises 11 state lawyers. There are 392 preliminary investigations still open and 627 convictions have been obtained. The sanctions add up to nearly 560 years' imprisonment. Diverse financial fines total DM 49 million. Damage to the public purse on the basis of these investigations amounts to approximately DM 78 million. This means that due to the work of Department XII, the perpetrators and their firms had to pay altogether about DM 127 million (or about US$ 60 million) to the public purse.

These numbers do not cover the separately led 791 investigations into the pharmaceutical area of allowances to doctors in the civil service.

There were only two acquittals in criminal procedures by the department.

3. Factors leading to or allowing for corruption

In the public administration, the following factors should be considered in order to prevent "calm biotopes", areas in which, with organisation and control, corruption structures develop, grow and prosper over the years.

- Because of the high number of orders, the critical areas are always departments of procurement, allocation of agencies, places which can give permission and concessions or carry out controls and forbid activities. These require greatest attention;

- In no case should the placing of orders, controls and payment orders for any significant procedures be under the control of one person;

- There are employees in these areas who have been engaged in the same activity for years and who even when ill or on leave appear in order to prevent checks by a representative into their area. They reject transfers – even if associated with promotion – and give rise to rumours because of their life style or economic situation. Such employees should be particularly closely watched and be examined repeatedly without prior warning;

- In the case of repeated or constant favouring of certain industrialists (so-called "favoured contractors") increased vigilance is likewise requested.

To these approved means the following measures should be added:
- Regularly job rotation;

- The general principle of double signature;

- Complete documentation of every step of procurement and payment;

- Basic training and education;

- Efficient control measures and control bodies.

For example, Munich uses a "measurement checking team" with great success. This team appears unannounced at building sites and checks whether the measurements are actually applicable. Enormous possibilities for manipulation of calculations exist with building projects, since they are based on the air passages.

4. Strategy and tactics

4.1. Co-operation

For intensive and effective investigations, it is very important to have open and early co-operation with and between the other authorities.

- The police authorities need adequate staff, including specialists such as accountants, banking experts and IT experts. A thorough, quick and targeted evaluation of seized documents is possible only by using such specialists;

- Intensive co-operation with the revenue offices is needed, in particular in the areas of fiscal investigation and audit. Here the legal situation in Germany notably improved with the loosening of what had been very strict tax secrecy laws. Since 1999, the revenue offices are obliged to communicate suspicions of corruption to the Public Prosecutor's Office. In response, the investigative authorities are obliged to convey any findings on the suspicions to the revenue offices for the purpose of establishing the taxes evaded. Bribes are actually almost never taxed. There are exceptions only where the payment of the bribe is covered by a falsified invoice of alleged work, which – allegedly – must be paid;

- Many authorities and municipalities have introduced the position of the "corruption representative". These employees – taken from the hierarchy – are indispensable partners, if suspicions are to be discretely examined. They have regular access to the IT that is used, and to the files. They are also extraordinarily helpful during the preparation of searches, arrests of officials and the security of evidence in offices.

In addition to further state bodies, with which the Public Prosecutor's Office co-operates, I wish to mention the Bavarian police authorities (intelligence service), in particular the Bavarian administrative office for the protection of the Constitution. The Bavarian law on the protection of the Constitution has obliged the administrative office since 1994 to dedicate themselves also to the "protection against organised crime", to observe such efforts, and to communicate any concrete suspicions.

In this area alone this year, two important events related to organised crime in the field of corruption have taken place. In one case, a source from the service was asked by an accused to extort a corrupt official. The official had threatened the accused that he would remove him from the kitchen equipment cartel because he was behind in bribe payments and would not use him any more in future transactions. It did not get that far. On the basis of the observations and the information from the service and after examination of the suspicious situation, three accused officials were arrested and 28 firms involved were examined, resulting in further arrests.

This case revealed something new. For thc first time it was not the companies who had actively approached the office-holders with offers of corruption. Rather the office-holders (two senior clerks and the department manager responsible for the procurement area) had united in a "gang". They determined which of the firms were accepted into the cartel and who therefore took part in the placing of orders. A condition was that the firm accepted the cartel conditions. In particular this meant that between 6% and 40% of each sum had to be paid to the officials in cash. This involved several million Deutschmarks over three years (and this was only for kitchens for schools, kindergartens etc. in the Munich area alone). Most of the perpetrators confessed. Unusually, the investigators found exact lists with demands, arrears and disbursement data for the bribes.

Another similarly organised case concerned the allocation of driving licences and the distribution of driving licence examinations. These investigations are still in their early stages.

4.2. Obtaining information and evidence

Which tactics and instruments are decisive for success in the fight against corruption, and how can we succeed in obtaining information and evidence?

Of course, statements and confessions of the perpetrators are extremely crucial. Corruption and fraud offences are constructed from the outset exclusively on the basis of collusion and cover-up.

It helps us that the danger of collusion is a serious ground for arrest in the German laws of criminal procedure and therefore, in the case of sufficient suspicion, such perpetrators can be held on remand. On the other hand, and independently of this, the risk of absconding can be easily eliminated by posting of considerable bail. This instrument of remand has proved to be extraordinarily necessary and also effective. Without an immediate decision to make an arrest – as numerous cases have shown – all the existing evidence is immediately destroyed and arrangements between the participants are made if this hasn't already happened. If this cannot be prevented, the success of the investigation is jeopardised.

These procedures of collusion and cover-up cause us problems of course in that they thereby reveal the criminal offence and the establishment of the perpetrator's guilt is made more difficult. The accused are often extraordinarily intelligent businessmen, who always include uncertainties in their considerations. The perpetrators are helped naturally to a considerable extent by the fact that each participant makes himself liable to be penalised, whether he takes or gives a bribe. He also makes himself liable to be penalised if he gives an "offer of protection" to the "competitor" and thereby helps him to make a fraudulent order at an exaggerated price. Not only is this punishable, but it also exposes the "provider of protection", the perpetrator, to the danger of having to make payment for the damages. All this usually means that each perpetrator can rely on the fact that all others will be silent, because all have completely parallel interests.

4.2.1. Cartel of silence

This applies in the same way to the bribed office-holders, because there is no real "victim". Those damaged are the honest competitors (who know or can prove nothing) and then, above all, the public authority. In order to break open this cartel of silence, the Public Prosecutor's Office nearly always relies on the confession statements of the perpetrator, particularly those leading to further perpetrators and punishable acts. However, like many things in life, such statements are not for free. For most of the accused, the outcome it will take is already decided at an early stage of the procedure. If an understanding is reached between him, his lawyer and the Public Prosecutor's Office regarding an acceptable measure of punishment (or the guarantee that the Public Prosecutor's Office will advocate a light punishment), many accused are willing to make a statement. The worrying alternative for the accused consists of holding his nerve and waiting to see if he himself is incriminated by others with the consequence that he does not receive a mitigation of punishment but a long prison sentence.

The present criminal instruments do not allow the possibility of granting such a perpetrator "chief witness" status, which may have meant the relevant court would even refrain from punishment. The Public Prosecutor's Office has been demanding such a regulation, which already exists in the area of narcotics criminality, for a long time – but so far unsuccessfully. This year an appropriate bill has been tabled again before the Parliament. So far only the Public Prosecutor's Office has the possibility of refraining from the prosecution of individual acts and of promising that the remaining acts will be dealt with leniently. Almost without exception, the courts do take these agreements into account, although an express obligation for this does not exist.

The above-mentioned bill also regulates the power existing to carry out bugging of telecommunications equipment when there is a suspicion of corruption offences. This new regulation will certainly be introduced and removes a deficiency in the instruments, which has been deplored for years. Bugging can only be carried out at present, if there are further offences involved – such as membership of criminal association, money laundering or "organised fraud group".

Recently, the Public Prosecutor's Office had a case in which several accused were simultaneously searched. A telephone conversation was overheard in which one of the accused informed her brother (the other accused) that the police were in the process of searching his apartment. The brother asked the reason for the search, and the sister replied that the search was being made because of "criminal association". This clearly implied that both the brother's and the sister's telephone calls were being intercepted. They therefore stopped contacting each other by telephone. Now that corruption offences permit phone tapping, this type of warning will no longer be possible and the effectiveness of the instrument of tapping will therefore increase.

Even though the accused know that it is possible their telephone is bugged, this measure nevertheless continues to prove extraordinarily effective. Not every call is planned and, despite the fear of being overheard, the accused often discloses a surprising amount of useful information.

4.2.2. Financial investigations

Thorough financial investigations are also important as they often lead to evidence. Of course, not only the known bank accounts of the accused and other responsible firms are to be checked. Here in particular, cash transactions, that is payments in and out, are to be checked. According to our experience, cash is still the lubricant that oils the wheels.

For large firms it is not at all easy to produce off-the-record funds and cash without leaving tell-tale traces. Large cash withdrawals with the alleged goal of paying foreign employees are a popular excuse. Further examples are alleged progress payments on the building site, or the payment for alleged support services to subsidiaries and others. By adjustment of the receiving accounts it can usually be ascertained whether the data is correct.

It is important to clarify the question as to whether the economic relationship between the accused and his known and legal income is explicable. Furthermore all credit cards and their use (even local) should always be investigated. Often one receives indications from this as to where the accused office-holder stayed, whether the person accused of giving the bribe was also there, and whether there are further bank accounts or properties in these places.

5. Future

How successful is the struggle against corruption? In some areas clear success has been achieved. It is illustrative that in recent years several very large projects in Munich (including the Fair) have been conducted within the projected cost framework, or even below it.

An interesting project has been the planning and construction of a specific tunnel. In the beginning of the 1990s this tunnel was planned on the city motorway in Munich. The calculated costs at that time (1992), in the tradition of the Munich cartel arrangement, were DM 220 million, based on the first tender. However, the project was delayed for political reasons. In 1997 the decision was made to nevertheless build the tunnel. On the basis of the very complicated procedure under public law, no new procurement procedure was carried out, but exactly the same object was set out. The offer from the building firms involved for this identical project was set, five years later, at DM 140 million – DM 80 million lower! Obviously prices had not fallen to this extent despite very much fiercer competition. This drop is probably due to the fact that the building firms knew that the Public Prosecutor's Office were aware of earlier fraud incidents and nobody wanted to run the risks again.

Negative experiences unfortunately accompany those successes. It is fair to say that, despite the work that has been done in this area, including all the publications, investigations and convictions, the necessary deterrence has not yet been achieved by any means. New cases of corruption have been discovered and investigated. The "kitchen equipment cartel" has already been mentioned in which officials from Munich asked for and obtained bribes, right up until their arrest in December 2000. Recently these perpetrators were sentenced to very long terms of imprisonment.

Another criminal procedure concerned bribes demanded and received by representatives of the Bavarian Red Cross for the material procurement of the blood donation service. This caused substantial damage and the perpetrators were sentenced to long terms of imprisonment. However, I am afraid that this has not been the last big corruption case for our department.

Nevertheless, some optimism is justified. The support of the international community and the overwhelming majority of the public for the work of the Public Prosecutor's Office helps to prevent the expansion of this phenomenon. Perhaps we are even succeeding in pushing these practices back.

As the estimate of the renowned non-governmental organisation Transparency International shows, there still remains a lot to do. In the ranking of the Corruption Perceptions Index (CPI) for 1999, Germany was in an acceptable 7th place.

However, Germany's ranking in 2000 dropped to 17th place, and – *horribile dictu* – for 2001 fell further to 20th place. Whether this suggests an increase in the criminal offences or only a higher consciousness of the problem and an increased number of well-known incidents, I am not able to judge. But it shows that further substantial efforts are necessary, in order to approach the common goal, both nationally and internationally.

We feel particularly obliged to achieve the goal of intensified international co-operation. With the newly created law for the prosecution of corruption in international business (*IntBestG*) our competence was extended. However, to date, only one concrete case from this area has been presented for examination by us.

Improved international co-operation proves increasingly important. We already have good experience with our neighbouring states in Europe and also with the Community bodies – such as the anti-fraud office in Brussels. We learned from the Munich experience that it takes close collaboration with all police authorities in confronting well-organised syndicates in order to be successful. Also internationally, it will be necessary to place a "cartel of the prosecution authorities" against the corresponding organisations of the perpetrators.

CHAPTER 4

The Battle against Corruption in the Context of a Developing Country: the Case of Indonesia

Adi Soetjipto

1. The map of corruption in Indonesia

Indonesia is a country having the most serious corruption cases in the world. The 28 October 1999 edition of the *Straits Times* quoted a report by the Berlin-based Transparency International that Indonesia was the third most corrupt country from a list of 99 countries. In all fields, especially in bureaucracy, from the lowest level to the highest level, people practice corruption whenever there is a chance to do so. It is not wrong to say that corruption has become common practice in Indonesia.

1.1. Common practice

Corruption is part of every day life in Indonesia. It could happen to you whenever you want to have fun, or when you are grieving. A permit to have a big party will not be issued in time unless you give the officers money (so-called "illegal levies"). Suppose your daughter is getting married and want to have a party with live music (not uncommon in our country). You will have to pay illegal levies to make sure that your plan can be carried out according to the schedule. When you are happy, you might not feel hurt by the request to make such payment. But imagine, if someone dies, you could also be extorted when you ask for necessary permits for the funeral and the certificate of death. This is surely too much. Unfortunately, it is common practice in Indonesia.

1.2. Public services

These illegal levies are part of the day-to-day life of Indonesia, and sums involved are quite small. A larger scale of corruption happens in government offices that

Cyrille Fijnaut, Leo Huberts (eds.), *Corruption, Integrity and Law Enforcement*, 59-72
©2002 Kluwer Law International, The Hague. Printed in The Netherlands.

offer public services, either at mayoral, regency, provincial or central government level. Of course, there are many "tables" there and to pass each table, you have to pay the illegal levy, otherwise, things will not run smoothly. What could take two or three days will require ten days or even longer. For example, in the mayoral office, funds for the construction of a school building or a road would be allocated not just to finance the project, but also to be distributed to officials handling the project. It is not surprising that many school buildings collapse only a few years after construction, and that many roads are seriously damaged a few months after they are built. This is because of the poor quality of materials – the amount of cement or quality of wood. How could that happen? Why is there no control from the Ministry of Public Works? Well, those who are supposed to make the controls are actually involved in the practice of collusion with the project officers, so they do not report the irregularities. It is evident that the dirty money is distributed among the project officers, the developers and the supervisors.

In the 21 April 2001 edition of the daily *Kompas* there was a report on the poor condition of elementary school buildings in West Kalimantan. According to the newspaper, 2,916 of 3,889 elementary school buildings in the province were damaged, 75% of them are seriously so. The local department of the national education office denied the allegation of corruption and collusion in the construction of those buildings, arguing that they were about 20 years old. But there was clearly corruption and collusion, because a good building should last about 50 years.

A similar situation applies to the roads. Suppose the construction of a road needs one tonne of asphalt. Only half a tonne is used for the road, the rest of the money finding itself being chanelled into certain pockets. No wonder public roads are in such bad condition.

What is possibly more difficult to imagine is corruption in the issuing of driving licenses. I have personal experience in this case involving my own servant. After he completed a 16-hour driving course, I found out that he was still far from being able to drive well. However, he could get a driving license by paying Rp. 275,000 (US$ 27) without taking part in the written examination or the driving test. Officially, to obtain a driving license you must pass the written and practical tests, and must also be in possession of an ID card. However, if you do not have an ID card, you can still buy one from the local authorities for Rp. 150,000 (about US$ 15). No wonder the traffic in Jakarta and Bandung is so chaotic – many motorists are not aware of traffic regulations or driving ethics.

In Indonesia, you must extend your vehicle title document once a year by producing the old vehicle title document, the vehicle ownership document and the ID card of the vehicle owner. If you are not the original owner of the car, you should first process the car ownership document under your name. But this rarely happens – even though the vehicle has been sold to another person, all documents are still possessed by the original owner. As a result, when one has to extend the vehicle title document, the ID card of the original owner is not available. But this can be solved with money. As the amount of the necessary bribe is less than the cost of processing the transfer of ownership document, only a few people transfer vehicle ownership to their own name.

1.3. Mega-corruption

There is also corruption involving large sums of money. This mega-corruption involves billions or even trillions of Rupiah. The money is kept overseas – it is estimated that overseas funds total about US$ 200-300 billion. This money is deposited in accounts in developed countries under a complicated money laundering system and was accumulated from the time former President Soeharto was in power. It was illegally deducted from the export of crude oil by state-owned Pertamina Gas and Oil Company, mining products (nickel, coals, gold, iron ore), logs, crops, marine products, as well as from the bonuses on, commissions for, and marking up and undervaluing of imports of machinery, ships, weapons and spare parts. It also came from projects of the state-owned electric company PLN and from oil refinery projects.

Almost all of the families of ministers in Soeharto's cabinet obtained business contracts because of their recommendation. From the time Soeharto became President until his resignation in May 1998, 148 ministers served under him. Of these, 96 (64.9%) were involved directly or indirectly in various businesses. The practice still took place under Habibie's administration, but the tendency declined – only 9 of 16 cabinet ministers were involved in businesses. Under President Abdurrahman Wahid's Government, ministers also had business interests. Of the 45 ministers in his cabinet, the President only 20 appointed of them – Soeharto or Habibie appointed the rest. And of those 20, 15 are involved in various outside businesses (*Kompas*, 11 April 2001, quoting data from the Business Data Centre led by Christianto Wibisono). It is not clear if these ministers also abused their power to win business contracts.

1.4. Law enforcement

What is really disturbing is the fact that there are also corruptors among law enforcers, police officials, prosecutors and judges. Even though the amount of money they receive is not as big as the amount of money obtained by corrupt ministers or business people, nevertheless the state suffers significant losses, including the loss of public trust in the law enforcement. Which also negatively affects the economy for which we are now paying the price. Foreign investors are reluctant to invest in Indonesia because they do not trust the legal certainty in the country.

1.5. Corruption is everywhere

That is what faces Indonesia: corruption is everywhere, like epidemic disease that spreads over the people and is difficult to combat. All efforts have been made, but the disease becomes more serious. The development of global trade and the removal of the state borders through various organisations and trade system and the free foreign exchange flow, for example through the World Trade Organisation and the Asia Pacific Economic Co-operation forum, together with the development of the telecommunication technology and computer (internet, e-mail, e-commerce) have boosted the practice of corruption in various forms.

In Indonesia, the development of corruption cannot be separated from the social form which in the beginning was based on paternalism, the obligation to provide "*upeti*" (gifts) to please the boss and the influence of feudalistic authoritarian lifestyle under Soeharto's 32-year nepotic and autocratic administration. Positions in the government were given to his favourites in order to guarantee his power in the administration. In the revolution (1945-1950), unscrupulous activities were shunned by the freedom fighters, as they believed an independent spirit could save them from disaster as long as they were clean. This happened until the establishment of political parties, who began to spread their influence to the public. To this was added the pressure of a lifestyle they copied from abroad. Even though the level of corruption was still low, this created unrest, thus repressive action was taken. Several officials were questioned and detained in 1957-1958, but this amounted to little more than politicking.

In other words, the efforts to combat corruption in Indonesia started 40 years ago with the establishment of anti-corruption teams, which all ended up in failure. The last one was the Joint Investigation Team for Fighting Corruption, which I chaired for seven months, but then resigned when I felt that it was failing.

2. The government's efforts to combat corruption

The last effort made to combat corruption when I was still chairman of the Joint Investigation Team for Fighting Corruption was to urge the government to declare the state of emergency against corruption so that emergency steps could be taken. Institutions assigned to combat corruption should be given extraordinary authority above the common authority based on the anti-corruption law. For example, the implementation of the retroactive system, the shifting of the burden of proof, protection for witnesses and the establishment of a special court to try corruption cases with ad hoc judges, changing the negative legal theory of evidence to positive legal theory of evidence, acknowledging the wider interpretation of laws and regulations and severe punishment for corruptors who were proven guilty were among the ideas that could be included in the abovementioned emergency steps. The idea to urge the government to declare the state of emergency against corruption is to find a reason for the government to make a "Government Decree in lieu of a Law". According to the Indonesia Constitution of 1945, the government can make a decree in lieu of a law only if there is a state of emergency. Unfortunately, up to now, the government has not reacted positively to our suggestion.

2.1. Lack of political will

Of course, it all depends on the government's will to seriously combat corruption. If the combat of corruption is only used as political commodity, as is happening in Indonesia, I am sure that in the next 40 years, corruption will still be as serious as now, if not worse. The political elite who in the past failed to take firm action against corruptors partly caused today's condition, even setting a bad example by conducting corrupt practices themselves. Now corruption is everywhere, and I think the only way to combat it is by declaring a state of emergency against corruption.

At first glance it seems that the Indonesian government takes the combat of corruption seriously, as proven by the issuance of the Decree of the People's Consultative Assembly no. XI/MPR/1998 on Clean Governance which is free from Corruption, Collusion and Nepotism; Law no. 28/1999 on Clean Governance that is Free from Corruption, Collusion and Nepotism; Law no. 31/1999 on Anti-Corruption; and the establishment of the Joint Investigation Team for Fighting Corruption based on Government's Decree no. 19/2000. But these laws and regulations are not of value unless they are implemented seriously.

The Decree of the People's Consultative Assembly no. XI/MPR/1998 stated, among other things, that to avoid the practice of corruption, collusion and nepotism, anyone entrusted with a government position should declare their wealth and be prepared to be audited, before and after they take up the position. Law no. 28/1999 which is the executing regulation of Decree no. XI/MPR/1998 stipulates that any state official must be willing to have their wealth audited before, during and after they hold the position, must declare their wealth, and must not conduct any practice of corruption, collusion and nepotism. Even though this stipulation is regulated by a decree of the People's Consultative Assembly, which means that it is of the highest order, this is only good on paper because the government does not seriously implement it.

Recently, the State Official's Wealth Audit Commission (KPKPN) was established. It is an independent institution, which has the duty to ensure clean governance, free from corruption, collusion and nepotism. The Commission started work, announcing the wealth of President Abdurrahman Wahid and of Vice-President Megawati Soekarnoputri. The announcement was made on 18 April 2001. Megawati and her husband own 14 properties in the form of land and buildings, obtained by them and from inheritance, worth Rp. 24.3 billion. The couple also have 12 cars and 10 motorcycles worth Rp. 1.5 billion and eight gas stations which bring in Rp. 31 billion. The total wealth is Rp. 59.8 billion. The wealth of the President in the same period, Abdurrahman Wahid, is almost Rp. 3.5 billion. This includes land and buildings, which he earned himself, worth Rp. 658 million, five cars at Rp. 314 million, a collection of gold and jewelleries, arts and antique objects worth Rp. 1.8 billion. A total of Rp. 1.72 billion of his wealth was a grant, which he obtained in the period of 1999 and 2000. Which means that in one year, he received a grant amounting to almost half of his total wealth. In comparison, *Warta Ekonomi* on 29 May 2000 estimated that the wealth of former President Soeharto is US$ 1.7 billion – approximately Rp. 17 trillion (*Kompas*, 19 April 2001).

This is an example of the wealth of just the President, Vice-President and a former President in the third most corrupt country in the world. We have not talked about the wealth of former or current ministers, or the six groups of state officials who have to declare their wealth:

- State officials at the People's Consultative Assembly;

- State officials at the Supreme Advisory Board;

- Governors and judges;

- Other state officials such as ambassadors, deputy governors, regents, mayors;

- State officials with strategic positions such as executives of the Bank of Indonesia;

- Executives of state universities, prosecutors, investigators, court clerks, project officers and treasurers.

In the case of the government's efforts to combat corruption, it is the wealth of the former President and former ministers who should have been audited first because they were able to carry out corrupt practices. I agree with the attorney general's effort to investigate former President Soeharto, the former director of Pertamina, the former Minister of Mine and Energy, the eldest daughter and the youngest son of Soeharto and the former Minister of Trade. But I wonder, how many others will be investigated and prosecuted? Will the prosecutors be able to carry out the job? Because, with so many cases, this is a complicated job, especially in the proof and the variety of the cases: from the field of agriculture to those of tax, customs and excise, and aviation. In short, there is corruption in almost every field. This is without mentioning the resistance from many parties who are not happy with the investigation of their wealth. Those who are not happy fight by using the loopholes of the law and regulations. Besides, the national leader does not support the efforts to combat corruption having made a statement that certain people should not be investigated.

2.3. Joint Investigation Team for Fighting Corruption

In an effort to combat corruption, the attorney general has established a Joint Investigation Team for Fighting Corruption, based on article 27 of Law no. 31/1999 on Anti-Corruption, which states: "In case there is a corruption case which is difficult to prove, a joint team can be established under the co-ordination of the attorney general". The Joint Investigation Team for Fighting Corruption was consequently established by Government Decree no. 19/2000. But the materials stipulated in the regulation were too broad – such as the arrest, detention, search, the freezing of a bank account, the opening of a bank secrecy and phone tapping – and need to be regulated by law. Therefore, in its judicial review decision, the Supreme Court annulled Government Decree no. 19/2000 on 23 May 2001 and declared it illegal. The Joint Investigation Team for Fighting Corruption therefore lost its legal basis and had to be disbanded.

As a matter of fact the Joint Investigation Team for Fighting Corruption had many weaknesses. It was not independent because it was under the co-ordination of the attorney general. The authority of the team was restricted to examining only corruption cases which were difficult to prove. And in order to decide that the case was difficult to prove, a decision had to be made by the attorney general. Within seven months of the team being established, it received more than 100 reports from the public, but the number which were difficult to prove, as decided by the attorney general, was only seven or eight. Of six cases on the team's priority list, none have been sent to court. It is for these reasons that I offered my resignation from the Joint Investigation Team for Fighting Corruption.

2.4. Justice, law and procedures

Why are no cases sent to court? What are the problems facing the team? The main problem is that the team often conflicts with law enforcement procedures. This could be explained by the "liberal culture", which includes the adoption of liberal law in some modern countries, including Indonesia. The liberal system puts weight on individual rights and freedoms and is implemented by, among other things, procedures which respect the protection of individuals so much that they often put aside truth, justice and humanity. As a consequence, there is a dichotomy between substantial justice on one side, and the enforcement of procedural law on the other side. Under such a system, law enforcement often overshadows justice. Worse, the system is combined with corrupt law enforcers. That is the case in Indonesia, where all efforts to combat corruption under normal and "obedient" principles can be easily challenged by the law enforcers themselves. As an example, Indonesia implements the negative legal theory of evidence. This means that even though the court examination finds enough legal evidence, if the judge is not convinced that the defendant really committed the crime as indicted, the defendant must be exonerated. It so happened that the first case handled by the team was a corruption case involving three Supreme Court justices. The team had to be very careful, because if there were any doubts cast in the minds of the examining judges, the three justices would have to be freed. It was not inconceivable that the judges who examined the case were afraid to punish their superiors or wanted to protect their corps. As for being "convinced", this is a very relative concept.

As for judges who protect their corps and resist the efforts of the Joint Investigation Team for Fighting Corruption, I have personal experience when the team was facing a law suit filed by the three justices before the pre-trial court of the South Jakarta District Court. The reason for the law suit was that the named team was considered to have no authority to investigate the three justices because the corruption they committed took place when the old Anti-Corruption Law (Law no. 3/1971) was still effective, the Joint Investigation Team for Fighting Corruption being established under the new Anti-Corruption Law (Law no. 31/1999).

Even though, according to the Code of Criminal Procedure, the judge of the pre-trial court has no authority to try the law suit filed by the three justices, the pre-trial court judge accepted the suit (decision by the South Jakarta District Court on 29 September 2000). According to the Code of Criminal Procedure, the judge of the pre-trial court has the authority to examine a law suit if there has been an illegal arrest, illegal detention or stoppage of the investigation. In the case of the three justices, they were neither arrested nor detained, and the investigation was not halted. The exception filed by the Joint Investigation Team for Fighting Corruption was turned down and the judge granted the suit on the ground of "the logic of law and the un-accommodated demand of justice". Furthermore, the judge of the pre-trial court had ruled beyond his authority by declaring that the Joint Investigation Team for Fighting Corruption could not investigate the three justices because the charges were covered by Law no. 3/1971. The authority to state that the Joint Investigation Team for Fighting Corruption did not have such authority was held by the Supreme Court, not the judge of the pre-trial court. Therefore, the judge of the pre-trial court took the position of the Supreme Court. But this was allowed to happen, a clear example of judges being resistant and clearly acting illegally in order to protect their corps.

The other procedural problem facing the Joint Investigation Team for Fighting Corruption concerns the procedures for police action against judges. According to the law, a judge could only be arrested upon the order of the attorney general and the approval of the Chief Justice and the Minister of Justice. The stipulation is further interpreted such that even the summoning of the judge should be made by the attorney general and must be approved by the Chief Justice and the Minister of Justice. The problem facing the Joint Investigation Team for Fighting Corruption is the impression that the Chief Justice is very reluctant to give the approval and will make various excuses not to do so.

Another example of how difficult it is to combat corruption comes from the Supreme Court. On 16 and 23 April 2001, someone who reported the three corrupted Supreme Court justices to the Joint Investigation Team for Fighting Corruption was brought to court upon defamation charges. Yet earlier (on 4 July 2000), the attorney general had issued a written statement saying: "for the sake of public interest, the attorney general will seriously consider to put aside the case involving anyone who reports a corruption crime as a witness and has the potency to reveal the network of the practice of corruption in the judicial institution". The Jakarta High Prosecutors' Office brought the case to the Central Jakarta District Court, ignoring the attorney general's statement. Why did a subordinate not obey the superior and why did the superior keep silent and took no action sanctioning the subordinate? This sends the clear signal that anyone who dares to report the practice of corruption to the Supreme Court runs the risk of being terrorised, intimidated and reported to the police for defamation, and then put in jail. As a result, the practice of corruption in the judicial institutions, especially in the Supreme Court, can run rampant.

3. The government's latest efforts to combat corruption

The government is preparing a Bill on the Establishment of an Anti-Corruption Commission. This is in accordance with the article 43(1) of Law no. 31/1999 on Anti-Corruption, which states: "within two years at the latest after this Law is implemented [16 August 2001], the Anti-Corruption Commission should be established". Ideally, this Commission is an independent body which, in carrying out its duty, is free from any influence or power from the executive, legislative, judiciary or anyone else. If this bill becomes law, the Commission will become the first independent institution for fighting corruption in Indonesia.

3.1. Independent Commission

Even though it is said that the Commission is an independent body, it is accountable to the President, and the House of Representatives has the authority to judge and evaluate its accountability report before it is submitted to the President. In addition, the fund to finance the activities of the Commission is taken from the State Budget, so the dependency of the Commission on both the government and the House is inevitable.

The Commission should not be wholly dependent on the funds from the state budget. The House and the government are in a strong position to influence the independency of the Commission altering its budget. The bill should stipulate the need for incentive funds for the Commission to be taken from the money that is returned after the corruption cases are settled. The incentive fund is important to maintain the independency of the Commission and should be up to 10% of the state gains that could be made.

One new thing in the bill, which is worth mentioning, concerns the establishment of a special court to examine and decide on corruption cases. But this is as yet only a bill and is being deliberated by the House, so we should not expect too much yet.

Many NGOs criticise the bill because it still relies on the role of police and prosecutors. If the government and the House want to combat corruption, according to these NGOs, they should be firm in breaking the "vicious circle" and give the Commission full authority on to probe, investigate, prosecute and even establish the ad hoc Court by itself.

I am pessimistic about the Commission's ability to combat of corruption in Indonesia because those who made the bill are not legal experts with the skill to draft the law. Even if they sought help from foreign experts, I am sure that there are still many loopholes in the bill which make it difficult to trap the cunning corruptors in Indonesia. After the bill is approved by the House, I expect it will be amended or revised. We have to admit that Indonesians are not like the Dutch, who produced the 100-year-old Criminal Code which is still used in Indonesia today.

Besides the Bill on the Establishment of the Anti-Corruption Commission to be submitted by the Government to the House, the Bill on the Revision of Law no. 31/1999 on Shifting the Burden of Proof, was submitted on 25 April 2001. The House's Special Committee, which deliberates the Bill on the Revision of the Law on Anti-Corruption is expected to deliberate the Anti-Corruption Commission Bill simultaneously, as the two are inseparable.

3.2. Efforts in perspective

Indonesia is one of the most corrupt countries in the world. The practice of corruption is common in all fields and in all levels in the society, from the lowest level to the highest level. Corruption occurs wherever it is given a chance to do so: you could be a victim of this practice whther you are having a party or in mourning. This istuation has been going on for more than 40 years. All efforts to combat corruption fail because they are loaded down with politicking.

The political elite, past and present, do not tackle the corruptors – on the contrary, they even set a bad example by conducting the practice of corruption themselves. Almost all of the families of ministers under the former President Soeharto's regime have business empires. They run various businesses, from the export and import of oil, crops and marine products to weapons, machinery and ships. This still continues today. How could you believe that a minister who runs a business does not abuse his or her power? If that is the case, how could they take a strict action against corruptors as they themselves also corrupt? How could former President Soeharto come down hard on corruptors when he was still in power, if he and his family owned an estimated US$ 1.7 billion? It is understandable that they prefer to keep silent – and if someone wants to reveal the corruption case involving a state official, that person will be in trouble.

When Soeharto, who resigned in May 1998 after 32 years in power, ruled the country with the style of nepotism and autocracy, positions in his government were given to his cronies to maintain his power, and the corruptor's empires became stronger and untouchable. But now, in the reform era started under President Abdurrahman Wahid, the condition has not changed at all. President Abdurrahman Wahid himself is not serious in his efforts to combat corruption. His statement when visiting Seoul, in 2001, to the effect that the attorney general should halt the investigation into three conglomerates on corruption charges, is evidence of his lack of seriousness.

In the efforts to combat corruption, the government should investigate the former President and former ministers first. Former President Soeharto was once sent to court on corruption charges, but the trial was halted because Soeharto was ill and never appeared in court. The case is still unresolved because Soeharto has yet not recovered. Besides Soeharto, his youngest son, Hutomo Mandala Putra was sentenced by the Supreme Court for eighteen months in jail for corruption, but he has escaped and is still at large. His other children have been questioned by the attorney general, but as yet none of them has been prosecuted. Soeharto's step-brother was also questioned, but this was not followed up. The only one to have been tried is the former Minister of Trade, who was sentenced to six years in jail on the Nusakambangan prison island, where the "big" criminals are jailed. Other officials who are being probed by the attorney general include the former director of Pertamina, and the former Minister of Mines and Energy.

4. Difficulties ahead

I wonder how many others who will be questioned and then prosecuted.Some will fight by using the weaknesses of the law and regulation procedures. This is as a result of Indonesia's "liberal culture" which attaches weight to the individual rights and freedom, so much so that it often overshadows truth, justice and humanity. As a consequence, there is a dichotomy between substantial justice on one side and the enforcement of procedures of law on the other side. Under such a system, the law enforcement often brings injustice to the people. Worse, in the case that the system is applied by corrupt law enforcers. This often happens in Indonesia, where the efforts to combat corruption in a normal and obedient way are easily squashed by the law enforcers themselves. It is suggested that the government declared a state of emergency to fight corruption so that it could take extraordinary measures, such as the issuance of a government decree in lieu of a law on the implementation of retroactive system, the establishment of a special court, shifting of the burden of proof, and severe punishment for corruptors who were proven guilty.

The establishment of the Joint Investigation Team for Fighting Corruption failed to combat corruption, lost its legal basis and had to be disbanded. In the spring of 2001, the government planned to submit the House of Representatives the Bill on the Establishment of the Anti-Corruption Commission, an independent institution which is free from the influence of the executive, legislative and judiciary. If it succeeds, it will be the first independent anti-corruption body in Indonesia. But, even if this Commission is established in the future, I am still not sure it can really be independent, considering the fact that it will be financed by the State Budget. It contributes to my pessimism about the Commission's ability to combat corruption in Indonesia.

PART III

CORRUPTION AND INTEGRITY IN THE LAW ENFORCEMENT SYSTEM

Corruption in Law Enforcement Agencies – Views from within the Criminal Justice System: Results from a German Corruption Study

Robert Mischkowitz

1. Definition of corruption

Every social scientist who wants to launch a research project about corruption faces the problem of defining corruption in the first place. It is well known that corruption can be defined quite differently, depending on the cultural context. Being aware of this problem and considering the fact that there is no legal definition of "corruption" in Germany, the research team had to agree on the elements that constitute the definition of corruption in its view. Since "corruption" should not be restricted to activities known as offering or taking a bribe or offering and accepting an advantage (sections 331-335 in the German Criminal Code), corruption has been defined as follows:

- The misuse of any public office in violation of a criminal law or service regulation;

- to the advantage of another person;

- committed upon the inducement of this other person or on the official's own initiative;

- with the intent to procure some benefit for himself or another person;

- resulting in (pecuniary) damage or other detriment to the police, judicial authorities, or customs authorities in respect of performing their duties.

Accordingly, the definition covers a wide variety of activities, but it does not include all kinds of deviant behaviour related to the misuse of any public office. For example it does not include direct criminal activities like burglaries and theft committed by

Cyrille Fijnaut, Leo Huberts (eds.), *Corruption, Integrity and Law Enforcement*, 75-90
©2002 Kluwer Law International, The Hague. Printed in The Netherlands.

officials while on duty, and it also does not include the excess use of force. Therefore, the definition is not as far-reaching as the famous definition by Roebuck and Barker or by Goldstein, but it does go beyond the sections of the Criminal Code quoted, and it covers activities belonging to the so-called "grey areas" (Roebuck & Barker, 1973; Goldstein, 1975). Persons who took part in the study were informed about the definition. In that way a common understanding of what should be seen as corruption was assured.

2. History and methodology of the study

Starting at the end of 1995 and up to its completion in 1999, the study being discussed in this chapter was conducted by the German Federal Criminal Police Office (*Bundeskriminalamt* – BKA) and the Police Management Academy (*Polizeiführungsakademie* – PFA) as a joint project.[1] From a thematic and methodological point of view, the investigation may be considered as a continuation of another BKA study which focused on corruption in trade and industry and public administration and was carried out by Vahlenkamp and Knauss during the first half of the 1990s (Vahlenkamp & Knauss, 1995). The empirical database for the new project – this time focusing on corruption in law enforcement agencies – consists essentially of four data files which were compiled by using different methods of collection.

1. A nationwide written questionnaire sent to representatives of the police force, the judicial authorities and the customs authorities (N=770);

2. A written questionnaire submitted to participants at various seminars at the Police Management Academy in 1996 (N=104);

3. A series of 85 partially structured interviews with experts; and

4. An analysis of 38 penal or disciplinary files.

The aim of the study was not to analyse all the legal offences involving corruption that had occurred during a precisely defined period of time. Rather, the goal was to reconstruct a (general) picture of corruption which conveys how experienced representatives of the state criminal prosecution authorities see the problem of corruption within their authorities.

---

[1] The results presented here are based on the publication of the *BKA-Forschungsreihe* Bd. 46 (Mischkowitz, R. *et al.*, 2000).

In this respect it is to some extent correct to speak of a "specialist study", which is further supplemented by the (documentary) analysis of a few individual cases. The study cannot be classified as a crime survey, although it contains some elements of such a survey. On the other hand, the database is not restricted to reported offences either. It is better to say that the study contains elements of both types of study, communicated via the experiential knowledge of the experts interviewed.

The core of the study consists of the nationwide written survey, which was conducted in the summer of 1997. The total level of response was 86% (N = 760). The questionnaire was distributed to employees in three authorities: the police, the judicial authorities, and the customs authorities. Since the focus is primarily on the police and "police corruption", the sample is dominated by employees of the police force, but the distribution of subjects between groups roughly reflects the relative proportion of the authorities taking part in the study (police force 76%, judicial authorities 12%, customs authorities 11%, and others 1%). Nevertheless, it is not correct to speak of a representative sample in a strict sense. In terms of research methodology, it is fair to say that we are basically dealing with a qualitative study.

The three groups that are mentioned can be divided further. Within the police, there is the distinction between the uniformed police and the detective branch, and within the judicial authorities between criminal courts, public prosecutors and penal authorities. These differentiations are decisive in respect of many research questions, since the action frame of reference, the opportunity structure and the civil service culture vary considerably between these groups.

Conducting a study about corruption is not an easy task. People are usually not that fond of being asked about their experiences with corruption, even when they are not asked about their own behaviour but rather their work experience with corruption cases. In order to avoid a high refusal rate, confidentiality of data was guaranteed and only a few questions about sociodemographic characteristics were included in the questionnaire. In that way the possibility of the subjects via information was avoided. Included, however, was a question about the time period of work experience, and it turned out that most of the subjects looked back on long professional careers. Almost 90% of the subjects had been in office at least 15 years, and only 1% less than five years. Consequently, the picture that can presented is based on the information of very experienced public officials.

The questionnaire consists of 15 groups of questions. Some of the questions were concerned with the extent of corruption within the subject's own institution and the view that is held towards other authorities; others dealt with indicators of corruption, the relationship between persons offering or taking bribes, and the "causes" of corruption. There was also an interest in the consequences and effects of corruption, and – of course – in the means to combat corruption. Finally some hypotheses were stated about the relationship between corruption and organised crime. Due to the variety of questions and the wealth of information, it is not possible discuss the results of the study in detail in this report; but some of the results can be briefly sketched.

3. Extent of corruption: self-assessment and external assessment

It is often said that what we know about the extent of corruption is only the tip of the iceberg. The police crime statistics and police situation reports give us information about reported cases and known offenders only, but this is simply one side of the story. The other side is that we must expect relatively high numbers of unreported offences. Why is this the case? One of the reasons is that there are often no personal victims of corruption. Both parties involved – giver and receiver – have a vested interest in not being discovered. Corruption offences are crimes with no victims, and the level of discovered offences depends on the efforts undertaken by the police. If the police intensify the fight against corruption, the numbers of reported offences will rise. Paradoxically, it seems that the more we fight corruption, the more corruption offences we will get – at least in regard of the numbers of reported offences. Another reason relates to the "fuzziness" of the concept of corruption. Sometimes people are not aware whether an activity is considered an act of corruption or not because "things have always been that way". Problems of the so-called "grey areas" are well known.

The study did not offer the opportunity to collect information about the numbers of unreported corruption offences. Therefore it was not possible to calculate prevalence or incidence rates of corruption. Like Transparency International (TI), a rating scale has been used in order to ascertain the perceived level of corruption in the authorities; but unlike the CPI (Corruption Perceptions Index of TI) the scale has only four degrees. The subjects could respond to the question: "To what extent do you think the following authorities are affected by corruption?" by a ranking from position (1) "not at all" to position (4) "very strong".

Figure 1 offers an impression of self-assessment by employees in the police and custom authorities only. By "self-assessment" we mean that people evaluate the extent of corruption within their own institution. Most of the officials in the uniformed police, the detective branch and the customs authorities think that there is only "a little bit" of corruption within their institution (70-80%). Very few believe that there is a high degree of corruption (only about 2%). Nevertheless, about a fifth to a sixth of the subjects consider the extent of corruption within their institution to be "fairly high".

Figure 1: *Extent of corruption – self-assessment by police and customs authorities*

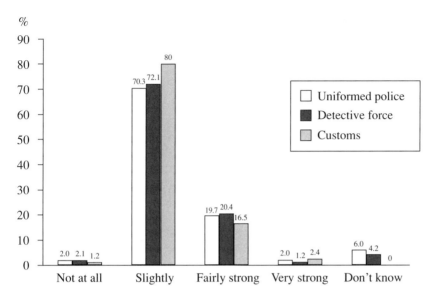

Figure 2: *Extent of corruption – self-assessment by judicial authorities*

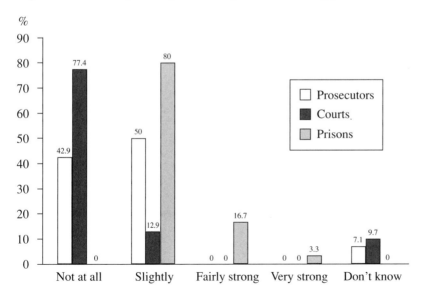

Figure 1 also makes it clear that there are only very small differences between the three groups with regard to their self-assessment.

The picture changes a lot when the responses of the judicial authorities are considered (Figure 2). None of the judges or public prosecutors said that there was even a fairly high degree of corruption within their institution. It is very clear for the judges. More than three-quarters of them were convinced that there is no corruption at all within their institution. Only about 13% "dared" to say that there could be "a little" corruption. Against the background of these results, one is tempted to say that the possibility of corruption is almost completely beyond the scope of imagination of a German judge when it comes to his own institution. Not so clear-cut but still following the same trend are the results of the public prosecutors. Half of them answered with "slightly affected".

Quite different, however, are the results of the employees within the penal authorities. Their response is almost identical with the response of the police and customs. About 80% said that there is a slight degree of corruption, and about one sixth that there is a fairly high degree of corruption. But none responded by saying that penal authorities have nothing to do with corruption. That is not an unexpected result. The work environment of the supervisory staff of a prison is very different from the work environment of a judge. Prisons are "total institutions" in the words of Erving Goffman (Goffman, 1961), and the way of life in a "total institution" is quite different from the way of life in the outside world.

The next step in the analysis was to ask whether there is a difference between self-assessment and external assessment. By external assessment, we mean that subjects evaluated the extent of corruption in institutions they do not belong to. One way of doing this is to contrast the answer of people within one institution with the answer of people not belonging to the institution. In respect of this comparison, one can basically say that the others perceive the level of corruption to be higher than do people within the assessed institution. This holds true for all groups considered and, from a social-psychological point of view, it does not seem very surprising. Quite often people are afraid of things they are not so familiar with, or things that seem to be foreign to them.

Another way of analysing external and self-assessment is by the construction of a matrix. The matrix makes it possible to distinguish how the subjects in different groups perceive the level of corruption within their own group and within all the other groups. In contrast to the example above, the category "other" has been broken down into different groups. External and self-assessment can be attributed to each group separately (see Figure 3).

If you consider the columns and rows of the matrix, the values in the columns tell you how the subjects in one group evaluate the level of corruption in their own

Figure 3: *Assessment matrix in respect of perceived extent of corruption*

Assessed authority	Assessing authority						
	Detective force	*Uniformed police*	*Customs*	*Prosecutors*	*Judges*	*Prisons*	*Average*
Detective force	**2.22**	2.45	2.50	2.24	2.26	2.48	2.36
Uniformed police	2.46	**2.23**	2.53	2.50	2.33	2.13	2.36
Customs	2.69	2.75	**2.20**	2.25	2.33	2.65	2.48
Prosecutors	2.00	2.08	2.00	**1.54**	1.50	2.13	1.86
Judges	1.71	1.84	1.75	1.31	**1.14**	1.65	1.57
Prisons	3.02	2.89	2.88	2.70	2.46	**2.23**	2.70
Average	2.35	2.37	2.31	2.09	2.00	2.21	—

group and in all the other groups. On the other hand, the rows show you how the level of corruption within one's own institution is seen by the other groups. We also can say that the values in the diagonal (marked in bold) represent the values for self-assessment, while the values outside the diagonal represent external assessment. The values in the last row and the last column are arithmetic means. According to the scale, the values could range from 1 to 4. It would be going too far to analyse the matrix in detail here, but four points should be emphasised:

1. Looking at the values in the diagonal (self-assessment), you naturally get the same picture as before. Judges and public prosecutors consider their authorities to be basically free of corruption; the police, customs and penal authorities concede a low level of corruption, and there is no difference between these four groups;

2. When we consider both external assessment and self-assessment (see the last column), the ranking goes from judges, prosecutors, the two police forces and customs to penal authorities. It is expected that the highest level of corruption might occur in penal authorities;

3. If you look at each row separately you will find that – with two exceptions – the values in the diagonal are the lowest values in the row. As has been mentioned before, people are more likely to suspect other authorities of having problems with corruption than their own;

4. The groups also differ in the awareness of corruption or the level of sensitisation towards corruption. The values in the last row give you an impression of this fact. But there are only minor differences. It is interesting, however, that judges have the lowest rating here as well.

Thus far we were dealing with perceived corruption. In order to avoid the impression that we were able to present only very subjective views and no "hard facts" about occurrences of corruption, another result of the study will be mentioned.

4. Conspicuous occurrences as signs of corruption

Within the framework of the nationwide written survey, 48 items referring to various incidents and conspicuous occurrences from the work and private environment that can be interpreted as signs of corruption were presented to participants with the request to indicate those that they had actually noted during their period of duty.

While about 13% of the respondents indicated that they had noted no conspicuous occurrences which could be described as signs of corruption, 87% of all respondents ticked at least one possible answer. Over a quarter of all those questioned noted more than ten different conspicuous occurrences in their work and/or private environment.

Examples of what is meant by these incidents and occurrences in the area of criminal prosecution are:

- The "disclosure of professional secrets/the passing of internal documents to third parties";

- The "discovery of internal documents of the authority in the possession of the criminal"; and

- The "disappearance of files on inquiries and prosecutions or parts of such files".

These three were overall most frequently mentioned as conspicuous occurrences of significance with regard to corruption.

Furthermore, there was a focus on conspicuous occurrences associated with the behaviour or the environment of the public employee, going beyond the work environment and tackling questions of their lifestyle and personality. Four of them should be mentioned here:

- Secondary employment activities and their concealment;

- Lack of interest, complete loss of motivation;

- Problems of addiction; and

- Various private contacts (with criminal offenders, representatives of the media, business employers, etc.).

It is very important to recognise that the answers only tell us what occurrences there were and how many of our subjects came to know about these occurrences. But we are not able to determine how many of these occurrences happened within a certain time period. It could be that several of the subjects referred to the same incident when they were answering the questionnaire because that incident had been made public. Thus the study is not a crime survey and does not give us precise information about the number of unreported incidents. In order to get an impression of the level of corruption, say the number of cases or suspects, we still have to look at the crime statistics and the police situation reports.

5. Crime statistics and situation reports: what do they tell us about corruption?

The total number of corruption cases and suspects varied in Germany in the 1990s. Figure 4 presents an overview of the development of total numbers from 1994 to 1999 (Bundeskriminalamt, 2000).

The upper figure gives you an impression of the development of the number of cases, the figure below of the number of suspects. Contrary to the broad definition that has been used in the study, "corruption" is seen here in a narrower sense, as defined in sections 331-335 of the German Criminal Code, mainly in the sense of bribery and acceptance or granting of an advantage.

Figure 4: *Police crime statistics: accepting/granting an advantage and taking/offering a bribe*

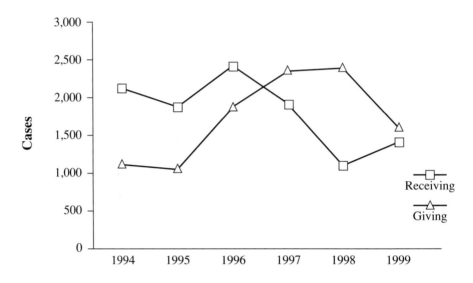

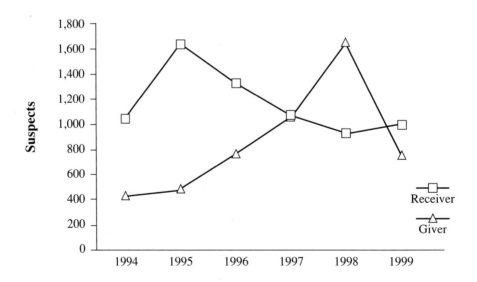

If we consider the cases, we see an upward-and-downward movement of the two lines representing total numbers; and if we differentiate between "receiving" and "giving" we recognise that the rise and fall of numbers must not be in the same direction. This contradictory development is even more prominent in the second set of figures. Whereas the number of "givers" decreases from 1995 to 1998, the number of "receivers" increases at least until 1998. Adding the numbers in each figure, we recognise that the total number of corruption cases varies within a range of approximately 3000 and 4000 cases and the number of suspects within a range of 2000 to 2500 suspects during that period of time.

The crime statistics of the police do not include any information on the professional background of the suspect. Thus we are unable to say how many policemen or public officials assigned to the authorities included in the study are involved in corruption activities. In order to get an impression of their number, we have to rely on police situation reports.

The police forces in Germany have been preparing situation reports on corruption since 1994. The reports include more information about corruption incidents and about offenders than the crime statistics of the police; and the numbers published in the situation reports are not identical with the numbers in the police crime statistics (Bundeskriminalamt, 1999). There is a variety of reasons for this. The main reason, however, is due to different times of recording. Whereas in police crime statistics known offences are recorded after completion of the inquiries by the police and prior to the submission of the files to the public prosecutor's office, offences in situation reports are recorded at the beginning of the inquiries.

In 1997, the year of data collection for the study, a total of 993 investigations was recorded with a total number of 858 suspects – suspects accepting an advantage or taking a bribe ("receivers").

Situation reports also offer information about the professional background of 699 "receivers" of bribes. About one third of them worked in the health sector and about one eighth in building authorities. Only 4% of them were policemen – a total of 27 persons. The year before, the percentage of policemen was almost the same: 4.3%. It rose to a high of about 12% in 1998 and declined to about 9% in 1999. In both years, the rise was due to three investigations in which several police officers were involved.

In 1998 the large number of suspects from police authorities can be explained primarily by two investigative proceedings in which a total of 70 police officers from three police stations was accused of accepting an advantage or taking a bribe.

In the case of one investigation, 32 police officers from two motorway police stations were accused of having accepted some of the goods (such as alcohol, tea, coffee, or tobacco) on trucks involved in motorway accidents from a tow truck service in return for giving the tow service preference when a tow truck was called. It turned out that the investigations of 28 of the aforementioned police officers were discontinued in accordance with Section 170 II of the German Code of Criminal Procedure.

In 1999 we had a similar case. These three cases make it clear that – due to the small total number of suspects – one single investigation can "inflate" the percentage rather drastically.

6. "Causes" of corruption

Another important part of the study refers to the "causes" of corruption. Who would not like to know the reasons why some people are corrupt and others are not? Or would like to know why corruption is prevalent in one institution while there is no corruption in another. Thinking about the causes of corruption usually involves thinking about theories that attempt to explain corruption. Therefore in the search for the causes of corruption and factors that favour corruption, the relevant literature was reviewed. The aim of the review was to find the causal factors as they are most frequently presented and discussed in the literature.

By reviewing the literature it became clear that there is no central cause of corruption, but rather that this phenomenon must be acknowledged as having many different causes. In this connection, classification of the causes according to various analytical levels is helpful. These are the level of society as a whole, the level of the institution or the authority, and the level of the individual. Of course, it is an analytical distinction, and some of the causal factors could belong to two analytical levels and not only one. It depends on the way of looking at the matter. Even more puzzling, some of the factors seem to contradict each other – for example, a lack of regulation and a high degree of regulation.

Explaining corruption is a very complex venture, and it was not the aim of the study to construct a theory of corruption or to be ready for theory testing. The only aim was to know what the subjects thought to be the main causal factors of corruption. Their answer certainly was not guided solely by their personal experience, but also by "everyday theories" and by discussions in the media. But anyway, it is revealing to see how the subjects responded to this question.

The answers verified – if one does not use the word "verified" in the strict methodological sense – that there is no central cause of corruption, even in the opinion of the subjects.

Clear agreement among the authorities can be noted in respect of two causes only: "society's declining values" and the "defective role model function of management and political representatives". More than half of those questioned regard these two causes as dominant, whereby only the subjects in the customs authorities rank the lack of the role model function ahead of "declining values".

The two factors were followed by variables concerning:

- *Financial aspects*: either in the form of concrete financial problems or, in the case of the public prosecutors and judges, in striving to achieve or attempting to preserve a high standard of living;

- *Character weakness, thoughtlessness, naivete*: these factors are considered particularly important for the penal authorities, the police force and the customs authorities;

- *Lack of administrative and professional supervision, insufficient checks*: this factor is mentioned by all the groups studied as the prime aspect affecting the institutional level. Only the penal authorities assign a higher ranking to certain other factors related to the civil service culture;

- *Lack of sensitisation to indicators of corruption*: the criminal investigation department, the penal authorities and the customs authorities, in particular, see this as a cause of corruption, while the police force and the public prosecutors and judges regard this aspect as less significant.

In summarising these results, it becomes clear that the causes of corruption are seen first in society as a whole and then in the sphere of the individual. Factors associated with the institutional level come next. Generally, a personalising tendency that is critical of society or the prevailing culture can be perceived in the responses. Prime "responsibility" for corruption is attributed to social developments that are difficult to influence and to human weaknesses, in particular in connection with situations involving financial difficulties. Institutional factors, i.e. factors related to the organisation of the authority and to the civil service culture, are mostly still viewed from a control perspective, i.e. from a perspective that is oriented to "external controls" like "inadequate administrative and professional supervision/insufficient checks".

Nevertheless, the importance of sensitisation regarding matters related to corruption and the associated allusion to "internal checks" is definitely also perceived, even if it is mostly classified as secondary. By "internal checks", we mean "internal" in relation to the public employee and not to the authority. This is, in a sense, equivalent to the concept of "super-ego".

7. Means for combating corruption

In addition to questioning the subjects about their views on the causes of corruption, they were also asked for their opinion about the means to fight corruption.

The public employees addressed in the nationwide survey mainly agreed that measures of prevention and of repression are equally important for combating corruption effectively. Overall, the following three variables were the most frequently cited by all those questioned as appropriate starting points for combating corruption:

1. Sensitisation; supplementing the general training syllabus (47.5%);

2. Improving administrative and professional supervision; intensifying controls (34.3%);

3. Reinforcing the role model function of superiors and trainers (33.1%).

The importance that should be attributed to sensitisation in connection with the prevention of corruption is indicated by the fact that 47.5% of all subjects (45% of the police officers, 67% of the public officials within the penal authorities and 62% of the customs officers) consider the item "sensitisation of employees and expansion of the general training syllabus to include topics related to corruption" to be the single most important starting point for combating corruption. This result corresponds with the fact that around a third of the subjects consider a lack of sensitisation with regard to corruption-related matters to be a significant cause of corruption.

In choosing their approaches, the uniformed police force, the penal authorities and the customs authorities generally place greater reliance on approaches to prevent corruption. They feel that "sensitisation", "strengthening of the role model function of superiors and trainers" as well as the establishment of "further training institutes on the topic of corruption" would contribute to building up internal controls and personal development in respect of professional ethics.

On the other side, public prosecutors and judges as well as the respondents from the criminal investigation departments place greater emphasis on the establishment of external supervisory bodies. Public prosecutors and judges recommend the following three approaches as more important than the aspect of sensitisation:

1. "Improving administrative and professional supervision; intensifying controls" (45.8%);

2. "Obliging the authorities to submit a report when there is a nascent suspicion/ rejection of the informal submissions procedure" (44.1%); and

3. "Obliging public employees to report all attempts at corruption – including those that are not punishable" (44.1%).

In connection with the assessment of the various approaches to combating corruption, the respondents were also asked what they could do personally to prevent corruption in their own area of responsibility or work environment. There was general agreement between the groups being studied that one's own exemplary, correct behaviour – i.e., to signal incorruptibility – and a rigorous refusal of every kind of gift or offer of advantage are seen as the most effective means of corruption prevention available to the individual. This is followed by the recommendation to "report dubious matters; not covering for colleagues under suspicion".

8. Internal and external controls

It has been mentioned before that combating corruption effectively requires careful analysis of factors that are favourable to corruption. The respondents' answer to the question about the causes of corruption must be considered in the light of their answers to the question about the means to fight corruption. It is important to note that, in addition to a general nucleus of measures, we have to pay attention to the specific structural contexts of authorities – by structural contexts, we mean, for example, written and unwritten rules of behaviour, traditions of leadership, or ethical codes.

Consequently, combating corruption effectively implies the right mixture of internal and external controls. Therefore you have to identify the "weak points" in the structural context of an institution. Perhaps you have to emphasise administrative and professional controls, or perhaps you have to put the stress on training, moral awareness and codes of ethics. Scientific analysis can help in that respect. This is, in fact, what should be accomplished with the research project. In any case, the project is considered to be only a first step in empirical research on the complex field of corruption; other steps must follow.

Before launching an empirical project, however, you need to know that corruption might be a problem. A certain level of awareness is required! Furthermore, you need the willingness to analyse the situation carefully and to take action based on the results of your study. Maybe this report can make a small contribution to both – to awareness and to willingness.

References

Bundeskriminalamt, *Lagebild Korruption Bundesrepublik Deutschland 1997/1998*, Bundeskriminalamt, Wiesbaden, 1999.

Bundeskriminalamt, *Polizeiliche Kriminalstatistik 1999*, Bundeskriminalamt, Wiesbaden, 2000.

Goffman, E., *Asylums. Essays on the Social Situation of Mental Patients and Other Inmates*, Anchor Books, 1961.

Goldstein, H., *Police Corruption. Perspective on Its Nature and Control*, Police Foundation, Washington, DC, 1975.

Mischkowitz, R., H. Bruhn, R. Desch, G.-E. Hübner & D. Beese, *Einschätzungen zur Korruption in Polizei, Justiz und Zoll*, Bundeskriminalamt, Wiesbaden, 2000.

Roebuck, J., & Th. Barker, *An Empirical Typology of Police Corruption: A Study on Organizational Deviance*, CC Thomas, Springfield, Illinois, 1973.

Vahlenkamp, W., & I. Knauß, *Korruption. Hinnehmen oder Handeln?*, Bundeskriminalamt, Wiesbaden, 1995.

CHAPTER 6

Corruption from a Police Perspective

Willy Bruggeman

1. Introduction

Corruption is a near universal phenomenon that takes many shapes and forms. Initially its study was largely confined to the work of political scientists who focused on public officials. Weberian bureaucracy was meant to have abolished particularism, nepotism and gift-taking because officials were salaried and trained to impartiality. In developing societies, however, low pay and the resilience of cultural patterns meant that civil servants were only stimulated into action by "speed money"; while in many countries the political machine undermined legal rules in order to preserve power. Officials were open to bribery, public employment was distributed as patronage, and relations with organised crime often meant that certain sectors of the economy were regulated and "milked" by criminals and corrupt officials working in concert. A number of scandals brought to light systemic corruption among politicians, judges and lawyers, public officials, and particularly among policemen.

Police corruption attracted a great deal of attention because it raised the eternal issue of "who controls the controllers"? Since then research and public interest have shifted towards concern with corporate crime and business deviance, governmental abuse of power, the increasing threat of organised crime, regulation and control, and new opportunities for corruption and fraud that are being created by a more open, global economy. Academic interest has expanded from political science, law and public administration to sociology, criminology, anthropology, organisations, accountancy and management. Indeed, open borders may stimulate new forms of deviance while, ironically, the rules for supra-national entities, such as the European Community, may even *create* possibilities for manipulation and for illicit profit.

Cyrille Fijnaut, Leo Huberts (eds.), *Corruption, Integrity and Law Enforcement*, 91-108
©2002 Kluwer Law International, The Hague. Printed in The Netherlands.

2. A definition of corruption

Corruption is a broad term that subsumes many different kinds of wrongdoing. It can range from a police officer's expectation of gratis services and products from the people he or she serves to more serious cases of theft and extortion. While examples of police corruption vary greatly in kind and degree, they all have elements in common:

- The conduct is prohibited by law or rule;

- The conduct involves misuse of position;

- The conduct involves a reward or personal gain for the officer.

Police corruption has been traditionally defined as an officer's misuse of police authority for personal gain.

Generally we view the police as being in the forefront of the fight against corruption and organised crime. It is particularly disturbing then, when we are confronted with cases of systematic police deviances because we have to turn our thinking around and consider organised crime within police agencies. Furthermore combatting police corruption raises in acute form the eternal conundrum: who controls the controllers? For the police are uniquely equipped as law enforcers to torpedo enforcement of the law agencies themselves.

According to Fijnaut (1990), one can categorise corruption as:

- Incidental corruption: to ignore or neglect a given operation (e.g. gambling) in the course of normal duty;

- Enabling corruption: a one-time bribe or another favour from organised crime when the criminal is wanting information on a particular subject;

- Conjunctive corruption: relying regularly on organised crime to accomplish official goals (accepting kickbacks in exchange of organised crime control or a public construction project);

- Integrated corruption: the official becomes part of the criminal enterprise.

In terms of effective enforcement, much will depend on the specific form the corruption takes, the extent to which a police department has been infiltrated by organised crime, and the nature of the political setting.

While solid evidence is hard to come by, there are indications that all forms of corruption – from incidental to integrated – have arisen in almost all countries. There are indications that the problem is becoming more and more dispersed and quantitively and qualitatively more serious. Indeed, the future would almost certainly contain an increasing degree of organisation in certain types of organised crime, and subsequent pressure on the police in this sensitive area.

3. Contemporary examples of police corruption

The problem for the police is threefold:

- Police corruption;
- Police as a facilitating factor;
- Corruption in the private sector.

Police corruption in particular deserves attention. Based on Gaspar's analysis the following inventory can be made.[1] Common allegations involve misuse of police powers, breaches in confidentiality, protection and pay-offs. Contemporary examples in our jurisdiction are:

- Theft of property during searches;
- Theft of drugs during searches;
- "Planting" of drugs or stolen property on individuals;
- Supplying confidential information about others;
- Supplying details of operations to subjects;
- Providing sentinel services to criminal associates;
- Extortion for withdrawal of investigative activity or reduction of evidence.

None of these activities is necessarily a simple single act of dishonesty. For example, where drugs are stolen during the execution of a search warrant, such drugs are either sold on through pre-existing criminal associates of the officers or used for "planting" on other suspects. When used in this second way, there are two options to benefit the officers; either an opportunity for extortion on the next suspect, or, if this fails, a further high profile but false arrest that enhances the status of the officers.

---

[1] Based on a speech given during the British National Criminal Intelligence Service conference in Brussels, May 2001.

The successful work gets them the approbation of their supervisors and protects them from scrutiny: after all who scrutinises the successful? Their hard working and committed approach to work is apparently demonstrated by their results.

If their peer group sees or suspects the corrupt activity, they also see the approbation of the supervisors and apparent encouragement of the corrupt activity in the form of rewards, such an extra overtime or better opportunities for further work, which are directed towards the corrupt. The difficulty for honest officers is whether they can trust their supervisors. The norm within the police service is that colleagues are protected. The strength of the peer group can be very powerful. Those with concerns will therefore be very conscious that any report they make about their suspicions will probably result in their own marginalisation rather than the isolation of the corrupt. Thus the corrupt hold a seemingly impregnable position.

Similar allegations of dishonesty during drug searches have been made involving the large cash proceeds that commonly ensue. With some pre-planning the removal and secretion of part of the proceeds is straightforward. The money involved can be such that large sums can be removed without the evidence being weakened. The suspect may be in a difficult position; he or she may be unwilling to admit that the remaining cash is theirs and therefore cannot admit knowledge of the full sum by identifying that a theft has taken place. Allegations such as this are not unusual.

A particular new trend in the past decade, but an area about which there have always been concerns, is the leaking of confidential information. The extent of such activity can vary extensively: at one end of the range is the apparently simple act of improperly revealing details of vehicle ownership from the police databases to a member of the public for quasi official purposes, such as to pursue traffic accident damage. At the most damaging end is the accessing of intelligence databases to provide information that individuals are the target of specific operations. As responses to organised crime are inevitably intelligence-led, this activity has the ability to completely neutralise complex and difficult investigations.

4. Why corruption exists

4.1. Constant factors leading to the risk of corruption

Sociological studies suggest that there is a number of universal and permanent aspects of police work which makes corruption possible or likely.

4.1.1. Discretion

A common feature of all western police services is the amount of discretion allowed to officers in the exercise of their duties. This legitimate discretion permits the opportunity for the illegitimate excrcise of discretion. The opportunity to conceal improper activity under the guise of properly exercised discretion is obvious.

4.1.2. Low managerial visibility

Some authorities draw attention to the difficulties brought about by designing our organisations on quasi-military lines. In the military role, individual decisions by the rank and file are not welcomed; training and managerial control is organised accordingly. In the police service, individual officers make the primary decisions but the military supervision model means that the supervisors can be far removed from the best position to monitor behaviour.

4.1.3. Low public visibility and awareness

The exercise of discretion or the completion of corrupt acts by individual police officers are seldom done within public view. Even if corrupt police activity is observed by the public, it would be unlikely to be separated from normal police activity (about which the public has generally only the television images to guide them) and therefore recognised for what it was.

4.1.4. Peer group secrecy

The police officer is isolated from the rest of the community. Friendships do of course exist outside the service but the honest police officer will chose the friends with care and avoid a whole group of society. This is the first component in peer group secrecy. The next is the isolation of work, its difficulty and danger. Those suspected and arrested for crime are thoroughly acquainted with complaints systems and the way in which the criminal justice system works. When such suspects misuse those systems for their own ends, the honest officer's isolation becomes more apparent. His or her safety is with the immediate group with whom they work and a natural defence of disbelief will be invoked to support any colleague who is similarly threatened.

4.1.5. Managerial secrecy

In Anglo-American police services, managers are invariably recruited from the ranks. This exacerbates the natural consequences of peer group secrecy as there is a tendency to protect juniors or minimise bad behaviour. Where the manager is or was also involved in corruption, they may see it as "acceptable" practice in others or they may adopt a protective stance in order to conceal their own vulnerability.

4.1.6. Status problems

How individuals within the police service regard the status of the service can also have an impact. Individuals who perceive that they and their work is undervalued, poorly regarded and isolated are less likely to have a high integrity ethic. Developments in human rights may be wrongly perceived as upsetting the balance of criminal justice and continue this undermining process.

4.2. The climate for corruption

Alongside these constant factors, there are other pressures that come to bear on individual officers.[2]

4.2.1. Visual economic pressures

Unemployment has affected the ability of partners of officers to hold down a job, and economic measures from the Government has eroded earnings. A squeeze on public spending found its way into the overtime budget reducing opportunities. Personal taxation rose either directly or indirectly, further eroding earning power. At the same time as this recession, an unusual phenomenon occurred – a slump in property values. Individuals within the police service had traditional invested in property and many now have negative equity in their property – owing more to the mortgage company than the property is worth. A trap which more than any other singles out this recession as the one which affected the police service more than any other in the past forty years. Such issues will, of course, vary from country to country but I am sure can be replicated in each.

---

[2] One may refer to the 1998-1999 report of the Service central de prévention de la corruption (Service des Gardes de Sceaux, Paris, 2000).

4.2.2. Hidden economic pressures

The principal hidden economic pressure is the extent of drug money available in our major cities. The drug dealer is aware of the substantial term of imprisonment which will greet his or her successful conviction. Consequently they are prepared to lose some of the drugs and/or money to buy their way out of a prosecution. An officer who removes cash or drugs at the scene of arrest provides the offender with a short-term gain and a long-term investment. The short-term gain is the reduction of the amount of evidence which they will face if a prosecution does follow: it also provides an indication that a further opportunity for corruption exists. As a long-term investment, for some it is the opportunity to move closer to an ally with whom a partnership can be formed to protect further dealing. For the organised criminal, investing in insider information makes sound business sense.

4.2.3. Siege mentality

The 1990s also brought the public confidence in most of the national legal systems into issue. A number of high profile miscarriages of justice and poor investigations have had an impact on normal everyday policing. It is more difficult to convict simply because of an increased level of doubt in the mind of the jury. On top of this, an additional burden of work has been brought about through the development of human rights legislation. The impact has been of increasing scrutiny of the process of investigation, increasing disclosure of sensitive techniques (which has an impact upon the next investigation) and more complexity of the criminal justice process which consumes more operational resources. The impact of these issues upon the police officer is an increasing impatience with the legal system which he of she sees as favouring the guilty at the expense of the victim.

4.2.4. Changes in investigative methods

Apart from the growth in materialistic values, the major change in the last thirty years is the explosion in communication and mobility. This has caused us in recent years to invest heavily in proactive investigations where intelligence, surveillance and prolonged covert work are prerequisites to a successful major investigation. Criminals are, of course, aware of this and find new opportunities, through corrupt police officers, to exploit the information channels in the many computerised databases which now exist. This is fertile ground for the corrupt officer to flourish. The reliance on computerised information, and the vast volume of it, allows an officer to place sentinels in systems so that he or she is warned of activity by other officers against protected individuals. The lack of properly designed audit trails can allow the careful corrupt officer almost free access to computerised databases. As officers are encouraged to make greater use of these systems for honest investigative work, so the limited but incredibly damaging corrupt enquiries become more secure.

I would argue that no trained professional group is more frequently tempted to misbehave, or is provided with more opportunities to succumb to temptation.

4.3. Types of corruption within police services

Police organisations which are corrupt take the form of one of three different types (Sherman, 1976). The most commonly held view is that a police force holds just a few rotten apples or at worst a rotten pocket of corruption. Generally it is thought this kind of organisation (a Type 1 organisation) may have a few "rotten apples" in the uniform or patrolling section of the service with "rotten pockets" confined to the detective or CID branches – even then thought by some to be confined to the more specialist detective units.

A different view of corruption is the Type 2 organisation – that corruption is pervasive and unorganised, existing in a majority of individuals who have little relationship to each other. Each takes what he or she can get. Some research suggests this sort of corruption is generally found in the developing nations where the poorly paid police services have a role in the issue of licences, the processing of endless paperwork and the granting of approvals for a variety of matters. In this type of corruption, the researchers argue that the prime purpose of the organisation is not distorted.

The Type 3 organisation has corrupt activity which is identified as pervasive and organised. It is argued that there is an hierarchical organisation which can extend outside the organisation variously into political groups, the criminal justice system and crime organisations. The major danger of this type of corruption is that it has subverted the purpose of the organisation. The major crime organisations will have tapped into the corrupt within the police service so that they are protected against major operations targeting them. In such a position, when they have a network of corrupt officers, warning of impending operations is only one of the services. They can enhance the status of their corrupt officers by providing information about other criminal activity against which police action can be taken and can even prompt action so that rival organisations receive police attention.

4.4. The pattern of corruption

There are a number of studies in America, Europe and developing nations which demonstrate a cyclic pattern of corruption.

Most organisations view themselves as a Type 1 organisation until something lifts the lid and reveals a tendency towards a Type 3 organisation. Scandal ensues and pressure from the media, government, political circles or the community force it into a reform phase. Typically new managers are injected into the organisation and a new leader may be introduced as the reformer.

A period of reform then follows, and such an atmosphere may exist for five or ten years. Cynics comment on the ingenious ability of bureaucrats to innovate around controls – once they know how the new controls work, they devise means of maintaining or reintroducing the former status quo. Inevitably other pressures and priorities arise and combine with complacency to force out the reform phase and circumstances relapse. Such a phase continues until a new scandal erupts whence the cycle is repeated.

Scandal tends to erupt either because of media pressure or through corrupters becoming increasingly intolerant with the level of demands placed on them. The history of police corruption is not exactly awash with examples of police services identifying the problem for themselves. It appears that unless we examine such data and evidence as becomes available, we will be at risk of complacency and slow to respond once that time of scandal arrives. It would seem that the best way to assess the extent of the problem lies in activating some of the remedies.

5. Dynamics of corruption

Corruption flourishes in a number of ways but secrecy is a key component. Therefore it is essential to determine the nature and extent of corruption within the organisation.

The first steps appear to be to turn the organisation into a telling organisation. This involves awakening in our people an understanding of the residual dynamics which are fundamental to the birth, thriving and safety of corruption. Tackling these seems essential to reducing corruption.

Basic goals are:

- To change behaviour by heightening the risk of detection;
- To reduce opportunity and temptation;
- To develop a value system and high ethical standards;

- To manage the culture of the department.

The first dynamic is the individual's descent into corruption. All police officers have been and will continue to be exposed to offers of free meals, free drinks and other small benefits such as free theatre or cinema tickets. Acceptance of these items requires no positive action by the officer and has an apparent innocence. The donor is generally happy to provide these items at a reasonable level – it brings the police nearer so that there is more likelihood of a positive response when help is needed. It may mean that parking tickets go elsewhere, that a police response is that bit quicker when trouble occurs or merely that the donor feels a little safer. The recipient will have to do nothing directly in return for the benefit. It will not be viewed as a corrupt gift but soon it will be normalised as a regular opportunity to save a bit of money. "Everybody does this – the man is pleased to see me".

The next step for some is to move from saving money to actively making a little more. Stretching the expense claim, exaggerating the overtime booked are two examples of this positive internal action. This behaviour again is easily rationalised – "I work hard; I am entitled to a little bit more because of that trouble I have. If I can get these benefits frequently, it will be normalised into my everyday budget".

The third step is to take external action involving the public or suspects. This action is negative in the sense that it is opportunistic. When a payoff is offered or a bribe given for taking non-enforcement of some matter, this is rationalised as an extension of a police officer's discretion, albeit that this is clearly not the case. If regular, this extra cash is normalised – "I deserve a better holiday or a new car: look at what my colleagues are able to afford, they must be doing this".

Such acts are of course wholly corrupt but there is a further stage where the officer creates the opportunity for the corrupt payment or activity. This is full positive external action and corruption at its most damaging. Here rationalisation is difficult but normalisation of the extra money makes it difficult for the officer to retreat. Indeed he or she may be hooked by the corrupter. In both these last two stages the officer is lost to the Service. It is arguable at what stage he or she really ceases to be a police officer and becomes principally a criminal.

The second dynamic is a similar descent into corruption for managers which entraps them into inactivity, according to Grieve.[3]

---

[3]   Based on an unpublished speech by J. Grieve on the dynamics of police corruption in 1994.

The first step is the involvement of management in mutually destructive relationships in an attempt to further a case. So where there are problems over the disclosure of information or details of an informant, economies are taken over the truth or small items of indirect material are re-written.

At the second level, specific lies are told because of operational difficulties, not really to change the evidence but "to make the system work". This is the so-called "noble cause" corruption. At this level many middle managers are sucked in partly because of their natural desire to assist their people and achieve a positive piece of work. Because the first step has already been taken, they are naturally drawn into this second activity.

For some, the slip into the third level of corruption is all too easy. If it is possible to tell lies for the system successfully, it is easy to tell lies for oneself. Informants will try to elicit more money out of the system, and the officers will consequently inflate the claim for a reward. If successful, the informant will be asked for the extra amount as a "drink" for the officers. It is a short step to removing part of the drugs or cash at the next seizure. There will be few managers actively involved in this but they will be powerless to intervene because of their involvement in stages one and two.

The final stage is the act of recycling drugs, corruptly receiving money, compromising operations and warning criminal associates. Management involvement will be rare and indeed the number of officers involved will not be large. However, should a manager be aware or suspect such activity, any involvement in the earlier steps will effectively draw them into concealing such suspicions.

I believe these two dynamics exist today, and any remedial strategy must take them into account.

6. Variable factors which affect corruption

6.1. Community structure

As Merton (1968) argued, there will be less corruption in a community with little dysfunction. Opportunities for corruption will be reduced, the police service will be less isolated, more respected and some of the corruption constants referred to previously will be absent. The absence of cultural conflict within the community is a key component restricting opportunities for corrupt practices to pass unobserved or unrecognised. Conversely where there is a community riddled with problems, the opportunities for corruption multiply. The overall quality of policing is therefore an essential component in corruption reduction.

6.2. Leadership integrity

Integrity of the leadership is essential. Poor and imprecise leadership creates a cynicism that is conducive to accepting bribes. By contrast, strong direct leadership promoting honest and positive values will undermine some of the corruption constants described earlier. Leadership, however, does not just mean the person at the top of the organisation. We have numerous examples where leadership from individual unit managers was essential to break the cycle of corruption and maintain the integrity of the work performance. Therefore all personnel must get full commitment from management to expose and eliminate corruption.

6.3. Reduction in work group solidarity

A reduction in regimented work group solidarity will reduce the opportunity for corruption to flourish. Tackling the siege mentality, sharing honest values and reducing the opportunity for concealment of corruption through the support of the peer group will contribute to the solution. These are issues for management at all levels to take to their people.

6.4. Less gradual steps

Tackling the gradual descent into corruption described earlier in both the individual officer and management cycle will support the honest officer and reduce the opportunity for compromise of officers and management alike. An officer may well slip down each of the gradual steps into full corruption when they would never contemplate going straight to the bottom of the well of opportunity.

6.5. Adopt a code of ethics and list activities that are specifically prohibited

The establishment of a code of ethics in connection with a list of activities that are specifically prohibited may also be of great help in containing corruption problems.

7. Corruption controls

7.1. Reactive initiatives

Investigations into corruption have to be conducted by external, specialised, highly professional police units. Investigation is difficult because police officers have a natural tendency to protect colleagues and to keep the police image up at the highest level. This can lead to dramatic situations as it has been experienced in some countries (e.g. in Belgium, the François case; in The Netherlands, the Van Traa enquiry, etc.).

There is frequent argument as to who should police the police. In America, a number of anti-corruption commissions have been formed, but the ordinary response is a strong, central internal affairs department. External commissions or investigation units have never successfully penetrated the police culture and have not had a major impact upon deterrence. By contrast, internal investigation units are considered to have the ability to increase the corrupt officer's perception of the risk of arrest.

I would argue that an internal body is essential because its presence within the organisation allows the assessment of changes in behaviour, trends and new developments as they occur. It can draw on the service for trained personnel and can put forward organisational remedies directly and in less threatening ways than an outside, politicised organisation. Perhaps of crucial importance, its position within the organisation as a data collection point will enable judgements to be made about the levels of corruption.

In England and Wales, a detailed complaints system is legislated by Parliament, investigated by police officers and supervised by the Police Complaints Authority. The system deals with all matters from rudeness to corruption, generally spending more time dealing with breaches of the disciplinary code rather than corruption but it provides the natural base from which anti-corruption work can commence.

7.2. A proactive response

The reactive response depends entirely upon the receipt of an allegation and nothing less specific will trigger an investigative response. This is the basis on which our complaint investigation system is organised but there are certain inherent problems. The complainant will invariably have a criminal record and almost always will stand to benefit substantially from making such an allegation. If the dishonest act occurred, the training of the officer will ensure that corroboration was absent, whether it be forensic evidence or an independent witness. This is a recipe for failure of the reactive approach through a lack of evidence.

The proactive response, however, acknowledges the cyclic nature of police corruption. In addition to dealing with the reactive public complaint system which we consider an important contribution to high regard in which our police service is held, the internal affairs department should take a proactive attitude to corruption, monitor and analyse data and prepare to use covert investigation methods similar to those adopted in the most serious crime investigations. The establishment of a proactive internal affairs unit also seems a valid organisational innovation.

7.3. Avoidance of amplification

One danger in the use of proactive investigative measures and strong leadership is that of amplification. That is the fear that the labelling of a whole section of the service as corrupt creates bitter resentment and prompts some to adopt corrupt practices in a form of revenge. I am far from persuaded by this argument. The numbers who would so react are probably exceeded by those who would be deterred by such steps. The difficulty of amplification in my view is the tendency we see in serious crime for the offenders to learn from the methods used by police and develop new ways of committing crime and avoiding detection.

I do not see this as an argument for not proceeding with proactive methods as we need to better the reactive response in such serious matters. However, it suggests that when such methods are being developed the moment of their impact should be carefully judged so that the greatest deterrence value is obtained. Thereafter a real test for the organisation is how to maintain an effective internal affairs unit, particularly after the reform phase is exhausted and relapse starts.

7.4. Vigorous media

Investigative journalism aimed at improper police practices is never welcomed by police managers. All the usual difficulties of assessing whether media reports are accurate, maintaining morale, defending the good, striking a neutral position during investigation and controlling the investigation during vigorous press activity will be present. The fact remains, though, that most serious outbreaks of police corruption have been exposed initially by the media. A free and uncensored press is essential.

8. Some comments on a proactive response

I have described some organisational changes which are considered important in reducing corruption. The main thrust of activity, though, has to come through an effective internal affairs department which uses proactive methods. This sounds relatively simple but in fact this approach brings with it a number of threats.

8.1. Staffing

How does the internal affairs unit determine whether those it is recruiting are honest. If proactive covert measures are to be used, experience and training will be at a premium, but those qualities will be principally found in that group of officers who face the greatest temptations to be corrupt. Our experience is that highly trained specialist squads and officers in technical support units have their own networks. Drawing personnel from these areas will introduce the risks of leaks, yet ignoring such recruitment areas will lead to a unit devoid of skills and the necessary depth of ability. Ethics training needs constant emphasis be it during initial or continued training.

8.2. Morale

Even if a recruitment process is devised which avoids the selection of corrupt officers, those selected face the unenviable task on working on their former colleagues. If police officers as a group are isolated, this group of internal investigators will be doubly isolated and put under great pressure. This extends outside the workplace. An example exists of an officer being followed from his place of work to his home address, and a clear threat was made to his family indicating it was known where he lived. In another case an officer had his son return from a game of football with the sons of other police officers to challenge him that his internal investigation activity had resulted in an officer being falsely accused and a criminal being released.

8.3. Resources

The major proactive work that a vigorous internal affairs unit would undertake would require a high degree of technical equipment and the provision of adequate resources. To draw such equipment from the same sources presents some serious difficulties. Knowledge of the radio frequencies used permits scanning and monitoring by those under investigation. Again, examples exist where suspect officers have been seen to scan the premises they were about to enter. The secretion of devices in premises and on people becomes very problematical when faced with a target who is used to deploying such devices. The effect is that the whole range of proactive activity has to be very carefully considered and expensively resourced. Such a unit must be constantly at the edge of technology and always looking for new methods.

8.4. Monitoring

Considerable thought needs to be give to the arrangements which support the unit's existence and work. For example, whether it is possible for officers outside the unit to interrogate audit trails on some networked computers to monitor the searches made by the unit. This means that before every enquiry is made on certain databases, the full implications and dangers of such action must be considered. Similarly, verbal enquiries of other units during an early stage of investigation must be carefully reviewed. Such restrictions on the investigation severely hamper the usual information gathering process. So there is the need for evaluation policy and procedures to constantly determine areas of vulnerability.

9. Making assessments on the extent of corruption

Judging the extent of corruption and whether an organisation is type 1 or type 3 is difficult and imprecise. At a corporate level, judgements can be made on the frequency, nature and extent of complaints against police or allegations. It may also occur as a common concern in reviews of failed operations or the failure to progress actions against major targets. Further assessment can be made upon media comment and, indeed upon parliamentary or commentator opinion.

At middle management levels, matters become more difficult to grasp but may provide vital data. The lifestyle of individuals should be monitored and considered in the light of the officer's work profile and those with whom he regularly associates. The individual's integrity will be obvious from his or her work practices and detailed intelligence must be objectively scrutinised. The proper action with this intelligence is essential.

10. Opportunities

Corrupt officers have a number of points of weakness. First, they must communicate with their associates outside of the police service, whilst they research, plan and prepare their illicit activities. In many cases, there will be a regular contact between criminal associates and the corrupt officer.

The next area of weakness for the corrupt officer is when they commit the act of corruption. This should be the point of focus of the proactive investigation but requires the full use of intelligence if it is to be successful.

The corrupt are also vulnerable when handling the proceeds of corruption. There is first of all the physical movement of the proceeds, then the long term gain which financial investigation may detect.

Against these weaknesses, there are similar problems for the investigators. This is a subculture which is designed to be hidden and may be protected by cellular construction. Understanding the links is crucial. Once links start to be identified, the familiar intelligence problem of analysis and identification of those areas upon which to concentrate arises.

It is, of course, evident that the corrupt's point of weakness is when they commit the act. The difficulty for the investigator is to identify that moment and collect the evidence of it. The moment may be short – the passing of a message – or it may be a series of events over a period of time. The receipt of the reward for these corrupt acts may not occur at the same time and may not even involve direct contact. It follows that obtaining evidence of this activity is immensely difficult, especially with sufficient corroboration to ensure that the appropriate criminal or disciplinary action is taken.

If I am right about the cyclical nature of corruption within the police service, successful methods of investigation will need to be protected for continued use. The corrupt are at their most vulnerable while they are unaware of the methods used against them.

It follows that the successful anti-corruption unit must be able to conduct its work without being observed by those it is acting against. Measures to protect the unit from infiltration is essential in the personnel selection policy, careful security measures are required around its work and the unit must have the ability to research activities within the service without being observed by those about whom there are concerns.

The problem is not insoluble but it does require detailed planning, sound direction, effective resources and a substantial commitment from politicians and criminal justice authorities, as well as from the police themselves.

References

Fijnaut, C., "De connecties tussen EG-fraude en georganiseerde misdaad", in H. den Doelder (ed.), *Bestrijding van EG-fraude*, Kluwer Rechtswetenschappen, Antwerp, 1990, pp. 87-97.

Merton, R., *Social Theory and Social Structure*, Free Press, New York, 1968.

Sherman, L., *Controlling Police Corruption*, Yale University Press, New Haven, 1976.

CHAPTER 7

Combating Corruption within the Metropolitan Police Service

Michael Taylor

1. Introduction

"A high command unwilling to acknowledge that the problem of corruption is extensive cannot very well argue that drastic changes are necessary to deal with the problem."

(W. Knapp (1972) Report of the commission to investigate alleged police corruption in New York)

This chapter seeks to provide a brief overview of the recent experience of the Metropolitan Police Service in London, in tackling the scourge of corruption, and the lessons learnt through difficult period. Particular regard will be made to the implementation of a corruption strategy to prevent many of the organisational and cultural failings that degraded our ability to deal with the issue of corruption effectively.

The police service has recognised its particular vulnerability to corruption and is leading the way in the development of effective counter-corruption strategies and investigative and preventative methodology. It is hoped that other parts of the public and private sector will follow.

2. Perception

It is important to keep the matter in context. The Metropolitan Police Service is a massive organisation with over 37,000 members of staff. It is a £2 billion a year organisation and is similar in size to the Royal Air Force. The number of officers

Cyrille Fijnaut, Leo Huberts (eds.), *Corruption, Integrity and Law Enforcement*, 109-116
©2002 Kluwer Law International, The Hague. Printed in The Netherlands.

involved in corruption is very small, but the damage they inflict is disproportionately high.

Most of our difficulties concerning corruption arise simply from our own perception of it. Essentially we have assumed in the past that it is an issue that does not intimately concern our own organisation or our close colleagues. In fact we have been quick to attribute it to other organisations and even other countries, never ourselves. When corruption has been detected, the response has reflected the belief that it was limited to a small group of rogue officers. This "mind set" is best evidenced by the organisation's complete failure for decades to use the tools that have been routinely deployed against other organised crime to combat corruption within our own organisation. Examples abound – we did not collect or maintain an intelligence database on corruption (a crucial failing), nor did we provide officers tasked with anti-corruption an adequate surveillance capacity to target some of the best-trained suspects in the world. We did not become effective until we came to terms with the fact that corruption will probably always be with us and must consistently and continuously be countered.

3. Areas of concern

There have been three key areas of concern relating to police corruption and malpractice in post-war Britain. The first was the excessive use of force, not only during arrest but also in extracting false confessions. Other than in isolated instances, unlawful force has not been a significant problem in Britain.

The second area of concern was interference with evidence as a form of corruption, which came to the fore during the course of the 1980s. Revelation after revelation of apparently deliberate wrongdoing by police officers, leading to miscarriages of justice, emerged from across the capital.

By the mid to late 1980s, the ability of police officers to interfere with evidence had been substantially undermined through the implementation of the Police and Criminal Evidence Act 1984 and other legislation which introduced clear scrutiny of process. A Royal Commission on Criminal Justice in 1992 introduced further safeguards, However, it is recognised that interference with evidence can lie beyond the scope of procedural restriction and cannot be said to have been totally eliminated.

The abuse of position and or power for gain is a more pervasive form of corruption and can take many forms. The introduction of new laws and new technologies opens up new opportunities for the corrupt police officer to abuse his or her authority and power. These abuses can relate to interference with evidence but also extend to the third area of concern. This was leaking of classified intelligence, the illegal use of computers, the provision of sensitive material to unscrupulous journalists and other media representatives and the protection of criminals from investigation and prosecution.

It is this last element of corruption, which has proved to be the main focus of the current Metropolitan Police Service anti-corruption campaign.

4. Corruption: durable and flexible

4.1. Adapting like a virus

The Police Service and the Metropolitan Police Service in particular failed in the past to recognise that corruption is not simply a scandal that periodically erupts and can be extinguished like a fire. With the benefit of hindsight, we know now that corruption is not cyclical in nature – rather it tends to be the effectiveness of the response to corruption that is cyclical.

Corruption has demonstrated remarkable durability and flexibility. Like a virus, it mutates and adapts to new environments.

The corruption of processes which had been seen in Britain earlier and often categorised as so-called "noble cause corruption", was by now clearly less common by virtue of much greater levels of scrutiny of the processes of arrest, detention, investigation and prosecution. ("Noble cause corruption" describes the fabrication of evidence to convict persons who officers honestly believe to be active criminals, whom the criminal justice system has failed to convict.) However, by the early 1990s, process corruption had changed emphasis in that where it occurred it was often for financial reward, for example, the destruction of evidence in return for favour or payment.

The exponential growth of drug-related crime during the course of the 1980s gave rise to the second mutation of corruption. Drug crime presented corrupt officers with new opportunities, and drug traffickers, having significant assets at their disposal, had the capability and motivation to corrupt officers to protect their business.

Another mutation grew from the developing capability of the Metropolitan Police Service to use intelligence and computers to fight crime. Police organisations are traders in information, some of which is extremely valuable to criminals, unscrupulous journalists and others. By the early 1990s, the incidence of the corrupt leaking of intelligence had risen sharply. The introduction of sophisticated IT systems makes all members of staff more effective. They can easily access information to make them work more productively. The benefits of this are obvious in a law enforcement organisation. However, this also makes an organisation considerably more vulnerable to subversion. Fewer corrupt staff can access the work of literally thousands of honest officers. Traditionally the Metropolitan Police Service has been very democratic in the way it allows all staff access to most of its intelligence. This was justified in the context of a belief that all our staff were honest. Certainly most are, but we now recognise that out systems need to be balanced by the need to freely access information with the need to provide protection against the few corrupt staff.

A further mutation of corruption in the United Kingdom was borne from the growth and sophistication of organised crime, including international drug trafficking. One only has to look at the experience of the United States to see the potential impact that organised crime with vast sums of money at its disposal can have on criminal justice and law enforcement agencies. The ability of drug traffickers to deploy very large quantities of cash to corrupt officers at all levels only increases our vulnerability.

4.2. Re-emergence

The last anti-corruption campaign in London concluded in 1977. Some 500 officers were expelled, and then other priorities took precedence. Little had been done to combat corruption until the recent campaign started in 1993. However, corruption was quietly undermining the effectiveness of the Metropolitan Police Service.

The spectre of corruption began to publicly re-emerge in the period between 1990 and 1993 when a series of major and organised crime investigations were inexplicably compromised. A number of significant prosecutions and trials also collapsed amid allegations of evidence being sabotaged and juries being subverted.

Also at this time, there was increasing anecdotal intelligence indicating the existence of corruption. This intelligence was running on informal networks within the Metropolitan Police Service and was being received from criminal informants and as an incidental product of technical surveillance. What became clear was that corruption was exacting a heavy cost on police efficiency. This cost was largely invisible but ran to many millions of pounds – the accumulating cost of compromised investigations and trials.

The Metropolitan Police Service in London was most affected by these issues. It is therefore not surprising that the current anti-corruption campaign began in London.

It was beginning to become clear that the reputation of the Metropolitan Police Service, where policing as we understand it in Western industrialised nations began, was under threat. The reputation of Scotland Yard had previously been synonymous with integrity and had become a brand name in policing. This reputation was now under serious threat.

5. Operation OTHONA

The new manifestations of corruption coincided with the appointment of Sir Paul Condon as Commissioner of the Metropolitan Police Service in 1993. Sir Paul was unequivocal in his response. The Metropolitan Police Service would not tolerate corruption. The Commissioner, along with a select group of senior colleagues, established what became one of the most secret operations ever undertaken by the Metropolitan Police Service.

Operation OTHONA was a radical intelligence gathering operation designed to penetrate the operational strata of the organisation using sophisticated and intrusive intelligence gathering methods in order to scope the extent of corruption and develop a strategic analysis of the threat.

Operation OTHONA ran from 1993 to 1997, revealed a number of unpalatable practices:

- Thefts of drugs and cash on searches;

- Sharing informant rewards;

- Fabricating informant reward applications;

- Destroying/fabricating evidence for payment;

- Selling operational intelligence;

- Drug trafficking;

- Arranging with informants for crimes to he committed and proceeds shared.

Operation OTHONA revealed that a very small number of police officers were engaged in serious corruption. It revealed that corruption was now far more covert and sophisticated in nature than had been the case during the last campaign in the 1960s and 70s.

Although a relatively small number of officers were involved, they were often highly skilled detectives in highly sensitive posts where they could inflict incalculable damage on the Service by betraying their office and public trust.

6. Anti-corruption strategy

The Anti-Corruption Command (C1B3) was launched in January 1998. Initially 150 handpicked detectives were directed to tackle corruption head-on.

Significant success has been achieved. Between January 1998 and November 2001, fifty persons were convicted and imprisoned for serious corruption offences. Of these, eleven were police officers and seven ex-police officers. The remainder were either officials in other parts of the criminal justice system or criminal who had corrupted Metropolitan Police Service staff. Currently at out Central Criminal Court (i.e., December 2001 at the Old Bailey) there are five trials in progress. A further 41 persons await trial for similarly serious corruption offences and 15 of these are serving police officers.

Corruption is a pervasive problem and can only be defeated through the implementation of a pervasive strategy that not only detects corruption but systematically addresses its causes and the vulnerabilities of individuals and the organisation.

In December 1998, the Metropolitan Police Service launched its Corruption and Dishonesty Prevention Strategy which has served the organisation well over the past three years. This strategy is now being revised in the light of experience. It comprises six key strands:

- Prevention and detection;

- Inclusion;

- Focus and accountability;

- Supervision and leadership;

- Security, screening and vetting;

- Corruption and dishonesty proofing.

In this chapter, I wish to focus only on the strand of prevention and detection.

A comprehensive armoury has been developed within the Metropolitan Police Service to tackle corruption. The weaponry deployed includes the following:

- A highly effective intelligence system, which pervades the organisation acting as an indicator of corruption;

- A high level capability to conduct covert and reactive criminal investigations;

- A similar capability for internal discipline investigations. This is particularly suitable where for same technical reasons criminal prosecution is not achievable;

- The use of cutting edge investigative methodology and technology, much of which will be unfamiliar even to the most experienced corrupt targets;

- A holistic approach to the issue of the investigation of police complaints from the public, to ethics, to integrity and professional standards. This overlays management information on complaints with that on corruption and links this with intelligence to achieve incisive analysis of not just problem individuals but trends and causes;

- Comprehensive witness protection arrangements;

- The Metropolitan Police Service Integrity Testing Program which is uniquely split into two specific tools, one acting as a scalpel to cut out corruption (intelligence led tests) and the other acting as an X-ray to look into the soul of the organisation to analyse behaviour and the drivers of corruption, dishonesty and malpractice (Quality Assurance Checks);

- The final tool is the Service Confidence Procedure, which is a backstop to protect the organisation where criminal or discipline disposals are unachievable, yet there is compelling material to indicate an individual is a threat to the Service.

For those who have not ventured into the arena of integrity testing, I would commend the program as one with immense potential to help address issues of corruption, dishonesty and malpractice. However, it is important not to see integrity testing as a panacea but simply one important weapon in fighting corruption and a useful tool in improving the ethics and integrity of large organisations.

7. Lessons to be learnt

A number of lessons can be learnt from the experiences of the London Metropolitan Police Service.

1. Recognition that any law enforcement agency will never be completely free of corruption;

2. The organisation must have a strongly established and credible strategy in place to combat corruption;

3. Corruption is not cyclical it simply mutates or adapts to an ever-changing organisational environment;

4. A law enforcement agency must actively collect intelligence about misconduct within its own organisation;

5. The tactics and systems used against crime should be utilised in internal investigations;

6. A strategy can only be credible if adequate resources are provided;

7. A credible system must be in place to support the reporter of misconduct;

8. In many cases the organisation's culture must change, so that officers sincerely identify with the anti-corruption ideology.

CHAPTER 8

Corruption Within the Judicial System: Some Remarks on Law and Practice in South Africa

Jan d'Oliveira

1. Introduction

Mrs C. Szczaranski, President of the State Defence Council of Chile, has correctly pointed out that it is the *rule of law* that is assailed by corruption in its many guises and forms.[1] She writes that the phenomenon of corruption is:

"a structural issue that injures the [basic] legal values of the rule of law: legal safety, certainty and equality ..."

She later adds that:

"[t]he judicial power is the maximum constitutional exponent of external control ... of the exercise of power."

In a recent judgement of our Constitutional Court, delivered by P. Chaskalson, the following was strongly expressed[2]:

"Corruption and maladministration are inconsistent with the rule of law and the fundamental values of our Constitution. They undermine the constitutional

---

[1]   See the reference to her speech in the Final Report of the Global Forum on Fighting Corruption and Safeguarding Integrity, The Hague, 2002.

[2]   *SA Association of Personal Injury Lawyers v. Heath and 3 Others*, 2000(1) BCLR 77 (CC), 80E–G, [4].

Cyrille Fijnaut, Leo Huberts (eds.), *Corruption, Integrity and Law Enforcement*, 117-134
©2002 Kluwer Law International, The Hague. Printed in The Netherlands.

commitment to human dignity, the achievement of equality and the advancement of human rights and freedoms. They are the antithesis of the open, accountable, democratic government required by the Constitution. If allowed to go unchecked and unpunished they will pose a serious threat to our democratic state."

The judicial system and its officers are the custodian of the rule of law and the bulwark against all that strikes against justice and integrity. How, then, is one to go about protecting the very custodian of the rule of law and eliminating conditions which could be exploited by those who seek to corrupt the judicial system?

The succeeding remarks will be confined to the central *personae* within the judicial system: judicial officers (judges and magistrates), officers of the court (prosecutors and practitioners) and – to a lesser extent – police or other officers who interact with the courts.

2. Range of measures

Effective enforcement of the criminal law is but one measure that is to be deployed in protecting the custodian of the rule of law by removing functionaries who engage in (or fall for) corrupt practices. Disciplinary regimes constitute a supplementary but more flexible and less rigid enforcement measure.

Naturally, the efficacy of enforcement measures presupposes the existence of appropriate rules (legislation and regulations) and depends on the integrity and effectiveness of enforcers. Importantly, enforcement structures must be accessible to the public, transparent in their operation and be seen to be effective and fair. This constitutes a necessary counter to corruption which thrives on secrecy or underhandedness.

Enforcement is but one arrow in the quiver. Another significant form of protection resides in the creation of structural conditions which discourage corruption and render the ground for its penetration infertile. Major protection would therefore appear to lie in the constitutional guarantees of independence and protected remuneration, and in transparent appointment procedures designed to enlist suitable candidates.

In addition to the latter "positive" measures, requirements of accountability and control (both external and self-regulated) would seem to be necessary adjuncts to judicial system organisation.

Besides strategies of enforcement and prevention, it is recognised internationally that building integrity and raising awareness are also parts of an anti-corruption strategy. Stated differently, ethical or moral dictates must continually inform those involved in the judicial system.

I will endeavour to illustrate the foregoing with reference to South African law and practice.

3. Preventive measures

3.1. Constitutional provisions

A constitutional foundation is a fundamental safeguard against corruption. Constitutional entrenchment (directly and indirectly) of the independence of judicial officers, of transparent appointment procedures, and guarantees of remuneration and against arbitrary removal from office reflect South Africa's priorities.

In respect of the judiciary, the constitutional and legislative arrangements are such that they create the necessary conditions for independence, including financial provision. Our Constitutional Court has had occasion to refer to those conditions in *De Lange v. Smuts NO and Another* 1998(3) SA 785 (CC). Citing Canadian jurisprudence, the Court stated[3]:

> "In the leading case *R v. Valente* three essential conditions of independence were identified that could be applied independently and were capable of achievement by a variety of legislative schemes or formulas. The first was security of tenure, which embodies as an essential element the requirement that the decision-maker be removable only for just cause, 'secure against interference by the Executive or other appointing authority'. The second was a basic degree of financial security free from arbitrary interference by the Executive in a manner that could affect judicial independence. The third was:
>
>> institutional independence with respect to matters that relate directly to the exercise of the tribunal's judicial function ... judicial control over the administrative decisions that bear directly and immediately on the exercise of the judicial function."

---

3   *Per* Ackermann J at 813H-814B.

The Republic of South African Constitution of 1996 provides that the judicial authority is vested in the courts which[4]:

"are independent and subject only to the Constitution and the law, which they must apply impartially and without fear, favour or prejudice."

Furthermore:

"[n]o person or organ of state may interfere with the functioning of the courts."[5]

Following on the Interim Constitution (Act no. 200 of 1993) which was implemented in April 1994, the final Constitution of 1996 provided as follows for the *appointment* of judicial officers. S. 174(1) states that:

"[a]ny appropriately qualified woman or man who is a fit and proper person may be appointed as a judicial officer."

In accordance with the differentiation between High Court judicial officers ("judges") and Lower Court judicial officers ("magistrates"), which harks back to British colonial history, the Constitution proceeds to deal directly with judges whilst laying down constitutional norms for legislation pertaining to magistrates.

3.2. In relation to judges

3.2.1. Appointment

A Judicial Services Commission (JSC) is established by s. 178 of the Constitution. It is a widely representative body applying the principle of transparency in appointments. Besides its involvement in special procedures relating to the appointment of Constitutional Court judges, the JSC's role is summed up in s. 174(6):

"The President must appoint the judges of all other courts on the advice of the Judicial Services Commission."

---

[4] S. 165(2).

[5] S. 165(3).

3.2.2. Remuneration

Section 176(3) protects the remuneration of judges in a terse prohibition:

"The salaries, allowances and benefits of judges may not be reduced."

Parliament must appropriate money specifically for the judiciary. The Judges' Remuneration and Conditions of Employment Act, no. 88 of 1989, illustrates the framework and details thereof.

3.2.3. Removal from office

Removal from office is provided for in the following constitutional provision:

"177(1) A judge may be removed from office only if –

a. the Judicial Service Commission finds that the judge suffers from an incapacity, is grossly incompetent or is guilty of gross misconduct; and

b. the National Assembly calls for that judge to be removed, by a resolution adopted with a supporting vote of at least two-thirds of its members."

If the resolution is adopted, the President must remove that judge from office.[6]

3.2.4. Discipline and complaints

There is at present no structured mechanism dealing with discipline and complaints. The role of the JSC seems to be confined to appointments and advice. However, a traditional and strong ethos of probity together with the principle of open courts, the duty to give reasons and the reviewability or appealability of decisions serve to ensure a transparency which is the antithesis of the secrecy that corruption would feed on.

Although there is at present no structured complaints body, it is significant that the judges themselves have drawn up proposals therefor and that legislation is envisaged.

From the above-cited s. 177(1)(a), it is apparent that a judge can lose his/her position if he/she commits gross misconduct.

---

6   S. 177(2).

3.3 In relation to magistrates

Concerning the magistracy, s. 174(7) of the Constitution provides that:

> "[o]ther judicial officers must be appointed in terms of an Act of Parliament which must ensure that the appointment, promotion, transfer or dismissal of, or disciplinary steps against, these judicial officers take place without favour or prejudice."

Prior to 1994, jurisprudence recognised that magistrates (who were career and not lay magistrates) were, in respect of judicial work ("on the bench"), just as independent as judges. However, in terms of appointment, remuneration, promotion and discipline, magistrates were public servants and, hence, subject to the Executive. They were also heads of sub-offices of the Department of Justice responsible for many administrative functions.

It is clear that this dual capacity was untenable as the possibility of at least indirect executive influence was too real. Furthermore, remuneration was dependent upon the general public service budget and was therefore notoriously depressed. The potential vulnerability was partially offset by collegial integrity and pride in incumbency of a magistrate's office.

3.3.1. Governance

In one sense, Lower Court judicial officers are ahead of judges in terms of self-regulation. Several functioning structures are in place.

The Magistrates Act, no. 90 of 1993, establishes a Magistrates' Commission which is also a representative body. Amongst the objects of the Commission is the implementation of the previously quoted s. 174(7) of the Constitution (see s. 4(a) of Act 90 of 1993). Other objects are[7]:

> "to ensure that no influencing or victimisation of judicial officers in the lower courts takes place,"

and:

> "to compile a code of conduct for judicial officers in the lower courts."

---

[7] S. 4(b) and s. 4(d).

The Magistrates Act provides for matters such as protection of remuneration: the salary payable to a magistrate cannot be reduced except by Act of Parliament. It may be added that magistrates' salaries were increased considerably.

3.3.2. Discipline and complaints

The Magistrate's Commission operates through a system of committees, an example of which is the complaints committee which is to be accessible to the public.[8]

Any conduct by a magistrate that is alleged to be improper or to have resulted in any impropriety or prejudice, may be reported to the committee which is to investigate and gather evidence. If misconduct is established after a hearing, removal from office could follow. A report on the findings of a tribunal is to be tabled in Parliament and if Parliament recommends the removal from office, the Minister shall remove the judicial officer.[9]

3.3.3. General

It is not possible to detail all the provisions of the Act within the space of this paper. Suffice it to say that governance by their own commission, the adoption of a code of conduct and accessibility (or transparency) are all hedges against the possibilities of corruption. To these are to be added the principle of public hearings and reviewability of decisions which also apply. South Africa also boasts an automatic process of review by the High Court of decisions of magistrates below a certain rank and involving certain threshold sentences.

Although the number of administrative functions has been reduced somewhat, it has not yet been possible to free magistrates from managerial and other administrative tasks. A process of reconstruction is under way which should ideally result in a court services component which frees both magistrates and prosecutors to concentrate on their respective professional tasks.

3.4. National Prosecuting Authority

There exists a duality here in the sense that appointments to the rank of Director of Public Prosecutions and higher are directly regulated by the National Prosecuting Authority Act, no. 32 of 1998, whilst all other ranks of prosecutors are still subject

---

[8] S. 6(b).

[9] S. 13.

to the laws governing the Public Service (as magistrates were). However, this is changing. The National Director is in the process of taking over responsibility from the Department of Justice for all prosecutors with a view to creating a single regime.

At present it is only the senior ranks (National Director, Deputy National Director and Directors) who are appointed by the President and receive remuneration determined statutorily. In respect of reduction in salary and removal from office, they are in a similar position to judges.

3.4.1. Independence

It has been long recognised that the prosecution service enjoyed a *sui generis* independence, notwithstanding a history of being overseen by the Executive. In the nature of its duty to pursue contravention of the laws, the existence of unacceptable apartheid legislation led to the prosecution being perceived as instruments of the previous regime – notwithstanding the prosecution's professional features. The democratic change has brought about a single authority that enjoys legitimacy.

The Constitution itself provides that[10]:

"[n]ational legislation must ensure that the prosecuting authority exercises its functions without fear, favour or prejudice."

Jurisprudence still recognises that the Prosecuting Authority is independent of the government, but not of the same order of the judiciary. In s. 179(4)[11]:

"[t]here is accordingly a constitutional guarantee of independence, and any legislation or executive action inconsistent therewith would be subject to constitutional control by the courts."

3.4.2. Accountability

The National Prosecuting Authority is accountable to Parliament through a reporting system. Internally, prosecutors are internally accountable through the institution's

---

[10] S. 179(4).

[11] *Ex Parte* Chairperson of the Constitutional Assembly: *in re* Certification of the Constitution 1996(4) SA 744 (CC), 819D-E [146].

hierarchy and subject to continual performance monitoring by a Court Management Unit. Naturally, prosecutors are accountable to the courts in their functioning under the laws and the Constitution. As with any other officer of the court, a prosecutor can be removed from the roll of practitioners for misconduct.

3.4.3. Discipline

In terms of its Act (no. 32 of 1998), the National Prosecuting Authority has drawn up a Prosecution Policy and Code of Conduct. It has also taken over the functions relating to discipline from the Department of Justice.

During 2000, its Court Management Unit established that there were about 72 prosecutors under suspension or investigation by the department, but that little progress had been made in processing these matters. In the course of the same year, the unit's disciplinary committees recommended, after hearings, that 16 prosecutors be dismissed – mostly for corruption.

Since instituting dedicated committees of peers to attend to disciplinary matters, the average time taken to finalise serious cases was reduced from three years to six months.

The lesson to be drawn from this is that dedicated attention and quick action to enforce a Code of Conduct is essential to buttress the positive institutional measures intended to lessen the threat of corruption.

3.5. Practitioners

In South Africa, other officers of the court are lawyers who may be advocates ("barristers") or attorneys ("solicitors"). The former are governed by the Advocates Act, no. 74 of 1964, and the latter by the Attorneys Act, no. 53 of 1979. The Attorneys Act governs, among others things, trust accounts of practitioners and requires that each holds an (annual) certificate to practice. It is strictly enforced.

Advocates and attorneys both have professional organisations which enforce their codes of conduct and legislation.

Before the democratic change, various individual and groupings of lawyers did not belong to the traditional associations. However, steps have been taken since 1994 to unite the various factions.

The process is not complete and the next step is the creation of an umbrella Council for Legal Practitioners. This is regarded as necessary to guarantee accessibility to the public and to ensure a transparent enforcement of discipline. A Legal Practitioners Bill is in the process of compilation.

At base, however, all practitioners are subject to the High Court which enrolls them. They can be removed from the roll on grounds of misconduct.

4. Presentation of a case

It is a cause of pride, and of solace, that the National Prosecuting Authority has never had occasion to enquire into the conduct or probity of any High Court judge. Regrettably, there have been a couple of occasions where suspicious conduct of judicial officers ("magistrates") of the Lower Courts has come to our attention.

Even more regrettable is the fact that the National Prosecuting Authority has had to take action against certain of its members. It is an unfortunate fact that law enforcement officials more easily fall prey to the lure of a reward, and criminal proceedings are more frequent.

A case which required much consideration was one where, on information, a magistrate, the prosecutor and the defence lawyer came under the spotlight. The facts of the case were as follows.

4.1. Facts of the case

One of the special police units assigned to the investigations of the highly prevalent thefts of motor vehicles noticed that the conviction rate in its cases had become exceptionally low. Further examination indicated that acquittals were the order of the day whenever a specific prosecutor, magistrate and defence lawyer dealt with the matters.

Faced with this intelligence but not having evidence of these irregularities, the question as to what to do with the information arose.

One option was to place a spy among the public attending court to observe in what way the prosecutor presented a case so as to achieve an acquittal. However, this option would not provide sufficient proof of corrupt conduct for purposes of criminal action.

The other option, which would secure evidence, was to register a false case of vehicle theft, to then arrest two (police) agents as accused and to take the matter to court. The services of the lawyer in question would also be secured. In other words a trap, based on a bogus case, would be set.

Ethical questions arose. Should one resort to using the court as a tool in the unmasking of corruption? The option entailed registering a false charge, opening a docket, arresting innocent persons and bringing them before a court and, if necessary, causing the court to hear fabricated evidence (for purposes of bail and/or the trial). It is a well-known principle that a court is not to be misled, nor to be used in this manner.

The option, in its full form, was decided against. But it was greatly toned down so as to eliminate the use of the court. A docket was opened with the agents as suspects. It was given to the prosecutor in question to make a decision on it and the lawyer was approached on the strength of that decision. The prosecutor, lawyer and his "clients" (the agents) did indeed proceed to negotiate a payment for the acquittal of the "accused". An arrest was made when the money was paid over.

Although one of the original targets, the magistrate, was abandoned, we were successful in the ensuing prosecution for corruption.

The case described was an exceptional one. In general, however, we are benefiting from an increasing public awareness of corruption. Once a member of the public, who has been propositioned by a court official with a "deal", reports the matter to the police, a special task team is utilised to monitor and/or set a trap, as circumstances require.

The National Office's continuing measurement of performance of prosecutors enables it to notice any disturbing trend. This is then examined and should indications of untoward conduct (combined with, for example, an unusual improvement of lifestyle) appear, an investigation is set in train.

But even here difficult questions do arise. Would it be an invasion of privacy to have surveillance equipment installed in, say, a prosecutor's office? In one case where a camera was installed in a female prosecutor's office, much more than was bargained for was recorded. A couple of defence lawyers became very nervous when the existence of the camera became known!

4.2. Attitude of courts

The South African criminal law pertaining to bribery and corruption was based on the Roman Dutch law. Interestingly enough, two *Placaats* of the States General of the United Netherlands (promulgated respectively in 1651 and 1715), were primary sources. They were interpreted widely by our courts. For example, the courts declined to limit the operation of the *Placaats* to cases in which an official's assistance is sought in a matter covered by his official functions. The corrupt intent was important. Furthermore, gifts made in respect of past favours as well as offers made in anticipation of favours to come, were covered by the *Placaats* (*cf. R v. Chorle* 1945 AD 487).

The consistent view adopted by our trial and appeal courts is captured in the following 1975 statement of principle[12]:

---

12 *Per* Holmes J A in *S v. Narker* 1975(1) SA 583 (A), 586 B.

"Bribery is a corrupt and ugly offence striking cancerously at the roots of justice and integrity, and it is calculated to deprive society of a fair administration. In general, courts view it with abhorrence; see *R v. Chorle* 1945 AD 487 at pp. 496-7; and *Limbada v. Dwarika* 1957 (3) SA 60 (N)."[12]

There is little doubt that criminal corruption will attract a severe sentence, which brings us to the subject of legislative measures and envisaged reforms.

5. Legislation and reforms

5.1. Political will

The development of an holistic anti-corruption strategy, including legislative reform and updating, is very much in the forefront of national priorities in South Africa.

Before 1999 a cabinet committee under the guidance of the Minister of Justice was appointed and mandated to make recommendations to Cabinet for a National Campaign against Corruption.

This was followed by a National Anti-Corruption Summit held in April 1999. The resolutions of the summit were grouped around the main themes, namely:

- Combatting corruption:
     (which includes a review of legislation and the establishment of a whistle-blowing mechanism);

- Preventing corruption:
     (which involves *inter alia* blacklisting of individuals, businesses and organisations that are involved in corrupt practices; establishment of a national hotline and disciplinary action against corrupt persons); and

- Building integrity and raising awareness:
     (including enforcement of codes of conduct and disciplinary codes in each sector and the promotion of training and education in ethics).

Furthermore, the 9th International Anti-Corruption Conference was held in Durban in October 1999. This served to commit South Africa to international endeavours.

Early in 2001, agreement was reached between representatives of the public sector, business and civil society on the establishment of the National Anti-Corruption Forum, which recognises that corruption occurs in all sectors of society and needs to be addressed by all sectors by way of partnerships. The National Anti-Corruption Forum is expected to be fully functional within a few months.

In order to support South Africa's efforts in the fight against corruption, the Minister for the Public Service and Administration signed a co-operation agreement with the United Nations Office for Drug Control and Crime Prevention on 9 March 2001. South Africa has also started participating in the United Nations' Global Programme against Corruption. In terms of this agreement, the following objectives are envisaged:

1. Between May and November 2001, a thorough assessment in all sectors will be conducted to analyse the causes and trends in respect of corruption and the effectiveness of anti-corruption measures in those sectors;

2. The information derived from this assessment, together with the expert advice received from the United Nations, will be fed into the National Anti-Corruption Forum processes with the view to establishing a national anti-corruption strategy with supporting legislation, if and where necessary;

3. Detailed assessments of the capabilities of anti-corruption mechanisms in selected government departments will be conducted in order to establish best practices and to facilitate training. This will then be rolled out to other institutions. Similarly, the capability of the Office of the Public Service Commission to address systemic risks and the capability of the National Director of Public Prosecutions to investigate and prosecute corruption will be enhanced;

4. Tailor-made provincial anti-corruption strategies will also be developed.

5.2. Inappropriateness of a piece-meal approach

In response to a Private Member's Bill proposing an amendment of the Corruption Act, 1992, to provide for the criminalisation of the misuse of public office, the Department for Public Service and Administration commented as follows:

"Successful anti-corruption strategies require a multiplicity of supporting operational plans, a key element being effective legislation. The current fragmentation of anti-corruption and related legislation has long been identified as a factor hampering effective anti-corruption action. The "logic" of the current legislative framework does not allow for a coherent approach to addressing corruption through systematic, administrative (disciplinary), criminal and civil means.

Whether anti-corruption legislation is located in one law or many laws is not the crucial question, but whether all elements and remedies support each other is.

In the present legislative regime the Act (Corruption Act, 1992) is one of a package of laws that addresses corruption. A piece-meal amendment to one of the laws in the package will serve little purpose in making anti-corruption action more efficient.

In principle, the criminalisation of misuse of public office is supported. However, two aspects need to be considered. Fundamentally, the Department for Public Service and Administration cannot support a view that purports corruption to be an offence that can be committed by a holder of public office only. This is in fact widely recognised internationally, regionally and domestically as can be seen from the National Anti-Corruption Forum process and fundamental principles. A review of legislation needs to criminalise corruption by those outside of the public sector. Secondly and more practically, the question of criminalisation cannot be considered in isolation of the administrative, prosecuting and judicial processes (which) criminalisation would lead to coupled with its financial and administrative burdens.

It is the Department for Public Service and Administration's view that the proposed amendment to the act –

- is premature in view of the absence of a thorough review of the legislative framework;

- does not recognise the complexity and deficiencies of the legislative framework; and

- fails to recognise corruption as a societal problem that must be addressed as such."

The National Director of Public Prosecutions, in agreeing that a piece-meal approach to amending legislation is inadvisable, has pointed out the importance of studying current international initiatives against corruption. He argues for the enactment of a new Prevention of Corruption Act as a matter of urgency, taking into consideration the proposals contained in the Global Programme against Corruption of the United Nations.

5.3. Some *lacunae*

There are no specific legislative provisions dealing with bribery and/or corruption of certain classes of officers. In Canada (and Australia), for instance, the bribery of judicial officers, or officers in the administration of criminal law, is penalised in separate enactments and/or by separate provisions.

South African law took a strange turn in 1992, following upon a report of the South African Law Commission, and promulgated a law which was intended to deal with bribery in all sectors, including the private sector. Whilst the intention was laudable, it was offset by the 1992 Corruption Act's repeal of the common law which was widely cast to include all state officials.

The events of the past decade, including the international developments in the field and the increase in the incidence of corruption have led us to the conclusion that the 1992 Act is too restrictive in scope. The realisation of the inadequacy of legislation has resulted in the establishment of a committee dedicated to remedying the *lacunae*. Substantive suggestions include the following:

1. Modern legislation tends to incorporate and develop a number of different provisions regarding various types of corrupt practices. The creation of offences by or in respect of the following persons is therefore suggested:

    i. Judges, magistrates or other judicial officers;

    ii. Any public servant;

    iii. Any private agent;

    iv. Parliamentarians and members of the provincial legislatures;

    v. Members of semi-governmental bodies, for example, Eskom and Telkom;

    vi. Members, and members of the staff, of constitutional institutions, for example, the Human Rights Commission, the Public Protector, etc.

2. Furthermore, the creation of offences in respect of the following corrupt actions is recommended:

    i. Bribery for giving assistance, etc., in regard to contracts;

    ii. Bribery for procuring withdrawals of tenders;

    iii. Bribery in relation to auctions;

    iv. Corrupt transactions with agents.

3. Creating the offence of "possession of unexplained property" similar to the provisions contained in the legislation of Hong Kong, Malaysia and India.

4. Creating the offence of conspiracy to commit an offence under the proposed Act.

5. Creating the offence of bribery of foreign public officials to give effect to the proposals contained in the Convention of Combating Bribery of Foreign Public Officials in International Business Transactions.

6. The establishment of an independent Anti-Corruption Commission or Bureau, and powers, duties and functions of such Commission or Bureau.

Although specific South African legislation needs to be developed, that has not hindered the investigation and prosecution of corrupt activities. After all, there are other common law rubrics which are utilised in order to supplement the 1992 Corruption Act. For example, offences such as fraud, theft and attempting to defeat the ends of justice are all part of the prosecutor's armoury.

5.4. Recent legislation

In conclusion, mention is to be made of recently enacted legislation which is relevant to the fight against corruption.

5.4.1. National Prosecuting Authority Amendment Act, 2000

Prior to 2000, there existed three investigating directorates within the National Prosecuting Authority. The subject-matter of each was:

- Serious economic offences;

- Organised crime; and

- Public violence and corruption.

The amending law consolidates the directorates into one Directorate of Special Operations, headed by a Deputy National Director. The main objects of this Directorate are to:

- Gather intelligence regarding, and to investigate offences which are identified in terms of, the proposed legislation as being of an especially serious nature;

- Ensure that the preparation for the prosecution and the prosecution itself, in respect of these offences, are carried out in the best possible manner.

5.4.2. Promotion of Access to Information Act, 2000 (Act no. 2 of 2000)

This Act, previously known as the Open Democracy Bill, gives effect to the right enshrined in Section 32 of the Constitution, namely the right of access to information. In terms hereof, everyone has the right of access to any information held by the state and to information held by another person when that information is required for the exercise or protection of any fundamental rights.

This legislation is intended to facilitate the demise of a secretive and unresponsive culture in both the public and private sectors which often led to an abuse of power and human rights violations and corruption. It will also foster a culture of transparency and accountability in public and private bodies.

5.4.3. Protected Disclosures Act, 2000 (Act no. 26 of 2000)

The Act is derived from Part 5 (whistle-blower protection) of the Open Democracy Bill, which was subsequently omitted from that Bill to be dealt with separately. (As stated above, the Open Democracy Bill has now been enacted into law and is known as the Promotion of Access to Information Act, 2000.)

The principal objects of the Act are to make provision for procedures in terms of which employees in both the private and the public sector may disclose information regarding unlawful or irregular conduct by their employers or other employees in the employ of their employers. It also provides for the protection of employees who make disclosures which are protected in terms of the Act.

6. Conclusion

This chapter attempts to convey the measures in place which specifically protect the judicial system from the insidious evil of corruption, and to indicate developments in progress.

It should be realised that judicial and other court officers can only be fully protected if there is in society generally effective anti-corruption strategies and legislation which buttress those strategies.

South Africa is moving in the desired direction. Fora such as these give our efforts impetus.

References

Case law

Rex v. Chorle, 1945 AD 487.

State v. Narker, 1975 (1) SA 583 (A).

Ex Parte Chairperson of the Constitutional Assembly: *in re* Certification of the Constitution, 1996 (4) SA 774 (CC).

De Lange v. Smuts N O and Another, 1998 (3) SA 785 (CC).

SA Association of Personal Injury Lawyers v. Heath and 3 Others, 2000 (1) BCLR 77(CC).

Legislation

Advocates Act, no. 74 of 1964.

Attorneys Act, no. 53 of 1979.

Judges' Remuneration and Conditions of Employment Act, no. 88 of 1989.

Corruption Act, no. 94 of 1992.

Magistrates Act, no. 90 of 1993.

The Constitution of the Republic of South Africa Act, no. 200 of 1993 ("Interim Constitution").

The Constitution of the Republic of South Africa Act, no. 108 of 1996.

National Prosecuting Authority Act, no. 32 of 1998.

Promotion of Access to Information Act, no. 2 of 2000.

Protected Disclosures Act, no. 26 of 2000.

National Prosecuting Authority Amendment Act, no. 61 of 2000.

PART IV

LEGAL INSTRUMENTS AND INSTITUTIONS

CHAPTER 9

Sanctions against Bribery Offences in Criminal Law

Barbara Huber

1. Introductory remarks

When looking closer to the subject of sanctions in the field of bribery offences, it appears that this part of criminal weapon has been neglected in discussions about legislative innovations. Much fantasy and legal wit has been heaped on tightening loopholes in the network of legal provisions against bribery, extending the net itself from national to inter- or supranational officials, loosening the causal link between promise or gift and the resulting acts of the civil servant etc. However, as to the consequences of the offence, not much has been done except perhaps an increase in the amount of punishment provided for and/or more possibilities to siphon off gains of the illegal acts. This is of course part of the general modern trend to confiscate financial means resulting from crime and is not a special feature of bribery laws.

Unfortunately, there is not much in the way of empirical studies in this field either. The practice of sanctioning so far has not been a topic of criminological research in many countries – perhaps the global study of the United Nations Inter-regional Crime and Justice Research Institute team in Turin will bring about more facts and data in this respect which may lead to new insights and perhaps to a new approach.

My survey will start with a look into the regulations of sanctions in the supra-national instruments and from there we shall proceed to the national systems of penalties and try to find a common platform for a more integrated approach to this subject.

Cyrille Fijnaut, Leo Huberts (eds.), *Corruption, Integrity and Law Enforcement*, 137-150
©2002 Kluwer Law International, The Hague. Printed in The Netherlands.

2. Sanctions provided in supranational instruments

By now there are several international or supranational agreements dealing (sometimes on a more limited geographical basis[1]) with bribery offences or with certain aspects of them. I have to mention here the Organisation of Economic Co-operation and Development (OECD) Convention,[2] the First Protocol[3] to the European Convention on the Protection of the Financial Interests of the Communities (EC)[4] and the EC Convention on the Fight against Corruption[5] all of which focus on foreign public officials in international business transactions or on officials of the European Communities or of the member states of the European Union.

The Criminal Law Convention of the Council of Europe of 1999 is of a more general nature dealing with the criminal side of bribery in a comprehensive sense.[6] Lastly, there is the European Union Joint Action on Corruption in the Private Sector of 22 December 1998, dealing with commercial bribery, a topic which is also part of the Convention of the European Council (article 7/8).[7]

2.1. Criminal sanctions

Besides dealing with the definition of the various kinds of corruption (sometimes limited to active bribery only: OECD Convention), with bribery and punishability of legal persons (all instruments) and with bribery in the private/commercial sector (Council of Europe Convention, Joint Action of the European Union), with jurisdiction (Council of Europe Convention), and with some connected offences like money laundering or accounting offences (Council of Europe Convention), there are also a few provisions to be found which refer to sanctions. In accordance

---

[1] Inter-American Convention against Corruption of 1996.

[2] Convention on Combating Bribery of Foreign Public Officials in International Business Transactions of 1997.

[3] First Protocol to the Treaty on the Protection of Financial Interests of the Communities of 27 September 1996 (96/C 313/01).

[4] Treaty of the European Union on the Protection of Financial Interests of the Communities of 26 July 1995 (95/C 316/03).

[5] Convention of the European Union on the Fight against Corruption of 26 May 1997 (97/C 195/01).

[6] Council of Europe Treaty, European Treaty Series no. 173, 1999.

[7] Joint Action on Corruption in the Private Sector of 22 December 1998 (98/742/JHA), Official Journal, L 358 of 31 December 1998.

with the obligations imposed by the defining articles of the instruments, the contracting parties are obliged explicitly to draw the consequences from the serious nature of the offences by providing for criminal sanctions.

There is, however, no concrete framework offered between the brackets of which such sanctions should be set by the national legislator. It is only said that such necessary sanctions should be "effective, proportionate and dissuasive". We find this general expression in article 19 of the Council of Europe Convention of 1999, in article 5 of the First Protocol and of the European Union Convention of 1997, in article 3(1) of the OECD Convention of 1997. This last-mentioned instrument wants them to be *comparable* to national sanctions. The criteria of effectiveness, proportionality and dissuasiveness have their roots in the well-known judgement of the Court of Justice of the European Communities which, in the (*Mais*) Case 68/86, stated:

"Member states must ensure in particular that infringements of Community law are penalised under conditions, both procedural and substantive, which are analogous to those applicable to infringements of national law of a similar nature and importance and which, in any event, make the penalty effective, proportionate and dissuasive."

All three conventions and the First Protocol demand that the penalties must always be of a criminal nature, in other words triable by courts. They need not always necessarily involve deprivation of liberty; it will also be possible to impose fines in addition or as an alternative to incarceration. But the national codes are obliged to provide, in serious cases, for penalties involving deprivation of liberty of a certain level which allow for extradition. In complying with this ruling, the member states have some discretion in determining the nature and severity of the penalties which may be provided for.

2.2. Corporate punishment

Besides providing penalties for natural persons, article 18 European Council Convention and article 2 OECD Convention oblige the parties to establish liability for legal persons, the problem of sanctioning such entities has to be tackled. While the European Union Convention relies on the other instruments which require the member states to consider the matter, article 3 of the Second Protocol to the Convention on the Protection of the European Communities' Financial Interests requires member states to provide for various forms of liability on the part of legal persons, including liability for active corruption involving the financial interests of the Community.[8] But the European Union Convention establishes a special liability of heads of business and decision-makers, as has been done in the Convention on the Protection of the European Union's Financial Interests (article 3) and is also contained in the *corpus juris* (article 14) (Delmas-Marty, 1997). This however involves the sanctioning of natural persons not for their own personal actions but because they have failed to fulfil a duty of supervision or control. Liability here is based on an offence distinct from corruption, and objective criminal liability could be attached for the actions of others.

Legal persons whose liability has been established shall also be subject to sanctions that are effective, proportionate and dissuasive. They can be penal, administrative or civil in nature. Being aware of the fact that not all criminal law systems subject legal persons to criminal liability, the conventions do not oblige the parties to impose criminal sanctions, but they should include monetary sanctions (OECD Convention article 3(2); Council of Europe Criminal Law Convention article 19 (2)). All these sanctions should however reflect the seriousness of the offence.

The European instruments since the Recommendation of the European Council of 1988 have already developed a broad spectrum of corporate sanctions: there are monetary sanctions (recognisance, skimming off extra profits, compensation, restitution, exclusion from advantages, fine or (total) confiscation of property/ forfeiture),[9] restrictions of entrepreneurial activities (prohibition of certain activities, removal of managers, closure of the enterprise/departments, winding up)[10] and other kinds of sanctions (warnings, publication of judgement) (Heine, 1999).

2.3. Secondary financial measures

In addition to the recommended effective, proportionate and dissuasive principal sanctions, most instruments provide that the parties shall adopt such legislative and other measures as may be necessary to enable it to confiscate or otherwise deprive the instrumentalities and proceeds of criminal offences established by the Conventions, or property the value of which corresponds to the proceeds (Council

---

[8] See Explanatory Report to the Convention on the Fight against Corruption involving Officials of the EC, 1997, commentary to article 6.

[9] EC Recommendation 1988; see also the recommendations of the Committee of Ministers of the Council of Europe no. R(88)(1988).

[10] EC Recommendation 1988 (note 9, *supra*).

of Europe Convention article 19(3)[11] in connection with the Convention on Laundering, Search, Seizure and Confiscation of the Proceeds from Crime, 1990; OECD Convention article 3(3); no such provision is contained in the European Union Convention).

The legal deprivation can also be civil forfeiture. These secondary sanctions or measures are based on the idea that confiscation of the proceeds is one effective method of combating crime. The expression "confiscate" refers to any criminal sanction or measure ordered by a court following proceedings or conviction for a criminal offence resulting in the final deprivation of property. Confiscation may be possible of objects that form the proceeds of the crime, or of other property belonging to the offender, the so-called substitute assets which equal the value of the directly gained illegal means.

2.4. Disciplinary aspects

The only instrument which refers to disciplinary consequences of a bribery offence is the European Union Convention on the Fight against Corruption of Community Officials (1997). Article 5(2) makes it clear that the provision does not intend to touch on the disciplinary powers of national authorities, but allows for taking into account of disciplinary consequences in sentencing if this is possible under the principles of the national criminal law.

2.5 Civil and administrative sanctions

Civil or administrative sanctions are mentioned in the conventions only in passing: in article 3(4) of the OECD Convention there is a vague proposal that "each party shall consider the imposition of additional civil or administrative sanctions upon a person subject to sanctions for the bribery of a foreign public official". Among the additional sanctions contemplated are: exclusion from public benefits or aid, temporary or permanent disqualification from participation in public procurement; judicial supervision and judicial winding up.[12]

---

[11] See earlier Guiding Principles, Resolution (97) of 6 November 1997, principle 4.

[12] See Commentaries on the OECD Convention, 21 November 1997, § 24.

2.6. Summary of the findings

To sum up this short *tour d' horizon* over the sanction scheme of the supranational instruments, it can be said that the framework offered to the parties is a very flexible one. Fixed cornerstones are:

- The characteristics of penalties: effective-proportionate-dissuasive; comparable with existing national levels;

- The demand for imprisonment for serious cases so that extradition is possible;

- Sanctions against corporations – allowing for discretion whether they are of a criminal, administrative or civil kind;

- The demand for secondary financial penalties which deprive the offender of his gains and assets; again, also civil measures may be chosen.

The process of integration of these international norms has two special features. First of all, there is no virgin terrain in the national systems waiting to be filled by the international demands; all national systems already have provisions against corruption, at least as far as public officials are concerned. The international model will therefore be re-shaped or formed by the national conditions.

A second characteristic of this process is the multiplicity of international instruments waiting for integration: the international law is already pluralistic in respect to its normative sources, the protected interests (democratic/economic), the ambit of its aims (regional/functional). The national systems therefore have to integrate a number of models. However, regarding sanctions the international dispositions do not demand conformity but only compatibility. This means that each state is left to implement, within the framework and requirements of its own system, with the relevant conventions and other instruments serving as a baseline or minimum standard which is determined by the vague concept of "necessity".

3. Sanctions (and sentencing practice) in the member states and beyond

The role of the supranational norms with respect to national systems can be threefold: depending on the proximity between national rules and supranational models it can be a source of inspiration, of impulse or of consecration (Mathonnet, 2001).

This leads us to the question whether the sanctions provided for by the national systems fulfil the conditions of being effective, proportionate and dissuasive.

The variations in incriminations in the national legal systems match enormous differences in the possibilities to sanction bribery offences. There are states which provide for relatively harsh penalties, like the United States Foreign Corrupt Practices Act. Under this act a criminal violation of the anti-bribery provisions by enterprises may result in fines of up to US$ 2.5 million per violation; individual persons not more than US$ 1 million or 10 years' imprisonment. Officers, directors, stockholders, employees or agents of issuers may also face fines of up to US$ 100,000 and/or five years' imprisonment, issuers up to US$ 2 million. Furthermore, if the offence causes a pecuniary loss or gain, United States law authorises alternative maximum fines equal to the greater of twice the gross gain or loss. Individuals may be fined on this basis or in the alternative up to US$ 250,000 and/or may be imprisoned for up to five years. In the Lockheed case (1995), the application of these provisions resulted in a combined civil and criminal fine totalling US$ 24.8 million.

European criminal codes are mostly more moderate, even an increase in penalty frames which generally occurs when the law is amended on the initiative and basis of OECD and European Union conventions would scarcely lead to such sanctions.

Penalty frames not only differ from state to state but also between the various forms of bribery. There is generally a different penalty provided for active and for passive bribery of public officers. It also makes a difference whether the act performed by the civil servant or asked from him is legal or violates his or her official duties. Some jurisdictions differ between serious and less serious cases. Bribery of judicial personal or of members of legislative bodies is generally considered to be an aggravated offence and is threatened with more severe penalties.

We generally find principal penalties and in addition ancillary sanctions which provide for the confiscation or forfeiture of the financial gains and, in case of officials, members of elected bodies or judges, the temporary or permanent disqualification from office and deprivation of the right to be elected or to vote.

3.1. Principal penalties

As a rule, principal penalties are imprisonment or fines. As far as I know only China and Vietnam provide for the death penalty for serious bribery offences, and China at least still executes it. Some countries, for example Greece and Turkey, still have two forms of deprivation of liberty for bribery offences: imprisonment or penal servitude can be imposed. This can be for a considerable period – between 5 and 20 years in Greece, depending on the amount of damage, and 4 to 12 years in Turkey for serious cases of active bribery. Imprisonment for life we only find in

Greece, all other jurisdictions being satisfied with periods of various length. On the less harsh side we find Belgium, Germany, The Netherlands, England, Austria, Sweden, Slovenia and Switzerland – penalties here start from 6 months (Germany, England, Belgium/8 days, Portugal) and can go up to 5, 6, 7 or 8 years (Belgium, Austria/except for abuse of office which can be punished up to 10 years; England (7), Sweden, Germany, Portugal (8)). Sometimes 10 or 12 years are provided for the most serious cases as in Germany or in The Netherlands if a judge is involved. Repeated active or passive bribery can be punished more severely: The Netherlands expressly provide for an increase of one third in this case.

Jurisdictions with harsher repression are France, Greece, Italy, Poland, Russia, Spain, Turkey, Japan and the United States. Here we find some forms of bribery offences and related crimes which can trigger high penalties not only in exceptional cases. There are penalties up to 10 years (France), 12 (Turkey), 15 years (Poland, United States), 20 years (Italy).

While some jurisdictions only provide for imprisonment for bribery offences (Italy, Greece), most jurisdictions offer fines which can be used instead of deprivation of liberty or cumulative to it in order to deprive the offender of his financial profits from the act. Sometimes we can find very detailed scales of fines and the amount depends of the value of the advantage offered or received (Spain, Turkey, United States). While some criminal systems provide for the same penalty for active and passive bribery (Italy, Greece, Belgium, Germany) others, like The Netherlands, differ between these two forms. Differences are also made if the demanded or granted official act is a breach of duty or not (Germany).

3.2. Financial measures relating to criminal gains

Deprivation of liberty and fines are supplemented by financial measures relating to criminal gains. In the fight against organised crime to which bribery often belongs, gain-orientated strategies of crime control hold a central position. Criminalisation of money laundering and confiscatory measures against the illegal gains are valued highly. The well-known slogan "crime does not pay" is most appropriate in relation to bribery offences which always include a financial aspect. So we find forfeiture, confiscation, restitution and compensatory measure in most jurisdictions. Sometimes they are an obligatory consequence (France, Italy, Germany when the act is committed under certain conditions (by a gang or professionally)), sometimes there is a judicial discretion for their use.

The classic measures like forfeiture of advantages gained by the offence and confiscation of objects used in or resulting from the commission of the offence are supplemented by new instruments which do not aim at concrete objects but at assets which are suspected of being gained from illegal acts or which form the whole property of the offender. In Germany, the application of these measures depends of certain conditions, for example if the completed or demanded act is a breach of official duties or if the offender is member of a gang. Under constitutional aspects these broad possibilities are heavily criticised. Since it is a penalty, this measure has to be proportional to the seriousness of the act and to the offender's guilt. For the evaluation of proportionality these supplementary measures have to be judged together with a prison sentence imposed for the offence.

The application and effectiveness of these additional sanctions are still far from ascertained (Kilchling, 2000; Hein, 2000). Despite the fact that the evidential burden as to the origin of the assets is frequently shifted to the offender and that the causal link between actual offence and assets has been loosened (for example in Italy) this measure has not yet been applied satisfactorily at all. In practice it seems to be too difficult to investigate assets in the same process by which the offences are adjudicated.

3.3. Disqualification and removal from office

Bribery offences involving state or municipal public servants, law enforcement officials, deputies, members of elected bodies etc. create a danger to the legal application of state authority, undermine public confidence in unbiased decision-making and are a misuse of official power. All jurisdictions therefore provide for suspension from office or disqualification of officials who are convicted for an offence of bribery or misuse of office. This supplementary penalty can be imposed even in connection with relatively short periods of imprisonment, such as in Germany for 6 months, or in Austria, 12 months. It can be for periods from two years up to three (Russia), five (Germany, England), 12 years (Spain) and unlimited (Italy) or for life (Spain). Under some laws these measures are obligatory, others contain discretionary powers in this respect. Further to criminal laws using this weapon against corrupt civil servants, disciplinary laws provide for removal from office.

These secondary penalties can have a great impact on the convicted person's professional and private life. It can mean the ruin of his future and of his reputation. German criminal courts therefore see the removal from office under disciplinary law as a reason for mitigation of the principal penalty. Cases from other jurisdictions show that courts rely heavily on this secondary penalty which guarantees that the civil servant will not have a chance to continue in a place where he proved to be vulnerable. Imprisonment is for a limited period only, suspension of short sentences or early release make the time to be served in prison even shorter; removal from office has a longer preventive result. On the other hand, in cases of serious bribery, the bribing enterprise sometimes offers employment to the removed civil servant thus making up for the loss he suffers as a consequence of his criminal behaviour.

Other secondary penalties are: a kind of forced unpaid labour in order to re-educate the convicted person (Russia), disqualification from a military career, or from certain legal posts (The Netherlands), loss of the right to vote or to be elected.

3.4. Punishing enterprises

By now, legal persons can be answerable to criminal charges under bribery laws and punished with criminal sanctions in more and more countries (China, The Netherlands, England, Belgium, United States, France, Portugal), other jurisdictions such as Sweden, impose corporate fines as secondary criminal penalty on legal persons if the crime has been committed in the exercise of business activities. Spain also knows several specific measures of uncertain legal nature against corporations who have committed an enumerated range of offences including bribery. Portugal however, though acknowledging corporate criminal responsibility until recently exempted bribery offences from this but is in the legislative process of changing the situation. A number of jurisdictions do not acknowledge the possibility of corporate criminal responsibility and therefore impose administrative fines: these are Germany, Greece, and Italy – the latter only introduced this possibility for a very limited range of crimes, including bribery offences, in April 2001. Greece limits this measure to enterprises, not to legal persons in general.

The range of sanctions in this context is broad: as a standard instrument there is the criminal or administrative fine which can run up to considerable amounts. Germany has set the upper limit to DM 1 million (500,000 Euro) for an intentional criminal offence.[13] The Netherlands at NLG 100,000 (50,000 Euro). In Greece corporations can incur a fine of up to three times the value of the advantage produced by the offence.[14]

The fine is flanked by confiscation and forfeiture measures, compensation and restitution, all of them having the same or even more disadvantages when applied against corporations as against individuals. The repressive or deterrent effect of such financial penalties, however high, is considered to be weak. For the enterprise it is simply a cost factor compensated for by adequate calculation. It is by no

---

[13] § 30 *Ordnungswidrigkeitengesetz (OwiG)*.

[14] Article 5 of Act 2656/1998.

means equivalent to imprisonment of natural persons. Modern legislation therefore has attempted to find more efficient sanctions against corporations. This can be noted especially in France and Spain. Such sanctions are:

- Dissolution or liquidation of the company or closing down of its premises (Spain, France);

- Temporary or permanent ban on conducting business (Greece, Spain, Italy);

- Disbarment from government procurement (Greece, France);

- Prohibition of carrying out certain activities, operations or transactions (Spain, France);

- Publication of the conviction in order to inform the public (Japan, The Netherlands, Switzerland, United States, France);

- Corporate probation (United States) or supervision by a court (France);

- Reprimands and adverse publicity (Italy).

Whether these standard and the new sanctions are efficient from a deterrent point of view or whether they generate their own ineffectiveness through reactive avoidance strategies, is a question of further discussion and in particular of more empirical research (Schünemann, 1999; Heine, 1999; Dandurand, 1999).

3.5. Penalties for acts of commercial bribery

A last special point touches on commercial bribery. This form is gaining more attention from governments and legislatures right now because of considerable economic and social changes in Eastern countries as well as liberalisation of commercial laws, growing professionalism of marketing, strong competition, growing anonymity and decline of ethical standards in Western states. Meanwhile, two supranational instruments have dealt with it.[15] This form of bribery and related behaviour of unfair competition is sometimes regulated for in the core criminal laws (Germany, The Netherlands, Sweden, England, Korea, United States, Poland (draft 1999)). Other jurisdictions chose special laws for criminalising such activities: commercial code or unfair competition laws (Korea, Japan, Switzerland), the Labour Code (France) or other legislation dealing at the same time with related offences

---

[15] See *supra* notes 6 and 7.

like fraud, economic espionage, bribery of witnesses, bribery in the context of television game shows or sport events.

The criminal penalties we find in core or ancillary criminal laws are, of course, the standard forms of imprisonment and fines. Incarceration is again provided for very diverse maximum terms: one year in The Netherlands, Korea and the Czech Republic – 10 years or even 30 in the United States legislation.[16] The average penalty ranges from between three and five years (Germany, Japan, Korea, Poland, Switzerland). Fines can be imposed as an alternative (Korea beginning the range with fine of up to one million Won) or in addition to imprisonment (England, United States).

Additional sanctions are similar to those provided for in respect of bribery of officials – additional fine (England, United States), forfeiture (Czech Republic, Germany, Japan, The Netherlands, Sweden, United States), confiscation of proceeds (France, Korea, Switzerland, United States, England), compensation (Japan, Sweden, United States, England).

Another form of sanctions in this field are restrictions of liberty; this can inhibit business activities or be a loss of licence (sometimes only used for by administrative bodies against enterprises). It can also be an order of community service on an individual offender (The Netherlands, Czech Republic) who would otherwise undergo a prison sentence of six months. Publication of the conviction is also a sanction in this field (The Netherlands, Switzerland, Japan and United States).

4. Summary and conclusions

This (necessarily short and therefore superficial) survey has shown a considerable divergence of kind and amount of principal and ancillary criminal penalties directed towards various forms of corruption. Countries with an elaborately structured sanction system provide a detailed scaling from a mild reaction of a few months of imprisonment or fine imposed for the basic crime to considerable penalties for the most serious form. In this scaling process legislation takes many factors into consideration, such as the legality or illegality of the demanded or rendered official act; bribery of ordinary public servants in the executive, or of members of the administration of justice; bribery of members of a legislative body; and finally bribery in commercial contexts. Aggravating factors such as commission by a gang

---

16 Netherlands Penal Code article 631; Korean Penal Code article 149; Czech Penal Code; United States Anti Kick-back Act; United States Bribery in Procurement on Bank Loans.

or as a habitual briber or bribee are decisive too. The amount of punishment provided in the law and imposed in practice depends on the national crime situation, on the immediate danger and anxiety caused by corruption in society, but also on the general approach to punishment as a means of social control and prevention.

Does such a system threaten corruptive networks, does it change a society prone to corruption? There are theoretical and practical doubts about this effect. Recent empirical data from Germany, for instance, show that of the cases under research, more than 40% of the investigations against suspects are discontinued, 30% because of lack of evidence. In less serious cases this mode of discontinuation (for lack of evidence) occurred in nearly 50% of cases, in serious cases it was still 35%. If a conviction is reached, prison sentences are more likely than a fine (16.3% in comparison with 1.8%). However, of the prison sentences which in 65% of the defendants ranged in the area where suspension was possible, all but one were suspended (Bannenberg, 2001).

So the question remains: which punishment is effective, proportional and dissuasive? Is criminal law at all effective considering the means of civil and administrative laws which already now protect the endangered fields of the state, the legislature, the economy? Whether criminal law can effectively influence or motivate societal behaviour is to be seriously doubted. It is ascertained criminological knowledge that changes of the ambit of criminal offences or changes of punishment frames as such generate nearly no effect on the legal consciousness of the public, nor is a strengthening of the preventive impact expected (Kerner & Rixen, 1996; Dölling, 1996; Kaiser, 1996). Increased and perfected repression without analysing the background and reasons for corruption only creates ephemeral success. The limited efficiency of criminal sanctions, the principle of last resort of the criminal law opens the view to the field of preventive measures (also secondary ones) outside the criminal law. Tax law, disciplinary reaction, financial contra-strategies like exclusion from tenders etc. may be more efficient than more repression by the criminal law.

It is easier to change situations than to change persons by way of punishment (in the sense of primary prevention). The implementation of measures of structural and situative prevention should therefore get high priority (Artz, 1998; Killias, 1998).

References

Arzt, G., "Filz statt Kriminalität", in *Festschrift für Kaiser*, Duncker und Humblot, Berlin, 1998, I, pp. 495-507.

Bannenberg, B., *Ergebnisse einer Bundesweiten Strafaktenanalyse zur Korruption*, 2001, unpublished paper.

Dandurand, Y., "Entertaining Realistic Expectations About the Effect of Criminal Sanctions Imposed on Corporate Entities: Canada", in A. Eser, G. Heine & B. Huber (eds.), *Criminal Responsibility of Legal and Collective Entities*, Max Planck Institute for Foreign and International Criminal Law, Freiburg, 1999, pp. 267-276.

Delmas-Marty, M. (ed.), *Corpus Juris. Introducing Provisions for the Protection of the Financial Interests of the European Union*, Economica, Paris, 1997.

Dölling, D., *Zeitschrift für die gesamte Strafsrechtswissenschaft*, 1990, pp. 1-20.

Hein, S., "Unrechtmässige Gewinne und ihre Bekämpfung in Italien", in V. Militello, J. Arnold & L. Paoli (eds.), *Organisierte Kriminalität als Transnationales Phänomen*, Max Planck Institute for Foreign and International Criminal Law, Freiburg, 2000, pp. 229-240.

Heine, G., "Sanctions in the Field of Corporate Criminal Liability", in A. Eser, G. Heine & B. Huber (eds.), *Criminal Responsibility of Legal and Collective Entities*, Max Planck Institute for Foreign and International Criminal Law, Freiburg, 1999, pp. 238-254.

Kaiser, G., *Kriminologie*, C.F. Müller, Heidelberg, 1996.

Kerner, H. & S. Rixen, "Ist Korruption ein Strafrechtsproblem?", *Goltdammer's Archiv für Strafrecht,* 1996, pp. 355-396.

Kilchling, M., "Unrechtmässige Gewinne und ihre Bekämpfung in Deutschland", in V. Militello, J. Arnold & L. Paoli (eds.), *Organisierte Kriminalität als Transnationales Phänomen*, Max Planck Institute for Foreign and International Criminal Law, Freiburg, 2000, pp. 241-270.

Killias, M., "Korruption: Vive la Repression! Oder was sonst?", in H. Schwind, B. Holyst & H. Schneider (eds.), *Festschrift für Schneider*, De Gruyter, Berlin, 1998, pp. 239-254.

Mathonnet, P., "La réception des instruments internationaux en droit pénal interne", in M. Delmas-Marty (ed.), *Criminalité économique et atteintes à la dignité de la personne*, vol. VII: *Les processus d'internationalisation*, Ed. de la Maison des Sciences de l'Homme, Paris, 2001, pp. 149-163.

Schünemann, B., "Placing Enterprises under Supervision ('Guardianship') as a Model Sanction against Legal and Collective Entities", in A. Eser, G. Heine & B. Huber (eds.), *Criminal Responsibility of Legal and Collective Entities*, Max Planck Institute for Foreign and International Criminal Law, Freiburg, 1999, pp. 293-300.

CHAPTER 10

Criminal Procedure: What Powers, Instruments and Safeguards Are Necessary for Adequate Law Enforcement?

Keonjee Lee

1. Introduction

Criminal procedure seems to be one of the last areas that could be harmonised on international level, since this is the mixture product of the concerned society's own political, economic, social and cultural components, and historical experiences.

When discussing the efficient fight against corruption in international fora, however, this aspect of criminal procedure often misleads the international society to overlook the importance of procedural aspects. It is needless to say that law enforcement without adequate and efficient means and instruments is just a "castle on sand". Despite this fact, very limited number of international conventions and declarations on corruption have handled procedural matters up until now.[1] And even when they touch on these issues, their language looks too cautious, reserved and declaratory to provide sufficient and meaningful guidelines and standards to governments.

As international and regional debates on corruption are becoming more matured, now is the right time that something concrete should be done in relation to criminal procedures on international level, and that more detailed guidelines should be developed to assist local society's fight against corruption. In this chapter, I will introduce the current measures, developments and difficulties in Korea in the context of criminal procedures, hoping that our experience could contribute to a constructive debate on criminal procedures for the effective fight against corruption.

---

[1]   The most detailed guidelines in relation to procedural matters so far can be found in *Conclusions of the 2nd European Conference of specialised services on the fight against corruption*, 27-29 October 1997, Tallinn, Estonia.

Cyrille Fijnaut, Leo Huberts (eds.), *Corruption, Integrity and Law Enforcement*, 151-160
©2002 Kluwer Law International, The Hague. Printed in The Netherlands.

2. Situation in Korea

During recent years in Korea, especially after President Kim Dae-jung came to office in February 1998, strong initiatives to eradicate corruption have been vigorously taken in the nation. Korea established a presidential joint committee on anti-corruption which reviews and develops the government's overall anti-corruption policies, set up special anti-corruption investigation units within the Supreme Public Prosecutor's Office as well as local public prosecutors offices to conduct and direct the investigation of corruption cases, and drafted bills for the enactment and amendment of various laws for the formation of the efficient anti-corruption infrastructures.

There have been many successes in the actual investigation of corruption cases (in 2000, 2276 persons were prosecuted under the charges of bribery offences) and this won the public's general support and confidence. But, there has not been much progress in the restructuring of the legal frameworks for anti-corruption infrastructure, and still, many debates are ongoing. Especially, the issue of investing law enforcement agencies with greater powers has been the most controversial one. Although the public generally agrees to the very necessity of eradicating corruption from the society, they also seem to have hesitations towards strengthening the powers of law enforcement agencies, due to their bitter memories from the past authoritarian regimes, during which there had been illegitimate use of powers and abuse of human rights by the law enforcement agencies. This roots from the time when the Imperialist Japan occupied the Korean peninsular. At that time, the resistance against the ruling government was regarded as good deed and, on the contrary, the obedience as a humiliation. In the long run, however, as the democracy gets matured in Korea, a sound balancing point will be found between the efficient law enforcement and the human right considerations.

3. Current measures and practical difficulties

In order to understand Korean criminal procedure, it is important to realise the role of public prosecutors in the country. Korean public prosecutors, whose political independence is strictly guaranteed by law, are empowered to conduct criminal investigation by himself or by directing the police or other investigative agencies, to make the final decision whether or not to prosecute a case, to conduct the trial proceedings as the plaintiff on behalf of the state and after the court sentence is finalised, to enforce the sentence imposed. Therefore, in Korea, public prosecutors practically play the leading role in the criminal procedures.

What is the existing criminal procedure and what are the difficulties experienced?

3.1. Arrest and confinement of a suspect

The investigation agencies may arrest a suspect with a warrant issued by a competent judge if certain conditions are met. A suspect may be arrested without a court warrant under certain conditions, in such cases where a suspect is apprehended while committing a crime, or where a person is reasonably believed to have committed a certain category of offences and there is urgent need to apprehend that person but no time to apply for an arrest warrant to a judge.

Arrested persons may be held in custody for up to 48 hours. The police and prosecutors may detain the arrested person for the maximum period of 10 days with another type of court warrant, i.e. a confinement warrant. When the police and investigative agencies other than the prosecutors seek to obtain a warrant of arrest, confinement or search and seizure, they should ask a prosecutor to apply a warrant to a judge on behalf of them. Only prosecutors may renew the detention period for another 10 days after obtaining the approval of a competent judge.

Thus, the period of the confinement of a suspect cannot exceed 30 days in total in the investigation phase (10 days by the police plus 20 days by a prosecutor). Even when the investigation is not completed within that period, the confined suspect should be released unless he is indicted.

Many prosecutors complain that the maximum confinement period is too short to successfully complete the investigation of complex criminal cases and that such restriction often results in insufficient investigation. But, human rights groups are generally in favour of shortening the period for fear of possible human right abuse by investigative agencies' confinement of a person.

An additional problem concerns members of the National Assembly who have been charged with corruption-related criminal offences. They have had improper recourse to their constitutional right of immunity from arrest or confinement, in order to escape from, or obstruct, criminal proceedings initiated against themselves. This practice naturally aroused much criticism from the public. While the Assembly is sitting, they may be arrested only with the consent of the Assembly, but practically it is almost impossible that such consent be given.

3.2. Search and seizure

Evidence and/or things considered to be confiscated may be seized with a warrant which is issued by a competent judge upon the request of a prosecutor. Search warrant issued by a judge is also available when necessary in criminal investigations.

3.3. Access to information on financial transactions

Law enforcement agencies have general power to demand other public or private entities to provide information necessary for criminal investigation under the Criminal Procedure Act. However, the bank secrecy law, titled "the Act on the Real-name Financial Transactions and the Protection of the Secrecy Thereof", strictly prohibits financial institutions from revealing the information about their customers' financial transactions to anybody including law enforcement agencies, unless relevant search and seizure warrants issued by a competent judge are presented. Any person who violates the bank secrecy provisions will be subject to up to 5 years in prison.

The act was the result of the then President Kim Young-sam's political determination in 1993 when he tried to exterminate prevailing "black" transactions conducted under fake or other person's name and at the same time, to make people feel secure about their secrecy on the financial transactions. Under the act, financial transactions conducted in violation of the duty to verify real identities and any person who did not conduct financial transactions in real names are subject to severe criminal and/or monetary sanctions. The act was a big success in that financial transactions had to be conducted in the transactors' real identities, and most non-real name financial accounts were converted into "real name" accounts. Of course, the law strictly requires investigative agencies to obtain "warrants" for their access to any information on financial transactions. Owing to this revolutionary system, Korean prosecutors successfully revealed and prosecuted many high-ranking officials and politicians under charges of corruption-related offences, as shown in the successful prosecution of two former Presidents involved in ugly corrupt scandals. This success shows that the bank secrecy law cannot obstruct successful investigation of corruption, if transparent financial transactions are guaranteed and proper measures for law enforcement are reasonably provided for.

Still, however, law enforcement agencies complain that the requirements for the application of search and seizure warrants for financial information are too strict to conduct efficient investigation on corruption cases, especially in cases where complex money laundering activities are involved. For example, the law strictly prohibits a comprehensive warrant. This means that, if the investigation agencies want to obtain the information on a number of related suspicious bank accounts, they are required to apply for a separate search and seizure warrant for every related bank account. In practice, this rigidity works as a heavy burden and accordingly, might seriously delay the investigation procedure on corruption.

In relation to money laundering, several bills for the enactment of comprehensive anti-money laundering laws are pending at the National Assembly at the moment.

In 2001, there is no comprehensive law which criminalises money laundering in general, no compulsory measures requiring financial institutions to report suspicious transactions, and no central authority specifically responsible for collecting and analysing information on possible illegitimate financial transactions.

3.4. Telecommunication interception

Wiretaps or other interception of electronic communications are available to investigation agencies, when certain statutory conditions are fulfilled and written approval is given by a competent court. The Telecommunications Secrecy Protection Act, which was enacted in 1993 in order to put the interception of electronic communications by law enforcement agencies within the ambit of strict judicial supervision, permits wiretapping, etc. only in relation to the investigation of a certain specified criminal offences ("the predicate offences"), including bribery offences.

The application of the approval for the interception, which is required to specify the method, the purpose, the object, the scope and the intended period of interception, should be made by or through a prosecutor to courts having jurisdiction over the residence place of the parties of the related communication. In light of the global nature of telecommunications, this narrow jurisdictional requirement often hampers investigation agencies' prompt application for the interception approval. Thus, a bill to amend the Act for the purpose of giving flexibility to the jurisdictional requirement is pending at the National Assembly. Originally the amendment bill was intended to strengthen the requirements of telecommunication interception and accordingly, to limit the powers of law enforcement agencies for the purpose of securing the people's freedom of communication. However, the lawmakers, having found that the narrow jurisdictional clause has no reasonable ground, agreed to amend that clause.

3.5. Confiscation and forfeiture

In general, the instrumentality and the product of criminal offences are subject to court confiscation or forfeiture under the Criminal Code. There is no general measure to confiscate or forfeit the "property laundered or transformed" from the product of criminal offences.

According to the Special Act on the Confiscation concerning Specified Public Officials' Offences, however, the "property laundered or transformed" from specified offences committed by public officials including passive bribery offences are subject to confiscation or forfeiture.[2] Under the Act, the burden of proof on the illegality of the concerned property is reversed to the defendant, and any criminal proceeds of specified public officials' offences such as passive bribery, whether it has been transformed or laundered, may be provisionally seized before the confiscation is finalised. The notion of "criminal proceeds from active bribery" is unfamiliar with the current criminal law.

3.6. Protection of witnesses, advantages to those co-operating with the investigation

So far, Korean law does not provide any special or separate measures for the protection of witnesses or whistle-blowers in relation to the investigation or the trial of corruption cases. Thus, investigation agencies are often faced with difficulties in getting assistance from possible witnesses or whistle-blowers.

Law enforcement agencies including prosecutors have no compulsory measures to secure witnesses' appearance or statement at their offices in the investigation stage. Prosecutors have insisted that such measures should be introduced in criminal procedures. The Ministry of Justice is currently reviewing this issue and will soon decide whether to include such measure within the future amendment of the Criminal Procedure Act.

Despite lack of special measures, however, to those persons who have been charged with corruption or other corruption-related criminal offences but assisted the disclosure and prosecution of corruption offences, by utilising traditional means under the current Criminal Procedures Act, several procedural advantages may be granted. In practice, Korean prosecutors frequently use their broad statutory, discretionary power on the prosecution and the custody of the suspect in order to get the assistance from such persons. They may not prosecute the suspect ("suspension of prosecution"), or may put the suspect to a summary trial in which the suspect is released from the custody and a sentence of fine not an imprisonment is sought against the suspect. Or they may prosecute him or her without detaining the person, or may promise to seek lighter punishment in the trial. In criminal trials, Korean prosecutors are entitled to give their opinion on the desirable sentence to be imposed on the accused, and in practice, the court usually pays due regard to

---

[2] The confiscation or forfeiture of "property laundered" is also available in relation to drug trafficking offences in accordance with the Act on the Prevention of Illegal Drug Trafficking, which is Korea's implementing law for the 1988 United Nations Drug Convention.

the prosecutor's opinion. Besides, according to the Criminal Code, a statutory mitigation in sentence should be given to those who have self-surrendered. There is no plea bargain procedure.

3.7. Prohibition of departure (ban on travel overseas)

Since the offenders of white-collar crimes including corruption-related offences frequently try to find shelters in foreign countries, immediate prohibition of the suspect's departure to foreign countries is very useful and important procedural means especially at the early stage of corruption investigations. Practically in Korea, when requested by investigation agencies with documents showing the necessity of departure prohibition, the Immigration Service takes very prompt measures to ban the suspect from leaving the territory of Korea.

3.8. International co-operation

Recently great efforts have been made in order to expand Korea's web of bilateral treaties on mutual legal assistance and extradition. Korea has also participated actively in many multilateral criminal conventions which provide for such international legal co-operation. As of May 2001, Korea has mutual legal assistance treaties with 9 countries and extradition treaties with 14 countries.

The International Mutual Assistance Act and the Extradition Act provide that mutual legal assistance or extradition may be granted to those countries with which Korea has not concluded any bilateral or multilateral legal instruments, under the principle of reciprocity. The responsible body for these matters is the Ministry of Justice. Any prosecutor wishing to make a request for mutual legal assistance or extradition should first make their request to the Ministry of Justice through the Prosecutor General. After the review of the Ministry of Justice, the request is forwarded to a foreign country through the Ministry of Foreign Affairs and Trade.

When investigating and prosecuting corruption cases where the suspect has escaped to a foreign country or where relevant evidence exists outside the territory of Korea, mutual legal assistance and extradition is very important. In practice, however, the strictness in the formalities and the documents required in making requests, together with time-consuming procedures, seems to make investigation agencies hesitant about making use of such formal measures more actively. Thus, Korean investigation agencies have developed close co-operative relationship and shared necessary information with their counterparts in some foreign countries. Though informal, sharing of various information among law enforcement agencies through these channels is very useful and efficient means that atone for the short-comings of the formal mutual legal assistance procedures.

4. Expected reforms

In order to restructure the overall framework for the efficient fight against corruption, several bills have been submitted to the National Assembly of Korea (the major bills are the Anti-Corruption Act, the Act on the Report and the Use of the Information on Certain Financial Transactions and the Act on the Regulation of Criminal Proceeds). The pending reformatory bills are currently under examination and debates by the Members of the Assembly. In relation to the delays in the legislation process, some people and civil groups supporting the reform have strongly expressed their concern that the lawmakers could be unduly influenced by those who do not wish the reform and that any subsequent political compromise might result in distortion of the intended reforms.

The major reforms and improvements expected in terms of criminal procedures are as follows.

4.1. Protection of witnesses

Any person, including public officials, who has provided any useful information, statement or material for the detection of corruption will have a right not to be prejudiced in his/her status or working conditions by the organisation that the he/she belongs to, on the ground that he/she has provided such information, and if prejudiced, that person is entitled to the right to request the Presidential Anti-Corruption Committee to take necessary measures to restore his/her original status or working conditions or to have his/her working place transferred. Such person's identity will be kept secret and he/she may demand appropriate measures of protection to the local police through the Committee. And, a reward may be given if the assistance resulted in the restoration of or increase in public funds.

4.2. Expanded criminalisation of money laundering and confiscation of criminal proceeds

The scope of predicate offences for money laundering will be expanded to include most serious offences including corruption-related offences, and any criminal proceeds directly or indirectly derived from those serious offences will be subject to criminal confiscation or forfeiture. Provisional measures and detailed procedures for mutual legal assistance in relation to the criminal proceeds will also be provided for.

4.3. Centralised monitoring of illegitimate financial transactions

A financial intelligence unit will be established within the Ministry of Finance and Economy for the purpose of efficient monitoring of possible illegitimate financial transactions concerned with criminal activities. Financial institutions will be required to report to this unit any financial transaction which is suspected to be concerned with any criminal proceeds or money laundering activities. And, when the unit deems it necessary, after reviewing the information received, it will forward the information to relevant law enforcement agencies for investigation. When necessary, the unit may exchange relevant information with foreign agencies.

5. Conclusion

Nowadays many governments, especially those in the developing stage, are strongly committed to combating corruption in their societies. For their efforts to be fruitful, however, more positive impetus should be given from the international society as well as on national level. Efficient law enforcement agencies, well equipped with adequate procedural powers and instruments, are an inevitable factor in the success-ful fight against corruption. However, it seems that, so far, international debates on the fight against corruption have not paid much attention to procedural measures for adequate law enforcement and have not sufficiently developed detailed guide-lines in this area. Subsequently, too much discretion in relation to procedural arrangements seems to remain in the hands of local governments. In light of the importance of procedural means for the efficient fight against corruption, it is not desirable for the international society to be relatively silent on the procedural matters. In conferences, declarations and conventions more attention should be paid to procedural aspects and more detailed guidelines should be developed on the powers, instruments and safeguards for adequate law enforcement.

CHAPTER 11

Corruption Cases and Their Consequences for Legislation and Judiciary in Belgium

Benoît Dejemeppe

1. Introduction

To some people, corruption may seem a nine-day wonder. But as the saying goes *nil novi sub sole*, and it suffices to reread the ancient history from Athens to Rome to see the proverb reconfirmed. Even when society has looked at the phenomenon of corruption in a somewhat changed perspective, the harshness of its judgement can be explained by a combination of various elements.

Corruption is not only an ethical question: the development of freedom of trade cannot continue endlessly without business taking a moral dimension. Corruption is also an economic issue. On the one hand, cynically enough, corruption seems a solution for certain market actors who do not hold back from cheating at the competition game, often with disregard for the political game as well. On the other hand, at a time when the economy takes on a global dimension and economic actors engage in fierce competition to dominate the emerging markets, certain well-established practices are unacceptable to companies.

Recent events have aroused almost universal feelings of inequality and injustice, justifying stricter sanctions. Besides, the growing interest in economic circles for corporate governance – the new way of managing a company in the best interest of all actors (shareholders, employees, creditors etc.) – fosters concern about corruption in the private sector as well.

2. Some examples

I shall first cite some examples I have gleaned from experience during recent trials before the Belgian courts.

Cyrille Fijnaut, Leo Huberts (eds.), *Corruption, Integrity and Law Enforcement*, 161-172
©2002 Kluwer Law International, The Hague. Printed in The Netherlands.

In common with most European countries, Belgium has faced corruption and misappropriation of public funds, especially in the context of secret political party funding at a time when law did not yet regulate this matter.

A first case took place in the 1980s: politicians had ordered various studies (relating to the impact of the economic climate on the subsidence level, the image of Belgium in certain parts of the world, etc.) as well as public opinion polls to be carried out by a specialist institute. Most of the work was paid for with public money, and guaranteed little interest or mere "paper work" without any real content. In fact, the opinion poll institute used part of the money to finance political activities, in particular election campaigns.

In the early 1990s, there was a second case involving international procurement contracts for military equipment such as Italian helicopters and French aeronautical equipment. When the contracts were concluded, several million Belgian francs were paid to representatives of political parties by companies that were in some way connected to the contracting parties via Swiss and Luxembourg bank accounts.

The setting of the third case was the Belgian Prime Minister's office. At the end of the 1980s, three of the Prime Minister's assistants set up a plan – without the Prime Minister knowing – to facilitate the introduction of a French specialist gas supply firm in Belgium. For years on end, legal advice was given to this firm and substantial lobbying was done when this firm negotiated for the required urban planning permits from the relevant local authorities to start laying down pipelines. These public officials received a considerable remuneration through tax-haven based offshore companies on Luxembourg bank accounts.

All of these cases resulted in sentences (respectively on 5 April 1996, 23 December 1998 and 7 March 2001) for a series of serious offences, including corruption.

Numerous legal problems arose when these cases were investigated by the judicial system. I shall confine myself to some of them.

First of all, there was a considerable time elapsed between the occurrence of the facts and the sentence: the investigations were indeed time-consuming and cumbersome. Furthermore, the cases were uncovered by coincidence, almost accidentally. In the first case, it was a public settlement of accounts between partners that made the Public Prosecutor sense that something was wrong; in the second case, the facts were uncovered during another investigation relating to the murder of a politician; in the third case, a tax inspector paying a routine visit to a tax payer, came across accounting records showing illegal transactions.

Secondly, the problem with the merits of the cases – a problem that is not typical of Belgium – lies in the field of application of the offence of corruption. At the time, it was necessary to prove that the corrupter and the corrupted person had concluded a deal before the actual accomplishment of (or failure to accomplish) the very act of corruption. Providing such proof was particularly tricky: one can hardly imagine that the partners to a corruption deal draw up a written contract – they generally deny the facts, which is their right. This experience was the starting point for a radical change in anti-corruption legislation.

At this point I would like to highlight two procedural issues.

The first one is typical of the Belgian institutional system, but fits in a European perspective all the same. As I have pointed out, ministers were involved in the first two cases. The Belgian Constitution – drafted in 1831 – allowed an exception in the case of ministers, to the effect that they were to be judged by the Belgian Supreme Court (taking on the role of a Belgian *tribunal correctionnel* deciding on misdemeanours) and the proceedings of such a ministerial trial were set by law. On the other hand, suspects who were not ministers and stood for trial at the same time, were deprived of the possibility of appeal, unlike the ordinary person seeking justice. However – a sign of the times perhaps – no other law was ever adopted, and with reason: no single minister was ever prosecuted throughout the 20th century. So the Belgian Supreme Court set itself the scenario of the trial and chose to act in accordance with the rules of the common criminal proceedings. Besides, Belgium's failure to adopt specific legislation in this field was one reason why Belgium was condemned by the European Court of Human Rights on 22 June 2000 (that was in the first case I have cited, the second is still pending at Strasbourg) – because the accused had been deprived of the right to a fair trial (the trial took place outside a formal legal frame of reference).

The second issue relates to the laboriousness of international co-operation. Proof of payments made abroad could only be provided when investigations were started in countries that have a reputation as bank and tax havens legally protecting the banking secrecy. Moreover, the co-operation with such countries revealed itself to be difficult, because of internal appeals that paralysed the proceedings for years. However, it is remarkable that in one of the above case, Switzerland agreed for the first time – and here we are talking about February 1994 – to disclose the identities of the economic beneficiaries of the bank accounts, which marked a breakthrough in the investigation.

3. Legislative evolution

3.1. The example of corruption in international law

During recent years, both the economic and the judicial worlds have sent out alarm signals that have set a legislative evolution in process. Growing use of international procurement contracts and the need to ensure that these are lawful made it necessary to develop a common definition of corruption, so that the nationality of a public official would no longer determine whether corruption were criminalised. Until then, in the sphere of international business transactions, it was impossible to bring a prosecution for bribing a foreign public official.

Worse, in the name of a certain form of economic realism, offering bribes was long encouraged by the fact that these were given special tax treatment, as is still the case in many countries. As a matter of fact, some countries still allow companies to tax-deduct secret commission fees when considered as a standard practice. This is no longer possible in Belgium when such payments relate to the award or continuance of public procurement contracts or administrative permits (section 7 of the Act of 10 February 1999).

The signing of the Organisation for Economic Co-operation and Development Convention on Combating Bribery of Foreign Public Officials on 17 December 1997 constituted a step forward. Thirty-four states undertook to make it an offence under their national law to bribe any representative of public authority abroad. Bribing an official in a foreign country is therefore treated in the same way as bribery of a national official. However, the convention is limited in scope; it sanctions those paying "commissions" to public officials, but not those accepting, and often even inducing, the payment of such bribes. This convention, drawing on American concepts, undoubtedly reflects a heightened awareness and establishes a new environment, but is still a mere incentive to amend domestic law. It came into force on 15 February 1999, and twenty countries have since brought their legislation into line with their international obligations under the convention.

We must not harbour illusions: a convention is not enough – and is in fact no better than a law – to bring about a fundamental changing in behaviour. Some signatory states are themselves banking and tax havens. What is really needed is action to eradicate these havens, which flourish everywhere, not least in Europe. Above all, steps should be taken to promote international judicial co-operation which is still somewhat in the Middle Ages, the criminals being well and truly of the 21st century. As long as these two issues have not been confronted, conventions of the above kind, signed in the media spotlight, will remain of little use, despite now permitting some form of judicial action.

3.2. Belgian anti-corruption legislation

In line with its international obligations, Belgium promulgated a Parliamentary Act on 10 February 1999, which may be regarded as one of the most advanced in Europe. Its strong points include:

- Corruption constitutes an offence as soon as a benefit is asked for or offered (a bribing deal is therefore no longer a condition for existence of the offence and attempted corruption is treated on the same footing as the act of corruption). The whole range of sanctions has increased in severity and their dissuasive effect has thus been heightened;

- Corrupting foreign public officials has been made punishable in the same way as corrupting Belgian public officials;

- The jurisdiction of the Belgian courts now also includes acts committed outside the Belgian territory relating to any person holding a public function in one of the European Union member states as well as in a non-European Union member state under the requirement of reciprocity. This last hypothesis is not likely to occur often, as the law of the state concerned must make corrupting a public official in Belgium punishable (requirement of reciprocity) on the one hand and, on the other, the authorities of the state concerned must officially notify the Belgian authorities;

- The Belgian courts now also enjoy jurisdiction with regard to any person suspected of corrupting a person holding a public function within the European Union institutions. Thus European public officials are put on a par with Belgian public officials, which is not an insignificant matter as numerous European institutions are based in Belgium;

- The distinction made so far between the concepts of the *public* official and the *private* operator has been done away with. As the media never failed to highlight, it was not forbidden to bribe a journalist, a player or a referee, or the head of the purchasing department of a certain firm to buy a particular product rather than the competing one;

- Logrolling (a three-party operation where the public official who is given a secret commission fee for exerting his real or alleged influence is not the person to be influenced in his decisions or actions) has also been made punishable.

Furthermore, under section 505, subsections 2 to 4, of the Belgian Criminal Code, laundering corruption money is made punishable under Belgian law, in the same way as laundering pecuniary benefits from any offence. Measures have also been taken to prevent the financial system from being used for money-laundering purposes, including the identification of clients and the obligation for banking, financing and stock exchange companies to report any suspicious transaction to an independent administrative body, the Financial Information Processing Office or the *Cellule de traitement des informations financières (CTIF)*.

4. Preventive measures and reforms in view of preventing and combating corruption

4.1. On the national level

4.1.1. Safeguards for the independence of members of the judicial system

Court judges in the European Union member states enjoy independence *statutum personale*. As a general rule, the principle of *trias politica* is a cornerstone of the Belgian Constitution. The guarantees of independence include appointment for life (subject to disciplinary punishment to be imposed by an independent body of the executive branch) pay set by law and a ban on exercising other political or commercial activities. In some states, irremovability is also a legal guarantee.

It is of equal importance that the public prosecutors – being the authorities in charge of supervising the application of criminal law in the name of society and in the general interest – enjoy autonomy to the largest possible extent. The Council of Europe drew general attention to this matter in its Recommendation of 6 October 2000 (2000-19, no. 11):

> "States should take appropriate measures to ensure that public prosecutors are able to perform their professional duties and responsibilities without unjustified interference or unjustified exposure to civil, penal or other liability. However, the public prosecution should account periodically and publicly for its activities as a whole and, in particular, the way in which its priorities were carried out."

When the public prosecution is subordinate to the government, the nature and the scope of its powers must be established in the Constitution or in an Act of Parliament. In particular, measures should be taken to guarantee that the government cannot interfere by giving negative injunctions or meddling in the way specific cases are dealt with (in Belgium, this guarantee is enshrined in section 151 of the Constitution).

The recruitment, the promotion and the transfer of court judges and public prosecutors must meet objective criteria and be carried out according to impartial proceedings, excluding the influence of any biased or corporatist element. Likewise, disciplinary proceedings should be governed by objective guarantees.

In numerous legislations, the appointment of a court judge or public prosecutor is subject to the threefold condition of a specific training, professional experience and a successful examination in professional proficiency before an independent jury.

Apart from these general considerations, it is also important to develop certain specialities within the criminal justice system by entrusting certain court judges and public prosecutors with specific powers in the fight against corruption.

4.1.2. Establishment of a special police bureau

Given the thousands of criminal rules that exist in every country, it is foolish to pretend every offence against any of these rules is sanctioned, and that action is taken on all fronts, although the complex nature of some cases justifies improvisation so that inefficacy is avoided. In this respect, forming specialist police forces creates considerable added value.

In Belgium, there is a special police force called the Central Anti-Corruption Police Bureau or the *Office central pour la répression de la corruption*. This unit is in charge of investigating serious crimes involving public office (including corruption in the private sector). Not only is the *Office central pour la répression de la corruption* engaged in tracing criminals; it also provides support to other police forces and manages a specialist information network.

4.1.3. Anti-corruption policy

Although the fight against corruption has induced some European countries to amend their legislation, it is still an established fact that the criminal justice system is traditionally targeted at prosecuting and sanctioning individual offences. Nowadays, it is not uncommon for those individual offences to fit within the larger framework of organised crime. In that case, priority should be given to dismantling the organisation the individual criminal belongs to, and to controlling the proceeds from such crimes.

In this context, an anti-corruption policy justifies a form of planning where the various specialist actors (of the administrative, police and justice system) join forces to outline a proactive approach in combination with repressive prosecution. As a matter of fact, charges are rare in this field.

4.1.4. Preventive administrative measures

One of the top priorities should consist in making the general public aware of the phenomenon of corruption, including administrative corruption. It would be useful to draw up a Code of Conduct for public officials, incorporating rules aiming at preventing corruption.

Moreover, members of Parliament and the government should be under the legal obligation to file a list of their offices and functions and to make a declaration of property both when taking up and when leaving office. These operations should be under a form of legal supervision.

4.1.5. Human and material resources

The fight against corruption is not only a question of legal instruments, it also poses the problem of having adequate resources available. And here court judges, public prosecutors and the police force often find themselves in an uncomfortable situation.

Along with a shortage of human and material resources, judges and public prosecutors have to contend with the dissatisfaction of parties to proceedings, of suspects, who often perceive judicial measures as unjust, and of victims, who criticise the judicial professions for their slowness, if not their failure or ineffectiveness.

It is essential to adequately gear the resources to the objectives that have been set.

4.2. On the international level

Legislative harmonisation is an indispensable tool for making headway on the international level, even if the road ahead may be long and the target slow to reach, given the traditions of the states.

In this context, the European Union has adopted a forward-looking approach by initiating a project known as the *Corpus Juris*, a set of rules defining offences against the European Union's financial interests, including corruption. It also recommends the creation of the office of European Public Prosecutor, with responsibility for directing both investigations and the prosecution of relevant cases in the national courts. The procedure adopted would ensure that a balance was struck between the effectiveness of prosecutions and strict respect for individual rights. The *Corpus Juris* is now part of the reforms to the Amsterdam Treaty proposed by the European Commission (Delmas-Marty & Vervaele, 2000).

Such proposals deserve careful consideration by the member states, because far from being Utopian, they outline a justice system that moves with the times (Van Gerven, 2000, pp. 296-318).

Although international co-operation has recently increased substantially, criminal proceedings remain embedded in a national concept, as each nation is inclined to consider its system to be the very best. Chauvinism is not the sole prerogative of the world of sports.

The conventions are too numerous and too complex (with their preambles, final clauses and reservations, not to mention their additional protocols), whereas the number of ratifications remains on the whole limited. Why continue on a diplomatic course which has not succeeded in providing the judiciary with effective tools? Is the time not ripe for a complete review of the judicial arrangements applicable, so as to propose a simple mechanism for obtaining evidence from abroad? (Vervaele & Klip (eds.), 2001, pp. 297-307; Flore, 1996, p. 379)

I might conclude with a few recommendations, based on the principles which should govern this field, so as to strike a balance between the right to a fair trial and the effectiveness of judicial action on experience alone:

- Execution of a request for assistance should no longer be subject to the dual criminal liability requirement (that the offence qualifies as such in both countries), where that rule still applies;

- Judicial authorities should communicate directly – in a language accepted by the requesting state – with the foreign judicial authority competent for executing a request, which should, in turn, directly transmit any evidence obtained, without the executive branch being involved in any way;

- Use of e-mail should become widespread;

- Compliance with requests for mutual assistance should be expedited, and, wherever possible, any deadline set in the request should be met, failing which explanations for the delay should be given;

- No appeal should be possible in the executing (requested) state, as this often constitutes a weak link in the chain, hampering the effectiveness of a request for assistance;

- With the foreign judicial authority's approval, a judge and/or members of his or her team should be able to participate in activities undertaken abroad in order to execute a request. Although a passive presence is commonly accepted, no rule currently guarantees the right to active participation, which can nonetheless be seen to be justified in practice;

- States should be willing to extradite their nationals, subject to the condition that it should be possible for a convicted person to serve any prison sentence imposed in his or her country of origin or of permanent residence. It is an anachronism that criminals should ordinarily enjoy freedom of movement, but once they are caught it is the principle of nationality which prevails, with the result that a French national arrested in Paris for a crime committed in Berlin cannot be sent back there for trial. A few countries, including the United Kingdom, constitute exceptions. Any national of a member state should be regarded as an European Union citizen, without being able to rely on his or her nationality to avoid being prosecuted. In this connection, disputes in matters of extradition and execution of foreign judgements should be a matter for the judicial authorities, without any interference by the executive;

- The secrecy which banks and other financial intermediaries owe their customers should not be used as an argument to counter a judicial investigation;

- It should be possible to use information and evidence collected abroad or received from a foreign country in all criminal proceedings. There should be an end to the speciality rule, whereby some countries even go so far as to require a written undertaking that information provided will not be used in other proceedings, for instance in respect of tax offences;

- The requested state should not be able to refuse assistance on the grounds that the charges are of a fiscal nature;

- Supervision should be exercised by the courts of the requesting country, which should ensure that the principles of a fair trial, in particular as regards the defendant's rights, are respected;

- Each country should designate members of the judiciary to fulfil the specific role of assisting foreign colleagues and ensuring the proper execution of letters rogatory;

- A documentation centre should be set up, so as to facilitate access to documents concerning the relevant national, cross-border and international rules for all states having signed the criminal law conventions;

- Work should begin on a general convention on mutual assistance in criminal matters, incorporating and reorganising the body of law contained in the existing instruments.

5. Conclusion

The idea of Europe had its origin in a dream – that of bringing down frontiers which had too long served as a pretext for violence and destruction. However, the more united Europe becomes, the greater and more impervious are the barriers posed by these frontiers in the light of the requirements of an extended form of judicial co-operation. I nonetheless share the hope that the desire to endow the judiciary with the capacities it needs will bear fruit, failing which we will find ourselves confronted with a real miscarriage of justice in the very near future.

Seeking to build a world of law and justice is not a moral cause; it is a matter of asserting a need of vital importance to the economy, to a balanced society and to the preservation of democracy. It is not possible to establish a single economic, monetary, financial and political area without giving it a legal and judicial system worthy of the name. For that reason, the representatives of civil society and political leaders must now make their voices heard, alongside those of members of the judiciary, the bar and other legal professions, to ask that the work done by the Council of Europe (initially through the conventions on extradition and judicial co-operation) be stepped up and conducted in closer co-operation with the European Union, which more recently began to concern itself with what is customarily designated the "third pillar". Care must be taken to avoid making progress solely within the narrow confines of the European Union, thus creating a two-speed Europe in terms of human rights and justice, which would run counter to the acknowledged universality of these two concepts, to which all nations aspire.

The rules governing judicial organisation, and in particular co-operation between public prosecutors, must be adapted if we do not wish the Europe of tomorrow – which is being built today – become a Europe of crime, a paradise for fraudsters. Europe will be what we make of it, and closing our eyes to the future will not make the impending dangers disappear.

References

Delmas-Marty, M. & J. Vervaele, *The Implementation of the* Corpus Juris *in the Member States*, Intersentia, Antwerp, 2000.

Flore, D., "Vers une justice pénale européenne; l'apport de l'Union Européenne", in *La justice pénale et l'Europe*, Bruylant, Brussels, 1996.

Van Gerven, W.,"Constitutional Conditions for a Public Prosecutor's Office at the European Level", *European Journal of Crime, Criminal Law and Criminal Justice*, 3, 2000, pp. 296-318.

Vervaele, J. & A. Klip (eds.), *Administratieve en strafrechtelijke samenwerking inzake fraudebestrijding tussen justitiële en bestuurlijke instanties van de EU-landen*, Wetenschappelijk Onderzoek- en Documentatiecentrum, The Hague, 2001.

CHAPTER 12

The Sentencing of Corruption

Peter Alldridge

1. Introduction

This chapter will address two major factors in the sentencing of corruption. The determination of the extent of punishment is crucial to the location of the response to corruption within a rational sentencing framework, and attention will first be given to some of the possible variables which should inform the punitive part of the post-conviction disposition. In recent years, part of the process of determining sentence has increasingly included the additional role of determining the extent of the liability of the criminal to disgorge the proceeds of crime. So this chapter will also consider the relationship between convictions for corruption and the seizure of the proceeds of crime. The system upon which I shall draw for concrete examples is that of the United Kingdom. However, the issues are, I hope, of far wider application forming the cutting edge of the increasingly internationalised criminal law (Kim & Kim, 1997). So far as concerns the punitive element of sentence, I shall write within a broadly retributive framework.

Some of the variables involved in sentencing will be the same as those involved in the definition of offences. Some jurisdictions have few, widely defined offences each with a wide sentencing discretion; others have more, and more narrowly defined (and, perhaps, banded) offences. Clearly the more factors which go to grading of offences, the fewer need to be considered in respect of sentencing (and *vice versa*).

2. Assessing sentence: some possible variables

On a guilty verdict, there will typically be a range of available sentences. In determining whereabouts an individual falls on the continuum, the sentencer will have regard to a range of considerations. The tightness of the controls on the discretion

Cyrille Fijnaut, Leo Huberts (eds.), *Corruption, Integrity and Law Enforcement*, 173-190
©2002 Kluwer Law International, The Hague. Printed in The Netherlands.

of the sentencer will vary from system to system. There is a set of issues dealing with sentence which are more or less equally applicable to all crimes – the differentials between first-time and repeat offenders, the especial significance of prison in sentencing white collar offenders, the relevance of remorse and so on. I will not deal with these aspects.

3. Corruption of government and of markets

The major claim I want to make is that there are two distinct, major wrongs against which the offences of bribery and corruption stand, and that no linear comparison may be made between those cases falling within the one category and those falling within the other. The first type of offence is to do with buying and selling goods which should not be bought or sold. Offences of corruption, by engaging in a market in an area in which this is an inappropriate distributive mechanism, were the first types of corruption with which legal systems concerned themselves: these were the offences of bribery of judges, sales of public offices,[1] the common law offence of extortion *virtute officii*, bribery of jurors or voters, and so on. These sorts of offence are, and should be, always serious. By creating black markets in important governmental functions they have the potential to undermine the legitimacy of government itself. A "normal case" of perverting the course of justice by a police officer taking a bribe will command in England and Wales a prison sentence of around ten years.[2]

---

[1] First criminalised in 8 R II c.3 (1383) and Sale of Offices Act 1551 (5 & 6 Edw VI c.16) respectively.

[2] *R. v. Donald (John Andrew)* [1997] 2 Cr App R (S.) 272 – D was a detective constable serving in a Regional Crime Squad. He accepted various sums from a man who was the subject of criminal proceedings to disclose confidential information about the inquiry and to destroy surveillance logs. D had agreed to accept about £ 50,000 and had actually received about £18,500. He was sentenced to of a total of 11 years' imprisonment. It was held that the sentence was severe but not manifestly excessive. See also *Attorney General's Reference (no. 70 of 1998)*, (perverting public justice; police officers; corruption; five year sentence of imprisonment lenient); *R. v. Brown (Raymond John)* [1999] 2 Cr App R (S.) 284 (nine years rather than 13 was the appropriate starting point when sentencing an ex-policeman for conspiracy to pervert the course of justice and conspiracy to corrupt a police officer. Compare *R. v. Patel (Mohammed Iqbal)* (1992) 13 Cr App R (S.) 550 – D accepted a payment of £ 500 to stamp a passport with leave to remain in the country. He was sentenced to two years' imprisonment.

The second type of corruption has to do, not so much with the violation of an existing legal duty under, for example, a contract between employer and employee, but on the effect which the behaviour of the agents have upon the operation of a market (Alldridge, 2001a). So if a company (or a government) puts out a contract to tender or engages in some other behaviour that implicitly promises that it will award benefits according to the outcome of competition on a "level playing field", and then awards those benefits to a party which provides a bribe, then the competitors have been deceived into expending resources in preparation of a bid, expecting normal competition would govern the allocation of the contract, and the consumer population has been deprived of the benefit of competition. In the allocation of employment, nepotism or other forms of jobbery takes away from others the possibility of being able to compete properly, and takes away from consumers the chance of securing the best possible people in the jobs in question.

In these corruption offences ("corruption of markets" as opposed to "corruption of government") the gravamen of the offence is that the defendant is denied the proper operation of competition, which, where it operates, is regarded as an instrumental good. The fact that sentences for the corruption of government offences must remain high does not mean that any other form of corruption need be punished in any particular way. Subject to the exigencies of international accords, therefore, the sentences for corruption of markets (where it is illegal) is a question within the sphere of national sovereignty. In fact, in England and Wales, the corruption of legitimate markets by bribes is not regarded by sentencers as having anything like the gravity of the creation or operation of illegitimate markets. In a "normal" case a defendant received commission amounting to £32,000 in respect of the renewal of contracts with another company by the company for whom he worked. The court held that "the coherence and propriety of the country's commercial life would be significantly destroyed if a prison sentence were not passed in cases of this kind", but then only passed a six-month sentence.[3]

Conceptually, the distinction between the two sets of cases is clear, but has proved sufficiently difficult to sustain in individual instances that the Law Commission for England and Wales has recognised its abolition and the instantiation of a single wide offence, covering both the public and private sector.[4] I have argued that the Law Commission could have made this distinction part of the proposed

---

[3]   *R. v. Wilcox (Robert Albert)* (1995) 16 Cr App R (S.) 197.

[4]   In Law Commission, Consultation Paper No 145, *Legislating the Criminal Code: Corruption* (1997) and Law Commission Report No 248, *Legislating the Criminal Code: Corruption* (1998).

legislative framework for corruption in England and Wales, and that it is better not left to the sentencing stage (Alldridge, 2001a). It is probably a mistake to have one offence on the statute book with more than one underlying rationale, because the task of sentencers in making comparisons is made commensurately more difficult.

Into which category will the case of the bribery of foreign officials to secure contracts – a case at which the Paris Convention of the Organisation for Economic Co-operation and Development is directed – fall?[5] This will depend upon the job of the official in question. Where the official is involved in a legitimate market (for example, the official is a buyer involved in government procurement), it may be argued, on the one hand, that the official just "happens" to be the holder of a public office, but is not really in a different position from a buyer for a private concern.[6] The contrary argument is that it is the fact of holding public office, disbursing public funds that makes the offence of abuse of public office which is necessarily of a different category from the same kind of behaviour as a part of a private concern. The cases at which the Paris Convention is directed appear to be those where the overseas official is involved in procurement or the granting of licences.[7] This raises the obvious question as to why there should be any limitation to the case where the overseas official is a public official, rather than any other individual charged with the award of these benefits.

4. Single transaction or continuing relationship corruption?

To someone trying to eradicate corruption, corruption of single transactions is far less of a problem than corruption within existing relationships – people doing each

---

[5] Convention on Combating Bribery of Foreign Public Officials in International Business Transactions, Paris, 17 December 1997 (Cm. 3994). The United Kingdom has now enacted legislation which, when brought into force, will make it compliant to the convention: Anti-Terrorism, Crime and Security Act 2001, ss. 108-110.

[6] And see *R v. Foxley* [1995] 2 Cr App Rep 523, 16 Cr App R (S) 879 – a Ministry of Defence procurement officer took large bribes received a penalty of four years' imprisonment and a confiscation order for £1.5m. See also *Ministry of Defence v. Foxley and Others,* Court of Appeal (Civil Division) 10 March 1995.

[7] Following complaints that the United States Foreign Corrupt Practises Act places United States businesses at a competitive disadvantage relative to businesses from countries which did not prohibit bribery of overseas officials.

other favours in the knowledge that sometime in the future there will be reciprocation. Should it make a difference to the sentence that the bribe changes hands as one transaction or as a series of payments. And if it does, which is worse? This is a matter that is generally able to be dealt with according to the rules of the jurisdiction in question as to the individualisation of criminal charges on indictments. It is possible to express the rules of criminal procedure so as to dictate particular answers to these questions, but beyond that it does not seem to me to matter whether the bribe is one transaction or part of a sequence.

5. The success of the corruption

There has been significant debate in other areas of criminal law as to whether the sentence for attempted offences should differ from those which are imposed for consummated offences.[8] Failure to complete the offence does not lessen the *culpability* of the defendant. In other areas of English sentencing law there is a convention that the failure of an attempt will generate a discount on the expected sentence of about one third. Whatever the merits of the discount elsewhere, the only sensible way to proceed in the case of offences of bribery and corruption is that it the "standard" sentence should be developed on the basis that the offence was an unsuccessful attempt. Offences involving attempted bribery are frequently not completed because the victim reports the offence to authorities or is acting in an undercover capacity.

There is a further consideration than simply the law of attempted crime. Is it a legitimate consideration in sentencing to take into account whether or not the profits of the crime were recovered? Is the fact that the criminal "got away with it", in the sense of not having to repay a profit which was made, something which should impact upon sentence. The position of this paper is that proceedings for the seizure of profits ought to be regarded as separate from proceedings for the predicate offence. A penalty to cover the non-payment of a confiscation order is legitimate, but increasing the penalty for the predicate offence is not.

---

[8] P. Glazebrook (1969) is one of many works which make the point that to make a significant distinction in sentencing between attempting and achieving "allow[s] chance to play an unnecessarily large part".

6. Are the victims identifiable?

The rise of the victims' rights movement has led to increased interest in the relationship between victim and sentence. The joinder of victims as civil parties is a time-honoured device in continental Europe, and attention there has been focused on the proposed victim's rights amendment and the specific question of victim impact statements. Now, whilst offences of bribery and corruption are sometimes presented (by their apologists) as "victimless" offences, in the category of corruption of legitimate markets the issue is really whether or not the loser is identifiable, and whether, if the victim is not identifiable, that should affect sentence. I suggest that where the harm involved in corruption is to the proper operation of a market, then it should not make any difference to sentence whether the victims can be identified or not. Wherever the victim is identifiable and a confiscation order could be made, a compensation order may be made in respect of the victim's loss, but the victim will probably receive more damages through bringing a civil action.

7. The amounts involved – lots, little or nothing

On the one hand, size is important. There is a principle in the sentencing of theft that, *ceteris paribus*, the greater the amount stolen the higher the sentence. So far as the cases of the corruption of legitimate markets are concerned, the same principle seems to apply to bribery. The larger the bribe or the larger the sums at stake, the heavier the sentence. The justification in both these cases tend to be standard (general) deterrent arguments. In neither the theft nor the corruption case, however, is the amount involved one of the principal determinants of the sentence. In the case of corruption by the creation or operation of illegitimate markets, the sums involved are much less significant. My moral intuition is that it does not make very much difference whether a judge, police officer juror or immigration officer takes a bribe of £1 or £1 million.

This raises a question which may be to do with the definition of the offence and may be to do with sentence – that is, does it actually matter whether there is a bribe or not?[9] Under existing and proposed English legislation, a bribe is necessary, but it is to be defined sufficiently widely (by including the mere conferment of

---

[9] At the moment, in England and Wales, it is a matter which goes to liability. On this see P. Alldridge (2001a).

gratification) as for the requirement of a bribe to have very little impact in excluding behaviour from the definition of bribery offences (Alldridge, 2001a). In particular, under the Law Commission proposals, conferring "gratification" might amount to a bribe.[10] If mere gratification is accepted as fulfilling the "consideration" part of the law of bribery, then there will never be any bribery charge that fails for lack of a bribe. Since it will not exclude any kind of favour from being a bribe there is no point in having it as an element of the offence, and the proscribed mental states (at the moment, in English law "corruptly", but invariably some descriptor of improper motive) should alone bear the entire weight of differentiating bribes from lawful favours. In the law of corruption the presence or absence of a bribe seems to determine whether or not there is to be a serious criminal offence. If the crime is to be defined on the basis of its intrinsic moral quality, then the presence or absence of an identifiable bribe can only be crucial to liability or to sentence if there is a morally defensible distinction between where there is and where there is not a bribe.

Should an offence be committed in cases where the behaviour is corrupt (in the sense of operating a market where there ought not to be one, or of denying the right to compete where it ought to exist) but where there is no identifiable bribe? In many cases there will be no identifiable "consideration" concomitant with a specific act of, for example, improper conduct in the allocation of jobs or contracts. There are three types of practice which are generally regarded as corrupt but would fall outside any definition bribery which restricted "bribe" to having economic value. First, if a powerful person "owns" the person charged with a decision, in the sense that, for whatever reason, they are able to require obedience, then they will not need to pay again. Nonetheless, their behaviour in requiring behaviour from that person can be called corrupt. Secondly, where there is a culture operating so that members of a particular group do each other favours, by, for example, exercising their discretion in favour of the other members of that group. It may very well be, for example, that the kind of corruption which is most dangerous is that where nothing is said and nothing need be said – where "old boys" look after one another and know that favours can be called in, implicitly or explicitly, later. Systems for the allocation of jobs or things that give access to income, like taxi permits, are at the centre of this problem. Thirdly, nepotism – preference for relatives and friends in the allocation of jobs and resources – is frequently not requested or engaged in for contemporaneous reward. In terms of its effect upon competition for jobs, and

---

[10] Law Commission 248, *Legislating the Criminal Code: Corruption* (1998) para 5.41.

upon the lives of people who are not properly considered for the jobs, the effects are equally serious whether or not money actually changes hands, or where there is no synchronicity of action and reward. A definition, or a set of sentencing criteria, for the crime of corruption that excludes these three cases is defective.[11]

At a more theoretical level, the relationship between gift and market is placed in question. Bordieu characterises indebtedness as arising from having received a gift as form of symbolic capital that can be converted into economic capital (Terdiman, 1987). Offer argues that the "great transformation" in economic history from customary exchange to impersonal markets is incomplete (Offer, 1997). Reciprocal exchange pervades modern societies. It takes the form of "gifts", reciprocated without certainty. Reciprocity is driven by the pursuit of "regard". Money is (generally) avoided in exchanges of regard, because it is impersonal. Instead, regard signals are embodied in goods, in services, or in time (attention). The personalisation of gifts authenticates the signal. Reciprocal exchange persists in family formation, in intergenerational transfers, in labour markets, in agriculture, the professions, in marketing, entrepreneurship, and also in corruption and crime. Exchanges of regard and a "favour economy" are not susceptible to governance by the clumsy distinction between gift and market. They operate in between. Whether or not a particular transaction is a gift or an "arms length" market transaction is something that will be culturally determined. The boundaries of the tolerable and the incidence of the prohibited also turns on the local culture (Pujas & Rhodes, 1999; Treisman, 2000).

There is a large realm of our dealings one with another which cannot best be typified in terms either (on the one hand) of a market or (on the other) of individual acts of kindness and of supererogation. Of course, the absence of a payment does not mean the absence of strings. Favours usually (or frequently) involve some sort of set of expectations – even if it is just the expectation that when this whole thing is over one of the participants will go away. What about when two people are in a continuing relationship in which, from time to time, they give and receive favours? On any given instance there will be no identifiable bribe, but the effects are just as

---

[11] The other argument for insisting that something in the nature of "consideration" be in contemplation for an offence of corruption is that it provides a valuable limitation upon the numbers of cases of alleged corruption that will come before the courts. We should beware of these sorts of "floodgate" arguments, however, particular in a system where the consent of a Law Officer has and will be required for prosecution. Home Office, *Raising Standards and Upholding Integrity The Prevention of Corruption*, Stationery Office, London, 2000, para 5.2-5.3.

much – in most cases more of the kind of social effect which the law is seeking to prevent. There will be many cases where the "one-off" bribe is significant (and they may frequently be in the overseas contracts cases), but there are also many where it is not.

8. Does it matter whether or not there is further illegality?

Under the United States' Federal Sentencing Guidelines, if a bribe is given to a law enforcement officer to allow the smuggling of a quantity of cocaine, the guideline for conspiracy to import cocaine would be applied if it resulted in a greater level of offence than for the corruption itself. This is really a question as to the way in which the legal system in question deals with a course of conduct which can either be characterised as one or several offences.

9. Does it matter whether the corruption is national or international in nature?

Before the advent of the movement for the internationalisation of the criminal law, the corruption of foreign markets was not regarded seriously at all. Not only was corruption not classified as a crime, but deductions could be made from taxable income in respect of bribes.[12] Monopoly power to deal with these matters was one of the clearest *indicia* of national sovereignty. Territorial prosecutions were thought preferable because crimes are best investigated and prosecuted in the country where they are committed, since that is where the evidence and witnesses are most readily accessible.[13] The countervailing force in recent years has been the assertion of a power, not so much in other individual countries, but in the "international community", to take an interest in matters which previously had been regarded as matters of internal sovereign governance. The explicit grounds in the case of

---

[12] Only recently have such payments ceased to be deductible. Income and Corporation Taxes Act 1988 s. 577A, inserted by Finance Act 1993 s.123, Finance Act 1994 s.141, implementing Organisation for Economic Co-operation and Development policy.

[13] Home Office, *Raising Standards and Upholding Integrity The Prevention of Corruption*, Stationery Office, London, 2000, para 2.17.

corruption are that they affect the "global economy" (Salbu, 1999).[14]

The burden of the change in thinking, underpinning the developments of which the Paris Convention was the most noteworthy, is that it those times are gone and that it does not matter what one country's nationals do when abroad, particularly if their behaviour abroad has economic benefits for that jurisdiction. In those jurisdictions in which the convention is in force, it should not make any difference whether the ultimate victims are, if identifiable, in the same country as the court or not. Suppose Company A in country X and Company B in country Y both tender for a job in country Z, but because of bribery Company A gets the contract. Company A and/or its directors or employees should be punished as if the job or the company deprived of the work by corruption had also been in country X.

10. Aggravation?

Under the United States Federal Sentencing Guidelines, where the court finds that the defendant's conduct was part of a systematic or pervasive corruption of a governmental function, process, or office that may cause loss of public confidence in government, an upward departure may be warranted. This kind of provision is difficult to justify: the reason the corruption of government commands such high sentences in the first place is because of the risk of corruption of that government function or loss of public confidence. To use these considerations as an aggravating factor is to risk punishing twice.

11. Confiscation and compensation orders

The other major element of the post-conviction disposition is the order for the confiscation of the assets of the criminal as constituting the proceeds of crime.[15]

---

[14] S. Salbu (1999) argues at 252 that "whatever mechanisms one state may put into its laws to avoid inflicting its values on other states, moral imperialism is an ineluctable reality whenever one sovereign entity seeks to alter or control behaviour inside the borders of another."

[15] This essay will not deal with the issue of *forfeiture* of the imedimenta of crime (under the provisions now to be found in the Powers of Criminal Courts (Sentencing) Act 2000 s.143). Although an argument may be made that the bribe itself is the means by which the crime is committed (and consequently liable to forfeiture under the provision) in the

One of the most significant developments in the legislative framework of the post-1985 world is the confiscation order and the giving of attention to the financial aspects of crime. Whilst confiscation orders have yet to be deployed substantially in the area of corruption, there is clear potential for them to have a very significant impact. It is in the area of the seizure of the proceeds of crime that the combination of recent developments in other areas of criminal law with the amplified interest currently given to corruption has great potential to radically alter the operation of the criminal justice system.

12. Reparation or punishment?

There may be two underlying rationales upon which the confiscation order is made: the objective of the order may be simply to deprive the offender of the *profits* of the crime(s) under consideration; or, the order might go wider and confiscate *proceeds*, including any sums the defendant acquired from the crime even though they did not constitute a profit. In the context of the seizure of the proceeds of drug sales, the issue comes down to the simple question whether or not the offender is entitled to deduct from the proceeds of sale of drugs the expenses involved in their procurement and sale. It has been held repeatedly that the power to make confiscation orders in England and Wales extends beyond the net profit that the defendant made.[16] The underlying aim is clearly one that rejects the "reparative" philosophy of Hodgson Report and shows an unequivocal commitment to the use of confiscation as a punitive device going far beyond the restoration of the *status quo ante* (Hodgson, 1984).[17] The supposed justification is that it is inappropriate to allow a deduction for expenditure on activity which is, *ex hypothesi*, illegal (Stessens, 2000, p. 53).

(heretical) opinion of the author, provisions permitting the forfeiture of property for no other reason than that it was used in the commission of crime ought not to survive challenge under first Protocol to the European Convention on Human Rights. The other major question as to liability and sentence which I shall leave over is that of the liability and sentencing of "legal persons" – bodies corporate – for these offences. The burden of the new internationalised crimnal law seems to be that there should be liability upon corporations in respect of these offences.

[16] *R v. Smith (Ian)* [1989] 1 WLR 765, [1989] 2 All ER 765; *R v. Banks* [1997] 2 Cr App R(S) 110 and cases there cited.

[17] The report by Hodgson (1984) formed the basis for the Drug Trafficking Offences Act 1986, the first United Kingdom confiscation statute.

Again, under the Criminal Justice Act 1988 (which deals with the confiscation of non-drug, non-terrorist money) predicate offences are "criminal conduct" which are offences listed in Schedule 4 of the Act[18] or indictable offences.[19] The significant part of the definition is that which extends to include all indictable offences (which is sufficient to include the miscellany of offences concerned with corruption).[20] Then, as to the *extent* of the confiscation order, the Act states:

71. (4) For the purposes of this Part of this Act a person benefits from an offence if he obtains property as a result of or in connection with its commission and his benefit is the value of the property so obtained.

(5) Where a person derives a pecuniary advantage as a result of or in connection with the commission of an offence, he is to be treated for the purposes of this Part of this Act as if he had obtained as a result of or in connection with the commission of the offence a sum of money equal to the value of the pecuniary advantage.

The benefit may be direct or indirect. "Proceeds of criminal conduct", in relation to any person who has benefited from criminal conduct, means that benefit.[21]

How does this apply to the proceeds of corruption? As an example, take the case where A obtains a job corruptly.[22] Upon his or her conviction for an offence of corruption, are his or her salary payments liable to confiscation, and if they are, should there be a deduction from the eventual confiscation order for: (i) the value of the work done; or (ii) tax paid on the salary? In English Law, where somebody obtains a job by deception he or she does not obtain salary payments by deception.[23] The theory is that actually doing the work is what triggers the payments, and that the payments are too remote from the original deception. It does not follow from this, however, that the salary payments are not recoverable as the proceeds of crime

---

[18] Which enumerates a series of offences dealing with specific ways of making money.

[19] Criminal Justice Act 1988 s.71(9)(c). Terrorist monies are subject to a different regime.

[20] As to which, see Law Commission, footnote 4 *supra*.

[21] Criminal Justice Act 1988 s.102(1), definition added by the Criminal Justice Act 1993, s 29(2).

[22] The argument identical for any other contract. I chose this example for its simplicity.

[23] This is the assumption of Theft Act 1968 s.16 (creating a specific offence).

under the confiscation legislation. It seems that the salary payments could be subject to a confiscation order.

Offences of corruption are now covered as predicate offences for the purposes of the confiscation legislation, and, on the face of things, there does not appear to be any case for a deduction for the market value of the work done. The statute states "a person benefits from an offence if he obtains property as a result of or in connection with its commission and his benefit is the value of the property so obtained".[24] There is no provision for deductions.

The answer to the question whether or not tax paid on the salary may be deducted may actually turn upon so trivial a matter as whether the tax was deducted at source (typical of an employment relationship) or not (as in the case of independent contractors) (Alldridge, 2001). The general approach appears very harsh indeed.[25]

As with something as small as a job, so too with the largest international contract. We must ask whether, in the event of a conviction, all payments under a contract entered into corruptly may be the subject of a confiscation order.[26] The answer appears to be in the affirmative.

13. *Ne bis in idem*

One of the reasons sometimes given for the denial of deductions for expenses, work done and tax when making confiscation orders, is that it is to put in place a further speculative enquiry (Stessens, 2000, p. 53). However, this enquiry is one which the court is obliged to undertake, because, so far as the confiscation goes beyond the profits of crime, it is part of the *punishment* for the crime charged, (in effect, it is a fine) and the *quantum* of that punitive element should be taken into account in the assessment of the overall punishment.[27] Failure to consider this is to

---

[24] The wording is, to all intents and purposes, identical for the purposes of the statute which is proposed as laying down the revised scheme: *Proceeds of Crime Bill Publication of Draft Clauses*, March 2001 (Cm 5066).

[25] *R v. Smith (David Cadman)* [2001] UKHL 68.

[26] As earlier, I leave aside the issue of the possibility of confiscation without conviction, which is the proposal under the Proceeds of Crime Bill.

[27] I leave aside here confiscation orders dealing with offences other than those alleged, under legislation which, when specified criteria are satisfied, allows all property acquired by the defendant during the six years prior to the conviction, the conceptual basis of which is – to the writer at least – wholly unclear.

punish twice, which is offensive to the principle of double jeopardy.[28]

Bribes are, in any jurisdiction which taxes unlawfully acquired income, taxable as income. A person who accepts a bribe and then fails to declare it for the purposes of taxation commits an offence of tax evasion. In the past it has not been the practice of the prosecuting or tax authorities in England and Wales to bring joined or discrete prosecutions on these questions. The amplified response to the perceived problem of the proceeds of crime is to include far greater co-ordination of the activities of tax and prosecution authorities.[29]

In the case where tax is paid and then the gross value of the property is confiscated as well there is clearly an issue of multiple punishment. The formal answer which English law gives is that if the confiscation provisions *are* taken to be punitive as well as reparatory,[30] the confiscation order is of the nature of a fine, and that the liability to tax arises independently of the criminality. In a jurisdiction where the professed aim of the confiscation proceedings is restricted to reparation (i.e. removal of the profit, with no punitive element) then there should be a set-off in respect both of work done (or other detriments occurred) and tax paid under a contract obtained corruptly.

14. Consequences

Once the notion of the profits or proceeds of crime for the purposes of the money laundering regime extends beyond the limited sphere of drug-related crime (and that has been the position in the United Kingdom since 1988[31]) there is no logical reason why the profits or proceeds of corruption should not be regarded as proceeds of crime for the purposes of either the existing or the proposed rules relating to the confiscation of assets, the reporting of suspicious transactions and the criminalisation

---

[28] The United Kingdom has not yet signed the eighth protocol to the European Convention on Human Rights, but has various common law principles outlawing double jeopardy.

[29] Cabinet Office Performance and Innovation Unit, *Recovering the Proceeds of Crime*, London, 2000; *Proceeds of Crime Bill Publication of Draft Clauses*, March 2001 (Cm 5066).

[30] This is the assumption of English law. The earlier arguments to the contrary folded after *Welch v. United Kingdom* (1995) 20 EHRR 247.

[31] Criminal Justice Act 1988 s.71 *et seq.*

of behaviour involving laundering.[32] Those regimes have not been enforced particularly vigorously in the United Kingdom, but the United Kingdom Government is clearly dissatisfied with what has been achieved, there are enormous international pressures for greater enforcement, and legislation early in the new Parliament appears certain.[33]

The consequences of the deployment of the confiscation provisions against the corrupt are not all beneficial. There are considerable economic costs involved in the instantiation of the money laundering regime so far as concerns corruption, and the value of privacy has already suffered derogation by the introduction of disclosure rules for banks. What is different about the profits of corruption from drugs, for example, is that there is *necessarily* nothing about any given payment which might indicate that its source is a payment under a contract entered into as a result of a corrupt business transaction. In consequence any regulatory framework which is able to achieve anything will need to review all transactions: even more than tax evasion (if that is to be the predicate offence for the purposes of money laundering) there are no *stigmata* to look out for.

The greater the attention that is given to corruption, the more damage will be done to security of transactions. If it is found that a transaction was entered into as a consequence of a bribe, questions will arise as to whether payments should continue, or whether the relationship is at an end. These will not aid commerce. Lastly, there are dangers of inconsistent law enforcement. The money laundering regime is a draconian one, and in an area where enforcement is so resource-intensive there will necessarily be selective application of the law. Issues of fairness and discrimination will arise. They are not trivial.

15. Conclusions

I hope to have very briefly set out some of the consequences of the coalescence of the international campaign against corruption with the international campaign in respect of the proceeds of crime. The propositions for which I have argued are (and they may be taken independently):

---

[32] *Proceeds of Crime Bill Publication of Draft Clauses*, March 2001, (Cm 5066).

[33] Cabinet Office Performance and Innovation Unit, *Recovering the Proceeds of Crime*, London, 2000.

- *Quantum* should be considered irrelevant to sentence in the case of corruption of government;

- Sentences for corruption of government are irrelevant to sentences for corruption of markets;

- Sentences for corruption should be jurisdiction-blind;

- The amount to be confiscated under confiscation orders should be computed so as to allow a deduction for work done and for tax paid.

More generally, I suggest that we should beware the "thin end of the wedge" type of argument for the extension of the powers in respect of the proceeds of crime. The powers were originally put in place in order to deal with drug-related profits of crime, which were construed at that time as the exceptional case. Even without the advent of a jurisdiction to seize without conviction, the logical consequences of the accumulation of legislated concerns about (a) corruption, and (b) the proceeds of crime is to take the law into areas which should have required fuller and better reflection than has so far informed the legislation in England and Wales.

References

Alldridge, P., "Reforming the Law of Corruption", *Criminal Law Forum*, 11, 2001a, pp. 287-322.

Alldridge, P., Are Tax Evasion Offences Predicate Offences to Money Laundering?", *Journal of Money Laundering Control*, 4, 2001b, pp. 350-359.

Glazebrook, P., "Should There Be a Law of Attempted Crime?", *Law Quarterly Review* 85, 1969, p. 49.

Hodgson, D., *Profits of Crime and their Recovery*, Heinemann, London, 1984.

Kim, J. & J. Kim, "Cultural Differences in the Crusade against International Bribery. Rice-Cake Expenses in Korea and the Foreign Corrupt Practices Act", *Pacific Rim Law & Policy Journal*, 6, 1997, pp. 549-580.

Offer, A., "Between the Gift and the Market: The Economy of Regard", *Economic History Review*, 50, 1997, pp. 450-476.

Pujas, V. & M. Rhodes "A Clash of Cultures? Corruption and the Ethics of Administration in Western Europe", *Parliamentary Affairs*, 52, 1999, pp. 688-702.

Salbu, S., "Extraterritorial Restriction of Bribery. A Premature Evocation of the Normative Global Village", *Yale Journal of International Law*, 24, 1999, pp. 223-256.

Stessens, G., *Money Laundering. A New International Law Enforcement Model*, Cambridge University Press, Cambridge, 2000.

Terdiman, R., "Translator's Introduction to Pierre Bordieu, The Force of Law. Towards a Sociology of the Juridical Field", *Hastings Law Journal*, 38, 1987, pp. 805-813.

Treisman, D., "The Causes of Corruption. A Cross-National Study", *Journal of Public Economics*, 76, 2000, pp. 399-457.

PART V

INDEPENDENT INSTITUTIONS

Independence in Investigation and Prevention: The Role of the New South Wales Government's Independent Commission against Corruption

Grant Poulton

1. Introduction

What is the notion and importance of "independence" in terms of the role and activities of anti-corruption institutions and what are the costs and benefits of combining investigation, prevention and education in such institutions? In order to assess the value of independence in undertaking anti-corruption work, this chapter discusses the role and work of the Independent Commission against Corruption (ICAC) of New South Wales (NSW) in Australia. The ICAC is an example of an anti-corruption institution that is independent and combines investigative, preventative and educative functions.

This chapter outlines the history of the ICAC, specifically how and why it was set up. The way in which the Commission is independent, particularly in its investigation functions is then described. The chapter then examines the ways in which the Commission's independence is tempered by accountability mechanisms and describes some of the costs and benefits of combining investigation and corruption prevention functions within one organisation. The chapter concludes with a brief discussion about whether the ICAC approaches can serve as a model for other jurisdictions seeking to establish an anti-corruption agency.

2. The New South Wales context

Australia has a federal system of government, with a national government, six states and two self-governing territories, and a system of local government in each of those states. New South Wales is the largest of these states which covers an area

Cyrille Fijnaut, Leo Huberts (eds.), *Corruption, Integrity and Law Enforcement*, 193-216
©2002 Kluwer Law International, The Hague. Printed in The Netherlands.

of over 800,000 square kilometres. Sydney is it's capital with a population of 4 million out of total New South Wales population of 6 million. In addition to Sydney, there are a number of regional centres spread throughout the state. The Commission is based in the state's capital, Sydney.

The New South Wales public sector is made up of the Parliament, the Executive Government, and the Judiciary. In addition, there are 173 local councils. Among the services provided primarily by the state government are education, health, law and order, transport, roads, community services, environmental protection, and the regulation of gaming. Universities are established by Acts of Parliament, and are therefore regarded as public authorities. There is also a system of Aboriginal Land Councils to administer lands held by indigenous communities in New South Wales. All of these institutions, services and authorities are within the jurisdiction of the ICAC.

The institution of the Independent Commission against Corruption was not one that was envisaged when NSW or Australia was colonised. Like the Ombudsman, it was not an institution that was factored into the governmental or legislative framework of the adopted Westminster system. But as we now see, the Ombudsman is an institution that has proliferated throughout common law countries such as Australia, New Zealand and Canada. And like the English language itself, which has had to adapt by adopting new concepts and making them its own, so has New South Wales taken on the challenge of establishing an anti-corruption body in the form of the ICAC. It has found its own place and now sits neatly in the parliamentary, judicial and legislative framework of the state.

3. Independent Commission against Corruption

3.1. Establishment of the ICAC

The ICAC was established at a time when corruption dominated the political debates of New South Wales and Australia. One of the seven judges on Australia's highest court had gone through several inconclusive enquiries and trials on corruption allegations. The chief magistrate for New South Wales had gone to jail on corruption charges. The minister for prisons ended up in one of the prisons he used to run after being convicted of receiving bribes to release prisoners before their sentence was complete. Two other ministers had been the subject of speculation and allegations of corruption. Indeed corruption was a regular and prominent feature of New South Wales' journalism, popular culture and political debate.

In 1989 New South Wales saw the ICAC come into being. Legislation had been passed the previous year to set up the Commission. The NSW Premier at the time, on introducing the legislation to establish the ICAC, said[1]:

> "Nothing's more destructive of democracy than a situation where people lack confidence in those administrators that stand in a position of public trust. If a liberal and democratic society is to flourish we need to ensure that the credibility of public institutions is restored and safeguarded and that community confidence in the integrity of public administration is preserved and justified."

The ICAC was established to expose and minimise corrupt conduct in the public sector in NSW through investigation, corruption prevention, research and education.

To deliver these functions, the Commission is organised into three divisions: investigations, corruption prevention and education, and corporate support. The Commission employs investigators, analysts, lawyers, assessment and enquiry registration officers, research officers, corruption prevention officers, education officers, technical support staff, as well as staff in information services and technology, records and evidence management, and support in such areas as media relations and corporate support.

3.2. Corrupt conduct

In the past, the term "corruption" meant something different to everyone. In fact, research undertaken by the ICAC shows that while people agree that "corruption" is bad, people also have difficulty in defining corruption.[2] The establishment of the ICAC assisted foremost as an educative tool for the public sector of NSW by insti-tuting a definition of corruption.

Corrupt conduct is defined by the Independent Commission against Corruption Act,[3] as any conduct that adversely affects the honest and impartial exercise of the

---

1   N. Greiner, (Member for Ku-ring-gai) Premier, Treasurer and Minister for Ethnic Affairs, Second Reading Speech for the Independent Commission against Corruption Bill, Legislative Assembly, 26 May 1988.

2   A. Gorta, *A Tool for Building Corruption Resistance*, ICAC.

3   Independent Commission against Corruption Act ("ICAC Act"), NSW, 1988.

functions of public officials in New South Wales.[4] It involves the misuse of public office or the misuse of information gained while performing public office. The misuse of information need not be for profit, or for the benefit of others.

A public official includes any person employed by a NSW government department or authority, ministers, Members of Parliament, judges and magistrates, local councils (including elected councillors), and university staff and academics.[5] It also includes people from the private sector who obtain government contracts. Findings of corrupt conduct are not limited to public officials. Any person may be found to have behaved corruptly if he or she acts in such a way as to adversely affect or potentially adversely affect the honest or impartial exercise of official functions by a public official.

The act lists some very specific types of conduct that it defines as corrupt conduct.[6] These include:

   a. official misconduct (including breach of trust, fraud in office, nonfeasance, misfeasance, malfeasance, oppression, extortion or imposition);

   b. bribery;

   c. blackmail;

   d. obtaining or offering secret commissions;

   e. fraud;

   f. theft;

   g. perverting the course of justice;

   h. embezzlement;

   i. election bribery;

   j. election funding offences;

   k. election fraud;

   l. treating;

   m. tax evasion;

   n. revenue evasion;

---

4   ICAC Act, s. 8.

5   ICAC Act, s. 3.

6   ICAC Act, s. 8(2).

o. currency violations;

p. illegal drug dealings;

q. illegal gambling;

r. obtaining financial benefit by vice engaged in by others;

s. bankruptcy and company violations;

t. harbouring criminals;

u. forgery;

v. treason or other offences against the Sovereign;

w. homicide or violence;

x. matters of the same or a similar nature to any listed above;

y. any conspiracy or attempt in relation to any of the above.

Conduct can be found to be corrupt even though it occurred before the commencement of the act in 1989, and even if the person or persons involved are no longer public officials. If the conduct occurred outside the state or outside Australia, or is a matter arising under the national law or under any other law, it may also come within the definition of corrupt conduct.

The corruption definition is very wide ranging. However, it is qualified by a requirement that, to make a finding of corrupt conduct, the conduct must be serious enough to warrant criminal charges or disciplinary proceedings. In the case of government ministers and Members of Parliament, the conduct must amount to a substantial breach of the relevant code of conduct. The test in relation to criminal charges is that the facts of the conduct must be so serious that if proved they would amount to a criminal offence.

So in effect the Commission is required to take three steps in determining whether or not corrupt conduct has occurred. The first step is to make findings of relevant facts. The second is to determine whether the conduct comes within the list of matters within the act. The third and final step is to determine whether the conduct meets the seriousness test.

The important thing to note about our definition of corrupt conduct is that it is not limited to the merely criminal. It includes those acts that fall short of criminal conduct but which are sufficiently serious to warrant disciplinary proceedings against public officials.

3.3. Receiving and assessing information

Amongst its powers, the Commission is an investigative agency but it is not a prosecutor and it is not a court.[7] It is responsible for investigating allegations of corrupt conduct. The Commission can commence an investigation from four possible sources:

- A complaint from a member of the public or a public official;[8]

- A notification from the chief executive of a public authority, who is obliged to advise the Commission of any matter that they suspect on reasonable grounds concerns or may concern corrupt conduct;[9]

- A reference from Parliament. If both Houses of Parliament make a reference to the Commission, then the Commission must undertake an investigation into the matter. In the eleven years of the Commission, this has occurred on three occasions;

- On the own initiative of the Commission.

The ICAC receives hundreds of calls, letters, reports and other pieces of information about suspected corrupt conduct. From June 2000 to June 2001, the ICAC received just over 1500 complaints. Table 1 shows how many matters were received during the July to June periods of 1998-99, 1999-2000 and 2000-2001 and how these matters were categorised.

Resources do not permit the ICAC to investigate every matter it receives. The focus therefore is on allegations of serious and substantial corruption, or matters that involve systems issues capable of assisting a number of public sector agencies.

However, every matter that comes to the notice of the ICAC is looked at in order to decide what should be done. An Assessment Panel makes this decision. The Director of Investigations, the Solicitor to the Commission and the Director of Corruption Prevention, Education and Research (or their nominees) comprise that panel.

---

7   Prosecutions are undertaken by a body independent of the ICAC, namely the Office of the Director of Public Prosecutions.

8   ICAC Act, s. 10. Complaints that are made by public officials are protected disclosures.

9   ICAC Act, s. 11.

Table 1: *Categories of matters raised*

Category	1998–1999	1999–2000	2000–2001
Section 10 This is a complaint that may be raised by any person, such as a member of the general public, as provided for in section 10 of the ICAC Act.	677	574	515
Protected disclosure This is a complaint made by a public sector employee, but not all such complaints will be defined as protected disclosures, as they may not satisfy the criteria set down in the Protected Disclosures Act 1994.	232	138	130
Section 11 This is a report from a principal officer of a public sector organisation, such as a chief executive officer of a state-level public authority or the general manager of a local council. These principal officers must, under section 11 of the ICAC Act, inform the ICAC of suspected corrupt conduct.	489	430	411
Information This is for matters which are not actual complaints about corrupt conduct, but do give information about a situation which may have the potential for corruption.	184	288	314
Dissemination This refers to information that is provided by government agencies other than NSW agencies, such as the Australian Federal Police, the National Crime Authority and the Commonwealth Ombudsman.	15	7	4
Referrals from Parliament This is where a matter is referred to the ICAC by the NSW Parliament, by resolution of both Houses.	0	0	0

Category	1998–1999	1999–2000	2000–2001
Inquiry This is when information is sought from the ICAC, usually by a member of the public, about whether a particular situation might indicate corrupt conduct, or similar matters.	22	33	9
Own initiative This is a matter initiated by the ICAC itself, without a complaint or report being received. Such matters may be prompted, for example, by media reports.	1	3	11
Outside jurisdiction These matters either do not involve corrupt conduct or do not involve the NSW public sector. Where possible, people making complaints outside the ICAC's jurisdiction are referred to a government agency that can deal with their complaint.	131	136	115
Total	1751	1609	1509

The Assessment Panel can make any one of four decisions.

1. An immediate referral to another investigating agency such as the Ombudsman, the Health Care Complaints Commission or no action in cases where the allegations does not involve corruption;

2. A request that the subject agency conduct an investigation and provide a report to the ICAC. This is done where it is appropriate for an agency to deal with the matter;

3. A preliminary investigation may be initiated in cases where the ICAC wants to look at it but a formal investigation is not warranted;

4. A formal investigation by the ICAC. This may occur in matters where there is a potential to expose significant and/or systemic corrupt conduct. The investigation has a specific scope and purpose which may involve using a number of powers including surveillance and hearings (both public and private).

Table 2 shows what the Assessment Panel decided on matters received in 2000-2001 and 1999-2000.

Table 2: *Initial action taken on matters received in 2000-2001 compared with 1999-2000***

Action taken by the ICAC in response to matters received	1999-2000		2000-2001	
	Number	%	Number	%
No significant investigative action taken by the ICAC after registration and assessment	863	76	762	73
Matters acted upon by the ICAC				
• Referred to Assessments for further inquiries	51	4	28	2.5
• Referred to Corruption Prevention for further action	68	6	94	9
• Referred to Investigations and/or Legal for further inquiries and/or investigation	161	14	165	15.5
Total number of matters acted upon by the ICAC	280	24	287	27
Total number of matters	1143	100	1049	**100**

* The figures in this table, reporting the decisions made by the Assessment Panel, differ from other reported figures, as this table records decisions made during 1999-2000 and 2000-2001. Matters received during a given year – recorded elsewhere in the report – may not be considered by the Assessment Panel during the same reporting year, particularly those matters received in June of each reporting year. It also excludes matters classed as information or outside jurisdiction from the outset.

A recent example of the investigation function of the ICAC is the formal investigation conducted into greyhound racing in NSW.[10] That industry is regulated by a government agency, the Greyhound Racing Authority. The investigation looked at the conduct of officials of the Greyhound Racing Authority and the activities of some of the owners and trainers of greyhounds. Using video-taped surveillance, telephone intercepts and listening devices, the ICAC officers captured the chief steward of the Greyhound Racing Authority tampering with urine swabs taken from greyhounds that had won races. It was part of his official functions to ensure the integrity of these samples until their delivery to a laboratory for analysis. Further evidence was obtained using search warrants and notices to produce documents.[11] Public hearings were held over nine days in April and May 2000.

The ICAC does not prosecute or discipline people as a result of its investigations, but it can recommend that consideration be given to those courses of action. The ICAC can recommend whether consideration should be given to action against a person. Recommendations may include the prosecution of a person for a specified criminal offence, disciplinary action for a specified offence and/or action with a view to dismissing a person from their position.

3.4. Powers used in conducting investigations

Unlike a traditional law enforcement agency, the ICAC can hold hearings, both in private and public. Hearings are part of the Commission's investigative strategy, and have the aim of getting to the truth. Hearings held in public also have the purpose and effect of exposing corrupt conduct.

Other powers of compulsion the Commission has to assist with investigations include:

- Issuing a summons to an individual to give evidence, or produce documents, or both at a hearing;[12]

- Issue a warrant for the arrest of a witness if the witness fails to appear for a hearing;[13]

---

[10] Independent Commission against Corruption, *Investigation Issues: The Greyhound Report*, August 2000.

[11] ICAC Act, s. 22.

[12] ICAC Act, s. 35.

[13] ICAC Act, s. 36.

- Issue an order that a prisoner in custody appear before ICAC;[14]

- Issue search warrants. An authorised Justice or the Commissioner may, upon application by an ICAC officer, issue a search warrant if satisfied that reasonable grounds exist.[15] A search warrant may be sought when an ICAC officer has a reasonable belief that there are on the premises, documents or other things that are associated with an ICAC investigation. It is ICAC policy to obtain search warrants only from authorised justices (rather than the Commissioner) unless there is an exceptional situation;

- Issue a notice for a public authority/official to provide a statement of information.[16] This notice requires a public authority or public official to provide a written statement in response to questions put in writing by the Commission;

- Issue notices requiring production of documents by public authorities, public officials or private citizens and companies;[17]

- The Commissioner can authorise ICAC officers in writing to enter specific premises occupied by a public authority or public official, inspect any document or thing in the premises and copy any document;[18]

- ICAC officers may apply to the Supreme Court for a warrant to use a listening device;[19]

- Telephone calls may be intercepted and recorded by the ICAC;[20]

- The Commissioner is able to authorise controlled operations.[21] These are operations that may involve ICAC officers or others in engaging in activity

---

[14] ICAC Act, s. 39.

[15] ICAC Act, s. 40.

[16] ICAC Act, s. 21.

[17] ICAC Act, s. 22.

[18] ICAC Act, s. 23.

[19] Listening Devices Act, 1984.

[20] Under provisions of the Telecommunications (Interception) Act, provided a warrant is obtained from a Federal Judge or a nominated member of the Administrative Appeals Tribunal.

[21] Under the Law Enforcement (Controlled Operations) Act.

which might be illegal if it were not for the approved controlled operation. An example is payment of a bribe to a public official in a "sting" operation. There are strict requirements under the relevant legislation and certain types of activities may not be authorised;

- Acquire and use assumed (false) identities. The Law Enforcement and National Security (Assumed Identities) Act 1998 permits the acquisition and use of assumed identities by officers of certain agencies, including the ICAC.

Because the hearings are part of the Commission's investigative capacity, there are certain related powers available to it that are not available to the courts. Witnesses are required to give evidence on oath or affirmation and are obliged to answer questions. If a witness formally objects to answering questions, the questions must still be answered, but the answers cannot be used against the witness in any subsequent civil or criminal court or disciplinary proceedings.

4. Independence and accountability

4.1. Independence

The ICAC is an independent institution in a number of ways. As outlined earlier, it does not sit within the usual structure of the executive in that it does not answer to a particular minister of the government. The ICAC requires this level of independence in order to satisfy its function of exposing corruption and holding public officials to an appropriate level of accountability.

The appointment of the ICAC Commissioner reflects a level of independence in that the Commissioner is appointed for a five-year term. During this time, only the State Governor can remove the Commissioner from their position on the address of both Houses of Parliament.[22] As the Commission is an independent institution, this method of appointment allows the Commissioner to make decisions and conduct investigations without having to jeopardise the security of his or her own position.

However, the independence of the Commission is best illustrated in its power to investigate all members of the public sector whether they are judges or politicians.

---

[22] ICAC Act, s. 6(2).

For example, in 1998, there was an investigation into the conduct of a certain Member of Parliament of NSW in relation to claims for travel allowances.[23] The investigation examined the conduct of that Member of Parliament in relation to five air charters organised by him. In each case, that Member of Parliament claimed that other Members of Parliament had travelled with him on the charters, when in fact they had not done so. The reason for these claims was so that he could used the vouchers issued to those Members, rather than him having to pay for the flights himself.

The purpose of the ICAC's investigation was to determine if the Member of Parliament's conduct might amount to corrupt conduct with the ICAC Act, 1988 and whether the trips made by him were for parliamentary or electoral purposes. The ICAC found that the conduct of the Member of Parliament constituted or involved the dishonest exercise by him of his official functions as a Member of the Parliament. The ICAC recommended that he be prosecuted for breaches of the Crimes Act and for the common law offence of breach of public trust. The ICAC also recommended that the Legislative Assembly reconsider his membership.

In other cases, the ICAC has found that there is no evidence of corrupt conduct following an investigation of powerful officials. However, as an independent body, it is necessary to be seen to investigate such allegations where allegations raise issues that are in the public interest. It is important for the public to know that such investigations can take place free from interference or inappropriate influences. For example, it was alleged that there had been a cover up of allegations that a Member of Parliament had indecently assaulted a young woman in Parliament House in September 2000.[24] It was not part of the ICAC investigation to ascertain whether the assault had occurred, but whether any person had acted to fabricate or withhold evidence or attempted to improperly persuade anyone not to report or seek proper investigation of the alleged assault.

At the conclusion of the investigation, the ICAC was satisfied that no one had acted corruptly. The ICAC investigated this matter because it was in the public interest to establish whether there had been any attempt to cover up the alleged indecent assault. The allegations of a cover up concerned the conduct of very senior

---

23 Independent Commission against Corruption, *Investigation into Parliamentary and Electorate Travel: First Report*, April 1998.

24 Independent Commission against Corruption, *Report on Investigation into Aspects Connected with an Alleged Indecent Assault at Parliament House on 14/15 September 2000*, December 2000.

members of the Legislative Assembly. The allegations were so serious that their immediate investigation was of compelling public interest. The ICAC's investigative powers were ideally suited to conducting such an investigation.

4.2. Accountability

Despite the high level of independence of the Commission, citizens have a guarantee that investigations will be conducted properly. That guarantee is grounded in the requirement of the Commission to adhere to the general law. Adherence to legal procedures and procedural fairness ensures that people will be treated fairly before the Commission and that the execution of the Commission's powers is monitored.

In 1992, the ICAC investigated a matter which resulted from a referral from the NSW Legislative Council and Legislative Assembly. A Member of the Legislative Assembly resigned from his position and was subsequently appointed to a senior position in the NSW public service.[25] The investigation found that the then Premier of NSW and the then Environment Minister acted corruptly in making that appointment in that it involved a partial exercise of their official functions and involved a breach of public trust. The two ministers appealed this decision in the Supreme Court. While both resigned their ministerial positions and from the Parliament, the Court of Appeal did declare the Commission's findings a nullity. In other words, the ICAC got the law wrong.

The Premier of New South Wales established the ICAC and yet his conduct was subject to its investigation powers. The Commission made a finding of corrupt conduct on his part and the Premier did resign from office. Following this, the Commission's decision was overturned in the Court of Appeal. This case provides us with a number of lessons. First, even the state Premier is not beyond the jurisdiction of the Commission in its endeavour to expose corruption illustrating the level of independence of the Commission. Secondly, notwithstanding the Commission's independence and broad powers, it is of course accountable to the rule of law.

It is with the balance of the two, independence and accountability, that the public interest is satisfied and that the Commission can continue to pursue its goal of exposing and preventing corruption while acting in the public interest. The ICAC Act itself establishes certain mechanisms for the accountability of the Commission

---

[25] Independent Commission against Corruption, *Second Report on Investigation into the Metherell Resignation and Appointment*, September 1992.

and the way in which it exercises its functions. These include the role of the Operations Review Committee,[26] the Parliamentary Joint Committee[27] and the public reporting of some of our investigations. In addition, the ICAC is accountable to the auditor-general in regard to its financial dealings.

4.2.1. Operations Review Committee

The Operations Review Committee (ORC) consists of government and community representatives. The function of the ORC is to advise the ICAC Commissioner whether the ICAC should investigate a complaint raised by a member of the public or if an investigation should be discontinued. The ORC can also offer advice on matters referred to it by the Commissioner.

The ORC generally meets once a month at the Commission. ORC members are provided with the reports a week prior to each meeting so that they have the opportunity to consider all the reports adequately. During the meetings, the ORC may reject or accept recommendations made by ICAC officers and/or request that future investigation be undertaken in relation to any matter reported to it.

The ORC provides an accountability mechanism for the Commission. It ensures that matters that should be investigated are not discontinued without proper justification.

4.2.2. Parliamentary Joint Committee

The Parliamentary Joint Committee is an oversight committee made up of Members of Parliament from Government and non-Government parties. The Committee is responsible for monitoring and reviewing the exercise of the Commission's functions, and considering the impact and performance of the Commission. It is not able to examine or reconsider individual operational matters or findings involving the Commission.

The Committee also has the ability to veto the nomination of the Commissioner prior to appointment by the Government. The constitutional convention in New South Wales is that the Governor of the State, who acts on the advice of the Executive Government, makes such appointments. Appointments to the judiciary are made the same way.

Some have the view that the Committee may affect the independence of the Commission in this way. At present, there are few, if any, acceptable alternative

---

26 ICAC Act, Part 6.

27 ICAC Act, Part 7.

processes for such appointments. The guarantee of independence is not so much the method of appointment but rather the security of tenure.

The Committee holds public hearings into the activities of the Commission, and this is a useful mechanism for public scrutiny and accountability of the Commission's activities.

4.2.3. Other mechanisms of accountability

The Commission may hold public hearings and in this way is exposed to media and, therefore, public scrutiny. This is an important aspect of the Commission's function as it not only satisfies the public's right to see the Commission acting in the public interest, but it also serves as a form of public education about corruption issues. However, it is important that there is a balance between the public's right to know and the rights of the individual who may be under investigation.

The Commission is accountable to the auditor-general of New South Wales for its financial management and performance. The Commission is also accountable to the Ombudsman for the proper exercise and recording of special powers, including telephone intercepts and controlled operations. The Commission is also subject to judicial review. On several occasions, Commission findings have been overturned on questions of statutory interpretation. Investigation reports and annual reports are made public, and are given wide media coverage.

A last mechanism to be mentioned is less institutional. Levels of accountability have also developed over time as part of the cultural context of the organisation. These include addressing an open and inquisitive media, forming strategic partnerships and developing work practices that ensure efficient functioning.

4.3. ICAC and other agencies

As a way of enhancing the relationship with other agencies, ICAC is looking at opportunities for joint operations and activities. Presently, the Commission relies on information and intelligence sharing arrangements with such agencies as the Police Service, the National Crime Authority (which deals with organised crime at the national level), and the New South Wales Crime Commission (which deals with organised crime and serious drug offences at the state level), as well as sources of information and intelligence such as the Australian Taxation Office and AUSTRAC (which monitors financial transactions).

For example, the ICAC conducted an investigation recently into the "rebirthing" of stolen vehicles.[28] This involved vehicles that were being stolen within Australia or imported from overseas and then given false vehicle identifiers and fresh registrations before being sold on. It was alleged that employees of the Roads and Traffic Authority were seeking to profit from this criminal activity. In order to conduct this enquiry, the ICAC obtained the assistance of the New South Wales Police Service, and the Roads and Traffic Authority itself.

The ICAC Act allows the Commission to receive complaints about corruption from members of the public. However, the Commission was not intended to be a complaints handling body in the sense that it provides redress for individual complaints. Other organisations in NSW perform this function. The most important of these is the Ombudsman, which has been in existence for 25 years in NSW. It can receive and deal with complaints about government departments, including the Police Service. There are also a number of specialist complaint-handling bodies, dealing with particular professions or social groups. These include the Health Care Complaints Commission, the Community Services Commission and the Legal Services Commission.

The existence of these bodies provides an avenue for many complaints about poor administration that might otherwise be referred to the Commission in the first instance. Even with the existence of these bodies, we receive a large number of matters that would be better handled by these other bodies, or even by the agencies the subject of complaint themselves.

If the ICAC was the only agency in NSW with the responsibility for investigating and dealing with corruption, without the support of government departments and authorities, the task would soon overwhelm ICAC. A key to its success has been identifying particular instances of corruption and drawing lessons from it that are of benefit for other government departments.

As the public sector is becoming more aware of issues surrounding corruption and the costs they incur as a result of corrupt conduct, they are developing ways of addressing the issue. These include developing Codes of Conduct that are specific to particular agencies and by which all employees are expected to understand their obligations regarding ethical conduct and their responsibility to act in the public interest. As mentioned earlier, the heads of public sector agencies also have an obligation to report allegations of corrupt conduct to the ICAC as they come to their attention.

---

28 Independent Commission against Corruption, *Rebirthing Motor Vehicles: Investigation into the Conduct of Staff of the Roads and Traffic Authority and Others*, November 2000.

The ICAC is now in a position to review the effectiveness of those mechanisms in the prevention of corruption. One approach that we have started to use is to work with agencies to see what potential there is for possible corrupt conduct even before we receive specific allegations. This program, called Corruption Resistance Reviews, looks at the characteristics of the department, and points out features of the department's functions and processes that are open to corrupt conduct. To ensure that these reviews can actually help agencies, we work with agency staff to identify potential problems and solutions.

4.4. Final reflection on accountability

The previous discussion on accountability is, as can be observed, longer than the discussion of independence. This reflects my belief, based on the NSW context, that is somewhat easier to create an independent institution but much more difficult to make sure that it is held to account. Ultimately, an independent institution that is held to account in ways that do not diminish its independence will be much stronger for being held to account. In other words, the Latin tag about who guards the guards does needs to be addressed.

5. Combining investigation and corruption prevention in one institution

What are the costs and benefits of combining investigation and corruption prevention functions in one institution? First, I will reflect on possible costs.

5.1. Costs

In the last decade, a Royal Commission was established to investigate allegations surrounding police corruption. That Commission was known as the Wood Royal Commission after Justice Wood who conducted the enquiry. Justice Wood criticised the ICAC, stating[29]:

---

[29] The commentary from the Royal Commission into the New South Wales Police Service is drawn from the *Royal Commission's Interim Report* (1996), and *Final Report*, Volumes 1 (Corruption) and 2 (Reform) (1997).

"It was of concern that both the ICAC and the Ombudsman in NSW have investigated, exposed and made recommendations about corruption in the New South Wales Police Service with little resultant change or acknowledgement by the NSW Police Service. This Royal Commission has had an advantage, in the power and resources accorded it, to expose the real nature and extent of corruption."

It was thought that the ICAC's responsibility for corruption investigation, prevention and education throughout the whole public sector may have limited or affected the attention given to the identification and elimination of serious police corruption. At the time, the ICAC had the largest jurisdiction of any oversight agency, with complaints about police making up approximately 30% of the Commission's intake.

The dual role of investigation and education/prevention might be seen to give rise to a conflict of interest, where a finding of corrupt conduct following an investigation might be seen as a failure of our education and prevention initiatives. The result of the Royal Commission was that a specialist body was established to investigate allegations of police corruption.

However, the ICAC maintains investigative and corruption prevention jurisdiction in relation to unsworn Police Service employees. The Commission also continues to have corruption prevention jurisdiction in relation to all aspects of the Police Service. The police have been identified as a unique case in that they may be better suited than other public sector employees to avoid detection of any corrupt conduct in which they may involved. The lesson from the Royal Commission is that there was a cost in combining a corruption prevention and investigation body in the oversight of the Police Service. That agency required a dedicated corruption fighting agency.

For this reason, in New South Wales, the NSW Ombudsman, the Police Integrity Commission and the Independent Commission against Corruption all have jurisdiction in relation to the conduct of police. While this may seem at first to be unusual or excessive, I believe that the Police Service make a special case and benefit from having separate institutions dealing with their complaints and customer service issues, the investigation of corruption, and the issues arising from corruption prevention.

On the establishment of the Commission, the Premier of New South Wales at the time stated[30]:

"... the Independent Commission is not a purely investigatory body. The Commission also has a clear charter to play a constructive role in developing sound management practices and making public officials more aware of what it means to hold an office of public trust and more aware of the detrimental effects of corrupt practices. Indeed, in the long term I would expect its primary role to become more and more one of advising departments and authorities on strategies, practices and procedures to enhance administrative integrity. In preventing corruption in the long term, the educative and consultancy functions of the Commission will be far more important than its investigatory functions."

Accordingly, the role of the Commission has evolved through the years. There has always been a substantial and significant investigative role. Even today, the investigative area makes up over half of the Commission's staff. In the past, a significant emphasis was placed on corruption education, believing that high profile investigations and hearings would have an educative and deterrent effect.

The current Commissioner, I. Moss, has established her priorities as actively identifying potential corruption risks, enhancing corruption resistance, and using investigative capacity in a much more active and strategic way. The recent initiatives of the Commission include:

- e-Corruption – highlighting the corruption risks in the use of electronic technologies by government agencies. The new technology is expected to bring some new risks for corruption through allowing greater accessibility to information and sensitive data, the downloading of inappropriate content and identity fraud;

- Corruption Resistance Reviews – a program designed to assist agencies in identifying corruption risks and ethical weaknesses and to develop strategies to reduce opportunities for corruption. This is achieved by identifying key risk activities and weaknesses in agencies and continuing to monitor the implementation of recommendations. The Commission is also creating a

---

[30] N. Greiner, (Member for Ku-ring-gai) Premier, Treasurer and Minister for Ethnic Affairs, Second Reading Speech for the Independent Commission against Corruption Bill, Legislative Assembly, 26 May 1988.

kit for agencies to use as a tool to conduct their own corruption resistance reviews.

5.2. Benefits

Some of the costs of combining corruption prevention and investigative functions have been outlined above. There are however a number of significant benefits. Corruption prevention work can be based on the findings of investigations. An investigation of a particular agency may result in outcomes that involve corruption prevention lessons for that agency and those that may be similar in nature. Investigation outcomes may allow for a corruption prevention plan that is tailored to a specific agency. The Commission may assist an organisation in establishing a plan containing corruption prevention strategies once an investigation is completed in regard to allegations of corruption conduct.

For example, the ICAC received a complaint that an employee of the State Rail Authority allegedly stole computer-related equipment.[31] It was alleged that the employee sold the equipment to a business, that business then sold the equipment back to the State Rail Authority. The employee was responsible for recommending the purchase of the equipment by the State Rail Authority and allegedly received a considerable sum of money from the purchase of the equipment. The ICAC's investigation revealed that the control of computer-related equipment was inadequate in the employee's department, providing an environment easily exploited by employees. The matter was referred for the prosecution of the employee in question. The ICAC has given the State Rail Authority advice on preventing corruption through the implementation of new asset control procedures.

Another benefit of combining functions is that not all corrupt conduct can be dealt with through the investigative process. As shown above, it is sometimes more appropriate to either liaise with an agency or act in an advisory capacity. This is especially fruitful when an agency is prepared to change and requests assistance in developing corruption resistance strategies. The ICAC attempts to encourage agencies to take responsibility for their own corruption prevention plans by allowing them access to its education and advice service.

Organisations such as the ICAC need to operate autonomously from constraints and external influences such as the political climate. Organisations that fight

---

[31] Independent Commission against Corruption, *Corrupt Networks: A Report into the Conduct of a Technical Specialist in the State Rail Authority*, April 2001.

corruption must also abide by the rule of law and understand that with the privileges of independence come proportionate obligations. In order to combat the potential for corrupt conduct, it is important to continue to be tenacious in using investigations to expose it. It is also important to work toward ensuring that agencies where this potential for corruption exists are in a position to identify it when it occurs and deal with it – in other words, to resist it.

6. Conclusion

From the perspective of New South Wales, there is an on-going need for the prevention and investigation of corruption. It assists the state in monitoring, sustaining and building the probity and integrity standards of its public officials. The public interest is clearly served by this work.

Ultimately, the ICAC of NSW is built upon the notion that public confidence in public officials and institutions is actually enhanced by having the corrupt behaviour of its officials publicly exposed. Some argue that such exposure could threaten public confidence in public institutions and officials. Arguably there might come a point in time were the exposures were of so deep and systemic that the public confidence might suffer.

In my view, the public of NSW have shown themselves to be a little more mature than that. Public confidence in our police service is growing now they know that something is being done to address police corruption. This confidence is growing despite the fact that during the height of the Royal Commission, there were embarrassing revelations on television, night after night, week after week. There might well be wisdom in the notion that strength comes through exposure.

6.1. Can the ICAC serve as a model?

Answers to the question as to whether some jurisdictions need independent institutions for prevention and investigation of corruption will depend on who is asking the question and the context in which the question arises. As outlined, the ICAC was a particular response to the particular circumstances faced in NSW – Australia's most populous state and host to the recent 2000 Olympics. It may be a model for export but whether it is or is not a suitable model for export, will depend almost entirely upon:

- The political and legal systems of the putative importer;

- The problems being faced by the importer;

- The cultural context; and, most importantly

- An institutional framework that reinforces independence but tempers that independence with strong accountability mechanisms.

The ICAC hosts many visits from international colleagues who are setting about establishing anti-corruption bodies. The ICAC message to them is straightforward: from the available models in existence, choose those aspects of those models that you believe will work in your circumstances.

CHAPTER 14

Maintaining Government Integrity:
The Perspective of the United States Office of
Government Ethics

Amy Comstock

1. Introduction

In the American experience, accountability of public officials is deeply ingrained within the constitutional framework of the country. The political and civic culture of the United States is based on the notion that public officials should always perform their duties in the public interest. For example, the Constitution begins with the words "We the People". These words signify that all government authority, whether exercised by elected or appointed officials, is ultimately derived from, and accountable to, the American people.

Given this conception of public service, misconduct on the part of public officials presents one of the greatest threats to citizen confidence in the Government. This truth is evident in the events and ramifications surrounding a variety of political scandals throughout United States history that at the time they occurred damaged public confidence in the integrity of the federal government. Many of these events have resulted in new legislation to deal with the perennial challenge of controlling misconduct and maintaining the public's trust. Certainly this is an appropriate response. If we are to create a democratic culture, if we are to avoid the cynical conclusion that public officials merely use their public offices for their own profit and advantage, if we are to ask people to have faith in government and to believe that all will be treated fairly, we must have institutions and systems that ensure that public officials are held accountable and that government operations are open to public scrutiny.

Cyrille Fijnaut, Leo Huberts (eds.), *Corruption, Integrity and Law Enforcement*, 217-228
©2002 Kluwer Law International, The Hague. Printed in The Netherlands.

2. Ethics infrastructure

When we look at the executive branch of the United States federal government today, we find a highly-developed ethics infrastructure. This infrastructure includes a variety of specialised agencies that carry out preventive, investigative, prosecutorial and oversight functions. These agencies implement a comprehensive framework of laws and administrative rules that are intended to preserve the integrity and impartiality of government operations and decision making, and maintain public confidence in democratic governance.

Much of the infrastructure that supports the current ethics programme was created in the wake of the Watergate crisis of the 1970s. The Watergate crisis vividly illustrated the dangers when those in power become too self absorbed and far removed from the people they are meant to serve. Perhaps more than any recent event, the perceived abuses of the Nixon administration threatened to put a wall of distrust and fear between the United States government and its citizens. This threat spurred the government to launch a series of ongoing initiatives to promote ethics and financial integrity in government programmes and operations and prevent the sort of abuse exposed during Watergate from occurring again.

For instance, the 1970s saw the creation of: the Federal Elections Commission (FEC), an independent regulatory agency to administer and enforce the Federal Election Campaign Act (FECA), the statute that governs the financing of federal elections. The duties of the FEC are to disclose campaign finance information, to enforce the provisions of the law such as the limits and prohibitions on contributions, and to oversee the public funding of presidential elections; the Merit Systems Protection Board (MSPB) which serves as guardian of the federal government's merit-based system of employment, principally by hearing and deciding appeals from federal employees of removals and other major personnel actions; and the Office of Special Counsel (OSC), an independent investigative and prosecutorial agency with the primary mission of safeguarding the merit system by protecting federal employees and applicants from prohibited personnel practices, especially reprisal for whistle-blowing.

Beginning in the late 1970s, inspector general (IG) offices were established in a few of the largest federal agencies and departments. Today there are 64 independent IG offices responsible for protecting the government against fraud, waste and abuse in agency programmes and operations. IGs play the major investigative role for ethics allegations.

As part of the post-Watergate reform effort, Congress also passed the Ethics in Government Act of 1978 which, among other things, established the United States Office of Government Ethics (OGE). OGE is a separate agency responsible for exercising leadership in the executive branch to prevent conflicts of interest on the part of public officials and to resolve those conflicts of interest that do occur. In partnership with other executive branch agencies and departments, OGE's mission is to foster high ethical standards within the public service and to strengthen the public's confidence that the government's business is conducted with impartiality and integrity.

While OGE plays a central role in the overall ethics programme of the federal government, it is important to distinguish its role of preventing conflicts of interest in contrast to the responsibilities of the individual ethics offices within every executive branch agency and department. OGE is a policymaking body responsible for issuing and interpreting the rules which govern the standards of conduct and conflict of interest policies. In this capacity, OGE establishes the ethics programme requirements which agency ethics offices are required to fulfill. In order to implement these requirements, agency ethics offices are responsible for carrying out the daily administration of the ethics programme within each of the 125 agencies and departments that comprise the executive branch. Through co-operation with one another, OGE and agency ethics offices strive to protect the integrity of the government and the federal workforce by administering systems designed to identify and resolve conflicts, and to provide counselling and advice to those who educate public officials about the rules that govern their conduct.

3. Prevention, investigation, prosecution

Each arm of the integrity infrastructure – prevention, investigation and prosecution – in the federal government has its own contribution to make. Effective enforcement is absolutely necessary to maintain the credibility of ethics laws and regulations. However, in one sense a prosecution for public corruption is an admission of systemic failure. Large numbers of arrests and prosecutions do nothing to reinforce the public's belief in the fairness and legitimacy of government institutions. While enforcement is vital, it is largely reactive. Preventive measures, on the other hand, are proactive. Each has an important role with the overall integrity infrastructure, and when performed effectively they can even have the added benefit of reinforcing one another. Credible law enforcement actions have the potential to encourage further compliance to the policies and systems that have been established to prevent misconduct. Likewise, preventive measures raise awareness among public officials of the rules governing their conduct and help them avoid unintentional wrongdoing that might result in enforcement actions against them. The ethics programme involves a series of preventive measures that are designed to help public officials avoid conflicts of interest that might jeopardise their own integrity and the integrity of government as well. Preventing misconduct avoids the corrosive impact corruption has on public confidence and the cynicism and disillusionment which it inevitably brings. Preventive efforts allow governments to take proactive approaches to addressing conduct that has traditionally been punished only after the fact through law enforcement efforts. In this respect, preventive measures can form a supporting pillar of a holistic approach to controlling official misconduct that eases the burden of a strict reliance on law enforcement while also enhancing ongoing enforcement efforts.

There is an ongoing debate about the state of public confidence in the federal government and its institutions. Some public opinion polls reported in the media suggest that public confidence in the federal government has declined, while others indicate that even though the public trusts career civil servants, popular opinion of the United States government is most often influenced by the conduct of elected officials and senior political appointees.[1] Despite differing notions of where the public has targeted its discontent, there is more agreement as to its cause. For example, when referring to the federal government, most Americans do not distinguish between the executive and legislative branches, or within the executive branch between the political and career civil servants. Since most publicised "scandals" concern political appointees or Members of Congress, it is easy to see why the entire government is often broad-brushed as tainted, albeit temporarily, by one person's alleged corruption. The criticism that is perhaps most often expressed with respect to the civil service is that it is too large, too powerful and should be more limited. This type of criticism is probably more prevalent than widespread concerns that the ethical standards of the average federal employee have declined. In fact, annual summaries of ethical violations at the federal level suggest that there are a relatively small number of such cases.[2]

Nevertheless, certain highly publicised cases involving senior appointed or elected officials can have a severe effect on public confidence in government. In

---

[1] For example, see the following public opinion polls that survey citizen trust and confidence in government: "Deconstructing Distrust – How Americans View Government", The Pew Research Center for the People and the Press, 1998; "America Unplugged: Citizens and Their Government", The Council for Excellence in Government, 1999.

[2] See the OGE website for lists of prosecutions under the criminal conflict of interest statutes at www.usoge.gov.

the United States there is continual and intense scrutiny of government officials and programmes, not only by the media but also by various public interest groups. Frequently, politicians and interest groups use this scrutiny as a forum for undermining and attacking a political opponent. Allegations of ethical violations, whether true or false, seriously damage personal reputations and erode public opinion. Related to this is the fact that criticism of the bureaucracy in Washington has been a feature of electoral politics for several decades. The cumulative effect of this rhetoric has been to generate an increasing degree of cynicism about government and public servants.

4. Ethics programmes

The OGE exists in part to combat cynicism about government and to foster a more positive image of the government in the eyes of the public. However, OGE does not act alone in this effort. As a small agency with oversight authority over roughly 3.5 million public servants, including the military, OGE relies on the individual ethics offices within each agency and department of the executive branch to give life to the ethics programme. Agency heads have ultimate responsibility for the quality of their agency's ethics programme. Agency heads are required to appoint a Designated Agency Ethics Official (DAEO) to lead the ethics programme.

It is vital that each DAEO has the full support of the agency leadership in order to run a successful programme. The agency head has ultimate responsibility for creating the political commitment within their agency to maintain a strong ethics programme. Agency leadership must sustain this political commitment by working closely with the DAEO and their staff when ethics issues arise, and by offering the DAEO a high level of access into agency processes. The decision by senior leadership to lend political will to the ethics programme is the predicate for how agency employees will perceive and comply with programme requirements. Employees will have less incentive to consider ethical conduct a priority if agency leadership fails to explicitly establish the connection between the agency's mission and the high ethical standards needed to achieve that mission. Therefore it is critical that DAEOs are appointed at a high level in order to provide them with necessary access to agency leadership and to communicate the importance of the ethics programme throughout the agency. Moreover, the value of such a visible demonstration of political commitment in support of ethics programmes is echoed in research on the role of ethics offices in private corporations and the success of their programmes (Trevino *et al.*, 1999).

DAEOs and their staff are responsible for the daily administration of the ethics programme. Under the supervisory attention of their DAEO, agency ethics officials interact with the employees within their agencies on a regular basis and are the most visible representatives of the ethics programme. In this role, they provide ethics counselling and training to every public official, from the most junior level employee to the Cabinet secretary level. While OGE's leadership and policymaking authority is essential to managing this highly decentralised network of agency ethics offices, the success of the ethics programme depends on the leadership that DAEOs exercise over the ethics programme in their respective agencies. Having a DAEO and an adequately staffed ethics office in every agency is critical because the DAEO is most likely to know the issues particular to their agency and how best to address ethics matters as they relate to agency initiatives with senior officials.

For this reason, no matter how detailed a policy OGE issues, it is the DAEO who "breathes life" into the ethics programme on a daily basis. Agency DAEOs are the primary intermediaries between the policies OGE issues and public officials. DAEOs accomplish this role by:

- Co-ordinating policy implementation with OGE;

- Reviewing financial disclosure reports;

- Conducting ethics education and training;

- Providing advice and counsel to employees on ethics matters; and

- Monitoring administrative actions and sanctions related to ethics policies.

In order to fully understand the interaction between OGE and agency ethics offices, it is useful to examine the scope of OGE's programmatic responsibilities. For example:

- OGE issues executive branch-wide regulations dealing with standards of conduct, financial disclosure, conflict of interest waivers, post-employment restrictions, and ethics training;

- OGE provides guidance and interpretation to agencies, including providing informal advisory opinions and publishing annually versions of selected opinions (without personal identifying information);

- OGE oversees systems of both the public and confidential financial disclosure systems and plays a key role in reviewing the financial disclosure reports of presidential nominees in the confirmation process;

- OGE provides leadership in ethics training to executive branch agencies; and

- OGE regularly reviews agency ethics programmes to ensure that they maintain effectiveness.

As this list indicates, the relationship between OGE and agency ethics offices determines the successful implementation of the ethics programme. Each side has to work with the other to ensure the programme is accomplishing its objectives and is operating in the most effective manner possible. However, the final measure of the ethics programme is whether it succeeds in strengthening the public's confidence in government institutions and processes, while at the same time giving appropriate and practical guidelines to employees. This is the ultimate challenge that OGE and agency ethics offices face.

5. Code of conduct and financial disclosure

The ability of the ethics programme to foster public confidence centres on the impact of the code of conduct and the financial disclosure system at both the policy level and the implementation level within the agencies.[3] The code and financial disclosure are intimately related. These programme elements reinforce one another to promote the high level of transparency the public has a right to expect from the government, and which public officials should expect of themselves. In conjunction with the written code to which employees must adhere, financial disclosure has the potential to engage the public in a proactive way that gives them insight, and ultimately a voice in their own government. Each element plays a critical role in helping to communicate OGE's commitment to strengthening the public's trust in government.

5.1. Code of conduct

The current code of conduct, in effect since 1993, provides a uniform set of standards applying to all executive branch officials. The code communicates the values and standards that condition government service to the public at large. These standards are based on important general principles, including the expectation that public officials should not use their public offices for their own personal gain; that they

---

[3] See Executive Order 12674, as modified by EO 12731, and the resulting regulation at 5 CFR Part 2635, "Standards of Ethical Conduct for Employees of the Executive Branch".

should avoid conflicts of interest; and that they should act impartially. The primary goal is not simply to achieve mere compliance with specific rules. Rather the goal is for public officials to have a clear understanding and a deep commitment to these principles and to abide by the rules as they fulfill the responsibilities of public office.

5.2. Financial disclosure

One of the central principles within the code of conduct is the notion that government officials must be impartial in fulfilling their official duties and cannot allow their professional judgement to be influenced by their private interests. This principle is crucial to maintaining public confidence in government. It is part of OGE's mission to provide information through financial disclosure in order to assure the public that government officials meet the expectations embodied in the code and remain free of conflicts that would affect their impartiality. In many ways, this is the most important function of the public financial disclosure. It is specifically designed to translate the code into a system that opens a window into government processes and creates a measure of accountability that might otherwise not exist.

Under the law, all senior officials – from the President and the Vice President, to political appointees and senior agency heads and managers, to general officers in the military – must publicly declare their assets, sources of income, and outside activities. Approximately 20,000 officials in the executive branch complete public disclosure reports every year. Officials covered by the statute must report their financial interests, as well as the interests of their spouse and dependent children. These interests include: stocks, bonds, mutual funds, pension interests, income-producing real estate, earned and other non-investment income, and honoraria. Officials must further disclose gifts, including food, lodging, and entertainment from non-government sources. Finally, liabilities must be reported, as well as outside positions and future agreements or arrangements for employment.

Ethics officials are expected to thoroughly review the contents of each financial disclosure report before making them public. Through their review of a report, ethics officials are then able to identify potential conflicts before they occur and work out appropriate remedies. Once the reports are made public they are freely available to anyone upon request. The very openness of this system is ensured by the ease of access to the reports. OGE regularly receives requests for disclosure reports from the media, non-government organisations, and other interested entities.

The high frequency of these requests is a healthy sign of the interest that citizens take in probing the conduct and integrity of public officials. One example of the public's interest in these forms is provided by the relatively recent experience of the Clinton administration. Before leaving office, and in keeping with financial disclosure requirements, President Clinton completed a termination financial disclosure report. When the report was made public, the media closely scrutinised its contents, and among other things drew particular attention to the fact the Clintons had accepted nearly $190,000 in gifts from various friends and political supporters. Using information provided on President Clinton's financial disclosure form, media reports created significant concern among the public and the political establishment over the value of the gifts and the circumstances under which they had been offered. The extent and value of the gifts they had accepted raised many questions of propriety. More significantly, the media raised questions about the connection between certain individuals who had offered significant gifts and controversial decisions made by the Clinton administration on the eve of its departure from office that favoured those individuals. Under the pressure of public outcry over these issues, President Clinton ultimately returned nearly half of the gifts he had received. This anecdote illustrates a very visible instance in which public financial disclosure provided the public with the information it needed to influence the political process in a fundamental way. Frequently observers focus on the role of OGE and agency ethics officials in eliminating conflicts of interest through disclosure. However, as the case of the gifts given to President Clinton demonstrates, solely focusing on this role of disclosure obscures its dual purpose to both identify potential conflicts that must be avoided, and also make transparent all other financial interests so they are open to public scrutiny.

In the United States we have come to rely on this level of transparency as a crucial check and balance on the government. Public scrutiny brings an added measure of confidence to our system of democratic governance and further reassures the American people that senior public officials uphold the highest standards of integrity. Moreover, public financial disclosure demonstrates the government's commitment to keeping the citizenry informed and involved in the decision making process of their leaders. It sends a clear message that citizens have a role to play in ensuring the effective and honest functioning of government. In addition to informing the public, financial disclosure provides ethics officials with a tool to counsel senior officials on possible conflicts of interest. The act of filing public financial disclosure reminds senior officials of the ethical standards they must meet and the high level of transparency and integrity that their position demands.

6. Disclosure, training, leadership

The results of a recent survey of executive branch employees confirms the positive impact of financial disclosure and ethics training on employee perceptions and awareness of the ethics programme. The survey report, entitled Executive Branch Employee Ethics Survey 2000, provided a number of interesting findings.[4] The study, designed to measure employee perceptions of the ethics programme, indicated the importance of financial disclosure and regular ethics training in enhancing awareness of ethics programme requirements. Officials who are required to file financial disclosure reports are also required to receive ethics training annually. According to survey results, these officials are more likely to be familiar with the rules of ethical conduct and to seek advice and counsel from ethics officials when ethics issues arise. Furthermore, survey respondents who attended regular training had a more positive perception of their agency's ethical cultural compared to employees who attended training less frequently. Of all available methods, employees indicated that in-person training led by an agency ethics official was most effective in raising programme awareness.

In addition to underscoring the relationship between training and programme awareness, survey respondents emphasised the role of strong supervisory and political leadership in the success of the ethics programme. Respondents who indicated a high level of awareness of the ethics programme also noted the importance of executive leadership in promoting ethical behaviour on the part of agency employees. According to survey responses, supervisory attention to ethics and executive leadership were the two highest factors in facilitating intended ethics programme outcomes. These results support the notion that leaders who strive to integrate ethical conduct within the mission of their agencies, and who demonstrate that commitment through their own conduct, are more likely to gain an equal commitment from agency employees. While the survey was designed only to measure employee perceptions, it provides useful data for assessing programme effectiveness and targeting resources in order to improve programme outcomes. Survey results, and further corroboration through empirical evidence from the private sector, supports the notion that executive and supervisory leadership is perhaps the most important resource in developing ethical conduct within government and in effect helping to earn the public's trust (Trevino *et al.*, 1999, p. 10).

---

4   The final survey report can be viewed on the OGE website at www.usoge.gov, under the section, "What's new in ethics 2001!"

As one private sector study on this issue summarised (Trevino *et al.*, 1999):

"Leadership was a key ethical culture factor – one of the most important factors in the study. Where employees perceived that supervisors and executives regularly pay attention to ethics, take ethics seriously, and care about ethics and values as much as the bottom line, all of the outcomes were significantly more positive. Employees paint all leaders with the same broad ethical brush. When it comes to ethics, leaders are leaders, and the level (supervisory or executive) doesn't seem to matter much to employees."

The concept of leadership is embodied in the structural design of the ethics programme in the executive branch. Leadership is diffused throughout the ethics programme on account of the decentralised network of agency ethics offices and the oversight role OGE plays in this system. OGE exercises leadership through its role in co-ordinating the efforts of agency ethics offices, while agency DAEOs strive to exert their own leadership over their ethics programmes. In this very practical way, leadership and ethics are intrinsic to one another. In order to be successful, the ethics programme must be actively promoted through proactive leadership, while leaders themselves must demonstrate their own ethical conduct as the foundation of their moral authority to serve as leaders.

7. Conclusion

While the ethics programme in the United States is designed to foster ethical conduct within government, its ultimate goal is to maintain public confidence that Government is serving the interests, needs, and demands of all citizens. The structure of the programme is only one model for achieving the challenging task of integrating accountability with democratic governance. It is designed to provide alternatives to relying strictly on law enforcement efforts to address wrongdoing by emphasising prevention approaches that both complement and enhance law enforcement efforts.

Over the years this structure has proven effective in accounting for the size, extent, and diversity of the executive branch, while implementing systems of prevention, such as a code of conduct and financial disclosure. These elements are only a piece, albeit an important one, of the larger mission to prevent conflicts of interest and provide the public with the access and information it needs to hold government accountable to the highest standards of integrity and honesty.

Ultimately we must reach for the standard Woodrow Wilson set in his classic work on democracy (1956, p. 187):

> "A sense of highest responsibility, a dignifying and elevating sense of being trusted, together with a consciousness of being in an official station so conspicuous that no faithful discharge of duty can go unacknowledged and unrewarded, and no breach of trust undiscovered and unpunished – these are the influences, the only influences, which foster practical, energetic, and trustworthy statesmanship."

References

Trevino, W. *et al.*, "Managing Ethics and Legal Compliance: What Works and What Hurts", *California Management Review Series*, 41, 1999, pp. 131-151.

Wilson, W., *Congressional Government*, World Publishing Company, Ohio, 1956.

CHAPTER 15

Anti-Corruption Agencies:
The Importance of Independence for the Effectiveness of
National Integrity Systems

Alan Doig and Jon Moran

1. Introduction

Both individual countries and donors continue their enthusiasm for independent
anti-corruption agencies (ACAs) as the lead institution to combat corruption. Such
agencies are also often seen as the lynchpin of the development of a country's
National Integrity System (NIS), a term used to encompass a range of institutions
and processes whose collective activity and inter-relationships produce an effective
anti-corruption strategy. Much attention is given to the need to allow both ACAs
and the NIS the freedom and independence to relevant agencies to work unimpeded,
individually and collectively. This chapter, based on research both for the Corruption
and Anti-Corruption Strategies project (funded by the United Kingdom Department
for International Development) and the Global Forum II conference for Transparency International (funded by The Netherlands' Government), suggests that the
issue of independence both for ACAs and the NIS are neither certain nor embedded,
despite the rhetoric of reform, because of operational, resourcing and political
issues.[1]

---

[1]   The DFID project involved a number of desk reviews and field visits relating to 13
      countries, briefing reports, desk reports (on issues ranging from money laundering and
      the vulnerability of micro-states to deforestation and corruption, and the work of
      multilateral donors) and bibliographies, source books and manuals. Much of this output
      has been published in journals and book format.
          The TI project involved the assessment of the NIS in practice in 18 countries, a briefing
      report on the NIS in theory and practice, and an overview report on the NIS.
          The views expressed here, and the use of representative material, reflect the views of
      the authors alone.

Cyrille Fijnaut, Leo Huberts (eds.), *Corruption, Integrity and Law Enforcement*, 229-252
©2002 Kluwer Law International, The Hague. Printed in The Netherlands.

An integrated database search across a global network of some 60 information sources between 1992 and 1997 correlating the words "political corruption" and "World Bank or IMF or OECD or UNDP" showed an interesting curve: 1992 – 32 references; 1993 – 69 references; 1994 – 70 references; 1995 – 303 references; 1996 – 247 references; 1997 – 297 references (Doig, 1998). While this may be a crude indicator, it does reflect the escalating concerns within international funding agencies in the early 1990s about corruption. At the time, for example, World Bank staff felt that corruption was almost an impossible problem that had to be tackled and that the Bank had to reverse its approach, described as an assembly-line approach to project preparation with an overemphasis on quantitative goals and quick allocation of large amounts to the neglect of supervision, accountability and institutional development.

By the late 1990s, however, addressing corruption was increasingly seen as a core prerequisite for the reinvigoration of the state's institutional capacity, for ensuring society's trust in its leadership and for protecting the fabric of public life (DFID, 1997; UNDP, 1997; UNDCP, 1997; World Bank, 1997). This emphasis was also made within the emerging development agenda which was prioritising the interests of the poor and marginalised in the context of an enabling state and higher ethical standards among donors. There is now a widespread acceptance among multilateral and bilateral donors that a limited, legitimate, honest, streng-thened and transparent state should be at the centre of the development process in both developing and transitional countries: "those most likely to succeed will have effective government, enlightened legislation, prudent budgeting and an efficient administration that responds to the needs of poor people" (DFID, 1997, p. 30).

The attention of both multilaterals and bilaterals on corruption during the 1990s has been sustained by the emergence of Transparency International (TI) as the leading international NGO committed to promoting anti-corruption initiatives in a number of developing countries in the world, encouraging the establishment of national chapters in both developed and developing countries, and ensuring that the issue of corruption remains firmly on the development agenda. With much of multilateral and bilateral donor awareness lacking any strategy, focus or operational expertise, TI has focused much of its efforts on an inclusive approach which sought to pull together individual countries' institutions and sectors in an anti-corruption strategy.

2. The concept of the National Integrity System

TI developed the concept of the NIS as a methodology concerned with the purpose of combating corruption, not simply as an end in itself but rather as part of the larger struggle against official abuse, misconduct, and misappropriation in all its forms, which is in turn part of a general effort to create more effective, fair and efficient government.[2] As such, the NIS was intended as a framework for existing institutions and practices to work together toward a just and honest government. Thus the NIS argues for a public aware of its rights and able to assert them as an informed consumer of services, and an honest election process which would yield a democratic legislature. This institution would in turn exercise accountability over the Executive, with the latter working to shape its delivery of public services to respond to the public and the scrutiny of the legislature which also represents the wishes of the public. In short, the theory of the NIS is about delivering good governance (Pope, 1997, pp. 5-6):

> "… the aim is not complete rectitude or a one-time cure or remedy, but an increase in the honesty or integrity of government as a whole …"

The NIS framework is a set of components (objectives), and elements (actions to be taken), to be delivered by or through key institutions, sectors or specific activities (the pillars) through an anti-corruption environment can be identified by:

- Identifying objectives – the policy components;

- Identifying actions – the elements;

- Identifying institutions, sectors or activities involved in delivering the NIS – the pillars.

Each has components and expectations to promote their effectiveness individually and collectively, as is shown in Table 1.

---

[2] The concepts, components and pillars of the NIS are developed in *The TI Source Book (1997)*, the latest version of which, J. Pope (2000), takes forward and develops the themes in the 1997 publication.

Table 1: *The National Integrity System*

NIS components

- Mechanisms supporting accountability and transparency in the democratic process, such as parliamentary and electoral processes;
- Building a creative partnership between government and civil society organisations;
- Administrative reform and countering conflict of interest in the public service;
- Administrative law as a common element in any system of probity and accountability of decision-makers;
- Appropriate mechanisms which provide public officials with channels for reporting acts of alleged corruption and also ensure independent monitoring of procedures and systems;
- Independence of judiciary and ensuring that legal procedures and remedies provide an effective deterrent to corruption;
- An open, genuinely competitive and transparent system of public procurement;
- Private sector self-regulation and the role of legal deterrence against corrupt practice;
- An alert press, free to discharge its role as public watchdog and increase public awareness of rights and responsibilities;
- Independent anti-corruption agencies and co-operation with other countries to assist in combating international corruption.

Elements of the NIS

- Clear commitment by leaders;

- Emphasis on preventing corruption and changing systems, not witch hunts;

- Comprehensive anti-corruption legislation implemented by agencies of manifest integrity;

- Identification of government activities that are most prone to corruption and a review of both substantive law and administrative procedures;

- A program to ensure adequate salaries of civil servants and political leaders;

- A study of legal and administrative remedies to ensure they provide adequate deterrence;

- The creation of a partnership between government and all elements of civil society;

- Making corruption a "high-risk, low-profit" undertaking.

NIS pillars/activities

- Civil society, public awareness, public participation;

- Public anti-corruption strategies;

- Good financial arrangements;

- Parliament;

- Public service;

- "Watchdog" agencies;

- Rule of law, the judiciary;

- Ombudsmen;

- Attorney-general;

- Public procurement;

- The media;

- The private sector;

- International actors and co-operation.

The reasoning behind the concept of an NIS reflected a concern over the failure of past efforts from a number of causes: the extent of corruption could not be addressed by a single individual or agency; the absence of top-level commitment; overly ambitious programmes; piece-meal and unco-ordinated reform; over-reliance on the laws as the vehicle for reform; lack of focus or uneven application; lack of sustainable institutional mechanisms. The NIS approach works through a number of crucial institutions, sectors or activities (the pillars) which ensure transparency, scrutiny, and accountability. The pillars are to be supported by related systems, laws, and practices, which themselves must be deployed together, and strategically, rather than separately and piece-meal, as had generally been the practice in the past. Such support is also very much predicated on making the individual pillars as resistant to corruption as possible in pursuit of their functions and to thus ensuring that the pillars could be effective within the overall NIS.

Much of TI's work during the 1990s has been to pull together the pillars, where the majority of pillars are deemed to exist in a way that would facilitate a collective approach, to work together toward the objectives, or to strengthen, on a priority basis, core pillars in an incremental approach to the development of an NIS, or work through one pillar to develop an agenda to tackle corruption. In many countries this has been the ACA, of whom the 1997 TI Source Book proposed (Pope, 1997, p. 103):

"Independent Anti-Corruption Agencies – 'As the corrupt grow more sophisticated, conventional law enforcement agencies are becoming less able to detect and prosecute complex corruption cases'. Anti-corruption agencies should be supported politically, with suitable leadership, access to evidence and operational independence. The appointment of the Head of the agency must be of the highest standard – agencies had the potential to fall under political influence or become corrupted – and the enabling legislation should ensure that the agency's relations with the host department, the DPP or parliament is carefully addressed. The agency would be expected to be responsible for monitoring the assets of senior officeholders, procurement contracts and so on, and have the powers to freeze assets, protect informants, and stop suspects fleeing abroad. It was suggested that such agencies be kept small, cultivate relations with the public, and develop links with related agencies at home and abroad."

3. Anti-corruption agencies

The difficulty in realising the intention is that, in practice, the establishment and roles of an ACA are fraught with constitutional, resourcing and operational constraints which may be summarised as follows:

- ACAs can only be effective organisations in combating corruption in a limited number of contexts, because the variables behind the success of an ACA are complex, and often specific to individual countries;

- ACA success is based on structural factors within which an ACA can be "embedded". These include: a favourable political climate; state capacity; the rule of law/professional legal system; a basic level of governance in terms of financial management/record keeping in institutions likely to be part of any inquiry or investigation;

- ACA success is also based on more predictable organisational features, which include: independence, level of funding, training, professionalism;

- Prior evaluation should be undertaken as to the feasibility of other anti-corruption programmes. Even if these are unlikely to be successful, the proposal of an ACA should not be adopted as a default response simply of the lack of other options;

- The establishment, support and sustainability requires a much greater level of assessment and planning than currently exists. The development and operations of an effective ACA should be based on standard institutional and environmental mapping, business planning and management approaches.

Overall, the effectiveness of an ACA within the NIS are likely to be affected by certain key factors: a favourable political climate; state capacity; appropriate funding; the rule of law/professional legal system; the activities of other agencies.

3.1. A favourable political climate

By the nature of their functions, ACAs operate in a highly charged political context. An ACA needs high-level political support to function as a credible, effective organisation. This is not to argue that an ACA requires *political will* – a meaningless concept since political leadership cannot (and should not) be actively engaged in promoting the work of any government agency (just as it should not actively interfere in the work of any government agency) if it also wishes to support the rule of law and discourage political compromising of the administrative arena – but rather the political and legal conditions under which it can operate successfully.

The context in which those ACAs recognised to have been relatively successful were established (for example, in Hong Kong, Singapore and certain Australian states) were complex and historically specific. For example the context in Hong Kong (McCoy, 1991) was highly specific and created the structural conditions for corruption to become a significant issue in which the British Government took steps to impose a genuine anti-corruption policy with the requisite contextual and institutional conditions (Moran, 1999). In Singapore from the 1960s the state's developmental policy involved creating a comparative advantage by establishing the conditions for attracting substantial foreign investment, which required a stable and reliable legal and economic system. Thus the state supported the creation of the CPIB as part of the wider objectives of the country's Prime Minister to make the country economically attractive to banks, computer software, financial services, information services, manufacturing, in preference to some other countries better endowed with natural resources, manpower and markets.[3]

The political context in which an ACA operates can of course be negative. If an ACA is established to settle political scores or enhance the position of an existing regime then the political support only exists as far as the ACA becoming a form of political police. In these circumstances the ACA may perform valuable work on individual cases but its targets will either be high-level opponents of the regime or low-level unimportant cases. In Botswana, where corruption is much less visible and controlled by an elite dynamic which is careful not to tarnish its political hegemony, the ACA – the Directorate of Corruption and Economic Crime (DCEC) – is located within the Office of the President. Perceptions over a lack of independence and a concern that very senior government and public service figures are not targeted has prompted internal proposals that the DCEC should report to a parliamentary committee or an outside review body to counteract such perceptions. In Pakistan, the framework for anti-corruption work (at least up to the latest military coup), including the Federal Investigation Agency, the Ehtesab Bureau and Khidmat committees, were heavily politicised and operated in a climate of feudalism, elite politics, pervasive administrative patronage and abuse of office, and corruption as the basis of political life.

---

[3] For a critical view of the Singaporean system of governance, see C. Tremewan (1996) and J. Quah (1989).

3.2. State capacity and support

An ACA requires a substantial level of effective governmental ringfencing alongside *formal* political independence to allow the agency to become established and integrated. In Hong Kong, the power of the governor, supported by the colonial government, allowed the introduction of an ACA and its investigations despite the opposition of the powerful interest group of the Royal Hong Kong Police. Similarly, despite a powerful business sector, the ICAC has continually focused on financial and other private sector corruption. With the return of Hong Kong sovereignty to China this may change and the ICAC may be more hampered in tackling powerful economic interests with ties to the mainland.[4]

In Singapore the CPIB is a smaller organisation. However the Singaporean state's developmental policy involved creating a reputation as a stable, legally reliable business zone. Thus the state consistently supported the CPIB, enabling the organisation to secure extensive compliance and co-operation from the public and private sector (Quah, 1995). In this respect Macao provided an instructive contrast with Hong Kong: "since the establishment of a High Commission against Corruption and Maladministration in 1991, there is still no evidence that Macao's bureaucratic corruption has been successfully curbed" (Lo, 1993, p. 36).

The Portuguese metropolitan power consistently lacked commitment to reform, whilst powerful interests within the colonial bureaucracy and in the gambling industry prevented the development of any independent corruption control system. The Commission itself has lacked the administrative and operational powers of the Hong Kong ICAC, a factor which has also been noted in Argentina where the limited scope of action granted to the Anti-Corruption Office has meant it can only monitor the functioning of the national public administration, excluding from its sphere of control the functioning of the judicial or legislative branches and provincial or municipal governments.[5] In Nepal[6]:

"the executive, civil service, anti-corruption agencies and public procurement sectors have not been found doing better in practice. Because they developed some sort of behind the screen understanding of working together for the sake

---

4   For a discussion of these and other issues relating to the ICAC see J. Moran (1999).

5   See S. Lo (1993) and S. Lo (1992).

6   Quoted in the TI Nepal country report presented to the Global Forum II conference, The Hague, 2001, p. 48.

of survival in accordance with the mood and dictates of the government of the day, they could neither follow the laws nor could listen to the voice of their conscience. They proved to be just the tool at the hand of the government."

3.3. Appropriate funding

The ICAC in Hong Kong is one of the most well-resourced ACAs in the world. Its 1300 staff include 900 in the Operations Department who are split into public and private sectors investigators (180 front-line staff in each), supported by some 300 personnel providing intelligence and surveillance functions. With some 300 in community relations and 60 in prevention, the expenditure of over HK$ 600 million (the ICAC in New South Wales with a staff of 135 cost some A$ 10 million) the government was clearly committed to a long-term and appropriately funded strategy. Few other countries have been prepared to fund the level of activity that would make an ACA functional; the argument that such figures should be seen as a percentage of government expenditure or GNP is spurious if that percentage does not produce "critical mass" staffing and resources levels. There is a point at which ACAs are too small to be effective and so small that they become unstable because of staff loss.

During the 1990s, the ACA in Uganda, the Inspectorate of Government (IG), received its budget allocations on a monthly basis. These were subject to fluctuations, impeding efforts to engage in long-term planning. Although there were annual increases in the IG's budget since 1992/3, these increases were not significant enough to increase capacity and wages, or to allow the IG to plan effectively and follow an efficient development plan. Because of inadequate funding, wages were relatively poor and the IG remained under its establishment level (it had an establishment of over 230 but for the first decade of its existence this never rose above half that figure). During that time it lost a number of experienced staff either to the private sector or to enclaved departments (those with higher salaries funded by donors, such as the Ugandan Revenue Authority), unsurprisingly after donor-funded staff training in a range of transferable skills

An issue still not fully grasped by donors is the crucial distinction between *skills training* focused upon the individual, and *procedures training* which enhances both capacity building and staff flexibility.

3.4. Rule of law/professional legal system

Effective legislation and an efficient criminal justice system is needed if criminal investigation is to be the core of the ACAs operations. An ACA requires special legal powers to investigate corruption, because the nature of corruption is that it is often a consensual, subtle relationship, is often protected by a culture of silence and loyalty, and in many countries (even developing ones), may involve sophisticated financial dealings, such as complex financial transactions and asset transfer, or procurement and contract corruption involving multinationals. Therefore special legal powers are usually required for the ACA. These may involve laws which frame an extensive definition of corruption, laws which place the burden of explanation on the suspect, such as "unexplained assets" offences which exist in Hong Kong, Singapore and Botswana; laws which facilitate extensive search and seizure, not only of the suspects records but those of his or her family; and laws which place the burden of proof of innocence on the suspect during questioning. These laws exist in a strong form in Hong Kong and Singapore, and in a weaker but still prominent form in the New South Wales ICAC and the Serious Fraud Offices in the United Kingdom and New Zealand.

Without oversight these powers can easily be abused, and the ACA can become oppressive. As Levi puts it in the United Kingdom context: "legislation on powers to investigate white collar crime seems often to diverge from that of 'ordinary' crime, largely because it is seen as analytically separable from it and does not attract significant civil rights lobbying: business people's rights do not interest many on the political left, and because of their social status and articulate familiarity with verbal combat, they are not seen to be at risk of miscarriages of justice" (Levi, 1995, p. 176). However in New Zealand: "the powers invested in the director of the SFO are considerable, in fact, they are among the greatest ever given to a law enforcement agency in New Zealand. Reflection, though, suggests that both the authority and the independence of the office are necessary" (Newbold & Ivory, 1993, p. 241).

Thus, agency operations must be subject to oversight. One of the major planks is the rule of law and a professional legal system, which would provide the space to, first, supervise the special powers of an ACA (important here is whether there are laws which empower the ACA to initiate prosecution or mandate referral to an independent judicial authority) and, secondly, challenge ACA operations in the courts. This means ACA operations, or the prosecutions brought as a result of ACA operations have sometimes been held up for years through appeals, as in the United States (in cases resulting from FBI investigations) or New South Wales (regarding cases brought as a result of ICAC recommendations). But it is only in such a complex context an ACA can operate effectively in terms of due process and respect for the rule of law. Furthermore, a professional and efficient legal system also needs to be in place to ensure that cases are brought up for prosecution within a reasonable time, and cases are completed within a reasonable time.

Thus the work of the DCEC in Botswana has often been held up due to problems in the court system because of, for example, the length of hearings where the absence of court clerks requires magistrates to take notes in longhand while confessions are only admissible if made before a judicial officer, usually a magistrate, who must complete the statement verbatim in longhand and then offer that evidence as a witness for the prosecution.

3.5. A basic level of governance in the financial systems investigated

Corruption offences often function in connection with economic crime offences such as fraud, embezzlement, bribery, money laundering, tax evasion, and so forth, where suitable paper records are evidentially crucial. In one Commission Inquiry established by the government of Gambia in 1994, charged with the responsibility for investigating corrupt activities carried out by businessmen in collusion with customs officers and customs clearing agents in order to evade paying customs duties, it was discovered that (IRMT, 1999, pp. 18-19):

> "by collaborating with various importers, many with very good contacts through-out the ruling government, large amounts of customs duties were either never levied or, where levied, never collected. False invoices were allowed to pass as genuine and customs entry forms, bills of lading and other relevant documents were indiscriminately discarded in a basement at the Department of Customs headquarters. Over time, these documents were nearly destroyed by pest infestations and damp conditions; some of the records became indecipherable. However, once discovered, the Commission's investigating team sorted through the remains to recover as much information as possible. Using whatever documentation they could salvage coupled with records obtained abroad from the shipping agents the team was subsequently able to recover the equivalent of US$ 10,126,294 in unpaid dues to the state."

4. The activities of other agencies

Invariably one of the central arguments for an ACA is that the police cannot investigate corruption because they lack the expertise or because they are themselves corrupt. While the latter was certainly responsible for establishment of the ICAC in Hong Kong, such evidence has hardly been forthcoming in many other countries. Botswana's DCEC was established because of a series of high-level scandals but there was no evidence that the police were especially corrupt or under political control (although the police, like the DCEC, fall under the remit of the Office of the President). In Uganda, there is a National Fraud Squad with over 130 officers who, in 1997, dealt with 33 cases of corruption (as many as the Inspectorate).

The establishment of an ACA begs the question of resourcing – are resources to be taken away from existing bodies, will the overall level of resource be spread more thinly – and also that of another body competing for cases, staff and lead responsibility. In a 1998 donor-funded consultancy into the possibility of an ACA in a region of Kazakhstan, it was proposed that the agency should be in existence for at least 10 years and that the donor could be willing to "support" it technically and operationally for at least its first two or three years. There was no record of the levels of funding required, of funding-linked measurement, or of who was to be responsible for the remaining eight years.

In many cases, the issue may be less to do with a new agency than the need to develop means for co-operative working, or sharing information, staff and intelligence. It may also emerge that the problems of effective investigation and prosecution are actually determined by other factors – most notably slow and corrupt criminal justice processes – which would equally impair the impact of a new agency as they have for existing agencies.

5. Permutation consequences

The presence of a favourable political climate, state capacity and support, combined with a functioning and credible rule of law and legal system and financial/administrative governance implies a certain level of political stability and at the least a system of "liberal authoritarian" rule. It should be pointed out that the rule of law and a professional legal system which can provide the basis for oversight logically implies a certain level of strength and independence in civil society. This balance means that those who expect an ACA to be a model independent "go-getting, crime busting" organisation in any context mislead themselves. Any police agency operates in a complex matrix of political, criminal justice and social co-ordinates.

Often both academic analyses and the recommendations of consultants and donor agencies do not take these factors into account; the application of landscape scanning or environment analysis techniques would go some way to remedy such failings (Quah, 1995).

Where the above issues negatively combine, then the implications for agency independence and effectiveness are even more circumscribed. The anti-corruption agency in Bangladesh (BAC) and the position of the anti-corruption office within the Argentinean NIS exemplify the issues[7]:

"The BAC is controlled and administered by the executive organ of the government, the officers of the higher grade such as the director general or the director are transferable in an ordinary manner. Its activities are not at all transparent nor is it accountable to the representatives of the people. It is mandatory to obtain prior clearance from PMO for deciding the course of action to be followed after investigations are complete ... since initiation of anti-corruption cases against government servants from mid to the highest level and against political office holders needs prior permission of the Prime Minister there is no instance of filing any corruption case against a political office holder belonging to or supporting the party in power."

The BAC took an average of some 20% of complaints to court where the average percentage of acquittals was as high as 57%. The TI report argued that this was mainly due to two reasons, firstly, weak framing of the cases at the investigation stage for inadequate or faulty information and secondly, weak pleading of the cases at the courts, which reflects the inability and lack of commitment of the public prosecutors. For Argentina[8]:

"The weakness of some of the control agencies (Anti-Corruption Office, National Auditing Commission) is revealed by their dependence – regarding the appointment and removal of authorities – on the authorities subject to their control. Accordingly, opportunities for the exercise of political pressure are created, thus restricting the capacity of carrying out rigorous controls, and publishing the outcomes of investigations. In the same manner, there is an absence of mecha-

---

[7] Quoted in the TI Bangladesh country report presented to the Global Forum II conference, The Hague, 2001, pp. 7-9.

[8] Quoted in the TI Argentina country report presented to the Global Forum II conference, The Hague, 2001, p. 22.

nisms to carry out substantive evaluations on public administration management, contract fulfillment or convenience, or the performance of public officials. At the same time, the poor performance of the judicial system regarding the enforcement of the law and the application of sanctions, generated in the bureaucracy of the judiciary and the dependence of some of its members on the executive branch, enhances the absence of controls ... The possibility of civil society to exert control is significantly hampered by the weakness of the control agencies –in charge of law enforcement and the application of sanctions– and the consequent low risk of being punished for the commission of irregularities which, added to the lack of mechanisms to produce and publicise information on the performance of public officials and the management of public agencies, operates as a system of protection for the commission of irregularities."

As the report from Argentina goes on to note, "the lack of planning and co-ordination between public agencies, impedes the efficient use of information collected by other public entities, and limits the exercise of rational controls of human and financial resources. This situation is reflected in the lack of databases of suppliers of the state, and of the contracting of services and personnel."[9] Indeed the Botswana report highlights both the specific difficulties of interaction, compounded by the location of control agencies, in its review of the activities of the DCEC[10]:

- The DCEC itself lacks the necessary personnel to carry out its mandate. For instance, it relies on the attorney-general's chambers for the prosecution of cases. These chambers itself is burdened with too many prosecution cases;

- Delays in prosecuting of cases are also experienced within the courts. All these seriously affect the outcome of cases investigated by the directorate;

- The directorate's independence is compromised by the fact that it reports directly to the President and not to Parliament.

---

[9] *Ibidem.*

[10] Quoted in the TI Botswana country report presented to the Global Forum II conference, The Hague, 2001, p. 7.

6. The nature of the state

A more constant issue affecting ACA independence and effectiveness is the true nature of the state. For some states, the veneer of democracy is being cemented over the old political systems and power plays which continue to operate beneath the surface, underlining the continuing predominance, of the executive or presidency in many countries. Whether the consequence of the legacies of colonial independence, communism or military rule, the Executive, invariably dominated by a single party or elite grouping, uses state resources for coercion and patronage in order to protect tenure of office and to disadvantage opponents. It has also has continued to reflect the traditional "high politics" configuration with a focus on elite gain or regime survival rather than the broader public interest. In such circumstances there are structural implications for – and thus for potential reform initiatives relating to – the development of an NIS itself, let alone the establishment of an effective ACA. For example, in Colombia and Ghana[11]:

> "The president of the republic is the head of state and the top administrative authority. He is empowered to freely name and remove the cabinet ministers. He directs international relations. He appoints diplomatic and consular staff. He directs the public forces and makes use of them as the top commander of the armed forces of the Republic. He directs war operations when he feels they are warranted. He opens and closes Congress' sessions. He regulates the laws. He appoints the presidents, directors and managers of public entities. He eliminates or fuses entities. He modifies the structure of ministries by making changes to the law. He oversees the strict collection of taxes and decrees how the income shall be spent in accordance with the law. He inspects and oversees the provision of public utility services as well as the performance of the persons who undertake activities related to finances, the stock exchange, insurance or any other occupation related to the management, use or spending of funds collected from the public. He organises public debt. He is accountable for the national debt. He inspects and oversees state-owned enterprises, among many other responsibilities."

On the face of the institutional arrangements in place are enough to promote national integrity. But the reality is different. The actual ability of the constitutional, legal

---

[11] Quoted in the TI Colombia country report presented to the Global Forum II conference, The Hague, 2001, p. 18; TI Ghana country report presented to the Global Forum II conference, The Hague, 2001, p. 2.

and political orders to promote national integrity and the control of corruption is undermined severely by a number of in factors. They include:

- Lack of operational and financial independence on the part of Parliament and the judiciary; executive/presidential dominance over those institutions. In the case of Parliament, Executive dominance arises from the constitutional fusion of powers, especially the extensive powers of the President, including appointment of Members of Parliament as ministers.

- Most of the existing integrity bodies such as CHRAJ and SFO depend on the attorney general for prosecution. But the position of attorney general is a politically partisan position and operates with a keen eye on political profit.

7. Conclusion: the external planning context

In 2001, the British House of Commons International Development Committee reported that the British Government's Department for International Development (DFID) had suggested that anti-corruption agencies require an environment which provided "real political commitment, administrative autonomy, independence from the police, adequate financial resources, power to investigate and prosecute, power to recruit directly, relevant laws and a functioning judicial system".[12] The Committee itself reminded DFID that its own preconditions should be met before funding to any agency was provided and that, where such conditions do not exist, government assistance "should be directed to creating the necessary conditions 'within the context of a programme for strengthening judicial integrity and accountability'".[13]

This self-evident suggestion is one, however, that multilateral and bilateral donors have yet to grasp, preferring to support the establishment or existence of a vehicle that appears to reflect commitment to and visible evidence of tackling corruption. Many multilateral and bilateral donors made mistaken assumptions about the impact of macro-reforms, such as democratisation or decentralisation, and thus failed to anticipate new or displaced corruption and the impact on the workload and effectiveness of existing ACAs (one African ACA used to "save up" the increasing number of cases arising from the decentralisation of funds for an annual investigation tour to economise on resources).

---

[12] *Fourth Report of the International Development Committee*, The Stationery Office, London, 2001, para 52.

[13] *Ibidem*, para 54.

Many existing country assessments are weak in that they may lack the depth of analysis or sources, relying on existing information or on a handful of individuals or on institutions in recipient countries. The picture that may emerge may be partial and superficial, with donors reliant on off-the-shelf solutions or support for inappropriate initiatives. For example, in a recent example of the proposal currently being considered by multilateral and bilateral donors for an ACA in a northern sub-Saharan African country with a federal political structure, the initiating report by an inexperienced consultant misunderstood the implications of suggesting a federal and a national body, and drew almost exclusively on the Hong Kong ICAC organisational structure. A federal ACA and a number of regional state ACAs would have significant legal, territorial, resourcing and co-operation implications. Even at operational levels, a further institutional tier would raise issues of boundary management, including service level agreements relating to the respective roles and responsibilities, case acceptance criteria, an agreed forum for liaison at a senior level, and means of ensuring the sharing and recording of information for the national database or index.

Such assessments often fail to map out the roles, strengths and weaknesses of existing institutions, not recognising that the capacity of police, public prosecutors and judiciary to fulfill their respective roles in dealing with corruption needs to be strengthened (and appropriately resourced) within an overall governmental strategy. In not doing so, therefore, any proposal for an ACA fails to address a range of agencies, all of them will be severely short of the financial and skilled human resources required to tackle the caseloads that they face. It is against this background that the creation of a new, and potentially costly, ACA needs to be considered in terms of ensuring the most impact from the organisation and use of existing resources and the following issues should be taken into consideration:

- Competition between agencies for scarce resources (not just money, but scarce skills and experience) and the potential for the dilution of the impact of anti-corruption initiatives;

- Substantial additional administrative costs in the setting up and running of the new investigative agency;

- Inflexibility in the allocation and use of resources, as well as in responding to changing priorities;

- The need to develop case allocation criteria, and to create and maintain an institutional means of resolving the inevitable "border disputes";

- Disputes over jurisdiction and responsibility between agencies whose activities substantially overlap;

- The development of an elitist culture in the specialist investigative agency; and weakening of police resources and de-motivation of police officers (exacerbated by any proposed differential salary structure for ACA investigators);

- Arrangements for case distribution;

- Arrangements for shared information;

- Arrangements for inter-agency co-operation, co-ordination and joint working.

8. Conclusion: organisational context

The proposal for a fully fledged ICAC model, noted in the previous section, failed to address either prioritisation or incremental development with all the implications of over-stretched resources, the likelihood of performance failure and the absence of any planning process. It is almost impossible for a newly established organisation to become effective immediately in all of its areas of responsibility or, given limited resources (financial, manpower, skill-base, etc.) at any one time, to give equal weight to each of these areas of responsibility. Questions that need to be considered in relation to fraud and corruption could include:

- Should the focus be on raising public awareness of the costs of fraud and corruption and creating sufficient ground swell of opinion to start having an effect?

- Should the ACA be investigating the systems and procedures within governmental and parastatal organisations and, where necessary, for example, developing, implementing and administering secure and corruption-proof tendering procedures?

- Should its efforts be directed towards the investigation of major fraud and corruption or should on petty corruption as this is perhaps the area of greatest concern to "ordinary" people?

- Is it a combination of these and others and if so with what relative priorities?

If the failure to address the legal, institutional and operating context of ACAs has a significant affect on there independence, then the failure to treat ACAs as any other business has an equally negative impact on their effectiveness. With the pervasive influence of public management in the organisation and delivery of public services in developing and developed countries, such issues could – and should – be addressed through business planning and management processes, where there is a range of techniques and tools to better shape and direct public institutions internally and externally.

Yet donors often seek to fund existing ACAs without any of the standard financial and management tools and techniques that would be applied to assess the likelihood of a successful investment. Where an ACA exists, there is often an explicit assumption that the presence of an organisational title, staff and activity indicates a functioning entity. The consequence of this for governments, donors and consultants is the assumption that the organisation is capable of absorbing organisational inputs, such as training, or departmental reorganisation, or expansion of activities, or additional equipment. In a number of cases, the outward appearance belied internal problems and raised the issue of planning techniques for internal and operational planning.

Forensic analysis of existing ACAs often reveal a lack of an organisational culture; an absence of functioning financial management and management information systems; an absence of effective organisational and administrative support systems; an absence of effective decisionmaking procedures, integrated with those concerned with resource allocation; no delineation of responsibilities; no realistic performance indicators or measurement; and so on. The overall organisation often does not reflect the organisation plan (just as job titles reflect a salary grade rather than a set of functions or a level of competency). There is usually no clear team structure, career structures, or job descriptions; no common approach to case intake, investigations and reporting; a failure to match skills to inquiries; duplication or overlap with other agencies and organisations; an over-reliance on prosecutions as the agency sanction; no integrated link between investigations and institutional reform; and, finally, records management is neglected (in itself and as an information or intelligence resource). Such organisational failings stem from the absence of a systematic approach using basic business planning techniques to determine what an ACA is intended to do, and how it is to do it

Further, many existing ACAs have not been in a position to appreciate, accept, assimilate and implement significant reform often expected by donors. Indeed, too much funding input, too much organisational reform and too much attention from a number of donors will lead to organisational dysfunctionality. Additional funding to expand, or introduce specialist equipment such as computerisation, will only compound the organisation's underlying structural problems.

The key to designing and developing an ACA is determining strategy – "the formulation, implementation and responsibility for plans and related activities vital for the central direction and functioning of the enterprise as a whole" – where organisational design and development work is needed to ensure that focus, reform and funding is fully translated into the anticipated improvement in the organisation's performance (Booth, 1993, p. 63). Organisational fragility or instability in both new and existing ACAs must be planned for through a generic management process to address issues of staffing and pay; decision-making and communication; staff development and appraisal; business planning, work allocation and resource management; case intake and allocation; decision-making and communication; delegation and devolution of operational staffing, decision-making and resources; operational performance prioritisation; case review, reporting and measurement; and general work planning and performance measurement.

Addressing the organisation's decision-making capabilities and financial and management information systems are essential to developing robust resource allocation procedures needed to ensure that all resources are directed to support core ACA activities, once these have been determined. Thus the need for a business planning process is fundamental:

- The importance of business planning – objectives, targets and action plans – to establish core functions and to ensure a prioritisation process;

- The need to ensure the inter-relations of the priorities – for example, new vehicles and enough fuel and maintenance to keep them on the road – and their sustainability in terms of core business;

- The ability of the organisation to underpin core activity with the appropriate decision-making, resource allocation, performance measurement and operational responsibilities devolved to front-line departments.

- Transparent and quantitative record-keeping, and management and financial information systems, to develop a clearer linkage between core indicators, the availability of staff and funding to the relevant departments, and the costing of activities in pursuit of their functions.

The trouble with consultants and donors is that they ignore the planning process to get to grips with the detection, investigation and prosecution of corruption – and consider that a focus on these will drive organisational change, adaptability and development. In practice, however, without addressing strategy, planning and management first, an ACA cannot align its organisational planning, budget and operational decision-making processes with its core functions. Before any effective anti-corruption work can be undertaken, an ACA must deliver in five general institutional development strands:

- Financial and resource management;

- Human resource management, including all training;

- Information and records management;

- Investigation and prosecution management;

- Communication and education management.

Effective ACAs are based a complex set of structural and organisational factors which condition their establishment and operation. Therefore the assumptions behind any recommendation for the establishment of an ACA, or funding proposals for existing ACAs, need to be carefully examined. Overall, ACAs can be effective but without the effective application for proven business planning techniques they, at their worst, can:

- Add another layer of (ineffective) bureaucracy to the law enforcement sector; divert resources from existing organisations involved in anti-corruption work;

- Function inefficiently if unable to target serious/high level corruption cases;

- Function as a "shield" to satisfy donors and governments not wholly committed to reform.

Ineffective or weak ACAs not only damage their own role, they undermine the overall impact and success of the National Integrity System.

References

Booth, S., *Crisis Management Strategy*, Routledge, London, 1993.

DFID, *Eliminating World Poverty*, TSO, London, 1997.

Doig, A., "Dealing with Corruption. The Next Steps", *Crime, Law and Social Change*, 29, 1998, pp. 99-112.

IRMT, *"From Accounting to Accountability. Managing Accounting Records as a Strategic Resource" – Report to the World Bank infoDEV Programme*, London, IRMT, 1999.

Levi, M., "Political Autonomy, Accountability and Efficiency in the Prosecution of Serious Fraud" in L. Noakes, M. Levi & M. Maguire (eds.), *Contemporary Issues in Criminology*, Cardiff, University of Wales, 1995, pp. 175-190.

Lo, S., "Civil Service Reform in Macao", *Issues and Studies*, 28, 1992, pp. 46-66.

Lo, S., "Bureaucratic Corruption and its Control in Macao", *Asian Journal of Public Administration*, 15, 1993, pp. 32-58.

McCoy, A., *The Politics of Heroin*, USA, Lawrence Hill, 1991.

Moran, J., "The Changing Context of Corruption Control. The Hong Kong Special Administrative Region 1997-99", *Journal of Commonwealth and Comparative Politics*, 37, 1999, pp. 98-117.

Newbold, G. & R. Ivory, "Policing Serious Fraud in New Zealand", *Crime, Law and Social Change*, 20, 1993, pp. 233-248.

Pope, J. (ed.), *The TI Source Book*, Transparency International, Berlin, 1997.

Pope, J. (ed.), *The TI Source Book*, Transparency International, Berlin, 2000.

Quah, J., "Singapore's Experience in Curbing Corruption", in A. Heidenheimer, M. Johnston & V. LeVine (eds.), *Political Corruption*, Transaction Publishers, New Brunswick, NJ, 1989, pp. 841-853.

Quah, J., "Controlling Corruption in City States. A Comparative Study of Hong Kong and Singapore", *Crime, Law and Social Change*, 22, 1995, pp. 391-414.

Tremewan, C., *The Political Economy of Social Control in Singapore*, St. Martin's Press, Oxford, 1996.

United Nations Development Programme (UNDP), *Human Development Report*, Oxford University Press, Oxford, 1997.

United Nations International Drug Control Programme (UNDCP), *World Drug Report*, Oxford University Press, Oxford, 1997.

World Bank, *World Development Report*, Oxford University Press, Oxford, 1997.

CHAPTER 16

Independent Anti-Corruption Commissions: Success Stories and Cautionary Tales

Michael Johnston

1. Introduction

If there is one near-certainty in the realm of fighting corruption, it is that at some point top governmental officials will create an anti-corruption commission. With great fanfare, leading figures will be introduced, the dangers of corruption decried (usually in the vivid, but misleading, language reserved for fatal diseases), and some sort of "war on corruption" declared. So frequently are such bodies created that in the United States, at least, we have a generic term for them – "Blue-Ribbon Commissions" – reflecting the prestige of their members and the language and symbolism that accompany their creation.

In several well-known cases – Hong Kong, Singapore, New South Wales, Botswana – independent commissions against corruption (hereafter, "ICACs", after Hong Kong's pioneering agency) have produced impressive reform successes (Johnston, 1999, pp. 217-226). But all too often that is not the case: some commissions hold hearings, issue a quick report, and go out of existence. Others are underfunded and understaffed – by circumstance or by design – or given overly restrictive remits and powers. Such agencies are likely to do little more than publicise the problem, promising reforms they can never deliver. Still others are political smokescreens: some are established mostly to give the appearance of action and create opportunities for claiming credit. Others are tools of political reprisal against critics and competitors, or ways to conceal corrupt dealings and protect those involved. Such failed or phony reform efforts do considerable harm in their own right. Public expectations are raised, and then disappointed, with cynicism as the likely end result. Scarce resources and political opportunities are wasted. The work and accomplishments of honest officials and dedicated opponents of corruption are wasted, while future anti-corruption proposals encounter perceptions of futility. Meanwhile, the dishonest learn to cover their tracks a bit more thoroughly.

Cyrille Fijnaut, Leo Huberts (eds.), *Corruption, Integrity and Law Enforcement*, 253-266
©2002 Kluwer Law International, The Hague. Printed in The Netherlands.

What can we say, based on events since the establishment of the Hong Kong ICAC in 1974, about the essence of this strategy? What are its advantages and its pitfalls? When is an ICAC *not* the right way to deal with corruption? In the scope of this short discussion I cannot provide an "assembly manual" or tool kit for reform. ICACs and reform campaigns have common elements and requirements, but to succeed they must be adapted to their social, political, and economic settings. Instead, I will spell out some minimal conditions for the ICAC model of reform, and discuss both the risks of ignoring those essential requirements and the need to link reform to broader interests in state and society.

2. What ICACs are – and what they are not

ICACs – free-standing agencies that specialise in corruption control, possess broad powers, and receive significant operating resources – are a tempting anti-corruption measure for many reasons. They draw public attention to the problem of corruption, and to the importance a government places upon reform. They are a focus for citizen reports and concern, and can mobilise impressive expertise and data. They need not, in choosing strategies and tactics, balance corruption off against other law-enforcement priorities. Most important, they avoid the problem, seen in many parts of the English-speaking world at any rate, of delegating anti-corruption activity to police forces – agencies that are themselves often the locus of major corruption. The well-known successes of the ICAC-style agencies mentioned above will naturally make independent commissions a major reform option.

But in fact there is no single "ICAC strategy". Some commissions have jurisdiction over both public and private-sector officials and organisations, while others work entirely within the public sector. Some develop extensive corruption *prevention* capabilities, and are involved in ethics training and risk-assessment activities; others serve primarily to investigate and prosecute cases as they arise. In some societies, anti-corruption officials have the power to reverse burdens of proof, backed up by sweeping access to private as well as public financial records; their counterparts elsewhere do not. ICACs in some jurisdictions have developed strong research capabilities, particularly as regards public opinion and the analysis of patterns of corruption; others have not. Most such agencies perform some public education functions, but the extent and effectiveness of such activities varies widely.

History matters too. Past patterns of corruption and other sorts of official abuses, and the number, strategies, and results of past reform efforts affect the current chances for reducing corruption. Size, affluence, and the extent of the rule of law vary significantly among societies; so do their economic foundations, regional settings, legal traditions, ethnic and linguistic divisions, and so forth. All can affect the resources – political as well as economic – available to an agency, and the sorts of friends and foes it will encounter. Cultural variations not only shape perceptions of corruption and its effects, but also have practical consequences: in some societies citizens react with enthusiasm and confidence when invited to report abuses to anti-corruption "hotlines", while elsewhere such reports are seen as suspect denunciations, and few citizens file complaints. A free press in one society may be a major ally for an anti-corruption commission, and in another might turn corruption issues into superficial but profitable scandals. In too many places today, good journalists face intimidating pressures – or, in fact, are in danger for their lives – and too often, reporters and editors themselves are corrupt. Even in many relatively open societies, restrictive libel and secrecy laws stymie the press. The political context is one of the most important variables: ICACs that enjoy strong, sustained, and widely-recognised support from top political leadership function in a very different setting from those whose political backing is less secure.

3. The essentials: minimal conditions and requirements

What are the essentials of the ICAC strategy? The most obvious – and most critical – is real *independence*. But independence in turn requires *permanence, coherence,* and *credibility.* Even when all are in place, they do not guarantee success: other factors, ranging from international and regional dynamics, to the skill and dedication of managers and agents, to pure good luck are also in the mix. But without these major elements, ICACs cannot succeed.

3.1. Independence

Genuine independence is important in several respects. One is captured in the ancient question, "Who shall guard the guardians?" In many places the police have long been entrusted with the task of investigating corruption; where risks of police corruption are anything more than minimal, the problems with this approach are obvious. Even where police corruption is not such a serious problem, corruption must contend with other law-enforcement priorities for time, resources, and commitment. A large and well-staffed agency may get around this problem by setting up a special section devoted to corruption issues, but in many places the available resources do not allow such an approach. Expertise and information may be serious challenges: corruption, after all, is not just another generic law enforcement task.

It is secretive almost by definition, takes on many forms, and evolves rapidly in terms of techniques and participants. Corrupt networks may reach well beyond jurisdictional boundaries, and the proceeds from major corruption may be moved around the world almost instantly. Investigators and prosecutors who deal exclusively with corruption will find it difficult enough to keep up with such changes; those who do not will be perpetually behind the curve.

Independence involves far more than figuring out where to put an ICAC in the overall government structure. Corruption is the abuse of public power and resources for private benefit, and thus poses fundamental questions about the relationships between wealth and power (Johnston, 2001, pp. 11-31). Simply put, there is no way to attack the corruption problem without raising *fundamentally political* questions about the ways people – both public and private – pursue and use power, and about the people and standards to which they should be held accountable. These questions are made all the more political, and all the more complicated, by the fact that terms such as "abuse", "public", "private", and even "benefit" may themselves be hotly disputed. Reform must be guided by what Susan Rose-Ackerman has called "a standard of goodness" – that is, a conception of what constitutes good government, and clear ideas about the ways wealth and power *ought* to be used (Rose-Ackerman, 1978, p. 9). Tempting as it is to reduce corruption to technical questions of administration, there is little point in resisting it unless we are clear about those ultimate values and goals – for they, in the end, are what justify the intervention of anti-corruption authorities into political processes (democratic or otherwise), and what set those interventions apart from the use of scandal or corruption issues for personal or partisan gain. Ultimately, both our understanding of corruption and our benchmarks for the progress of reform must be integrated into a broader conception of what makes for good and accountable government.

Too often, however, corruption investigations do become weapons in partisan conflicts, and tactics of reprisal; this is just as true of established democracies as of other societies. Where corruption investigations are politicised, powerful officials can "protect their own" and conceal evidence. In fact, as the policy differences among major parties in liberal democracies continue to narrow, allegations of corruption become even more common features of party contention. Scandal becomes a cheap, and poor, substitute for politics. Ironically, while much anti-corruption policy quite rightly consists of preventing excessive political influence over administration, particularly in a democracy an ICAC may find itself cast in the role of defender of the political process.

Independence has other dimensions too. An ICAC must be able to follow evidence of corruption wherever it leads, while resisting pressures to conduct investigations and prosecutions of political targets. It must be able to publicise itself and its activities freely, and conduct its own affairs in a transparent manner. It must be able to guarantee citizens that the evidence they give will be taken seriously, and that they can file reports without fear of reprisals.

These propositions make intuitive sense, and they are nothing new. But maintaining real independence will be a continuing challenge. It is perhaps an irony, but certainly no accident, that two of the earliest and most successful ICACs were established in undemocratic city-states – Hong Kong and Singapore – where top leadership could define commission structures, functions, and powers, and provide critical resources, more or less by *fiat*. That the Commissions benefited from such top-level support is beyond dispute. But in a more competitive and open political system one party or another is likely to take the lead in establishing an ICAC, and will have to obtain consent from representative bodies. The Commission will almost certainly face charges of partisanship when it investigates members and backers of other parties. Likewise, funding and access to information must be guaranteed in ways that prevent them from being used to pressure the Commission or its agents.

3.2. Permanence

An effective ICAC will have to be a long-term initiative. Short-term morality campaigns or prosecutorial crackdowns are unlikely to win public confidence, or to change the behaviour of corrupt officials in lasting and fundamental ways. This means *core resources* – political backing, funding, and access to information chief among them – must be guaranteed over the long run. Clearly committed top leadership is essential in that regard; but an effective and genuinely independent ICAC must also build its own base of support over time, both in the population at large and among government and political elites. The ways leaders and citizens can benefit from reduced corruption are familiar by now; the key to winning their support, however, may lie in enlisting them as parts of the reform effort as early and often as possible, and then allowing them to share the credit for the agency's successes. In democracies, it may then become politically risky to cut support for an ICAC. Where democracy is not in place, or is weak, the situation is more difficult to predict, and depends greatly upon personalities and goals of those in power. In some cases, outside pressure may be required to win support for reform, but in other cases even undemocratic regimes may come to see that they have an interest – be it economic growth or increased popular legitimacy – in backing an anti-corruption effort.

Permanence also requires that *prevention of corruption* and the *institutionalisation of reform* be major priorities. The two are similar but not identical concerns:

the former refers to changing the ways public – and, where appropriate, private – officials and organisations do business, through vulnerability assessments, procedural and personnel changes, training, and so forth. The latter entails both the continuation of monitoring and specific anti-corruption measures within agencies and broader efforts to enlist society at large in the reform effort.

Journalists, trade and professional associations, researchers, political parties and interest groups, and citizens at large must be persuaded that anti-corruption policies are credible, that they are here to stay, that they themselves stand to benefit from them, and that they are important to the chances of success. Many may have tolerated corruption because they saw few real alternatives, or because they saw themselves as benefiting from it in the short run. Persuading them that non-corrupt ways to do business, conduct politics, and make a go of everyday life really can and do exist is critical.

When that perception begins to take hold, the costs of corruption – particularly over the long term – and the spurious nature of the "security" it appears to buy in the short term, can be made more apparent and compelling. Most important, the belief that corruption is inevitable must be dispelled. Clearly, these tasks require sustained effort. They are, again, tasks involving considerable research and education: people need to be made aware not only that they pay a large price for corruption – larger, in all likelihood, than most of them realise – but also that there are real alternatives. To the extent that these things can be accomplished, the same energies and interests that at present drive corruption may be mobilised as forces sustaining reform.

3.3. Coherence

Anti-corruption efforts that follow no overall design, and are not based on a sound understanding of the origins of the problem, may be as bad as no reform at all. In the short term they may give the appearance of action – always a tempting response in political terms – but as time goes by they may amount to little more than cover for continuing corruption, open up new opportunities for abuse, and foster public cynicism. The seriousness of corruption problems, and the fact that opportunities for action may be infrequent, create inevitable temptations to bombard the problem with good ideas – to act now and ask questions later, or to resort to a "tool kit" approach, trying whatever seems to have worked somewhere else and then discarding the idea when success is not immediate. But these approaches can waste scarce resources and good will, and may only deepen the public perception that reform is futile. Worse yet, some attempted reforms – even those that seem effective elsewhere – may just make matters worse.

As a practical matter, if permanence is a value and reform a long-term challenge, the anti-corruption strategies and tactics we choose are going to be with us for a long time. Here it is good to remember the importance, discussed above, of long-term goals and values. But it is equally important to develop an analytical understanding of how and why corruption develops, of the forces and incentives that sustain it, and of its broader consequences for society. Despite the recent tendency to treat "corruption" as a synonym for "bribery", and to apply essentially similar analytical and reform models to significantly differing cases, the fact is that there are many forms of corruption. They are best understood as symptoms of deeper political, economic, cultural, and institutional problems in societies. Punishing malefactors without attacking underlying causes and incentives will accomplish little; attacking those deeper causes in contradictory ways may only increase the delays, inefficiencies and problems of accountability that encourage and protect corrupt dealings in the first place (Della Porta & Vannucci, 1999; Rose-Ackerman, 1999).

Much the same can be said about effects. Anti-corruption reforms, like any other kind of policy, have unintended consequences. Implementing remedies without careful consideration of how they fit into the broader political and economic setting, and without plans for assessing impact and progress, is to invite consequences that may undermine the ICAC's effectiveness and base of support. And how should an agency gauge its own effectiveness? An ICAC should not look to "corruption indices" to document success. Even the best have considerable shortcomings as measurements; moreover, an effective ICAC that is actively reporting evidence of corruption, bringing cases into court (and into the headlines), and attracting a wide range of corruption reports from various parts of society, may well find that perception-based ratings will *worsen* for a time because of the agency's very effectiveness (Johnston, 2002). Instead, reformers would be much better-advised to use routine, quantifiable indices of government performance as their indicia (Klitgaard *et al.*, 2000). How long does it take to get a passport, or a telephone connection? How many steps are involved in obtaining a small business license? How much time, in a given year, do citizens and business people spend filling out forms or dealing with inspectors? How much does it cost to provide a school meal in one jurisdiction, compared to others?

Corruption itself will forever defy measurement, but the delays, "squeeze points", and related costs that it can create, and that make corrupt connections comparatively attractive, can more easily be assessed. A government that is streamlining its routine operations, bringing costs into line with reasonable norms, and is cutting back on opportunities for bureaucratic delay is also likely making corruption less tempting, profitable, and easy to conceal. The value of effective and accountable government, after all, is one of the main reasons we are concerned about corruption in the first place.

A final aspect of coherence brings us back, once again, to public education. Citizens must be informed as to what to expect as the results of reform. This is true both with respect to how long and difficult reform will be, and also as regards the effects of specific anti-corruption measures. In the United States, for example, citizens were encouraged to think that the campaign finance reforms of the 1970s would usher in a new era of clean politics in which money played only a minor role. When the reforms were enacted, however, the political action committees created under the new system served as conduits for contributions from a wide range of interests, and disclosure procedures provided clear evidence of large amounts of money in the political process.

Both aspects of the new system did exactly what they were intended to do, and what anyone familiar with the existing realities of political finance should have expected. But most of the public quickly came to regard the system, and the data it produced, as the embodiment of worsening corruption, because people had been encouraged to expect results the law could never have delivered. The result has been a continuing corrosion of public trust in politics and, ironically, in many reformers. An ICAC should promise only what it can deliver, and then it deliver on those promises.

3.4. Credibility

Public perceptions of an ICAC's independence and effectiveness are critical, as noted, and may be difficult to sustain. What will the public and the political stratum see as real evidence of independence – or as compromising the agency? What will it see as coherent, reasonable, even-handed remedies? Contrasting patterns of investigations and prosecutions will inevitably develop across parties, regions, ethnic groups, and kinds of corrupt activities, particularly in the short run. "Big fish" may have large political followings, often built and rewarded in ways that conflict with the core values of good government.

An ICAC cannot redress the imbalances by setting quotas for investigations or prosecutions. Similarly, as the agency begins to win early credibility, new allegations of corruption will surface. Some of these will be well-founded, but others will reflect thinly disguised political grudges. The agency will inevitably end up pursuing some cases vigorously while setting others aside (precisely as it should do). But again, how can the public be persuaded that such decisions do not reflect a political agenda?

There is no simple answer, particularly in democracies. Even agencies such as the New South Wales ICAC, which in my view has gone to great lengths to remain politically independent in fact as well as in appearance, cannot take public trust for granted, and must devote continuing attention to making sure that their procedures and initiatives are as widely understood as possible. But one answer may be to focus on procedures, standards of good politics and government, and ultimate goals, as well as on specific cases and personalities – that is, to emphasise how the agency does its business, and the goals and values that guide its actions and decisions.

Results remain essential, of course: Hong Kong's capture and imprisonment of a top police official who had fled the territory was an essential step toward winning public confidence. But if the public believes that all complaints will be carefully considered, and pursued as far as the evidence takes them; that investigatory and monitoring functions are sustained and broadly employed; that prevention activities are available to all; that choices and priorities are guided by a vision of the overall good, rather than by expediency or partisan gain; and that the agency itself is incorruptible (no small challenge in its own right), a credible image of independence can be built up over time.

Similarly, long-term public education campaigns, backed up by regular soundings of public opinion, should emphasise not only the evils of corruption but also the independence, effectiveness, and long-term goals of the ICAC. Such campaigns are complex and expensive, but should be viewed as a continuing investment in the credibility of the commission itself.

Finally, understanding what citizens regard as corrupt, and what they see as appropriate punishment, will help an ICAC do its work in ways that correspond with, and reaffirm, public values. Acquiring this sort of knowledge means an investment in research, and in training and re-training within the agency; but in the long run it will help ensure that the commission is seen as fair and credible – as neither failing to do its job nor as seeming to exceed or abuse its legitimate powers.

Unless it maintains its credibility, an ICAC's reports and initiatives will quickly become suspect or seen as futile. When that happens, citizen responses change: instead of confronting corruption directly – making reports, providing evidence, and refusing to pay up – citizens will respond evasively or illicitly, avoiding corrupt pressures, looking the other way, or fighting corruption with corruption, because they believe their evidence will be ignored, or that making a report is to put oneself in danger (Alam, 1995).

4. Problems of the ICAC strategy

So far, we have seen that while ICACs are by no means a simple anti-corruption strategy, they can be, and have been, effective when the core concerns and requirements are kept in view. But when is an ICAC *not* the right approach? And what are the risks of ICACs? In this brief concluding section I will offer just a few points.

4.1. Hostile circumstances

However compelling the political incentives to establish an ICAC, there are situations in which it would not be recommended. The most obvious are those in which independence and permanence cannot be assured. There are, for example, societies where corruption – even though it may be severe – is not the most immediate challenge for government. In parts of Africa, for example, civil war and the AIDS crisis are simply more important problems than corruption, at least for now. But even in less dramatic situations ICACs may be inappropriate. Where elite and popular consensus are weak, where society is so deeply divided along regional or communal lines that high-level leaders are not trusted, and where the rule of law is not functional at some minimal level, ICACs will accomplish little. Where the state is simply a vehicle for the interests and domination of well-entrenched elites, an ICAC is likely to do more harm than good.

At the other extreme, societies that have had low levels of corruption for long periods of time are clearly controlling the problem by other means, ranging from social consensus to elite political culture. Imposing an ICAC on the situation may disrupt existing anti-corruption forces, touch off unwanted competition with existing law enforcement agencies, and raise public worries or expectations in counter-productive ways. ICACs are also less likely to succeed where the news media are subject to political or official control, where civil society is weak or intimidated, or where recent reform efforts and agencies have failed. Finally, in any society, corruption control requires sustained high-level support, as already noted. Where such support is absent, success is unlikely at best.

4.2. Risks and challenges

Other problems must also be noted. One obvious risk is that the commission itself may become corrupted – and that when this occurs, effects upon official and citizen support for reform may be devastating. At one level, independence itself is its own best protection, and at others, corruption-prevention mechanisms common to many other kinds of organisations will be required. But maintaining both the prestige of the agency, and as far as possible paying staff very well, may be of particular value both for attracting the best staffers and making the threat of losing an ICAC job particularly effective as a corruption deterrent.

Different sorts of abuses may occur if the agency and its agents get out of control, even if out of an excessive moral zeal. Such excesses may become serious problems, particularly where an agency possesses the power to act in both the public and private sector, and to reverse burdens of proof. A population should respect and support an ICAC, not fear it; and here too public perceptions are worth careful monitoring. The accountability of the ICAC itself to top leadership, and to society at large where such is feasible, is of extreme importance – indeed, must be a condition for the powers, support, and resources that the agency needs to operate. Transparency in routine operations, extensive publicity regarding policies and operations, citizen participation and review processes, and open relationships with the press will prove to be more than just good ideas; they will be essential if the commission is to know the boundaries of its own power.

A different sort of problem has to do with "scaling up" the ICAC model from small and undemocratic societies to larger and more open systems. This, in my view, is one of the most difficult challenges involved in generalising the ICAC model. As noted, the two most prominent ICAC success stories have taken place in small and undemocratic places. In larger and more complex societies, and those where politics is more open and contentious, it will be much more difficult to establish credible anti-corruption agencies by decree: opposition groups will very likely view such efforts with skepticism at best. Agencies established through routine political processes may be seen as serving the interests of those who created them, and may find their roles and resources diminished after the next election.

Opportunities for corruption may be more frequent and incentives much larger in large societies, and it may well be easier to conceal corrupt activities and flows of funds. Meanwhile, links between people and government may be weaker, more complex, or cross-cut by ethnic, partisan, regional, and other sorts of divisions, making it more difficult to build support and credibility for an ICAC and harder to get people to participate in its efforts.

But where it has been decided that a commission is needed, the most successful ones will be those most closely integrated with other parts of the normative framework – the courts, civil society, the press, the political culture, and accepted bounds and methods of political and economic competition. Given our earlier emphasis on independence, this might seem a contradiction, but it is not. At one level, it is only to observe that a society that intends to control corruption over the long run cannot rely on an anti-corruption commission alone, but must also draw a wide range of other forces and institutions into the process of reform. It is also, though, a matter of building a consensus – a base of common goals and values that does not tolerate corruption.

An analogy can be made to the courts. Many societies benefit from, and actively support, a judiciary that remains independent and free to act. The support, and the continued independence, both grow out of the fact that the courts are generally seen as enforcing legitimate rules in a fair and effective manner, and thus serve the best interests of all. That sort of consensus can take a long time to build, and cannot be taken for granted once it is in place. But when it has been attained, reform has been institutionalised, and the practitioners of corruption will find it difficult to hide.

References

Alam, M., "A Theory of Limits on Corruption and Some Applications", *Kyklos*, 48, 1995, pp. 419-35.

Della Porta, D. & A. Vannucci, *Corrupt Exchanges. Actors, Resources, and Mechanisms of Political Corruption,* Aldine de Gruyter, New York, 1999.

Johnston, M., "A Brief History of Anticorruption Agencies", in A. Schedler, L. Diamond & M. Plattner (eds.), *The Self-Restraining State. Power and Accountability in New Democracies*, Lynne Rienner, Boulder, CO, 1999, pp. 217-226.

Johnston, M., "The Definitions Debate. Old Conflicts in New Guises", in A. Jain (ed.), *The Political Economy of Corruption*, Routledge, London and New York, 2001, pp. 11-31.

Johnston, M., "Measuring the New Corruption Rankings. Implications for Analysis and Reform", in A. Heidenheimer & M. Johnston (eds.), *Political Corruption. Concepts and Contexts,* Transaction Publishers, New Brunswick, NJ, 2002, pp. 865-884.

Klitgaard, R., R. Maclean-Abaroa & H. Parris, *Corrupt Cities. A Practical Guide to Cure and Prevention,* ICS Press, Oakland, CA, 2000.

Rose-Ackerman, S., *Corruption. A Study in Political Economy,* Academic Press, New York, 1978.

Rose-Ackerman, S., *Corruption and Government. Causes, Consequences, and Reform,* Cambridge University Press, Cambridge, 1999.

PART VI

REFLECTIONS ON LAW ENFORCEMENT STRATEGIES

CHAPTER 17

A Multidisciplinary Approach for Detection and Investigation of Corruption

Tom Vander Beken

1. Introduction

Although Belgium was one of the first countries to establish an anti-corruption service in the beginning of the last century, the issue has only received significant policy attention over the last decade.[1] This is due to the fact that in this period Belgium was confronted by a number of incidents that have tarnished its reputation in relation to corruption. Evidence of this is reflected in the *2000 Corruption Perceptions Index* of Transparency International (TI) in which Belgium ranks 25th. Of all European Union member states, only the perception of the corruption situation of Greece (35th) and Italy (39th) is worse. All in all, compared to the years 1999 (equal 29th, together with Namibia), 1998 (28th, after Costa Rica) and 1997 (26th, after Greece), the Belgian result of 2000 is the "best" of the last years (Transparency International, 2000a, 1999, 1998, 1997).

The present Belgian government is aware of the seriousness of this issue and has declared the restoration of the faith in the Belgian institutions as one of its most important ambitions. Consequently, the fight against corruption has been explicitly adopted as part of its governmental agenda, in particular finding expression

---

[1] In 1910 a High Control Committee (*Hoog Comité van Toezicht*) for the railways and post was established. Although its competences were broadened to the control of all state departments, the Committee only had administrative (preventive) powers until 1962. From that date the officers of the Committee had both administrative and repressive powers. In 1998 the Committee was replaced by the Central Office for the Repression of Corruption. This office has only repressive powers and forms part of the Federal Police. (For an overview of the history see Vander Beken, Carion, De Ruyver, 1999, pp. 51-69; Van Heers, 2001, pp. 60-62.)

Cyrille Fijnaut, Leo Huberts (eds.), *Corruption, Integrity and Law Enforcement*, 269-282
©2002 Kluwer Law International, The Hague. Printed in The Netherlands.

in the discussions within the Federal Safety and Security Plan (Belgian Government, 1999, 2000).

In these policy proposals the fight against corruption is placed within an integrated and multi-disciplinary approach that combines both prevention and repression. The basic idea of this approach is that corruption should be defined in a way that covers more than the criminal act alone, so that action at several levels and by several actors can be undertaken.

This paper analyses to what extent such a comprehensive approach can contribute to a better investigation and exposure of corruption. The analysis is based on Belgian experiences and a number of case studies. However, since our study of the meat sector is the first and only in-depth Belgian case study on this matter, it will be used as main point of reference (De Ruyver, Bullens, Vander Beken, Siron, 1999).

2. Corruption as a (new) policy issue

2.1. The definition phase: Belgian Parliament opts for a broad definition

Following the publication of a book of a Belgian journalist on trafficking of human beings in Belgium, a Parliamentary Enquiry Commission was established in 1992 (De Stoop, 1992). In 1994, this Commission published its final report and pointed to serious problems regarding police corruption (Belgian Government, 1994). In particular it was in the cities of Antwerp (Fijnaut, 1994) and Ghent (De Ruyver, 1994) where the reaction and the investigation of police corruption was considered to be insufficient. Interestingly the experts of the Commission pointed at the fact that police corruption is more than the specific criminal act, but also includes other forms of unacceptable behaviour (Fijnaut, 1994, p. 119). In that framework, De Ruyver introduced the concepts of "corruption", "corrupt behaviour" and the "blurring of norms" (*normvervaging*) to stress the importance of seeing corruption as a process, and not only as a single act that can be prosecuted before criminal courts (De Ruyver, 1994, pp. 198-199).

According to this conceptualisation, the first phase of the corruption process can be the "blurring of norms" which is the lowering of ethical standards that lead to behaviour which is not in accordance with the accepted deontology. This process opens the door to corrupt behaviour that is behaviour that may lead to criminal conviction if it is possible to prove all elements of the crime. The last, but in many cases the least visible phase of the corruption process, is the actual corruption in its penal sense, were there is proof of all elements of the crime and conviction by the criminal court is possible (De Ruyver, 1995, p. 96; De Ruyver, Bullens, Vander Beken, Siron, 1999, pp. 170-171).

In August 1996 the Belgian police arrested M. Dutroux, who was suspected of the kidnapping, rape and murder of several young girls. Since there were questions regarding the management of the investigation, a Parliamentary Enquiry Commission was set up to find out if the allegations regarding the investigation were true (Belgian House of Representatives, 1997-1998). In the second part of its report – the report in which the Commission was investigating the possible protection of the suspects from prosecution – the Commission decided to distinguish between corruption, corrupt behaviour and "blurring of norms". The Commission stated, as had the Commission on trafficking in human beings, that such an approach was far more effective to understand and detect the real ambit of corruption problem (Belgian House of Representatives, 1997-1998, II, pp. 13-23).

In its conclusions, the Parliamentary Enquiry Commission stresses the importance of building anti-corruption strategies which rest on this broad vision of corruption and encompassing both repressive and preventive measures. Especially with regard to the aspect of repression and investigation, the Commission reiterates that a singular focus on corruption in its penal sense is not useful and that criminal investigation should complement internal and external controls.

2.2. The Belgian meat sector in crisis

2.2.1. An urgent call for anti-corruption strategies for the meat sector

On 20 February 1995, K. Van Noppen of the Veterinary Inspection Institute was murdered. Since Van Noppen was very active in the fight against the illegal use of growth promoters in cattle, it is believed that he was the victim of the so-called "hormone mafia". Later in 1996-1997, when it became clear that some criminal groups used the BSE crisis to commit significant meat frauds, the phrase "meat fraud mafia" was often used for criminal groups in Belgium related to this sector (De Ruyver, 1995, p. 96; De Ruyver, Bullens, Vander Beken, Siron, 1999, p. 1).

From 4 to 6 June 1996, a special meeting was held with all actors in the fight against illegal growth promoters. One of the conclusions of the meeting led to the decision of the government to appoint an expert charged with the task of developing anti-corruption strategies with regard to the fight against the illegal use of growth promoters (Timperman, 1998-1999, p. 899).

Following the considerable problems identified in meat fraud, the government asked for policy proposals for a multi-disciplinary approach to tackle the issue. As a result it was decided to extend anti-corruption strategies to the fight against meat fraud.[2]

Finally, the Minister of Justice charged our research group with the study to develop strategies for corruption related to the illegal use of growth promoters and meat fraud. The research period was from 1 July 1998 to 31 March 1999 (De Ruyver, Bullens, Vander Beken, Siron, 1999).

2.2.2. The meat sector anti-corruption study and its findings

The study on anti-corruption policies in the meat sector consists of three major parts. In the first part a systemic analysis is made of the meat sector as a whole, focusing both on the meat production chain and on the control chain. The idea was to detect the weak points in these chains by describing their functioning. In the second part a conceptual study with regard to the definition of corruption was made and applied on the findings of the first part on the sector itself. In line with the above-mentioned conclusions of the Parliamentary Enquiry Commissions and literature, the choice was made to develop strategies that aimed at behaviour which goes beyond the criminal law definition of corruption. Similarly, the situation in the meat sector showed that it would have been useless to limit the scope of the study to "penal" corruption alone. Although there were clear indications that there was a corruption problem in the sector, virtually no case ever reached the stage of conviction (De Ruyver, Bullens, Vander Beken, Siron, 1999, p. 169). In the third and final part, the findings from the previous parts were combined and used to develop anti-corruption strategies for the sector.

The most important conclusion of the first part is that the meat production chain consists of numerous different sections which should be covered and controlled by as many different services of the control chain. A multi-disciplinary approach and a close collaboration between all these services is needed, but is not yet established.

---

2   The problems were also addressed in other Parliamentary Commissions. In the final report of the Belgian Senate, *Parlementaire Commissie van onderzoek naar de georganiseerde criminaliteit in België; eindverslag uitgebracht door de Heren Coveliers en Desmedt* (Parliamentary Enquiry Commission on Organised Crime), 1-326/0, 1998-1999, p. 297, explicit reference was made to the meat sector and its problems with organised crime and corruption. Also a special Commission on the follow up of the problems regarding meat fraud was established, see House of Representatives, *Subcommissie belast met de opvolging van de problemen inzake fraude in de vleessector; verslag namens de commissie voor de volksgezondheid, het leefmilieu en de maatschappelijke hernieuwing*, 1905/1, 1998-1999.

An additional complication is that regulation in the meat sector is to serve two, not always compatible, goals. On the one hand the regulation is designed to safeguard the quality of the meat in order to guarantee a healthy human consumption. On the other hand, regulation and control have an enormous impact on the economic aspects of the sector. In practice, control services find it hard to strike the right balance between economic interests and public health. Therefore, it was found that the growing financial aspects of the sector and the difficult market situation had an important influence on the frequency and the thoroughness of the controls.

It is especially in such a situation that the "blurring of norms" and "corrupt behaviour" flourish. A typical example is the existence of close friendships between farmers and controlling officials.[3] The fact that both farmer and controller believe that the governmental policy which prohibits all use of growth substitutes is not feasible and basically unfair compared to the limited control efforts abroad, appeared to drive them towards each other. This leads to situations where farmers were warned before controls were to take place or where planned controls got cancelled and certificates were signed without any form of control.

Regarding the corrupt behaviour, the overall conclusion of the research was that nearly all controlling officials active on the field have been in situations where there was active corrupt behaviour. In nearly all cases, it was very difficult to qualify the situation as penal corruption as such and prosecute the case. Very often the offer of the bribe was too implicit or the person who offered the bribe could not be identified. A typical example of that is the controller who hangs his jacket on a coat-hanger in the morning and finds money in his pocket at the end of the day (De Ruyver, Bullens, Vander Beken, Siron, 1999, pp. 178-180).

These findings illustrate the complexity of the corruption phenomenon and the variety of possible causes. Limiting the scope of the strategies to one aspect alone is therefore not useful. In most cases, corruption is not an individual problem but an organisational problem. Approaches that only aim at removing the rotten apple from the barrel therefore cannot be successful. Ideally what is required is an approach that aims at the barrel, rather than just the apple (Punch, 1994, pp. 19-45).

For this reason we suggest that anti-corruption strategies that aim at structural results should be focused on as many causes as possible and should therefore always be multidisciplinary and integrated. As a consequence it is necessary to have both

---

[3] These relations sometimes went very far. We found examples where the controller was being asked to be the godfather of the farmer's son and where controller and farmer had joint holidays abroad (De Ruyver, Bullens, Vander Beken and Siron, 1999, p. 176).

repressive and preventive strategies in the project (De Ruyver, Bullens, Vander Beken, Siron, 1999, pp. 221-282; Savona, 1995, p. 23). The purely individual punishment of corruption is just a matter of the last stage of the corruption process and comes too late anyway. Besides, in such a manner the level of purely fighting the symptoms is never exceeded in any way and the deeper structural causes remain untouched (Anechiarico & Jacobs, 1996, p. 207).

2.3. Anti-corruption strategies as a general policy issue

The meat sector case study showed that anti-corruption strategies are not only useful for one sector, but should be supported by a general anti-corruption policy. For this reason the Minister of Justice asked for a new study to get recommendations about the way to develop a general anti-corruption policy for Belgium. This research, which also addressed the problem of the actors involved in the anti-corruption policy (the anti-corruption services), was carried out by our group in 1999 (Vander Beken, Carion, De Ruyver, 1999). Most of the conclusions where accepted and cited in the government's *Federal Safety and Detention Plan* of 2000.

The starting point of the study was the same as in previous research. Corruption is to be seen as a complex phenomenon of which the causes are situated at different levels. Because the problem broadly exceeds criminal law but should, nevertheless, be dealt with within one coherent policy, it is essential to develop these strategies in a multidisciplinary and integrated manner. This implies that within a general anti-corruption project at least as much attention should be paid to prevention as to repression.

3. The advantage of a multi-disciplinary approach for detection and investigation

Although the detection and investigation of corruption is necessarily situated within the repressive framework, the choice of a multi-disciplinary approach has an impact on that level as well. First, it implies that the detection strategies will not only focus on the criminal act as such, but also extend their scope to the whole corruption process, including corrupt behaviour and "blurring of norms". Secondly, the approach will have consequences on the organisational characteristics of the investigation of corruption since traditional criminal law enforcement bodies cannot cover the whole field and therefore need non-law enforcement partners.

3.1. Detecting corruption in his broadest sense

The understanding that corruption in its penal sense is mostly the result of a whole corruption process implies that it is not useful to focus the detection only at this last phase.

Rather than the traditionally reactive response, a proactive approach is needed in order to be able to detect and understand what is happening. From a strategic point of view this underlines the importance of a good and reliable knowledge base and a comprehensive understanding of the current situation in terms of corruption. However, in most cases this overall picture is not available and there remains a great deal still to be done at national and international levels to develop a methodology to draw that picture in terms of a strategic assessment (Vander Beken, 2001; United Nations, 2000; Amundsen, Sissner, Søreide, 2000).

Given the complexity and breadth of corruption at an aggregate level it is to be recommended that such a strategic analysis must rely on a risk-based methodology by which vulnerable points within the society and the various sectors can be detected, even without knowing if corruption has actually taken place.[4] Such a methodology could list and rank the risk situations and form a reliable tool for detection and the prioritisation of investigation in the same way that the European Union annual report on organised crime needs a better methodological focus.[5]

The idea that corruption is to be seen as a process with the criminal act at the very end also has consequences at the operational level because it points to the need of a very early detection and intervention method. Therefore, a proactive approach by which special investigative techniques can be used is needed.[6] The

---

[4] For a methodology for measuring the threat of organised crime see C. Black, T. Vander Beken & B. De Ruyver, *Measuring Organised Crime in Belgium. A Risk-based Methodology*, Maklu Publishers, Antwerp-Apeldoorn, 2000.

[5] See e.g. *II Forum on the Prevention of Organised Crime* (Council, 9433/00 CRIMORG95, 22 June 2000) and *Forum on the Prevention of Organised Crime*, 18 May 2001. At the European Union Conference *Towards a Knowledge-based Strategy to Prevent Crime* (Sundsvall, 21-23 February 2001) the conclusions of workshops 1 and 2 were formulated as follows: "Risk-based methodologies as developed in Belgium and those already present in industry could contribute to the further development of a European Union Organised Crime Threat Assessment Methodology".

[6] See the Conclusions of the Workshop Integrity and Corruption on the *International Conference on EU and US Strategies in Combating Organised Crime*, Ghent, Belgium, 23-26 January 2001.

present state of affairs, however, shows that the use of these techniques in corruption cases is not allowed in all countries (Siron & Vander Beken, 2001, p. 30).

3.2. Co-operation between different services and partners

The process-based approach to the fight against corruption also has organisational consequences, since an early intervention in the corruption process cannot be done by proactive policing alone but requires the involvement of other partners. Detection of corruption and action to tackle the phenomenon is not purely a police task, but is to be done within the different departments and services on the work floor as well. This implies that the role of disciplinary authorities within both the public and private sectors cannot be underestimated. They are the natural and necessary partners of law enforcement agencies in tackling corruption.[7] A key issue in this debate is the organisation of the relationship between these actors in such a way that they complement each other in a multidisciplinary and integrated approach without denying the specificity of each actor, or indeed spurring unproductive competition. Challenges are especially located in those issues surrounding the organisation of the information flow, as well as issues of professional secrecy, privacy and of course, practicality.

The role of the public, and civil society in more general terms, as a partner in the detection of corruption also merits mention (Transparency International 2000b; Fijnaut, 1993, p. 32; Kwan, 1992, pp. 3-5; De Ruyver, Bullens, Vander Beken, Siron, 1999, p. 230). For instance, changes in cultural attitudes, especially when the public believes in the legitimacy and effectiveness of the anti-corruption project, can significantly alter the ability of authorities to counter corruption. The public can deliver very useful information and data on corruption by informing the relevant authorities, especially when given access and/or incentive (New York Box 100, p. 1; New York 1993, p. 23). Therefore, by way of example, special rules on whistle-blower protection (Council of Europe, 1997; Transparency International, 2000b)

---

[7] The idea that law enforcement and private sector should collaborate in tackling problems relating to organised crime and corruption is explicitly recognised by the European Union by establishing the *Forum on the Prevention of Organised Crime* (first meeting 17/18 May 2001) in which both governmental and private sector representatives are united.

276

can be very useful to facilitate reporting on corruption and to break down codes of silence.[8]

In the study we undertook for the Belgian government about the question of the organisation of the anti-corruption strategies a number of recommendations were made (Vander Beken, Carion, De Ruyver, 1999). Following our recommendations, the Belgian government has opted for a combination of repressive and preventive anti-corruption services. The repressive service is situated within the Federal Police and has an operational and supporting task in the detection and investigation of corruption as defined by the criminal code (Van Heers, 2001, pp. 60-63). The idea of a complementary preventive service is taken up within the reform of the Belgian civil service. A new horizontal federal department is tasked with the control on the budget and the management of all federal departments. Within this service all departments are represented, thus allowing for a multidisciplinary and multi-focussed approach. Time will show if this system will work, if all requirements are fulfilled resulting in all the actors being on the same wavelength, and indeed if a change in both public and international perception and support is achieved.

4. Conclusion

By way of conclusion, we think that a multidisciplinary and integrated approach towards corruption is the best way to tackle it. A broad view of the phenomenon with action at all phases of the corruption process offers far more guarantees than the traditional repressive and purely reactive action to individual offences.

At the strategic level, the need for a good understanding and knowledge of the phenomenon and risk-based strategic analysis was stressed in a way that detection and investigation priorities can be set.

At the operational level early and proactive action is indispensable and requires adequate tools such as special investigative techniques. An early intervention and

---

[8] For comparative research on this issue see e.g. S. Kutnjak Ivkovich & C. Klockars, "Comparing Police Supervisor and Line Officer Opinions about the Code of Silence: The Case of Croatia"; M. Pagon & B. Lobnikar, "Comparing Police Supervisor and Line Officer Opinions about the Code of Silence: The Case of Slovenia", and F. Kremer, "Comparing Police Supervisor and Line Officer Opinions about the Code of Silence: The Case of Hungary", in M. Pagon (ed.), *Policing in Central and Eastern Europe. Ethics, Integrity and Human Rights*, College of Police and Security Studies, Ljubljana, 2000.

detection also implies the involvement of other actors than the traditional law enforcement bodies and the establishment of partnerships with the active participation of various departments, the private sector and the public. And this practical implementation of the multidisciplinary approach is the real challenge for the future.

References

Amundsen, I., T. Sissner & T. Søreide, *Research on Corruption. A Policy Oriented Survey Commissioned by NORAD*, December 2000, www.unifri.ch/pol-wis/ lehre/cours/docsonline cours2andvig_jens_2000_research_on_corruption. E.pdf.

Anechiarico, F. & J. Jacobs, *The Pursuit of Absolute Integrity*, University of Chicago Press, Chicago, 1996.

Belgian Government, *Federaal veiligheids- en detentieplan* (Federal Safety and Security Plan), Brussels, 2000, http://194.7.188.126/justice/index_nl.htm.

Belgian Government, *De brug naar de eenentwintigste eeuw; regeerakkoord* (The Bridge to the 21st Century; Coalition Agreement), Brussels, 1999, http:/ /verhofstadt.fgov.be/policy/brugn03.html.

Belgian House of Representatives, *Parlementair onderzoek naar een structureel beleid met het oog op de bestraffing en de uitroeiing van de mensenhandel* (Parliamentary Enquiry for a Structural Policy on the Punishment and Eradication of Trafficking in Human Beings), 673-7-91/92 BZ, 1994.

Belgian House of Representatives, *Parlementair onderzoek naar de wijze waarop het onderzoek door politie en gerecht werd gevoerd in de zaak* "Dutroux-Nihoul en consorten" (Parliamentary Enquiry into the Way the Investigation was Conducted in the Case "Dutroux-Nihoul and Consorts"), 713/6, 1997-1998.

Belgian House of Representatives, *Subcommissie belast met de opvolging van de problemen inzake fraude in de vleessector. Verslag namens de commissie voor de volksgezondheid, het leefmilieu en de maatschappelijke hernieuwing*, (Subcommission Responsible for Following up the Problems Concerning Fraud in the Meat Sector, Report on Behalf of the Commission for Public Health, the Environment and the Regeneration of Society), 1905/1, 1998-1999.

Belgian Senate, *Parlementaire Commissie van onderzoek naar de georganiseerde criminaliteit in België; eindverslag uitgebracht door de Heren Coveliers en Desmedt* (Parliamentary Enquiry Commission on Organised Crime), 1-326/0, 1998-1999.

Black, C., T. Vander Beken & B. De Ruyver, *Measuring Organised Crime in Belgium. A Risk-based Methodology*, Maklu Publishers, Antwerp-Apeldoorn, 2000.

Council of Europe, *Programme of Action against Corruption*, Part III A, http://www.coe.fr/corrupt/eaction3c.htm, 1997.

De Ruyver, B., F. Bullens, T. Vander Beken & N. Siron, *Anti-corruptiestrategieën. De aanpak van corruptie en beïnvloeding bij de bestrijding van de hormonendelinquentie en de vleesfraude: een case-study* (Anti-Corruption Strategies. The Approach towards Corruption and Influence in the Fight against Hormone-Delinquency and Meat Fraud: a Case Study), Maklu Publishers, Antwerp-Apeldoorn, 1999.

De Ruyver, B., "Tussen wet en werkelijkheid; bespiegelingen over tuchthandhaving en rechtshandhaving" (Between Law and Reality. Reflections on Discipline and Law Enforcement), in F. De Mot (ed.), *Politie en gezag; overheden-controle-tucht*, Politeia, Brussel, 1995, pp. 93-107.

De Ruyver, B., "Annex: Ghent", in Belgian House of Representatives , *Parlementair onderzoek naar een structureel beleid met het oog op de bestraffing en de uitroeiing van de mensenhandel* (Parliamentary Enquiry for a Structural Policy on the Punishment and Eradication of Trafficking in Human Beings), 673-7-91/92 BZ, 1994, pp. 133-203.

De Stoop, C., *Ze zijn zo lief, meneer. Over vrouwenhandelaars, meisjesballetten en de bende van de miljardair* (They're so Nice, Sir. About Traffickers in Women, Girl's Ballets and the Gang of the Billionaire), Kritak, Leuven, 1992.

European Union, *Towards a Knowledge-based Strategy to Prevent Crime*, Sundsvall, 21-23 February 2001.

European Union, *Forum on the Prevention of Organised Crime*, 18 May 2001.

European Union, *II Forum on the Prevention of Organised Crime*, (Council, 9433/00 CRIMORG 95, 22 June 2000)

Fijnaut, C., "Annex: Antwerpen", in Belgian House of Representatives, *Parlementair onderzoek naar een structureel beleid met het oog op de bestraffing en de uitroeiing van de mensenhandel* (Parliamentary Enquiry for a Structural Policy on the Punishment and Eradication of Trafficking in Human Beings), 673-7-91/92 BZ., 1994, pp. 31-132.

Fijnaut, C., *Politiële corruptie in Nederland* (Police Corruption in The Netherlands), Gouda Quint, Arnhem, 1993.

Kremer, F., "Comparing Police Supervisor and Line Officer Opinions about the Code of Silence: The Case of Hungary", in M. Pagon (ed.), *Policing in Central and Eastern Europe. Ethics, Integrity and Human Rights*, College of Police and Security Studies, Ljubljana, 2000, pp. 211-219.

Kutnjak Ivkovich, S. & C. Klockars, "Comparing Police Supervisor and Line Officer Opinions about the Code of Silence. The Case of Croatia", in M. Pagon (ed.), *Policing in Central and Eastern Europe. Ethics, Integrity and Human Rights*, College of Police and Security Studies, Ljubljana, 2000, pp. 183-195.

Kwan, W., *Community Relations and Corruption*, Fifth International Anti-Corruption Conference, 1992.

New York, Department of Investigation, *Box100*, www.ci.nyc.ny.us/html/doi/html/bs100.html.

New York, Department of Investigation, *Report to the Mayor 1990-1993*, New York City, 1993.

Pagon, M. & B. Lobnikar, "Comparing Police Supervisor and Line Officer Opinions about the Code of Silence: The Case of Slovenia", in M. Pagon (ed.), *Policing in Central and Eastern Europe. Ethics, Integrity and Human Rights*, College of Police and Security Studies, Ljubljana, 2000, pp. 197-209.

Punch, M. "Rotten Barrels. Systemic Origins of Corruption", in E. Kolthoff (ed.), *Strategieën voor corruptiebeheersing bij de politie*, Gouda Quint, Arnhem, 1994, pp. 19-45.

Savona, E., "Beyond Criminal Law in Devising Anti-corruption Policies. Lessons from the Italian Experience", *European Journal on Criminal Policy and Research*, 3, 1995, pp. 21-37.

Siron, N. & T. Vander Beken, "Comparative report", in T. Vander Beken, B. De Ruyver & N. Siron (eds.), *The Organisation of the Fight against Corruption in the Member States and Candidate Countries of the EU*, Maklu Publishers, Antwerp-Apeldoorn, 2001, pp. 13-33.

Timperman, M., "Over de bestrijding van hormonencriminaliteit. Een stand van zaken; of hoe assepoester het muiltje paste maar toch blootsvoets liep" (The Fight against Hormone Delinquency. A State of Affairs; Or How Cinderella Put on the Crystal Slippers but Still Walked Barefoot), *Rechtskundig Weekblad*, 1998-1999, pp. 897-916.

Transparency International, *2000 Corruption Perceptions Index*, www.transparency.de/documents/cip/2000/cpi2000.html, 2000a.

Transparency International, *The TI Source Book*, www. transparency.de/documents /source-book.html, 2000b.

Transparency International, *1999 Corruption Perceptions Index*, www.gwdg.de/ ~uwvw/1999 Data.html, 1999.

Transparency International, *1998 Corruption Perceptions Index*, www.gwdg.de/ uwvw/CPI1998.html, 1998.

Transparency International, *1997 Corruption Perceptions Index*, www.gwdg.de/ uwvw/rank-97.htm, 1997.

United Nations, *Tenth United Nations Congress on the Prevention of Crime and the Treatment of Offenders. Background Paper for the Workshop on Combating Corruption*, Vienna, 10-17 April 2000.

Vander Beken, T., B. De Ruyver & N. Siron (eds.), *The Organisation of the Fight against Corruption in the Member States and Candidate Countries of the EU*, Maklu Publishers, Antwerp-Apeldoorn, 2001.

Vander Beken, T., "General Conclusions and Recommendations", in T. Vander Beken, B. De Ruyver & N. Siron (eds.), *The Organisation of the Fight against Corruption in the Member States and Candidate Countries of the EU*, Maklu Publishers, Antwerp-Apeldoorn, 2001, pp. 409-410.

Vander Beken, T., T. Carion & B. De Ruyver, *Een geïntegreerd anti-corruptie- beleid voor België. Krachtlijnen en actoren*, (An Integrated Anti-Corruption Policy for Belgium. Lines of Force and Actors) Maklu Publishers, Antwerp- Apeldoorn, 1999.

Van Heers, I., "Belgium", in T. Vander Beken, B. De Ruyver & N. Siron (eds.), *The Organisation of the Fight against Corruption in the Member States and Candidate Countries of the EU*, Maklu Publishers, Antwerp-Apeldoorn, 2001, pp. 49-68.

281

CHAPTER 18

Dilemmas of Corruption Control

James Jacobs

1. Introduction

There are surely lessons to be learned from the massive investment the United States has made in fighting corruption, especially since the Watergate scandal in the early 1970s. Because of its resources and politico-legal capacity to implement new laws and policies, the United States can be thought of as a laboratory for policy experimentation in anti-corruption control. Nevertheless, as we shall see, since there has been hardly any evaluation of the United States anti-corruption project, it is difficult to reach confident conclusions about what works and what does not.

Let me summarise the argument at the outset. The Watergate scandal involving President Nixon stimulated an outpouring of outrage about governmental corruption. Corruption became a more salient political issue, so that political opponents sought to define each other as, in one way or another, corrupt, while they themselves claimed to be above reproach in every respect. Our normative expectations for official conduct increased dramatically and perhaps unrealistically. Federal, state and local governments invested heavily in diverse anti-corruption controls.

One consequence has been much more scandal-sensitive politics, whose implications for American democracy are not clear. Another consequence, and the one highlighted in F. Anechiarico's and my book, *The Pursuit of Absolute Integrity* (1996), is that government has become less effective and less efficient because many anti-corruption controls tend to reinforce the pathologies of bureaucracy. What we have tried to show is that corruption controls entail costs, and that, in some cases, these costs outweigh any benefits as measured by reduced corruption. The challenge, of course, is to find the optimal type and amount of corruption controls; as we shall see, this is no easy task.

Cyrille Fijnaut, Leo Huberts (eds.), *Corruption, Integrity and Law Enforcement*, 283-292
©2002 Kluwer Law International, The Hague. Printed in The Netherlands.

2. The ever-expanding definition of corruption

Ironically, we are the victims of our own moral crusade. Our ambitions in the area of corruption control are constantly increasing. Over the course of the last half century and especially since the Watergate scandal, the concept and definition of corruption has steadily expanded (which, undoubtedly, also has something to do with the 1960s protests against authority and the traditional style of politics). More types of officials' public and private conduct are labelled corrupt. There are more corruption offences on the books (e.g. anti-gratuity laws and conflicts of interest laws), and more expansive interpretations of traditional corruption-type crimes (e.g. the statute on punishing violation of existential right to honest government under mail fraud). The campaign finance laws, in effect, have defined America's traditional interest group politics as corrupt and have turned every political candidate into a potential criminal. In the field of corruption, law, and especially criminal law, is seeking to change mores rather than reinforce them. There is a widening gap between law and reality.

Not only is the official behaviour of government officials under scrutiny, but so is their private, even sexual, behaviour. Evidence of Senator Hart's adultery drove him out of the 1982 presidential election. President Clinton's relationship with Monica Lewinsky led to his impeachment and trial in the United States Senate. Whether Governor George W. Bush experimented with illicit drugs a quarter of a century ago seemed at times to be the most important "issue" in the 2000 presidential campaign. American politicians and top administrative officials must now be holier than Caesar's wife – over the course of their entire life. President Clinton's White-water land deal was the subject of investigation throughout his presidency even though the events in question took place more than fifteen years before he became President. According to the anti-corruption standards of the times, there must be no instances of drug use, adultery, cheating, campaign donations or expenditures and especially dubious investments and financial deals at any time over one's entire life. Given such unrealistic expectations of public and private conduct, it is fairly easy to expose public officials as flawed, tainted, and corrupt.

All sorts of corruption controls have become popular since Watergate. In the area of public contracting, we have widespread "reform" in the guise of the lowest responsible bidder system. In the personnel sphere, there are laws and rules outlawing patronage appointments (i.e. appointing people to public position on the basis of personal or political ties), and promoting whistle-blowing (reporting the wrongdoing of colleagues and superiors). In the field of administration, complex accounting procedures, comprehensive audits, and inspectors general have been set in motion. Corruption has become a much higher priority for law enforcement agencies. In the United States, federal investigation and prosecution of state and local public officials has become routine.

3. The disadvantages of corruption politics

It is generally recognised that a corrupt political system leads to a dispirited and alienated citizenry and to all sorts of inefficiencies and distortions in government operations and services. But ironically a political system that is hypersensitive to corruption can produce the same results. Our anti-corruption wars have not improved the peoples' confidence in government or politicians. We often hear that "all politicians are corrupt" or that "the system of campaign donations makes the whole political system corrupt". The consequence may be that a large percentage of the citizenry becomes disaffected from political life and views the government as contemptible. This is a problem even in stable democracies like the United States, where voter turnout is very low, and suspicion of government increases. It becomes harder to recruit capable people into government service because government service is not respected and some prospective appointees fear unfairly becoming the targets of special prosecutors and congressional inquiries. Weak support for government means insufficient support for competitive government salaries; again, recruitment and retention suffers. Under such conditions, it is hard for the government to mobilise support for important social initiatives.

Countries going through a political transition from dictatorship to democracy may be especially vulnerable to too much corruption and too much anti-corruption ideology. Where "getting ahead" has long been seen as suspect, successful people may immediately be suspected of being corrupt. If a large segment of the population defines the governors and the government as corrupt and illegitimate, they may be receptive to demagogues and extremists. There is also the danger that corruption becomes an excuse for foreign governments and banks not to invest in a developing nation, and an excuse for putting off or cancelling much needed political and economic steps. The point is that an expansive definition of corruption, that leads to labelling of many or most government officials and government programs as corrupt, may well undermine democracy while having little impact on reducing hard core corruption.

Obviously, the Watergate investigations weakened the United States government severely, at least at the time. Indeed, for many months the Nixon administration could hardly act at all. There was certainly no possibility of implementing legislative or foreign policy initiatives. It could perhaps be argued that the Watergate scandal strengthened democracy and the national government in the long run. But did it?

Or did it lead to a scandal "pay-back" politics, whereby every future President's life, in and out of office, would be scrutinised for moral flaws which, when found, would undermine the legitimacy of his administration? Clearly the long investigation into possible corruption by President Clinton in the so-called Whitewater development weakened his presidency. And the exposure of sexual immorality almost destroyed it. For many months the United States government was paralysed.

4. The costs of the anti-corruption project

Corruption is not just a crime problem, it is a political and public administration problem. A corruption scandal can trigger a political and governmental crisis. It can topple governments even in stable democratic countries. Good government groups, the media, and the political opposition demand that governmental units do all in their power to prevent corruption, and they hold high officials responsible for corruption that occurs on their watch. At the height of our intolerance for corruption, any amount of corruption is considered unacceptable, a blight on the record of the administration, the agency, and managers up and down the chain of command. Lately, "zero tolerance" has become a slogan associated with "quality of life" policing in New York City and elsewhere. It indicates increased attention to low-level offences that might have escaped much if any attention before. But no one really expects that disorderly street behaviour will be reduced to zero; no one will hold the police department responsible if some instances of disorderly street behaviour occur; nor will the police department go through a public hand-wringing and catharsis if it appears that street prostitution, public drunkenness or graffiti still take place. To take another example, the police department and the department of transportation may launch a multi-faceted campaign to "stop drunk driving", but they will not be excoriated when it turns out that some drunk driving continues or even if drunk driving remains unaffected by the campaign. More likely it will be the drunk drivers who are vilified for their anti-social personalities and weakness for drink.

4.1. Goal extravagancy

Compared with other crime control initiatives, anti-corruption control is far more extravagant in its public goals. Publicly, at least, the chief executive has to be committed to zero tolerance. It is not enough to promise to punish corruption when it comes to light; it is necessary to demonstrate that precautions have been taken and strategies adopted to prevent any corruption from occurring. We are ideologically committed to corruption-free government. Any amount of corruption, even the appearance of corruption is unacceptable. Policymakers have to promise far more than can be delivered. They thereby set themselves up for powerful criticism and cynicism if any corruption comes to light on their watch. Ironically, greater commitment to preventing and punishing corruption has not been accompanied by greater public confidence in government integrity. On the contrary, the expansion of the concept of corruption, greater sensitivity to ethics in government, more hearings, investigations and prosecutions has been accompanied by declining public confidence in the integrity of governmental officials.

4.2. Ratio of resources

Because the political costs of corruption can be so high, there is great deal of attention paid to prevention, or at least to the appearance of prevention. Indeed, when it comes to corruption control, the ratio of resources spent on prevention to the resources spent on punishment is probably higher than for other crimes. Thus, unlike most other crimes, government is expected to change the way it does business in order to prevent corruption. Hence, the emergence of an entire panoply of prevention strategies – ranging from procurement and contracting regimes, to the inspector general movement, to accounting systems and corruption vulnerability audits. Preventing corruption can become an end in itself so that a corruption-free administration is a successful administration, never mind whether important socio-economic and diplomatic problems have been addressed.

It is the thesis of Anechiarico's and my book that the structure and operation of government at the federal, state and local levels can be significantly accounted for by layers of anti-corruption reforms that have usually been put in place after corruption scandals. Take, for example, such staples of government and governing as civil service, procurement and contracting rules; conflict of interest codes and financial disclosure rules; inspector general systems; accounting and auditing programs; and whistle-blower protections; or such strategies as agency reorganisations; dividing authority; structuring multiple oversights; frequently moving personnel around; and undercover integrity testing.

4.3. Consequences for effectiveness and efficiency

The problem is that these administrative anti-corruption strategies all entail costs varying, of course, on how they are implemented. The important point is to question the assumption that every administrative "reform" undertaken in the name of attacking corruption, also serves the purpose of more effective and efficient government. This is simply not true.

Consider civil service. It was originally seen as a remedy for nepotism and sale of office. Those who promoted civil service also considered it compatible with, if not a requirement for, governmental efficiency. They did not recognise any trade-offs between corruption control and efficiency. Over the years, civil service has become a general anti-corruption palliative. If some civil service protection was good, more was better. Non-civil service appointments came to be seen as corrupt. And civil service protections have been extended beyond hiring decisions to promotions and demotions.

Only recently have the dysfunctions of civil service been taken seriously. In many governmental units, agency heads cannot easily recruit, promote or demote their subordinates. They lack both punishments and rewards to motivate the men and women who work for them. Excellent performance cannot be rewarded. Mediocre or even unsatisfactory performance cannot be penalised. The result is inefficiency and even paralysis.

To take another example, consider government contracting. The lowest responsible bidding (LRB) system is meant to prevent government officials from awarding contracts on the basis of favouritism, including personal financial interests. Any other procurement system is considered suspect and potentially corrupt. But the consequence of a slavish adherence to the LRB system has produced a procurement system that neither saves money nor prevents fraud. The whole process is often tied up in incredibly time-consuming procedures. Under a strict version of the LRB system, in awarding a contract the government procurer cannot take account of the contractor's past performance on public or private contracts; the only question is whether the contractor's bid is lowest. It does not matter that a contractor did an excellent job in the past; no favouritism can be shown him. True, a hideous previous performance may be enough to label the contractor "non-responsible", but it takes fortitude to trigger the procedures that might produce such a determination. At a minimum it takes a great deal of time and effort to have a bidder disqualified. The LRB system puts government agencies at arm's length from their contractors. The government agency does not enjoy a long-term relationship of confidence with its contractors as is the case with many private sector companies which develop relationships of trust and confidence with their contractors. Such relationships would be considered suspect and potentially corrupt in the public sector.

Unfortunately, the LRB system has stimulated a different kind of corruption. At least in New York City, contractors tend to bid low and then increase the value of the contract by manipulating change orders, sometimes fraudulently, from harried government contract managers. The final cost of the contract may amount to several times the bid price. Anechiarico and I found that many New York City government officials suspected all private contractors who bid on government contracts to be potential criminals. Obviously, such a situation undermines effective and responsive government.

Whistle-blowing protections which became popular after the Watergate scandal also illustrate how the anti-corruption project imposes costs on public administration. Perhaps the encouragement provided to whistle-blowers by protecting them from negative personnel actions stimulates reporting of agency corruption and thereby deters such corruption, but this is only a perhaps. I know of no evidence. However, a proper evaluation of whistle-blowing reforms would have to consider possible costs on public administration. For one thing, some whistle-blower protection laws almost presume that government managers will not handle corruption charges properly and, worse, will punish employees who make such charges. This certainly doesn't enhance the status of public managers or their morale. For another thing, encouraging whistle-blowing provides a weapon for disgruntled and poorly performing employees to use against their supervisors. An employee with a grudge against a supervisor or an apprehension of being fired may file a bogus corruption charge and thereby trigger whistle-blower protections for himself. Once recognised as a whistle-blower, an employee is untouchable. He or she may remain on the job for months and even years while the case is being investigated. His or her continued presence in an agency whose director wished to fire him or her illustrates the impotence of the agency head. Should the outside investigators conclude that a negative personnel action against a whistle-blower was improper and must be reversed, the authority of the government manager may be seriously undermined.

5. Trade-off: the reduction of corruption

Anti-corruption controls can and do have costs for public administration. The question that must be asked is whether those costs are worth bearing. Isn't it reasonable to pay a price to reduce corruption? Obviously, the answer is "yes". It is worth some decrease in efficiency to reduce the amount of corruption. The question we now must turn to is: how much corruption is reduced by various corruption controls?

Unfortunately, there is an insuperable obstacle to answering this question: we do not know whether a particular anti-corruption strategy, or spate of strategies, is "working". Unlike almost all other crimes, we have no data whatsoever on the official corruption rate. How much corruption is there? Is the rate rising or falling? Is there more corruption now than in previous decades? Is there more corruption in one city than in another, in one department than in another? Has corruption decreased after implementation of a set of managerial reforms? Corruption cannot be estimated through the Uniform Crime Reports, based on crimes reported to the police, nor through the National Victim Survey, based upon interviews with a national sample of individuals. It is hard to think of any other crime which so lacks an indicator of prevalence. For example, some estimate of the level of drug trafficking can be obtained by surveys of high school students and others, drug testing of arrestees, drug seizures by customs officials and police, and changes in retail price. There are no similar or comparable indices of corruption.

Very little thought has been given to how to measure corruption or how to construct an offence rate. For example, should corruption be measured by the percentage of officials who have engaged in any corrupt act in a year, decade, or over their careers? Would a better measure be the percentage of official transactions involving corruption? Or the amount of money involved in corrupt events as a proportion of an individual's, agency's or governmental unit's total budget?

Not only do the conceptual and practical problems inherent in assessing the amount of corruption seem insuperable, politicians and government officials have strong disincentives to undertake honest evaluation. The ideal position for an agency official operation in a country or jurisdiction where there is a great deal of concern about corruption is to have all sorts of anti-corruption strategies in place and to have no instances of corruption revealed. Revelations of corruption may subject the administrator to criticism for tolerating it. An agency might be engulfed for weeks or months in a scandal, thereby jeopardising its provision of goods or services. Whether the official could have prevented it or not, he or she may become the scapegoat, i.e. held responsible for the scandal and fired (even prosecuted) to assuage media criticism and public anger.

The point is that we should not assume that administrative prevention strategies, instituted in the name of corruption control, actually limit or reduce corruption. It is precisely those New York City agencies with the most anti-corruption controls that have the most corruption scandals. Of course, this does not mean that corruption controls cause corruption, or that corruption controls have no effect on corruption. Since we do not know the underlying incidence of corruption, no such conclusion can be drawn. Still, our study should serve to caution scholars and policy analysts against drawing the conclusion that highly visible and touted corruption controls mean that there is less corruption.

6. Optimal corruption control

As odd as it may at first sound, there must be an *optimal* amount of corruption, i.e. an amount such that the costs of any further reduction would outweigh the benefits. This truism reminds us that the goal of public administration cannot be the total elimination of corruption. Instead, the goal must be to identify:

1. The most costly types of corruption;

2. The most cost-effective anti-corruption strategies.

Not all corruption is equally damaging, and various types of corruption are damaging in different ways. Some corrupt acts merely impose financial costs, while others undermine democratic institutions. I would suggest that judicial corruption (the sale and purchase of justice) is extremely deleterious for a democracy because it fundamentally undermines the rule of law. Likewise, election fraud directly undermines the legitimacy of the political regime. Certain types of conflicts of interest and patronage may be at the other end of the continuum. Government service may still be well provided, even if it is provided by firms and individuals with ties to the party and people in power. It also seems likely that corruption by high-level officials, who are closely associated with the functioning and therefore the legitimacy of the state, is far more deleterious than corruption by low-level functionaries. In any event, we need to generate and test, as best we can, hypotheses like this.

Not all corruption controls are equally efficacious in preventing corruption, nor equal in their impact on bureaucracy and public administration. The problem is that, even in the United States, we do not know, for example, to what extent certain personnel assignment strategies (e.g. frequent rotation of personnel through assignments), accounting procedures, contracting rules, and whistle-blower protections have succeeded or failed in preventing corruption.

We have a better chance of finding out which corruption controls take the largest toll on efficiency. I would hypothesise that accounting procedures and auditing would likely have the most potential for promoting both governmental efficiency and corruption control. It is hard to imagine that an agency could run efficiently without having in-place financial controls that allow officials to determine how much is being spent, by whom and for what. Of course, "accounting and auditing" are not self-defining terms. In some agencies, accounting and auditing aimed at corruption control rather than at informed management have become burdensome and costly for administrators.

7. Conclusion

For generations we have implemented anti-corruption strategies without any effort or even hope of determining whether the strategies worked. Perhaps the whole point of the exercise is to assuage public resentment, to provide political cover, and to demonstrate that public officials have proper values. If no further scandal occurs in the short term, the political elite implementing the reforms can take credit. If another scandal occurs, the political elite can at least claim that previous anti-corruption recommendations had been followed and that everything possible was done to prevent a recurrence.

Every major corruption scandal has produced new anti-corruption mechanisms and procedures. At the time, these "reforms" are devised and implemented to satisfy the political demands of scandal politics, without much, if any, regard for their impact upon public administration. Wide ranging rules on conflicts of interest, financial disclosure, "revolving door-ism" are good examples. They may provide political cover, but at the cost of discouraging good people from entering or remaining in government. In certain circumstances we end up with both a corruption problem and a corruption control problem.

This essay is not a brief for doing nothing about corruption. It is a brief for taking corruption control very seriously, indeed for treating corruption control as a science. At present there is no "off the shelf" package of corruption controls that, simply by being sprinkled around a corrupt agency, can make corruption disappear while improving the quality of government services. Practically all corruption controls involve costs and trade-offs. Therefore, they should carry the label "use with caution".

Reference

This essay draws heavily on the research and ideas developed in F. Anechiarico and J. Jacobs, *The Pursuit of Absolute Integrity: How Corruption Control Makes Government Ineffective*, University of Chicago Press, Chicago, 1996. The book also contains an extensive bibliography on the United States scholarly literature on corruption and corruption control.

CHAPTER 19

Law Enforcement or a Community-Oriented Strategy Toward Corruption Control

Frank Anechiarico

1. Introduction

Is it possible to control corruption, without the plethora of rules and regulations that grow with each scandal and without the difficulty that this control regime entails for public administration? This chapter argues that it is possible to control corruption without further burdening public administration. In addition, it is argued here that lessons learned by the civil society movement can be applied to the prevention of corruption. The ultimate premise is that democratic government can be made to reinforce integrity, a proposition that runs counter to the conventional wisdom that seeks to separate the people from public administration (Anechiarico & Jacobs, 1996).

2. Law enforcement: the current paradigm in the pursuit of absolute integrity

The most draconian programs around the world are generally held to be successful, having turned broadly corrupt political economies into models of integrity, inside and out – that is, inside the government and between the government and the private sector.[1] The restoration of integrity is in turn held responsible for the enormous

---

[1]   This assessment is made by a former director of the Hong Kong Independent Commission against Corruption, B. de Speville, *Hong Kong Initiatives against Corruption*, Development Centre of the Organisation for Economic Cooperation and Development, Paris, 1992; J. Hsiung, *Hong Kong the Superparadox. Life After Return to China*, St. Martin's Press, New York, 2000. The assessment is supported by Transparency International's

Cyrille Fijnaut, Leo Huberts (eds.), *Corruption, Integrity and Law Enforcement*, 293-306
©2002 Kluwer Law International, The Hague. Printed in The Netherlands.

growth in several locales, such as Hong Kong, as financial and trading centres. This seems to be a story without losers, but it becomes complicated.

The story of the Hong Kong Independent Commission against Corruption (ICAC) is told well elsewhere in this volume. It suffices to say here that the integration of Hong Kong with the Peoples Republic of China challenges the independent nature of that agency and its power as a bulwark against corruption.

More generally, the law enforcement paradigm comes into conflict with the nascent democracy movement in many places around the world that seek to become more open as their governments become more honest.[2] The singular example of Singapore, a relatively closed and honest society, demonstrates the limits of the current paradigm. Singapore also reflects more about its own administrative and political culture than the power of the sanctions it has put in place. The fact is, some populations, though fewer than a decade ago, are willing to accept a limitation of freedom and citizen participation in corruption control, in order to prevent official malfeasance. Accounting for differences in administrative and political culture ought to be relevant to the ranking of integrity published each year by Transparency International, which ranks Singapore highest in Asia, in spite of the cost in openness and democracy. However, Transparency International is only interested in a nation's reputation for integrity and has no way to measure difference in the relationship between citizens and government that are the basis of administrative culture.[3]

Susan Rose-Ackerman (1997, p. 108), a highly respected student of comparative corruption control argues specifically in favour of the law enforcement case, as well, though her qualifications about its long-term viability are worth noting:

"Yet, an independent anticorruption commission is not without problematic aspects. Its widespread powers could be abused in systems less committed to the rule of law. The Hong Kong case indicates that a tough, independent

---

Year 2000 Perceptions Index [www.transparencyinternational.org] which rates Hong Kong second in integrity in Asia only to Singapore, and also by L. Huberts, "Anti-Corruption Strategies. The Hong Kong Model in International Context", *Public Integrity*, II, 2000, pp. 211-228.

2 Section 10 of the ICAC law allows the presumption of guilt from what may be considered excessive material possessions and permits the search of premises for such evidence. See W. Fong, "Hong Kong's Bill of Rights: Two Years On", Faculty of Law, University of Hong Kong, Hong Kong, 1994.

3 *Ibidem.*

anticorruption agency can be a potent tool so long as it represents a credible long-term commitment and includes checks on its ability to be misused for political ends."

There are a number of diverse reasons that the current law enforcement paradigm developed in a variety of countries. If it is possible to generalise, one can say that the professionalisation of public administration began in Europe at the end of the 19th century and spread to the United States and then (often through colonial administration, as in Hong Kong) to parts of industrialised Africa and Asia and the Third World. The basic premise of making public administration professional was to take it out of the hands of non-experts who were, in many places, susceptible to conflicts of interest and basic nepotism; that is giving public jobs and public contracts to relatives and friends or to others as favours. The focus on expertise went hand-in-hand with the prevention of corruption. Even further, the lack of expertise became identified as corrupt in itself. It was only with the code of ethics that accompanied professional practice that the public could be assured of integrity in the delivery of public services – or so it was argued (Hong, 1998).

The ideal is to put the prevention of corruption completely in the hands of an expert executive branch, which is governed by independent overseers. This was the reigning paradigm up until the very recent past, when it became apparent that professional administration was less than democratic and, in many cases, less than efficient.[4] In fact, the worst of both worlds seemed to obtain: administrative in-efficiency and no appreciable reduction in corruption in the most problematic agencies.

The essential paradox of professionalism is pointed out by S. Brint in his historical analysis of the phenomenon. He argues that professionalism started out with a "trustee" mentality in the late 19th and early 20th century. The clear idea was to return to society what it had given to the professional in training and support in a particular field. The ethics of professions follow from this mentality. Integrity was the governor of the *quid pro quo* between professionals and society. However, by the mid-20th century, change began in the professions. Longer training was necessary. Loans needed to be paid back and the entire culture became more aware of material, as opposed to ethical status. Brint labels the current era one of expert professionalism, an atomised, status-driven era that has little training in or use for ethical standards (Brint, 1994).

---

4   "History of the Legislature", http://www.legco.gov.hk – 2 February 2001.

The movement toward professional administration is described as inevitable by historians like W. Nelson (Nelson, 1982). The "scientism" of the mid-19th century along with the moral movement against slavery in the industrial world combined to build an ethic of expert dedication among those providing public services. The natural inheritor of the moral movement behind abolitionism was the civil service movement which was based on the same moral imperatives as its predecessor. As Nelson explains it, the problem with basing public administration on morality was the ambiguity of morality. The first few years of reconstruction after the Civil War in the United States found the federal courts split about the treatment of African-Americans, much less the authority of professional government employees. In brief, no clear ethic emerged from the first era of professional public administration. The resultant compromise was bureaucracy.

Bureaucracy, as we know, develops a series of pathologies over time that make it relatively difficult for professionals to work within an ethical framework. The rule-bound nature of bureaucracy, its strictures on middle management, and erosion of morale all work against the discretion that professionals need to respond to varying situations in an ethical way. The bureaucratic ethic, if such a term can be used, holds that discretion is corruption-inducing and that professionalism is to be tightly controlled. Over time, the conflict between bureaucracy and professionalism drove professionalism, as Brint describes it, out of the public service. The caricature of the civil service comes from this period, generally timed between the two World Wars of the 20th century. The civil servant turns into a mechanical, unfeeling cog in the wheel of the state. Weber's grim description of the "splintering of the soul" caused by bureaucracy is the nadir of this process (Weber, 1962).

In the meantime, corruption continued. Politicians, who were detached from the administrative process, still had their hands on budgetary and a good deal of procurement policy. Further, we must remember that Weber's mechanical description of the bureaucracy was one part of a segmented ideal type. It was seldom found as he described it. In most polities, there were at least some corrupt bureaucrats or at least "fixers" as they were known in New York City: people who knew how to manipulate the system to the advantage of their patrons, friends, and family.

The absorption and then excretion of professionalism from public administration has led to a *democratic vacuum* in governance. At the same time, democratic government seeks the most honest, efficient government possible and also a system of government close to the people. Professionalism achieved, at least initially, one of those goals: an honest and efficient government. However, now that most democratic governments of any size are characterised by bureaucracy, there is little emphasis on either integrity in the way that it was interpreted by professional ethics, nor is there an openness to the public, since bureaucrats tend toward closed systems, in both the public and private spheres.

3. Accountability

A variety of questions is raised by the vacuum of democratic governance: How does this vacuum effect the delivery of government services and the basic functions of planning and budgeting? Do anti-corruption rules reinforce the vacuum? In a recent study, E. Lai notes the growing influence of the People's Republic of China in Hong Kong, in a pessimistic assessment of corruption control in the post-1997 regime there. Lai (1997, p. 735) argues that the political priorities of Bejing bureaucrats will trump the democratic intentions of the ICAC, which is generally considered to be a model of professional corruption control:

> "The greatest potential problem of political integration, as far as the economy is concerned, is probably corruption. The author's concern is that the Chinese Communist Party princelings – the sons and daughters of the high officials in the Chinese Party – will bring with them the business practice of exchanging favors (which is effectively giving and receiving bribes) to get things done, and that the Hong Kong SAR government will not have the authority to restrict such practices, if those involved have connections with the highest officials and influential figures in China. ... It is doubtful that the independent status of the ICAC can be maintained after 1997."

Positive assessment of professional corruption control has become the accepted position internationally, but there are signs that change may be coming. Several political historians argue that an essentially corrupt political culture underlies many "reformed" systems. That while the approach to corruption control has been different, there are signs that the old systems are reemerging in the developed world, emerging nations and in newly democratic Third and former communist nations (Lau). Basically, there are but few examples of national or subnational governments that have managed to maintain corruption control that is both democratic and efficient. Further, in many cases, the controls that are in place are not only inefficient in the prevention of corruption, but often impose control burdens on operating agencies that make the delivery of services inefficient, if not impossible (Lau).

One more point needs to be made about the professionalisation of public administration. In addition to being a response to the corruption of the political party machine, it has often been characterised as a middle-class revolt against proletarian politics in many big cities in the industrial world. This gives too much credit to the machine. A close examination of most of the party machines in American, European and Third World cities, reveals closed systems primarily interested in self-preservation and the sort of self-dealing that made many a small time pol quite rich by knowing where the next road or tunnel was going to be built (Gosnell, 1968; Bryce, 1913).

That leaves us between the devil and the deep blue sea. The machine was justly charged, in many cases, with corruption, while it provided little access to political power to the general public. That is not to say that its welfare function did not play an important role, but to note that the nostalgia for the machine's place in industrial politics may be overplayed. On the other side, newly professional government employees of the late 19th and early 20th century, were purposely disconnected from the public so that the excesses of the supposedly democratic machine would be eliminated. Unfortunately, as noted above, the trusteeship of the new public professionals did not last and, in short order, the hard-won reforms of a century ago turned into the pathologies of bureaucracy. These bureaucracies were both inefficient regarding the delivery of services and ineffective in the eradication of corruption.

4. Corruption control and efficiency in public administration

This chapter will not recommend rapid change in political culture. The results of such attempts in China and elsewhere have been disastrous. However, one of the linkages made during cultural revolutions deserves more dispassionate, rational consideration as a treatment for corruption. That is the linkage between corruption and bureaucracy. The foregoing discussion leads to the proposition that construction and the protection of bureaucratic structures requires the construction of parallel structures to oversee them, and then the use of countermeasures to circumvent the overseers in order to provide services to citizens. As one highly placed informant in New York City put it, "it's more important for me [as a bureaucrat] to look honest than to get anything done, substantively".

In hundreds of interviews with program officials and government bureaucrats that underlie the following conclusions it was quite clear that the law enforcement paradigm was and remains a dominant force in the work of service delivery. A slight infringement of the rules, or a well-meaning but irregular attempt to get a project completed more rapidly is not looked upon kindly by anti-corruption officials. The lack of due process guarantees or basic democratic oversight that has made the law enforcement approach a "success" in the eyes of Transparency International and others, makes it a fearful obstacle in the way of efficient and effective service delivery.

This is not to say that nothing gets done, but many bureaucratic pathologies have come to characterise the current paradigm. Among these pathologies are: decision making delay, overcentralisation, inadequate mid-level authority, defensive management, goal displacement, poor morale, barriers to intergovernmental co-operation, and maladaptive strategies (end-runs) (Anechiarico & Jacobs, 1996).

The interviews establish a basic maxim: corruption control and bureaucracy are mutually dependent. Further, as the two grow in tandem – corruption control supporting bureaucracy and bureaucracy being maintained and legitimised by anti-corruption rules – corruption itself flourishes as a way to by-pass the obstacles presented by these twin structures. J. Jacobs and I also found that in two agencies where controls were most evident and where structures were most bureaucratic – the New York City Police Department and the New York City Department of Buildings – corruption was a regular, endemic part of business (Anechiarico & Jacobs, 1996). The two pathologies that appear to be most significant and comprehensive are goal displacement and maladaptive strategies.

Goal displacement was most succinctly defined by R. Merton as "following the right rules rather than achieving the ultimate goal" (Merton, 1940). It clearly applies to what is found in agencies adhering to the current, rule-bound paradigm. The law enforcement orientation, implying the panoply of sanctions of the criminal justice system, including accusation, arrest, and punishment, is attached to the rule orientation. The rule orientation becomes so important, because potential costs displace the public mission of a given government agency.

In order to make up for this displacement, well-meaning public officials will often attempt to get around the rules in order to deliver effective services or, in many cases, to prevent their agencies from grinding to a halt. As mentioned above, in many cities and large polities characterised by the law enforcement paradigm, there is a person variously known as a "fixer" or "connection" who has the political power to waive rules in order to move key projects ahead and gain prestige or other rewards for the current political administration. "Fixing" or "connecting" comes close to corruption in many cases. It is especially evident in building inspection, where a delay in granting a certificate of occupancy can cost the builder a great deal in payments on an untenanted building. The collapse of so many buildings in Taipei in the wake of the recent earthquake was blamed by review commissions on the connections of building inspectors and owners who were anxious to complete buildings that needed additional work to be safe.[5]

This is not to say that bureaucracy always creates corruption. However, once corruption becomes a political issue, the response of bureaucrats, both executive and legislative, is to create rules and regulations designed to combat malfeasance. These rules and regulations are administered by civil servants who work for bureaucratic organisations. These civil servants become interested, quite naturally, in doing more and better each year, and so the bureaucracy of control grows. At least this is the hypothesis Jacobs and I tested in New York City and which I tested elsewhere in the United States, in The Netherlands, and am in the process of testing in Hong Kong:

- Is the future of corruption control, not less corruption, but more bureaucracy?

- Is democracy a positive or negative influence on the amount and nature of corruption in a particular society?

On the latter point, it is a good idea to be clear about what is meant by democracy. Democracy was widely criticised by the founders of the American system, which is structured not as a democracy, but as a republic (one recently famous aspect of which is that it is an Electoral College, not the majority of the popular vote, that selects the American President). Originally, only white men who were property holders were given the vote. It was not until 1920 that all American women could vote in federal elections. In addition, it was the same era of Progressive reforms that ratified a change in the selection of United States Senators from votes by each state legislature to the majority of the state electorate.[6] So, it might be said that the United States has relative little and relatively tentative experience with democracy. It should also be noted that it was not until 1965 that the United States Voting Rights Act enabled the federal government to oversee state procedures related to minority access to the polls.

A precise definition of democracy must include the express preferences of the populace and their direct involvement in the operations of governance. Preference

---

5   According to the seismic engineering firm, EQE, in San Francisco, many buildings in Taipei and surrounding areas were poorly built for a seismically active area. Basically, no "3rd party review [or dynamic analysis] is required if the building is less than 50 meters" (www.equ.com/revamp/taipei13/html).

6   The election of United States Senators by the state electorate, rather than by state legislatures, had been changing piece-meal up through the 19th and into the 20th century. However, state legislative election of United States Senators was a part of the Constitution of 1789.

and involvement are the two pillars of what is known as the public choice school of political economy (Ostrom, 1987). This approach is recognisable in the community-based movements in many service provision areas in current public administration. Community-based policing, community-based planning, and community involvement in other service areas are centred on citizen preference and involvement and are being used as palliatives for citizen complaints, cost overruns and also corruption.

The basic idea of community-based integrity runs counter to the reforms at the beginning of the 20th century in the United States and elsewhere. As noted above, reformers sought to remove public administration from the reach of the people (and infamous political party machines). The less connection there was between an increasingly professional civil service and the public, the better. Community-based service provision, with its focus on citizen preference and involvement, turns the Progressive ideal on its head and creates a new anti-corruption paradigm. Community-basing argues that the greater the involvement between service providers and service consumers the less likely it is that there will be complaints and the more likely it is that community ethical standards will be upheld. The degree of community scrutiny in genuine community-basing is the equivalent of what Jane Jacobs called "eyes on the street" in describing what kept a neighbourhood safe in a large city (Jacobs, 1961). Empty streets, like isolated, unobserved civil bureaucracies, are prone to danger – in the latter case, that danger is corruption.

5. A new paradigm for corruption control

J. Jacobs and I found much of the "reinventing government" movement appealing, but the movement raised obvious concerns by recommending entrepreneurial bureaucracy without monitors (Osborne & Gaebler, 1992). The idea of an unfettered bureaucracy may seem to be what we are recommending, but we are quite clear about the inadvisability of "reinventing corruption". Is it a case of damned if your do (reform) and damned if you don't? Not, we argue, if community-based corruption control is taken seriously. It has become quite clear that communities that have intensive citizen involvement also have reputations (in some measurable way) for ethical public service.

Many subnational units in the American West and other parts of the industrial world never went through the cycle of corruption and reform that some American cities did. Some of the unreformed cities had the attributes of an oligarchic economy in the early days of the 20th century, but by the 1950s, had become models of what urban reformers were recommending. Many had strong city management that served at the pleasure of a council or legislature. In such a situation, city management makes a big difference. In many such situations the new, more democratic corruption control paradigm requires that each of a polity's departments include methods of citizen evaluation and oversight. Several in the American West turn out to be textbook examples of community-based corruption control and citizen centred service evaluation. Both, it was determined from interviews, seemed to work.

The price of this Elysium, wherever it is found, is intensive training and frequent refresher courses for government employees about how to behave within the organisation of government and how to behave toward citizens. These training sessions are required and are included in job evaluations. In other words, the ethics espoused by a particular government are tied to each employee's paycheck and to his or her potential mobility in the organisation.

6. Back to political culture and its constituent parts

Polities are understood as relatively corrupt or prone to corruption due to what I have called *political culture*. It may be more accurate to split the concept in two and think of political culture as a combination of the traditions that make up *administrative culture* (the traditions and continuing patterns of behaviour that influence the relationship between government and citizens) and also *civic culture* (the tendency of the local populace to become involved in collective decision making).

The two are interrelated. Many cities and other units of government caught in the law enforcement paradigm have an isolated administrative culture, based on a tradition of machine politics, that is matched by a fairly inactive civic culture. In such cities, there are relatively few institutions available to connect individuals. Others, such as those referred to in the American West, are nearly the opposite, with an active and engaged citizenry on the civic side and a receptive civil service on the administrative side, constituting the new paradigm. Many political units like New York City and Hong Kong are a good deal more complex, because of their size. However, in the 1990s, neighbourhoods in both cities were empowered by the creation of community boards that have a degree of review authority over zoning and changes in city law that influence the quality of life in a given area. The community boards and hundreds of not-for-profit organisations in New York and Hong Kong have produced vibrant civic cultures. However, those civic cultures are only occasionally matched by a receptive administrative culture. For example, community policing in New York City has taken a back seat to strategic targeting (called Compstat, a system of enforcement concentration based on computer statistics) that is very aggressive and not favoured by most neighbourhoods where it is employed. Likewise, planning and inspectional service are not overseen by citizens. A ray of hope in New York City is that the Procurement Policy Board, which makes rules for letting contracts in the city, has, on the basis of various critiques, decided to cut by half the rules necessary to contract with the city and to clarify and simplify the rules in order to encourage more competition for city work. Similarly, Hong Kong's ICAC is highly bureaucratic, though it is well-known for its educational function. In each case, the receptivity of government is a measure of democracy.

It is important to note that an uncensored press and a variety of media can keep the lines open between the populace and the government. This is perhaps not optimal, but it is a requisite of the kind of democracy I am taking about here, the kind that brings administrative culture together with civic culture. Civic cultures and administrative structures do not easily change, as Ostrov (2000) puts it in his study of smuggling, it requires a great deal of political will, and the media can generate political will:

"If nothing else, [recent steps to combat corruption] suggest the political will exists to put an end to smuggling – though the odds of achieving long-lasting success are perhaps limited. As corruption is rooted in the monopolistic character of the [PRC] regime, China's government can do little more – short of trans-forming itself – to fight smuggling at its roots."

7. In sum

Those concerned with the procedures by which ethical government is maintained must also be concerned with the manner in which administrative culture and civic culture interrelate. If bureaucracy develops without citizen involvement, even with the best of intentions regarding the reduction of corruption, administrative culture will remain isolated and pathologies will become more evident. If civic culture is not engaged in governance, it will atrophy and encourage either counter-agendas or cynicism. Overall, the most basic research tool in understanding this interrelation is the nature of democracy in a given political economy. The less democracy there is, the more distance there will be between administrative and civic culture. The more democracy there is, the more closely connected the two aspects of political culture will be.

Once again, qualification is necessary. Cynics will dismiss the view of democracy presented here as either Utopian or naïve. It is neither. The civil society movement argues that without recognition and improvement of the connection between citizens and government, the improvement of services is left to chance, to bureaucracy or to both. The qualification is that just as the growth of bureaucracy is the product of drift, inattention and self-dealing, the development of civil society connections is the product of concentrated effort in several areas. A summary of that effort follows[7]:

- *Ongoing discourse concerning significant political questions.* Once an issue comes to closure, it becomes bureaucratic turf, and civic engagement declines. This decline is what has happened to corruption control in the United States. The desire to end a dispute "once and for all" establishes winners and losers, and cuts off discourse. However, ongoing discussion requires continuous adjustment in the allocation of benefits.

- *A coalition-style forum for policy development.* Tocqueville's township is gone, but multiple, conflicting viewpoints should remain legitimate, and the "horizontal" associations that represent them should be affirmed and strengthened by inclusion. The role of the state as generator of citizen engagement in public decision making and as facilitator in private sector disputes creates a broad meeting ground that is neither public nor private.

- *Development of trustee professionalism in public agencies.* The shift toward expert professionalism in the 20th century is considered an obstacle to civic engagement. The limited number of people who involve themselves in corruption prevention is evidence of the expertise considered necessary to enter this field. The trustee model draws on earlier values of collaborative work between citizens and those with specific training in a field.

- *Civic alternatives to public consumerism.* The use of the market model in the design and delivery of public goods shifts definitions of government effectiveness and administrative reform away from broad participation and common enterprise. Non-market models allow for a definition of citizenship based on contribution and ethical values, rather than entrepreneurship.

None of these elements looks very much like much of the world as we find it, which may be why corruption prevention has become either bureaucratic, autocratic

---

[7]   The civic culture elements in this section are adapted from F. Anechiarico, "Administrative Culture and Civil Society", *Administration and Society*, 30, 1998, p. 14.

or ineffective in many places. However, as parts of a new social contract about public integrity, these elements are the basis of a beginning.

References

Anechiarico, F., "Administrative Culture and Civil Society", *Administration and Society*, 30, 1998, pp. 13-34.

Anechiarico, F. & J. Jacobs, *The Pursuit of Absolute Integrity: How Corruption Control Makes Government Ineffective*, University of Chicago Press, Chicago, 1996.

BBC, www.bbc.co.uk: 9 August 2000.

Brint, S., *In an Age of Experts. The Changing Role of Professionals in Politics and Public Life*, Princeton University Press, Princeton, NJ, 1994.

Bryce, J., *The American Commonwealth*, Macmillan, New York, 1913 (new edn.).

Dittmer, L., "Hong Kong Returns to China. The Problem of Corruption", *Asian Journal of Business and Information Systems*, 2, 1997, pp. 53-86.

EQE, www.equ.com/revamp/taipei13/html.

Fong, W., "Hong Kong's Bill of Rights. Two Years On", Faculty of Law, University of Hong Kong, Hong Kong, 1994.

Gosnell, H., *Machine Politics. Chicago Model*, University of Chicago Press, Chicago, 1968 (2nd edn.).

"History of the Legislature", www.legco.gov.hk – 2 February 2001.

Hong, Y.-H., "Communicative Planning Approach Under an Undemocratic System: Hong Kong", Lincoln Institute of Land Policy, Cambridge, 1998.

Hsiung, J., *Hong Kong the Superparadox. Life After Return to China*, St. Martin's Press, New York, 2000.

Hsu, C., "Corruption and Morality in the People's Republic of China", Indiana East Asian Working Papers Series on Language and Politics in Modern China, no. 8 (East Asian Studies Center, Indiana University, Bloomington, Ind, 1996).

Huberts, L., "Anti-Corruption Strategies: The Hong Kong Model in International Context", *Public Integrity*, II, 2000, pp. 211-228.

Jacobs, J., *The Death and Life of Great American Cities*, Vintage Books, New York, 1961.

Lai, E., "The Economic Implications of the Reunification of Hong Kong and China", *Vanderbilt Journal of Transnational Law*, 30, 1997, pp. 735-752.

Lam, J., *The Political Dynamics of Hong Kong Under Chinese Sovereignty*, Nova Science Publishers, Huntington, NY, 2000.

Lau, S., "A Foretaste of Chinese Rule", *Asian Business*, 29, pp. 19-28.

Lu, X., *Cadres and Corruption. The Organization and Involution of the Chinese Communist Party*, Stanford University Press, Stanford, CA, 2000.

Merton, R., "Bureaucratic Structure and Personality", *Social Forces*, 1940, pp. 560-568; reprinted in R. Merton (ed.), *Reader in Bureaucracy*, Free Press, New York, 1952, pp. 362-371.

Nelson, W., *The Roots of American Bureaucracy, 1830-1900*, Harvard University Press, Cambridge, MA, 1982.

Office of the HKSAR in Bejing, http://www.info.gov.hk/bjo/e/zzjg.e.htm: 25 January 2001.

Osborne, D. & E. Gaebler, *Reinventing Government. How the Entrepreneurial Spirit Is Transforming the Public Sector from Schoolhouse to Statehouse, City Hall to the Pentagon*, Addison-Wesley, Reading, MA, 1992.

Ostrom, V., *The Political Theory of a Compound Republic. Designing the American Experiment*, University of Nebraska Press, Lincoln, 1987 (2nd edn.).

Ostrov, B., "The Fight against Smuggling", *The China Business Review*, July/August, 2000, pp. 44-47.

Rose-Ackerman, S., "The Role of the World Bank in Controlling Corruption", *Law and Policy International Business Review*, 29, 1997, pp. 93-114.

De Speville, B., *Hong Kong Initiatives against Corruption*, Development Centre of the Organisation for Economic Co-operation and Development, Paris, 1992.

Transparency International's Year 2000 Perceptions Index, www.transparency international.org.

Weber, M., *Basic Concepts by Max Weber*, Citadel Press, New York, 1962; original text: *Wirtschaft und Gesellschaft*, part III, ch. 6, pp. 650-678.

PART VII

INTERNATIONAL ORGANISATIONS AND CORRUPTION

The United Nations' Approach to Helping Countries Help Themselves by Strengthening Judicial Integrity: a Case Study from Nigeria

Petter Langseth and Oliver Stolpe

1. Background

In response to the growing concern about corruption as a global problem and the need for global solutions, the United Nations Office for Drug Control and Crime Prevention established a Global Programme against Corruption in March 1999.[1] The primary functions of the programme include examining the problems associated with corruption with a view to supporting specific efforts of countries which request assistance in developing anti-corruption strategies and policies, and serving as a forum in which information from different countries can be shared in order to bring an element of international consistency, to allow each country to learn from the successes and failures of other countries, and to support the process of developing a global strategy against corruption that meets the needs of United Nations member states.

The programme employs a systematic process of "action learning" intended to identify best practices and lessons learned through pilot country projects, programme execution and monitoring, periodic country assessments and by conducting a global

---

[1] A series of resolutions of the General Assembly and ECOSOC call upon the Secretary General to take various actions against corruption, including General Assembly Resolutions 51/59, 51/191, 54/128, 55/61 and 55/188. The decision to refer the matter to the United Nations Office for Drug Control and Crime Prevention and the Centre for International Crime Prevention reflects the predominant view of member states that, while the fight against corruption goes beyond the criminal justice field in many aspects, the perception is that most forms of corruption should be seen as crimes for purposes of research, analysis and the development of preventive and reactive countermeasures.

Cyrille Fijnaut, Leo Huberts (eds.), *Corruption, Integrity and Law Enforcement*, 309-334
©2002 Kluwer Law International, The Hague. Printed in The Netherlands.

study on corruption trends. The global study will gather information and analyse and forecast trends about the types, levels, costs, causes and public awareness of corruption around the globe, as well as trends in best practices and anti-corruption policies. Within the programme, attention is also given to institution building, prevention, raising awareness, education, enforcement, anti-corruption legislation, judicial integrity, repatriation of foreign assets derived from corruption, as well as the monitoring and evaluation of these things.

Since its inception, the Programme has seen the endorsement of many member states,[2] and between 1999-2001, the number of countries which participate in or have asked to join the programme increased from five to twenty and the number of active pilot countries has increased from three to seven.[3] Numerous documents have been prepared and made available, including a *United Nations Manual for Anti Corruption Policy* and a *United Nations Anti-Corruption Tool Kit*, and a new internet web page featuring this material and other information about corruption and the fight against it, has been launched.[4] The programme also sponsors or participates in meetings on corruption and where feasible, publishes information about them.[5] A growing area of concern is the need to deal with the problem of assets which have been derived from cases of "grand corruption" and transferred abroad by the offenders.[6] The sums involved are often enormous – in the hundreds of millions, and in some cases billions of dollars – and their recovery is critical both to deterring future abuses and to assisting governments in repairing the social and economic damage done in such cases. In this area, policies against money

---

2 See, for example GA/Res/55/59, annex, "Vienna Declaration on Crime and Justice: Meeting the Challenges of the Twenty-first Century", paragraph 16, in which countries at the Tenth United Nations Congress on the Prevention of Crime and the Treatment of Offenders undertake to consider supporting the programme.

3 As of August 2001, pilot projects were planned or ongoing in Benin, Colombia, Hungary, Lebanon, Nigeria, Romania and South Africa, and others were under consideration for Indonesia, Iran and Uganda.

4 http://www.ODCCP.org/corruption.html

5 For example, expert group on the "Global Programme against Corruption – Implementation Tools", Vienna, 13-14 April 2000 and workshop on integrity in the judiciary, Vienna, 15-16 April 2000. A report on the latter meeting appears on the Global Programme web page.

6 See General Assembly Resolution 55/188 of 20 December 2000 and United Nations Commission for Crime Prevention and Criminal Justice, *Report on the Tenth Session*, E/2001/30, E/CN.15/2001/13, paragraphs 17-24.

laundering and corruption are intertwined, and the United Nations Global Pro-grammes against Money Laundering (GPML) and Corruption (GPAC), are jointly working to develop general policies and specific measures which can assist the countries involved in tracing, identifying and obtaining the return of such assets.

In order for this initiative to be successful a series of crucial lessons which have emerged clearly in the course of the past decade should be internalised by all stakeholders involved. These include:

1. *Economic growth is not enough to reduce poverty.* Unless the levels of corruption in the developing world are reduced significantly there is little hope for sustainable economical, political and social development. There is an increasing consensus that, if left unchecked, corruption will increase poverty and hamper the access by the poor to public services such as education, health and justice. However besides recognising the crucial role of good governance for development, the efforts undertaken so far to actually remedy the situation have been too limited in scope. Curbing systemic corruption will take stronger operational measures, more resources and a longer time horizon than most politicians will admit or can afford. The few success stories, such as Hong Kong or Singapore, demonstrate that the development and maintaining of a functioning integrity system needs both human and financial resources exceeding by far what is currently being spent on anti-corruption efforts in most countries.

2. *Need to balance awareness raising and enforcement.* The past decade has mainly be characterised by an substantive increase of the awareness of the problem. Today we are confronted with a situation where in most countries not a day passes without a political leader claiming to eradicating corruption. However, it increasingly emerges that this increase in the awareness of the general public all too often is not accompanied by adequate and visible enforcement. In various countries this situation has led to growing cynicism and frustration among the general public. At the same time it has become clear that public trust in the government anti-corruption policies is key.

3. *It takes integrity to fight corruption.* As obvious as this might seem, there are countless initiatives that have failed in the past because of the main players not being sufficiently "clean" to withstand the backlash that serious anti-corruption initiatives tend to cause. Any successful anti-corruption effort must be based on integrity and credibility. Where there is no integrity in the very system designed to detect and combat corruption, the risk of detection and punishment to a corrupt regime will not be meaningfully increased. Complainants will likely not come forward if they perceive that reporting corrupt activity exposes them to personal

risk. Corrupt activity flourishes in an environment where intimidating tactics are used to quell, or silence, the public. When the public perceives that its anti-corruption force can not be trusted, the most valuable and efficient detection tool will cease to function. Without the necessary (real and perceived) integrity, national and international "corruption fighters" will be seriously handicapped.

4. *Building integrity and credibility takes time and consistency.* It is fair to say that, in the eyes of the public, most international agencies have not demonstrated sufficient integrity to fight corruption. These agencies have not accepted that integrity and credibility must be earned based upon "walk rather than talk". The true judges of whether or not an agency has integrity and credibility are not the international agencies themselves but rather the public in the recipient country.

5. *There is a need for an integrated approach.* It has emerged clearly that national institutions cannot operate successfully in isolation but there is a need to create partnerships across all sectors and levels of government and civil society in the fight against corruption.

6. *Importance of involving the victims of corruption.* Most donor-supported anti-corruption initiatives primarily involve only the people who are paid to fight corruption. Very few initiatives involve the people suffering from the effects of corruption. It is therefore critical to do more of what Independent Commission against Corruption in Hong Kong has done over the past 25 years. For example, the Independent Commission against Corruption interfaces directly (face-to-face in awareness-raising workshops) with almost 1 percent of the population every year.

7. *Managing public trust.* While Hong Kong has monitored the public's confidence in national anti-corruption agencies annually since 1974, few development agencies and/or member states have access to similar data.[7] The larger question is whether the development agencies, even with access to such data, would know how to improve the trust level between themselves and the people they are supposed to

---

[7] In Hong Kong the trust level is considered critical for the effectiveness of any complaint or whistle-blower measures and is monitored closely. In 1997, 85.7 percent of the public stated that they would be willing to report corruption to ICAC and 66 percent were willing to give their names when reporting corruption. As a result more than 1,400 complaints were filed in 1998, up 20 percent from 1997. See: Richard C. LaMagna, *Changing a Culture of Corruption,* United States Working Group on Organised Crime, 1999.

serve. Another question is whether they would be willing to take the necessary and probably painful action to improve the situation.[8]

8. Money laundering and corruption. Even though these two terms are synonymous, they seem to be treated as different problems. The media frequently links "money laundering" to illicit drug sales, tax evasion, gambling and other criminal activity.[9] While it is hard to know the percentage of illegally gained laundered money attributable directly to corruption, it is certainly sizeable enough to deserve prominent mention. It is crucial to recognise the dire need for an integrated approach in preventing both activities. When we accept the idea that lack of opportunity and deterrence are major factors helping to reduce corruption, it follows that when ill-gotten gains are difficult to hide, the level of deterrence is raised and the risk of corruption is reduced.

9. Identifying and recovering stolen assets is not enough According to the *New York Times*, as much as US$ 1 trillion of criminal proceeds is laundered through banks worldwide each year, with about half of that moved through American banks.[10] In developing countries such as Nigeria, this can be translated into US$ 100 billion stolen by corrupt regimes over the last 15 years.[11] Even if Nigeria, for example, receives the necessary help to recover its stolen assets, does it make sense to put the money back into a corrupt system without trying to first increase the risk, cost and uncertainty to corrupt politicians who will again abuse their power to loot the national treasury?

10. Need for international measures. Quality in government demands that measures be implemented worldwide to identify and deter corruption and all that flows from it. In the United States, attempts are being made to pressure banks to know who its clients are and to monitor the accounts of foreign officials and their business partners. However, the powerful banking industry is blamed for preventing legislative

---

8 Results from "client satisfaction surveys" conducted between multilateral agencies and the public in the past were often so bad that they were given limited circulation and/or ignored.

   Even within the international development agencies the trust level between their own staff and their internal complaints function is rarely monitored.

9 *International Herald Tribune*, 8 February 2001.

10 *New York Times*, 7 February 2001.

11 *Financial Times*, London, 24 July 1999, "Nigeria's stolen money".

measures from becoming law. The good news is that the disease of corruption is getting more attention than ever before. Abuse of power for private gain can only be fought successfully with an international, integrated and holistic approach introducing changes both in the North and the South.

2. United Nations' integrated approach to build integrity to fight corruption

Lessons learned from countries where anti-corruption programmes have been pilot-tested suggest the key to reduced poverty is an approach to development which addresses quality growth, environmental issues, education, health and governance. The element of governance includes, if not low levels of corruption, then the willingness to develop and apply effective anti-corruption strategies. It has been argued that development strategies must be: *inclusive, comprehensive, transparent, non-partisan, evidence-based and impact-oriented*, and the same is true for anti-corruption strategies.[12]

2.1. Inclusive

Including as broad a range of participants or stakeholders as possible raises the expectations of all those involved and increases the likelihood of successful reform. This is true not only for senior officials, politicians and other policymakers, but also for general populations. Bringing otherwise marginalised groups into the strategy empowers them by providing them with a voice and reinforcing the value of their opinions. It also demonstrates that they will have an effect on policy-making, and give a greater sense of ownership for the policies which are developed. In societies where corruption is endemic, it is these individuals who are most often affected by corruption, and who are most likely to be in a position to take action against it, both in their everyday lives, and by supporting political movements against it.[13]

---

[12] P. Langseth, *Helping Member States Build Integrity to Fight Corruption*, Vienna, 2001.

[13] One example of this is Hong Kong's Independent Commission against Corruption. Over the past 25 years it has conducted workshops involving almost 1% of the population each year. This gives those consulted input, allows policy-makers to gather information, and generally raises popular awareness of the problem of corruption and what individuals can do about it.

The establishment of strategic partnerships has also proven to be valuable, both in bringing key stakeholders into the process and developing direct relationships where they will be the most effective against specific forms of corruption or in implementing specific strategy elements. Examples include strategic partnerships between NGOs and international aid institutions, such as the partnership between the World Bank and Transparency International, which has resulted in excellent national and international anti-corruption awareness raising.

While the need for integration is manifest, the means of achieving it in practice are not as straightforward, and are likely to vary from country to country. A major requirement is the need for the broadest possible participation in identifying problems, developing strategies and strategic elements, and effective communications between those involved once the process of implementation begins. Broad participation in identifying needs can assist in identifying patterns or similarities in different social sectors which might all be addressed using the same approach. Broad participation in developing strategies ensures that the scope of each element is clearly defined, and the responsibility for implementing it is clearly established, but that each participant is also aware of what all of the others are doing and what problems they are likely to encounter.[14] Plans to develop legislation, for example, should also give rise to plans to ensure that law enforcement and prosecutors are prepared to enforce the laws and that they will have the expertise and resources to do so when they are needed. Effective communications between the participants – using regular meetings for example – can then ensure that elements of the strategy are implemented consistently and on a co-ordinated schedule, and can deal with any unforeseen problems which arise during the process.

2.2. Comprehensive

Corruption is a complex, cross cutting, international and dynamic problem which requires comprehensive, transnational and dynamic responses, addressing as many aspects of corruption and as many of the different factors which contribute to it as possible. To be effective, however, these responses must also be integrated with one another into a single, unified anti-corruption strategy (internal integration). Strategies must also be integrated with other factors which are external, such as the broader efforts of each country to bring about such things as the rule of law,

---

[14] United Nations pilot projects have successfully used national integrity systems workshops for this purpose.

sustainable development, political or constitutional reforms, major economic reforms, or major criminal justice reforms. As many aspects of modern corruption have proven to be transnational in nature, external integration increasingly also includes the need for integration between anti-corruption strategies or strategic elements being implemented in different countries.

No single factor causes corruption, but a wide range of factors have been shown as supporting or contributing to it, and in many cases these factors are inter-related in such a way that if one is eliminated, increased activity in another may simply take its place. This requires that anti-corruption strategies be comprehensive, addressing as many different factors at the same time as possible. The bribery of public officials, for example, has been linked to low status and salaries, a lack of effective laws or law-enforcement, sub-cultural values that make it acceptable for applicants to offer bribes and for officials to take them, and a lack of effective transparency and monitoring with respect to the officials' duties and the way they carry them out. Acting against only one of these factors – increasing the severity of bribery offences, for example – is unlikely to produce results unless some or all of the other factors are also addressed. As many aspects of modern corruption have proven to be transnational in nature, external integration increasingly also includes the need for integration between anti-corruption strategies or strategic elements being implemented in different countries. In this context the Centre for International Crime Prevention initiatives are mainly geared towards facilitating the development of the necessary international legal framework. In December 2000 (General Assembly Resolution 55/61) the United Nations recognised the desirability of an effective legal instrument against global corruption and the elaboration of such an instrument began. The mandate was further broadened through General Assembly Resolution 55/188. As a matter of fact, the new instrument will be the first one to address the issue of preventing and combating the transfer of funds of illicit origin as well as of returning such funds. While there have been many developments in international law, the picture remains incomplete. Legal instruments which are binding in nature are not universal or global in their application, and efforts of a global nature are thus far not legally binding.

At the same time the centre is supporting the ratification and implementation of the Convention against Transnational Organised Crime.[15] The convention is principally focused on the activities of "organised criminal groups", but recognises that corruption is in many cases both an instrument and an effect of organised crime activity, and that a significant portion of the corruption associated with organised

---

[15] General Assembly Resolution 55/25, annex, of 15 November 2000.

crime is sufficiently transnational in its nature to warrant the development of several provisions in the convention. It is presently open for signature and ratification, and may achieve the necessary number of ratifications (40) to come into force during 2002 or 2003. In addition to establishing a corruption offence (article 8), the convention also requires the adoption of measures to prevent and combat corruption (article 9). The mandatory corruption offences capture both active and passive corruption: "the promise, offering or giving" as well as "the solicitation or acceptance" of any "undue advantage". In both offences the corrupted person must be a "public official", the advantage conferred must be linked in some way to acting or refraining from acting in the course of official duties, and the advantage may be conferred directly or indirectly.[16] States parties are also required to criminalise participation as an accomplice in these offences. In addition to the mandatory offences, they are also required to consider criminalising the same conduct where the person promising offering or giving the benefit is in one country and the public official who solicits or accepts it is in another. They are also required to consider criminalising other forms of corruption. In cases where the public official involved was involved in a criminal justice system and the corruption was directed at legal proceedings, the convention offence relating to the obstruction of justice would also generally apply.

In addition to the criminalisation requirements, the convention also requires the adoption of additional measures against corruption. The text calls for "legislative, administrative or other effective measures to promote integrity and to prevent, detect and punish the corruption of public officials". It does not specify details of the measures to be adopted, but does require further measures to ensure that officials take effective action, including ensuring that the appropriate authorities possess sufficient independence to deter inappropriate influences on them.

Other convention provisions, notably the articles establishing the money laundering offence and providing for the tracing, seizure and forfeiture of the proceeds of crime may also prove useful in specific corruption cases. The convention requires states parties to adopt, to the greatest extent possible within their domestic legal systems, provisions to enable the confiscation of any proceeds derived from convention offences and any other property used in or destined for use in a convention offence. Courts or other competent authorities must have powers to

---

[16] Article 8, paragraph 4, provides that "public official" includes any person who provides a public service as defined in the domestic law and as applied in the criminal law of the state party concerned. See also *travaux preparatoires* note, A/55/383/Add.1, paragraph 19.

order the disclosure or seizure of bank, financial or commercial records to assist in tracing, and bank secrecy cannot be raised as an obstacle to either the tracing of proceeds of crime or the provision of mutual legal assistance in general. Once proceeds or other property have been confiscated, they can be disposed of in accordance with the domestic laws of the state which has confiscated them, but that state is required to give "priority consideration" to returning them to a requesting party in order to facilitate compensation of victims or return of property to its legitimate owner.[17]

The application of the convention is generally limited to cases which involve an "organised criminal group" and events which are "transnational in nature". This does not apply to the corruption offence itself, which must be enacted by countries in a format which criminalises the specified acts of corruption whether they involve organised crime and transnational aspects, or not. The requirements of transnationality and organised criminal group involvement would have to be met, however, to invoke the various international co-operation requirements in corruption cases.[18] Where these requirements are met, a wide range of assistance and co-operation provisions would apply to assist in investigations and ultimately, to secure the extradition or prosecution of offenders among states which are parties to the convention.[19]

2.3. Transparent

Transparency in government is widely viewed as a necessary condition both to effectively control corruption, and more generally for good governance. Populations should generally have a right to know about the activities of their government to ensure that public opinion and decision-making (e.g. in elections) is well-informed. Such information and understanding is also essential to public ownership of policies

---

[17] Article 14, paragraph 2. The *travaux preparatoires* will also make reference to the use of confiscated assets to cover the costs of assisting and protecting witnesses in organised crime cases. See A/55/383/Add.1, paragraph 25.

[18] A broader standard also applies to mutual legal assistance, which is often needed to establish the involvement of transnational organised crime as a prerequisite of applying other convention provisions.

[19] Where a country does not extradite a fugitive because the individual is one of its nationals, there is an obligation to prosecute the case in the same manner and with the same priority as if it were a domestic case.

which are developed, and this is as true for anti-corruption policies as for any other area of public policy. A lack of transparency with respect to anti-corruption strategies is likely to result in public ignorance when in fact broad enthusiasm and participation is needed. It can also lead to a loss of credibility and the perception that the programmes involved are corrupt or that they do not address elements of government which may have succeeded in avoiding or opting out of any safeguards. In societies where corruption is endemic, this will generally be assumed, effectively creating a presumption against anti-corruption programmes which can only be rebutted by their being clearly free of corruption and by publicly demonstrating this fact. Where transparency does not exist, moreover, popular suspicions may well be justified.

2.4. Non-partisan

The fight against corruption will generally be a long-term effort and is likely to span successive political administrations in most countries. This makes it critical that anti-corruption efforts remain politically neutral, both in their goals and in the way they are administered. Regardless of which political party or group is in power, reducing corruption and improving service delivery to the public should always be a priority. To the extent that anti-corruption efforts cannot be made politically neutral, it is important that transparency and information about the true nature and consequences of corruption are major factors in an anti-corruption strategy, because these generally operate to ensure that corruption is seen as a negative factor in domestic politics. Where corruption is endemic, the popular perception is that individual interests are best served by predicting which political party will hold power and therefore be in a position to reward supporters. A major focus of anti-corruption strategies must be the reversal of this attitude so that the perception is that any political faction which is exposed as corrupt is not acting in the public interest and is therefore unlikely to remain in power for long.

Multi-partisan support for anti-corruption efforts is also important because of the relationship between competition and corruption. Just as competition in the private sector leads companies to resort to bribery to gain advantages in seeking business, competition between political factions can lead participants to resort to political corruption in order obtain or maintain advantages, or to offset real or perceived advantages on the part of other factions. Common problems in this area include the staffing of public-service positions with political supporters to reward them and ensure further support and to influence areas public administration in their favour. Critical public service positions in this context include senior law enforcement, prosecutorial and judicial offices, senior positions in the military or security forces, and officials responsible for the conduct of elections. Similarly, supporters in the private sector may be rewarded (or opponents punished) using the allocation of government spending on goods or services. A major challenge in this regard is distinguishing between legitimate political contributions from individuals or companies to parties or candidates whose policies they support, and contributions made in the belief or expectation that the contributor will obtain a reward or avoid retaliation if the recipient is elected.

2.5. Evidence based

It is important that strategies be based on concrete, valid evidence at all stages, including preliminary assessments of the extent of corruption and need for counter-measures, the setting and periodic reassessment of strategic objectives, and the assessment of whether objectives have been achieved or not. In countries where corruption is seen as endemic, the external gathering or validation of this evidence is often seen as an important factor in the credibility of the evidence, and hence the credibility of strategic plans based on that evidence as well as periodic assessment of progress against corruption. The United Nations Global Programme against Corruption has established a comprehensive country assessment to assist in this process, where such assistance is requested. This includes a review of all available information about relevant factors to establish information as a "base-line" for future comparison and an initial qualitative and quantitative assessment of the forms and general extent of corruption (see below).

Sources of information may vary, but will generally include opinion surveys, interviews with relevant individuals such as officials or members of companies which deal with the government, focus group discussions about the problem of corruption and aspects of the problem or measures against it which may be unique to the country involved, the preparation of case-studies, an assessment of anti-corruption laws and the agencies which are intended to monitor, prevent and/or prosecute corruption cases, and assessments of other key institutions. Also critical is a more general assessment of strengths and weaknesses in civil societies, national cultures or other areas which may be important in the development of a successful and effective anti-corruption strategy. Many factors will vary from country to country, which makes it important that comprehensive country assessments be custom-tailored to each country, and that much of the actual design be done domestically.

Country assessments and other sources of evidence should be used to assess corruption in both qualitative and quantitative terms, considering the full range of corruption-related activities, their effects, and how they operate in the circumstances of each country, the extent and relative prevalence of these activities, as well as the overall extent and impact of corruption in the country as a whole. At the policy-making level, the evidence should then form the basis of the development of anti-corruption strategies and policies. At management levels, the knowledge that evidence will be objectively gathered and assessed should encourage result-oriented management, and a clear understanding of exactly what results are expected. At operational levels, service providers should gain an understanding of what corruption is, how it affects them and what is expected of them in terms of applying anti-corruption policies in their work. The users of the various services should have the same information, so that they come to expect corruption-free services and are prepared and equipped to speak out when this is not the case. The international element in country assessments should serve as a validation of the evidence, a source of objective and independent analysis and reporting, and form the basis for international comparison, the communication of information about problems encountered and solutions developed from one country to another, and the development of a coherent international or global strategy against corruption.

Once anti-corruption strategies are in place, further country assessments should review both actual progress made and the criteria by which progress is defined and assessed. In practical terms, this gives participants at all levels an opportunity to comment, providing valuable feedback about both results and policies, and helping to protect a general sense of ownership and support for the programme. The need for popular participation makes credibility or legitimacy a critical factor in controlling corruption. For this reason, further assessments should consider not only evidence about whether the programme is actually achieving its goals, but about the perceptions of key figures and the general population.

It is important that the process of gathering and assessing evidence be seen as an ongoing process and not a one-time event. One term used to describe this is "action research", which has been described as embracing "principles of participation and reflection, and empowerment and emancipation of groups seeking to improve their social situation".[20] Common among most is the concept of using dialogue between different groups to promote change through a cycle of evaluation, action and further evaluation, as illustrated in Figure 1 below.

---

[20] K. Seymour-Rolls and I. Hughes, "Participatory Action Research: Getting the Job Done", *Action Research Electronic Reader*, University of Sydney, 1995.

Figure 1: Cyclical Research Process[21]

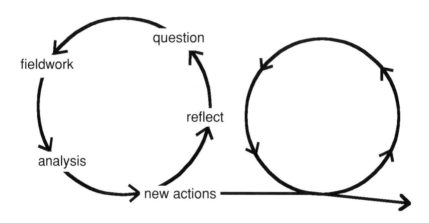

2.6. Impact-oriented

As discussed above, it is critical that clear and realistic goals be set and that all participants in the national strategy be aware of these goals and the status of progress made in achieving them. The complexity of the corruption problem and the difficulty in gathering valid "baseline" and progress data make this difficult, but it is critical. Initial evidence is used to provide the basis for comparison and to set initial goals, while periodic assessments of what has been accomplished monitors progress, identifies areas which may need more attention or a different approach, and supports ongoing revision of the initial goals of the programme. Validated evidence can also play an important role in reforms in other areas. Evidence that corruption is being reduced supports confidence in national economies, for example, and evidence of the nature and consequences of political corruption will lend support to democratisation and similar political reforms.

National anti-corruption strategies involve long-term and wide-ranging policies, and it is essential that planning and philosophy make allowances for periodic

---

[21] Y. Wadsworth, "What is Participatory Action Research?", *Action Research International*, Paper 2, 1998. Available on-line: http://www.scu.edu.au/schools/sawd/ari/ari-wadsworth. html.

monitoring and assessment and for adjustments based on those assessments.[22] The need for such adjustments should not be seen as evidence of failure: indeed, changes are as likely to be triggered by elements which are more successful than expected or which succeed in unexpected ways as by the need to re-think elements which have fallen short of the desired or predicted results. Adjustments may also be triggered or advised by outside information or changes in external circumstances, such as successes achieved in other countries or the development of international agreements or instruments.

In concordance with this approach the project on strengthening judicial integrity will involve a series of different actors at the national, international and sub-national level including the judiciary at the federal and the state level, the International Chief Justices' Leadership Group, the Independent Corrupt Practices and Other Related Offences Commission (ICPC), the victims of corruption, the media, the private sector, the NGOs and the international donor community.

3. The International Judicial Integrity Leadership Group

The Judiciary Integrity and Capacity Project in Nigeria is a result of the successful outcome of the Workshop of the Judicial Group on Strengthening Judicial Integrity, convened by the Centre for International Crime Prevention (Global Programme against Corruption), at its Headquarters in Vienna, in April 2000, in co-operation with Transparency International. It was hosted by the centre in conjunction with the Tenth United Nations Congress on the Prevention of Crime and the Treatment of Offenders. The workshop, in which eight Chief Justices and senior judges from countries of Africa (including the Chief Justice of Nigeria) and Asia participated, was conducted under the chairmanship of former World Court Judge C. Weeramantry, with Justice M. Kirby of Australia acting as rapporteur.[23]

This Judicial Group considered means by which to strengthen the judiciary against corruption and to effect judicial reform across legal systems. The Global Programme against Corruption found this to be most likely to yield the best results in terms of combating judicial corruption. In the view of the authors, some important lessons, which might help overcome the impasse against corruption, were learned in this experience. The unusual partnership, based on mutual trust, exemplified by

---

[22] See below for detailed discussion on monitoring and assessment.

[23] Nigeria, Uganda, Tanzania, South Africa, Sri Lanka, India, Nepal and Bangladesh.

the group, and the self-evaluative and remedial or "indigenous" nature of the recommendations of the justices themselves demarcate the road to progress and future effectiveness in combating judicial corruption. In this regard Centre for International Crime Prevention has found this promising approach to assessment and remedy as a forerunner to the transfer of such judicial know-how among senior judges in different parts of the world.[24] In fact, the insightful and practical recommendations made by the participating justices highlighted the importance of involving senior practitioners of the sector which is a target of reformative action.

In focussing on ways and means by which to strengthen judicial integrity against corruption, the Centre for International Crime Prevention point to the many challenges that should be met. One such challenge has to do with a process that must necessarily involve all stakeholders in order to have ultimate success. Designing and launching such processes would change (mis)perceptions about corruption that might be deeply entrenched in the public consciousness and the political life of a state, yet contrary to the public interest and a great burden to the state. One such misperception is that public figures have license to dispense favours and they are above others before the law.

The group's recommendations provided the overall framework for the Judicial Integrity Promotion Programme:

- Generate reliable court statistics;

- Enhance of case management;

- Reduce court delays;

- Increase judicial control over delays;

- Strengthen interaction with civil society;

- Enhance public confidence in the judiciary;

- Improve terms and conditions of service;

- Counter abuse of discretion;

- Promote merit based judicial appointments;

- Enhance judicial training;

---

[24] The findings and recommendations of the first meeting of justices, documented by M. Kirby, can be accessed on the web page of the Centre (http://www.ODCCP.org/corruption_judiciary.html).

- Develop transparent case assignment system;
- Introduce sentencing guidelines;
- Develop credible and responsive complaints system;
- Refine and enforce code of conduct.

4. Strengthening judicial integrity: case study Nigeria

One component of the Judicial Integrity Promotion Programme is a Project for Strengthening Judicial Integrity and Capacity in Nigeria. It is designed to assist the Nigerian authorities in the re-establishment of the rule of law in the country and to create the necessary preconditions for handling complex court cases in the area of financial crimes and by doing so, to support the development of a functioning institutional anti corruption framework to contribute to the prevention of illegal transfers.

In the absence of an in-depth knowledge of the current capacity and integrity levels within the judiciary and consequently of an evidence-based anti-corruption action plan for the judiciary, this project will focus on supporting the Nigerian judiciary in the action planning, implementation and monitoring process. The pre-conditions for evidence-based planning will be made available through the conduct of capacity and integrity assessments of the criminal justice system in three pilot states including: a desk review of all relevant information regarding corruption in the criminal justice system; face-to-face interviews with judges, lawyers and prosecutors; opinion surveys with court users; an assessment of the rules and regulations disciplining the behaviour of judges; a review of the institutional and organisational framework of the criminal justice system; and the conduct of focus groups.[25]

Based on the outcomes of this assessment, the Centre for International Crime Prevention will assist the judiciary in three pilot states to conduct integrity meetings to develop plans of action focusing on the strengthening of judicial integrity and capacity. Finally, the Centre for International Crime Prevention will support the judiciaries within nine pilot courts across the three pilot states to launch the implementation of the state level actions plans.

---

[25] The assessment of judicial integrity and capacity will be conducted following the recommendations made by the second meeting of Chief Justices on "Strengthening Judicial Integrity" held in February 2001 in Karnataka State, India.

At the end of the project, it is expected that the judiciary, supported by Centre for International Crime Prevention, will have conducted, developed and pilot-tested an evidence-based, impact-oriented, non-partisan, inclusive, transparent and comprehensive National Integrity Strategy and Action Plan for the judiciary forming the basis for a sustainable process of the re-establishment of the rule of law in the country. The political will for change, already existing at the level of the federal Supreme Court, will have been transmitted to the state level and will be supported by a critical mass of judges of all levels.

Different from past initiatives by donor agencies trying to assist in the reform of judiciaries, the Judicial Integrity and Capacity project is characterised by a strong commitment towards maintaining and strengthening judicial independence and at the same time making the judiciary more accountable. It is therefore crucial to note that within the context of all the various components of the programme the judiciary itself, headed by the Chief Justice of the federation, owns and controls the entire planning, implementation and monitoring process.

Even though limited to the judiciary in its immediate scope, the programme takes a wider perspective aiming at the promotion of integrity, efficiency and effectiveness of the entire criminal justice system. It will comprise an exhaustive assessment of the levels, causes types, locations and effects of corruption within the judiciary and provide hereby the basis for an integrated approach to change. At all stages of this process particular attention will be given to the empowerment of the general public and the court users through social control boards and other forms of participatory channels.

The programme, furthermore, focuses on the building of strategic partnerships reaching across institutions and branches of government, the legislative and including representatives of the civil society. In concordance with the action learning process which is applied by Centre for International Crime Prevention in general, the centre will pilot test various measures within three pilot states in nine courts. The outcomes will be collected documented and further cross-fertilised through broad information sharing and dissemination, both at the state and federal levels. At the international level the lessons learned will be analysed by the international Chief Justices' Leadership Group at its future meetings.

In October 2001 the project was launched with the conduct of the First Federal Integrity Meeting for Chief Judges in Abuja, Nigeria. The Chief Judges and senior high-level judges spent two days identifying within the broad framework provided by the International Chief Justices Leadership Group those measures most relevant for Nigerian judiciary.

The process of prioritisation was facilitated by a survey among the participants of the workshop. Out of 55 workshop participants 35 filled out and submitted the questionnaire. Out of the 38 Chief Judges, G. Kalis and other senior judges present, 33 participated. The participants in the survey were asked to prioritise the problem areas identified by the International Judicial Leadership Group at their first meeting in Vienna in April 2000 (see above).

Out of the 17 areas, the participants rated five as "top-priorities". These were court records management, judicial training, public confidence in the judiciary, judicial control over delays caused by litigant lawyers and a merit based system of judicial appointment.

Areas considered by the participants as "high" or "very high" priorities

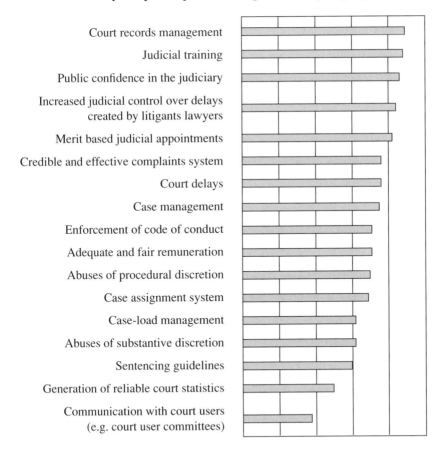

Medium priority was given to the establishment of a credible and effective complaints system, the reduction of court delays in general, the enforcement of the Code of Conduct, the reduction of abuse of procedural discretion and an improved case assignment system. In this context it was interesting to observe that adequate and fair remuneration, one of the generally preferred reform recommendations of most judiciaries in developing countries and countries in transition, was only given medium priority.

Relative low priority was given to improved case load management and the creation of reliable court statistics. Also the abuse of substantive discretion and consequentially the necessity of sentencing guidelines was not seen as a matter of urgency. Astonishingly, by far the lowest priority was given to an improved communication with the court users. There are some doubts whether the question was correctly understood by most of the respondents since at the same time increasing public confidence within the courts was seen as one of the top priorities.

Based on this prioritisation, as well as on the general plenary discussion during this meeting, the judges increasingly focused on identifying measures within the four areas which were considered to be the most neuralgic within the Nigerian justice system:

(i) public access to the courts;

(ii) quality and timeliness of justice;

(iii) public confidence in the judiciary; and

(iv) efficiency, effectiveness and transparency in dealing with public complaints.

Further discussions were conducted in small groups, each of which concentrated on one of the above-mentioned four areas. These groups managed to identify 17 measures that would greatly contribute to the improving the overall situation within those four broad target areas. Also, the groups agreed upon a list of 59 impact indicators, which given the successful implementation of the above measures would show a measurable impact.

The next challenge now consists in translating the consensus reached among the Chief Judges at the national level into concrete action at the court level within three pilot states.

5. Conclusion

Already at this early stage, the integrated approach applied by Centre for International Crime Prevention in the context of its Global Programme against Corruption seems to yield positive results. The integrated approach emphasising key aspect, such as being comprehensive, evidence-based, impact-oriented, transparent, inclusive and non-partisan ensure at each stage of the planning and implementation phase the consistency and sustainability of the process. Also, the approach applied throughout the development and implementation of the Global Programme against Corruption is being transferred to the national level in the context of the action planning process.

As far as the thematic focus of the programme is concerned, there are not only practical reasons for Centre for International Crime Prevention to concentrate on judicial integrity as a niche. Mainly this strategic choice is based on the consideration that any efforts to eradicate corruption within a society are useless unless the very institutions that are designed and expected to protect the individual's rights and to ensure adequate sanctioning of the perpetrators of these rights are either to corrupt and/or inefficient to carry out their institutional mandates.

Among the criminal justice institutions again it is the judiciary that for a variety of reasons needs to be addressed first. The judiciary stands at the summit of the criminal justice process. Where judges are incorruptible and possess the necessary professional skills, no matter how poor the results are that police and prosecutors produce, they will still lead to conviction. On the contrary if police and prosecution are effective but the judiciary is not, cases will be brought to trial, expectations will be raised and ultimately destroyed once the courts do not come up with appropriate convictions because either they lack integrity or capacity. Such a scenario easily leads to frustration within police and prosecution as well as by the general public and ultimately will confirm the view that corruption pays.

Finally, in most countries, the judiciary is the smallest of the criminal justice system institutions. Technical assistance is therefore more likely to have an impact. In particular, integrity and capacity building training can easily target a considerable part of the judges.

References

Anderson, N., *Evidenced-based Planning. The Philosophy and Methods of Sentinel Community Surveillance*, EDI, 1996.

Beckhard, R. & W. Pritchard, *Changing the Essence. The Art of Creating and Leading Fundamental Change in Organisation*, Jossey-Bass Publishers, San Francisco, 1992.

Buscaglia, E., *Comments on Corruption. Proceedings of the Annual World Bank Conference on Economic Development*, The World Bank, Washington, DC, 1997.

Buscaglia, E. & W. Ratliff, "Judicial Reform in Developing Countries. The Neglected Priority", *Annals of the American Academy of Political and Social Sciences*, March 1997, pp. 1-54.

Buscaglia, E., "Judicial Reform in Developing Countries. Its Causes and Economic Consequences", *Esssays in Public Policies*, Stanford University Press, Palo Alto, CA, 2000, pp. 1-24.

Buscaglia, E., Paper Presented at the World Bank Conference on Justice, St. Petersburg, Russia, 3-6 July 2001.

Buscaglia, E., "A Governance-based Analysis of Judicial Corruption: Perceptional vs. Objective indicators", *International Review of Law and Economics,* 2001, pp. 34-45.

Buscaglia, E. & W. Ratliff, *Law and Economics in Developing Countries*, Stanford University Press, Palo Alto, CA, 2001.

Buscaglia, E., *An Analysis of the Causes of Corruption in the Judiciary*, The World Bank, Washington, DC, 2000.

Bryson, J., *Creating and Implementing Your Strategic Plan. A Workbook for Public and Nonprofit Organisations*, Jossey-Bass Publishers, San Francisco, 1996.

Chong, A. & C. Calderón, *Institutional Efficiency and Income Inequality. Cross Country Empirical Evidence*, Mimeograph, World Bank, Washington, DC, 1998.

CIETinternational, *Uganda National Integrity Survey 1998. Final Report*, EDI, World Bank, Washington, DC, 1998.

CIETinternational, *Performance and Perceptions of Health and Agricultural Services in Uganda*, 1995.

Dalziel, M., *Changing Ways. A Practical Tool for Implementing Change within Organisations*, American Management Association, New York, 1988.

Fink, A., *The Survey Kit* (9 vols.), Sage Publications, Thousand Oaks, CA, 1995.

Goerzen, J. (ed.), *Service Delivery Surveys. Applying the Sentinel Community Surveillance Methodology. Country Overviews*, EDI, 1996.

Grindle, M., *Challenging the State. Crisis and Innovation in Latin America and Africa*, Cambridge University Press, Cambridge, 1996.

IRIS, *Governance and the Economy in Africa. Tools for Analysis and Reform of Corruption*, University of Maryland at College Park, 1996.

Kaufmann, D. & C. Grey, "Corruption and Development", *Finance and Development*, 35, 1998, pp. 7-10.

Kaufmann, D., "Corruption. The Facts", *Foreign Policy*, Summer 1997, pp. 134-141.

Klitgaard, R., *Controlling Corruption*, University of California Press, Berkeley, CA, 1988.

Kpundeh, S. & P. Langseth (eds.), *Good Governance for Sustainable Development. Proceedings of a Workshop for Parliamentarians in Kampala, Uganda*, The World Bank, Washington, DC, 1997.

Lai, A.,*Corruption Prevention. A Hong Kong Perspective. Proceedings from the 9th SPAC Conference in Milan*, 19-20 November 1999.

Lai, A., "Building Public Confidence. The Hong Kong Approach", *Forum on Crime and Society* (forthcoming 2002).

Langseth, P., *Value Added of Partnership in the Fight against Corruption*, OECD's Third Annual Meeting of the Anti-Corruption Network of Transition Economies in Europe, Istanbul, 20-23 March 2001.

Langseth, P. & O. Stolpe, "Strengthen the Judiciary against Corruption", *International Yearbook for Judges*, Australia, 2001, pp. 53-71.

Langseth, P., *Integrated vs Quantitative Methods. Lessons Learned*, NORAD's Conference in Oslo, October 2000.

Langseth, P., *International Co-operation. Its Role in Preventing and Combating Corruption*, Conference of Central and East European Countries on Fighting Corruption, Bucharest, 30-31 March 2000.

Langseth, P., *Prevention. An Effective Tool to Reduce Corruption*, ISPAC 1999 Conference on Responding to the Challenge of Corruption, Milan, 19-20 November 1999.

Langseth, P. *et al.*, *Building Integrity to Fight Corruption in Uganda*, Fountain Publishing House, Kampala, Uganda, 1998.

Langseth, P., R. Stapenhurst & J. Pope, *The Role of a National Integrity System in Fighting Corruption*, World Bank, Washington, DC, 1997.

Langseth, P., "How to Fight Corruption on the Ground", *Economic Reform Today*, 2, 1998, pp. 27-30.

Lippit, G., P. Langseth & J. Mossop, *Implementing Organizational Change*, Jossey-Bass Publishers, San Francisco, 1986.

Mauro, P., "Corruption and Growth", *Quarterly Journal of Economics*, 110, 1995, pp. 681-712.

Mauro, P., *Why Worry about Corruption?* International Monetary Fund, Washington, DC, 1997.

Miller, M. & T. Miller, *Citizen Surveys. How to Do Them, How to Use Them, and What They Mean*, ICMA, Boulder, CO, 1991.

National Performance Review Office, Office of the Vice President of the United States, *Putting Customers First. Standards for Serving the American People* (Report of the National Performance Review), Washington, DC, 1994.

Pope; J. & Transparency International, *The TI Sourcebook,* Transparency International, Berlin, 2000.

Pope, J. (ed.), *The TI Source Book*, Transparency International, Berlin, 1996

Pope, J. (ed.), *National Integrity Systems. The TI Source Book*, World Bank, Washington, DC, 1997 (second edition).

Presidential Commission of Inquiry against Corruption, *Report of the Commission on Corruption*, Dar-es-Salaam, 1996.

Presidential Commission of Inquiry against Corruption, *Service Delivery Survey. Corruption in the Police, Judiciary, Revenue, and Lands Services,* Dar es Salaam, 1996.

Rose-Ackerman, S., *Corruption and Development*, Paper prepared for the Annual World Bank Conference on Development Economics, Washington, DC, 30 April – 1 May 1997.

Selener, D., *Participatory Action Research and Social Change*, Cornell Participatory Action Research Network, Cornell University, Ithaca, NY, 1997.

Seligson, M., *Nicaraguans Talk about Corruption*, Unprocessed, 1997.

Smith, S., D. Williams & N. Johnson, *Nurtured by Knowledge. Learning to Do Participatory Action-Research*, The Apex Press, New York, 1997.

Stevens, R., *The Independence of the Judiciary. The View from the Lord Chancellor's Office,* Oxford University Press, Oxford, 1993.

Stone, A., *Listening to Firms. How to Use Firm Level Surveys to Assess Constraints on Private Sector Development*, World Bank Working Paper Series no. 923, World Bank, Washington, DC, 1992.

Urban Institute, *Selected Urban Institute Staff Reports and Publications on Performance Measurement and Program Evaluation*, Urban Institute Press, Washington, DC, 1998.

Wei, S., *How Taxing is International Corruption*, NBER Working Paper no. 6030, 1997.

World Bank, *Helping Countries Combat Corruption. The Role of the World Bank*, World Bank, Washington, DC, 1997a.

World Bank, *World Development Report 1997*, World Bank, Washington, DC, 1997b.

CHAPTER 21

The Fight against Corruption: Substantive Criminal Law Issues in the Organisation for Economic Co-operation and Development Convention

Manfred Möhrenschlager

1. Introduction

After the failure to reach agreement on a United Nations convention at the end of the 1970s (Tiedemann, 1979; Bassiouni, 1995), the Organisation for Economic Co-operation and Development (OECD) took new and ultimately very successful steps over a decade ago, at the initiative of the United States, to fight corruption at an international level (Heidenheimer & Moroff, 2001, p. 945; Korte, 1999, p. 81; Möhrenschlager, 1996, p. 822; Möhrenschlager, 2000; Zagaris & Ohri, 1999, pp. 66-67). An ad hoc Working Group on Bribery in International Business Transactions was established in 1989. It started its work modestly but became more and more ambitious:

- First with a comparative review of national concepts, laws and regulations in different fields, including not only criminal, but also civil, commercial, financial and administrative law areas;

- Secondly with the development of various recommendations in 1994, 1996 and 1997; and

- Thirdly and lastly with the adoption of a convention at the end of 1997, which entered into force on 15 February 1999, a turning point in the international fight against international corruption.[1]

---

[1] Convention on Combating Bribery of Foreign Public Officials in International Business Transactions, adopted by the Negotiating Conference in Paris on 21 November 1997, laid open for signature and signed on 17 December 1997 (reprinted in OECD Document

Cyrille Fijnaut, Leo Huberts (eds.), *Corruption, Integrity and Law Enforcement*, 335-348
©2002 Kluwer Law International, The Hague. Printed in The Netherlands.

In relation to our topic the breakthrough came with the development of so-called "Agreed Common Elements of Criminal Law and Related Measures", included as an annex to the "Revised Recommendations" adopted by the OECD Council in May 1997.[2] At the initiative of France and Germany, who submitted a draft convention in the spring of 1997, the new instrument took the form of a convention in preference to a mere recommendation. Underlying this was the conviction that only a co-ordinated approach on the basis of a binding international agreement can guarantee effective suppression of corruption at the international level. The negotiations in the Working Group and, ultimately, at an international diplomatic conference, included not only the 29 OECD members but also five non-members from South America and Eastern Europe.[3] The new convention has become a great success. Over thirty of the advanced industrialised countries have bound themselves to criminalise and prosecute foreign and international bribery through a new anti-bribery convention. The number of countries involved may increase even further. The convention is open to accession by non-members who become full participants in the OECD Working Group and accept, *inter alia*, the Revised Recommendations of 1997.[4]

DAFFE/IME/BR(97)20 of 8 April 1998, pp. 3 *et seq.*). An important and decisive role for the interpretation of the convention is played by the "Commentaries on the Convention", also adopted on 21 November 1997 (reprinted in the same Document, pp. 12 *et seq.*). An overview of the content together with a comparison with other relevant international conventions and legal instruments is contained in the United Nations document "Existing International Instruments, Recommendations and Other Documents Addressing Corruption – Report of the Secretary General", E/CN.15/2001/3 of 2 April 2001 (United Nations, Economic and Social Council, Commission on Crime Prevention and Criminal Justice, Tenth Session, Vienna, 8-17 May 2001, Item 4 of the provisional agenda), the article by D. Flore (1999), pp. 17, 53-56, the report (in print) of M. Möhrenschlager (1996) and in B. Zagaris & S. Ohri (1999), pp. 68-73.

[2]   Reprinted in OECD document of 8 April 1998, pp. 19-24.

[3]   Namely, Argentina, Brazil, Bulgaria, Chile and Slovakia.

[4]   Such as Slovenia in 2001.

2. Bribery offences of the convention

2.1. Structure of the bribery offence

Although the OECD takes a multifaceted approach to fighting bribery, the main purpose of the new instrument is to prevent and repress bribery in international business transactions by requiring parties to the convention to establish the criminal offence of bribing a foreign or international public official with adequate and effective sanctions against natural and legal persons involved, and to provide for co-operation among the parties to the convention in fighting such crimes.

Bribery is, in sum, defined as the offering, promising or giving of any undue advantage to a foreign public official, in order to influence him in the execution of his duties with the aim of obtaining or retaining an improper advantage in the conduct of international business (article 1, para. 1).

In contrast to other conventions, the OECD convention therefore deals only with so-called "active bribery", i.e. the conduct of the person offering or making the bribe. The term "active bribery", however, has not been inserted to avoid the impression that the briber has to take the initiative and the recipient is only a passive victim. In a number of situations, the recipient takes a more active role himself by inducing or even pressuring the briber.

The convention does not cover "passive bribery", i.e. the conduct of the bribe recipient. In this respect it follows the approach of the Foreign Corrupt Practices Act in the United States, where the legislature in the 1970s was somewhat reluctant to also include the possibility of prosecuting foreign ministers, members of parliament and other foreign and international public officials. It has been pointed out that "pursuing the officials themselves would raise unsolvable jurisdictional issues and open them to the criticism of interfering with the sovereignty of other states" (Sacerdoti, 2000, pp. 29, 34). Another – in my view not wholly convincing – explanation why "passive corruption" is treated less rigorously refers to the fact that "bribed officials would in usual practices not be employees of the OECD signatory governments, but officials of developing countries" (Heidenheimer & Moroff, 2001, p. 948). In the meantime the development has progressed. In principle, the Council of Europe conventions treat the "active" and the "passive" sides equally. The concern raised against such an extension is less convincing, for example, if the bribery occurs in the country which also prosecutes the briber.

The convention covers the main cases of international bribery. It does not cover bribes paid to foreign public officials for purposes other than obtaining or retaining business, or other improper advantage in the conduct of international business. At the level of the OECD, in view of its competence, it would have been difficult to go further. This is different for organisations such as the Organisation of African States, the Council of Europe or the European Union, which have consequently taken a much broader and more general approach.[5] It cannot be ruled out that a future United Nations Convention may go further, too.

As with the United States Foreign Corrupt Practices Act, the convention does not cover bribes paid to private persons, at least not in a comprehensive manner. The competence of the OECD as such would not have excluded an extension in this direction. Trends towards and calls for privatisation of more and more government functions provide a valid argument to address this area much more intensively in future than is the case now – otherwise loopholes could develop and a danger of avoiding international obligations could be created. This will not be an easy task, as the present national situations show. On the one hand, there are countries in which bribery in the private sector or in commercial life is not yet an offence. On the other hand there are a number of countries which apply the same concept to the bribing of public officials as to employees and managers of private companies.

These divergences are reflected at the international level, too. The Council of Europe convention includes a broad provision on bribery in the private sector, but at the same time provides for the possibility of a reservation.[6] The European Union went one step further in a so-called Joint Action with a new provision which has, however, a very limited binding scope due to the need for compromising between different approaches.[7] Nevertheless, the topic of bribery should continue to be included in future discussions at the international level on the development of a comprehensive anti-corruption strategy.

---

[5] Inter-American Convention against Corruption of 29 March 1996 (OAS Convention), articles VI, VII (reprinted in 35 *International Legal Materials* (ILM), 1996, p. 724); Criminal Law Convention on Corruption of the Council of Europe of 27 January 1999 (European Treaty Series no. 173), articles 2-11; Convention on the Fight against Corruption Involving Officials of the European Communities or Officials of the Member States of the European Union of 26 May 1997 (Official Journal of the European Communities no. C 195/1 of 25 June 1997), articles 2 and 3.

[6] Articles 7 and 8.

[7] Joint Action on Corruption in the Private Sector of 22 December 1998 (Official Journal of the European Communities no. L 358/2 of 31 December 1998), articles 2 and 3.

2.2. Elements of the bribery offence (article 1 of the convention)

The offence of bribery can be said to include six basic elements.

1. Following a model in many national legislations all over the world, article 1 of the convention requires not only that the actual giving of a bribe be included in national legislation as an intentional act, but also the preceding act of promising and offering, regardless of whether it is done directly or through an intermediary. Due to this extension there is no obligation to introduce the punishability of the attempt as such, since the act of promising or offering can be regarded as a kind of specific attempt at (or even preparation for) the act of giving. Only where national law already goes further in relation to the bribing of national public officials does an obligation to apply the same concept to the bribing of foreign public officials exist (article 1, para. 2, sentence 2). The discussion at OECD level has shown that there are differences in understanding, especially in the delineation of the acts of "offering" and "promising". That does not matter as long as one-sided acts are included.

2. The subject of the offence is the offering, promising or giving of a "bribe" described in the convention as an "undue pecuniary or other advantage". It therefore covers not only a sum of money or other gifts or services with a monetary value, (i.e. economic, material or tangible advantages), but also advantages of an immaterial or intangible nature, such as sexual favours. Whether the bribe goes to the public official himself or to a third party does not matter. A third party is not only a person close to the public official such as a spouse, relative or friend, but can also include institutions, political parties or even charities. The examinations at OECD level show that in certain countries such an extension – based on court interpretations, for example – is included in the general understanding of the offence even if the "third party" is not expressly mentioned in the text. In Germany, the situation used to be different. In the past, the courts applied a more restrictive interpretation. Therefore the German Parliament decided in 1997 to insert the explicit reference to third parties into the text.[8]

---

8 §§ 331 *et seq.* of the German Criminal Code ("*Strafgesetzbuch*"), as amended by "*Das Gesetz zur Bekämpfung der Korruption*" ("Act to Combat Corruption") of 13 August 1997, *Bundesgesetzblatt*, Teil II (Federal Law Gazette, Part II) no. 58 of 19 August 1997, p. 2038). These provisions are reprinted in English translation in Bundesministerium des Innern (ed.), *Texte zur Korruptionsprävention*, 2000, pp. 99 *et seq.*

3. In the OECD convention, the offence is applicable to the bribery of foreign public officials. This extension is the essence of the whole convention and the real turning point in the fight against international corruption. The conventional approach of national bribery statutes in dealing only with the bribing of national officials has proven to be insufficient. Although the bribed public official could be prosecuted in his home country, there are often insurmountable difficulties in catching the briber, especially if they are foreigners or foreign companies and the crime is committed abroad. In a well-known case of international bribery in Germany which went up to the Federal High Court (*Bundesgerichtshof*) and which involved large-scale bribing of the medical head of a department in a public hospital by an Italian company furnishing parts of heart transplants, only the bribed person could be prosecuted and convicted.[9] Therefore the emphasis of the convention lies on creating the prerequisites for the prosecution of the bribers of foreign public officials. This restriction may be also a consequence of the emphasis in the OECD context on fostering fair international trade relations. It was left to other international organisations to go further in this respect by also covering the area of bribery of national public officials. What is most important in this regard, too, is the inclusion of the bribery of foreign public officials of all (foreign) countries of the world and of all public international organisations (*cf.* article 1, para. 4), which is an extremely ambitious approach and concept. The offence of bribery is therefore not restricted to the bribing of public officials of parties to the convention, as in instruments of the European Union.

The meaning of the term "foreign public official" is laid down in article 1, para. 4 of the convention. In essence it is "any person exercising a public function [i.e. an activity in the public interest] for a foreign country" and "any official or agent of a public [not a private!] international organisation". The convention clearly contains an expansive definition, not only expressly including "any person holding a legislative, administrative or judicial office of a foreign country" but also "any person exercising a public function for a public agency or a public enterprise". The last example is very important, since it also includes even private enterprises (stock corporations, companies with limited liability) over which a government exercises a dominant influence. Therefore, in the case of privatisation, the convention covers at least the area where the private sector is entrusted with public tasks. Due to differences of opinion, party office holders or members of a political party and

---

9   Bundesgerichtshof, Decision of 19 October 1999 of the First Senate, file 1 StR 264/99, reprinted in wistra 2000, p. 22 and in *NStZ* (*Neue Zeitschrift für Strafrecht*) 2000, p. 90.

candidates for public offices were not expressly included, but are still a topic for further discussion.

4. Traditionally, the offence of bribery mostly requires a so-called "*quid pro quo*" agreement or relationship (in Germany this is called an "*Unrechtsvereinbarung*") between the act of bribery (offering, promising or giving) and an at least intended act of the official (in the form of an active act or an omission to act) "in relation to the performance of official duties". Explanations of the convention – the "Commentaries" – show that flexibility is granted for the implementation of the convention.[10] It is expressly stated therein, for example, that the requirements of the convention could be fulfilled by bribing "to induce a breach of the official's duty provided that it was understood that every public official had a duty to exercise judgement or discretion impartially". Therefore, a concept restricting the implementation to cases of breach of duty including influencing discretionary decisions or acts of the public official would be in line with the requirements of the convention. A more restrictive approach along these lines is followed in the instruments of the European Union and can also be taken in the implementation of the Council of Europe convention by way of a reservation.

5. The OECD convention covers only the case where the bribing is done "in order to obtain or retain business or other improper advantage in the conduct of international business". This not limited to the procurement of contracts, but also includes, for example, the obtaining of an operating permit for a factory which fails to meet the statutory requirements. It is irrelevant whether the person or company involved was in fact the best-qualified bidder or could properly have been awarded the business.

6. It is quite clear that it is not a punishable offence if the advantage is *required* by the written law or regulations (including case law) of the foreign public official's country. This covers, for example, the case where the law requires that a certain fee has to be paid for the (legal) official act. In such a case, German courts already deny the element of "advantage". It is also not a punishable offence if the acceptance of the advantage is *permitted* by law. Local custom or tolerance of the acceptance by local authorities is not, of course, sufficient ground for justification. Following the model of the Foreign Corrupt Practices Act, small so-called "facilitation payments", for example, to induce foreign public officials to perform their functions,

---

[10] "Commentaries" (note 1, *supra*), p. 12 no. 3.

shall also be excluded from the scope of the offence. An exception which has, however, led to a certain degree of criticism.[11]

2.3. Sanctions and measures against natural and legal persons (article 2, 3 of the convention)

Each party must establish effective, proportionate and dissuasive criminal penalties, a formula often used by the European Court of Justice in Luxembourg. The range of penalties must be comparable to that applicable to bribery of the party's own public officials. It has to include imprisonment at least as an alternative sanction sufficient to enable extradition. The convention also addresses the liability of legal persons, but only in a very general manner. It is left to the parties to apply the concept of criminal liability or to impose non-criminal sanctions, which, however, must include monetary sanctions. Due to the differences in national legislation – especially between Anglo-American and European continental countries – no effort was made to include details on the prerequisites of the liability of legal persons. Therefore, the convention requires only that the liability of legal persons be established in accordance with its legal principles. However, outside the OECD, the development has gone further. Virtually identical models have been developed in instruments of the European Union and the Council of Europe. It is my understanding that those countries which meet the requirements laid down by these organisations also applicable to the area of corruption are in compliance with the OECD convention.

In addition, each party must make the bribe and the proceeds of the active bribing, including property to a value corresponding to that of such proceeds, subject either to seizure and confiscation or to a part of monetary sanctions (article 3, para. 3).

2.4. Procedural requirements

Article 6 (Statute of Limitations) requires an adequate period of time for the investigation and prosecution of bribery. Such investigation and prosecution, although in general being subject to the internal rules and principles of the party concerned, may nevertheless not be influenced by considerations of national economic interest, the potential effect upon relations with another state or the identity of the natural or legal persons involved (article 5 on enforcement).

---

[11] "Commentaries" (note 1, *supra*), p. 13 no. 9.

2.5. Jurisdiction

The scope of the jurisdiction clause (article 4 and article 10, para. 3 of the convention) was debated at great length in Paris. The real issue was how to establish rules which guarantee the possibility of effective prosecution of international bribery if a national of a party commits the offence abroad. Civil law countries apply the concept of nationality jurisdiction whereas common law countries usually exercise jurisdiction over criminal matters on the basis of the concept of territoriality supplemented by the possibility to extradite their own nationals.

Both concepts are ultimately applied in the convention. To meet criticism of the principle of territoriality its notion was extended with a broad understanding so that it would also apply where the offence is committed only in part in the territory of a party (article 4, para. 1). Countries applying the nationality principle in general have to apply it to the offence of bribing of foreign public officials in the same manner ("according to the same principles"), article 4, para. 2. In addition, each party is obliged either to extradite its nationals or to prosecute them (article 10, para. 3, sentence 1). Civil law countries which do not extradite their own nationals are therefore also obliged to submit the case for the purpose of prosecution by applying the principle of *aut dedere aut iudicare* (article 10, para. 3, sentence 2). Anglo-American countries have the possibility of extradition on the basis of a request.

In the context of an effective prosecution of bribery of foreign public officials, this solution is – from my view point – not wholly satisfactory. Where the principle of territoriality together with the possibility of extradition are applicable, no prosecution and punishment is possible if, for example, no request for extradition is submitted.

Despite the general attractiveness of the nationality principle, it has its weaknesses. If a businessman, being a national of state party A, bribes a public official of state B at a location in state C, the classical requirement of the principle of nationality that the offence is punishable at the place of the commission of the offence may lead to non-prosecution. In most countries which are not parties to the OECD convention, the bribing of a foreign public official is not yet punishable. The requirement of double criminality is not met if only the bribing of a national public official is punishable. Therefore this requirement for a successful prosecution in state A may be missing if a territorial link of the offence to state A or at least to state B cannot be established. If the intended act of the bribed public official is to be executed in the official's home country, however, it might be that in such a case, the offence is considered to be committed in this country, too. Additional problems may arise in countries applying the nationality principle if prosecution is made dependent on a request of the country where the crime has been committed or of the public official's home country.

In the light of these facts, it is not surprising that the convention obliges all parties to "review whether its current basis for jurisdiction is effective in the fight against the bribery of foreign public officials and, if it is not", to take "remedial steps" (article 4, para. 4). Such a reassessment has, for example, led to a governmental proposal in the United Kingdom for the introduction of nationality jurisdiction (in England and Wales).[12] To overcome possible difficulties, some countries, like the United States and Germany, have even introduced the unrestricted nationality principle.[13] The extent to which there is a real danger of an important loophole existing is, however, disputed. It belongs to the horizontal issues which will be examined and reviewed on the basis of practical experiences at OECD level in the future. The problem of introducing even an unrestricted nationality principle does, of course, lose some of its weight if a future United Nations convention including the bribing of foreign public officials is ratified by a large majority of United Nations member countries.

3. Other provisions of the convention – additions related to other areas of criminal law and other legislation

The OECD convention contains additional provisions relating, for example, to criminal law, international co-operation in criminal law, and the law of accounting.

In article 7, it requires that each party that has made active or passive bribery of its own public officials a predicate offence for the purpose of the application of its money laundering legislation shall do so on the same terms for the bribery of foreign public officials. Such an extension is not automatically a consequence of the ratification of the convention, but, if the existing national law does not already cover this situation, it does require an additional legislative act of assimilation. The place where the bribery occurred plays no role in this context. The extension is not restricted to the area of criminal law but also has an impact on the scope of

---

12 Home Office (ed.), *Raising Standards and Upholding Integrity. The Prevention of Corruption*, 2000, pp. 13, 21.

13 15 United States Code §§ 78dd-1 *et seq.*; article 2 § 3 of the *Gesetzes über internationale Bestechung* (Act on Combating International Bribery) of 10 September 1998, *Bundesgesetzblatt*, Teil II (Federal Law Gazette, Part II) no. 37 of 21 September 1998, p. 2327; reprinted in English in *Texte zur Korruptionsprävention* (no. 12), pp. 111 *et seq.*

accompanying non-criminal money laundering legislation, e.g. in relation to reporting obligations.

According to articles 9 and 10, states parties to the OECD convention are committed both to providing mutual legal assistance, which cannot be declined for criminal matters on the grounds of bank secrecy (article 9, para. 3), and to granting extradition in cases of bribery of foreign public officials. If necessary, the convention (article 10, para. 2) provides the legal basis for extradition in respect of an offence of bribery of a foreign public official. Article 9 para. 1 sentence 1 also includes the case of mutual legal assistance in relation to proceedings against a legal person if these are – as in Germany, for example – of a non-criminal nature. Article 9, para. 2 and article 10, para. 4, sentence 2 address the issue of identity of norms in the concept of dual criminality. Where a party makes mutual legal assistance or extradition conditional upon the existence of dual criminality, dual criminality shall be deemed to exist if the offence for which the assistance is sought is within the scope of the convention. Therefore parties with a statute prohibiting the bribery of agents generally and a statute directed specifically at bribery of foreign public officials should be able to co-operate fully regarding cases whose facts fall within the scope of the offences of the convention. Without prejudice to other arrangements between parties, each party must notify an authority or authorities responsible for making and receiving requests (article 11).

Article 8 on accounting supplements section V of the 1997 OECD Recommendations (Accounting Requirements, External Audit and Internal Company Controls). Each party shall take the necessary measures, within the framework of its laws and regulations regarding the maintenance of books and records, financial statement disclosures regarding their material contingent liabilities, and accounting and auditing standards, to prohibit the establishment of off-books accounts, the making of off-book or inadequately identified transactions, the recording of non-existent expenditures, the entry of liabilities with incorrect identification of their object, as well as the use of false documents, by companies subject to those laws and regulations, for the purpose of bribing foreign public officials or of hiding such bribery. To give effect to these obligations (civil, administrative or criminal) sanctions have to be imposed for omissions and falsifications in respect of the books, records, accounts and financial statements of companies (article 8, para. 2).

4. Measures of control and outlook

The Revised Recommendations and the convention represent an ambitious undertaking of the OECD to fight worldwide corruption effectively in the business area together with its members and those countries which are also party to the convention. It has taken on a leading role in the battle against international bribery. This is also true for a strong commitment to regular reviews of steps taken by the OECD and participating countries to monitor and promote the implementation of the recommendation (*cf.* section VIII) and of the convention (article 12). Full implementation is not an easy task as the introduction of the liability of legal persons reveals, for example. For many continental countries this requires basic changes of national concepts built on the classical notion of *societas non delinquere potest*. The first phase of a systematic follow-up monitoring with the examination of the conformity of the implementing legislation with the convention is nearly finished, a result for which the OECD can only be congratulated. The Working Group involved noted that there was overall compliance with the convention's obligations in the great majority of countries. Some specific recommendations for remedial actions were made. Certain "horizontal issues" affecting the implementation need further studies. This process will soon be supplemented by an additional examination (phase 2 of the monitoring), where the emphasis lies on the examination of the parties' structures to enforce the laws and their practical application, including visits to the national judicial and administrative authorities entrusted with the application and enforcement of anti-corruption measures. The results will have an impact on the efficiency and enforcement of other international instruments too, including the future work at the level of the United Nations.

References

Bassiouni, Ch., & E. Wise, *Aut Dedere Aut Iudicare: The Duty to Extradite or Prosecute in International Law*, Martinus Nijhoff, Dordrecht, 1995.

Flore, D., "L'incrimination de la corruption. Les nouveaux instruments internationaux. La nouvelle loi belge du 10 février 1999", in *Dossiers de la Revue Pénal et de Criminologie* 4, 1999.

Heidenheimer, A., & H. Moroff, "Controlling Business Payoffs to Foreign Officials: The 1998 OECD Anti-Bribery Convention", in A. Heidenheimer & M. Johnston (eds.), *Political Corruption. Concepts and Context*, Transaction Publishers, New Brunswick, NJ, 2001.

Korte, B., *Der Einsatz des Strafrechts zur Bekämpfung der internationalen Korruption*, wistra, 1999.

Möhrenschlager, M., "Strafrechtliche Vorhaben zur Bekämpfung der Korruption auf nationaler und internationaler Ebene", *Juristenzeitung*, 1996.

Möhrenschlager, M., "Die Bekämpfung der Korruption auf internationaler Ebene" in *Deutsch/Brasilianische Juristenvereinigung*, Jahrestagung 2000 (in print).

Sacerdoti, G., "To Bribe or not to Bribe?", in OECD (ed.), *No Longer Business as Usual*, Paris, 2000.

Tiedemann, K., *Multinationale Unternehmen und Strafrecht*, Carl Heymanns Verlag, Cologne, 1979.

Zagaris, B., & S. Ohri, "The Emergence of an International Enforcement Regime on Transnational Corruption in the Americas", *Law and Policy in International Business*, 30, 1999.

CHAPTER 22

How to Make a Convention Work: the Organisation for Economic Co-operation and Development Recommendation and Convention on Bribery as an Example of a New Horizon in International Law

Gemma Aiolfi & Mark Pieth

1. Introduction

The corruption of one person by another is as old as human nature itself, and efforts to regulate its perpetration by individuals, governments and industry span the centuries. In very recent years the fight against its deleterious effects have taken on a dynamism hardly credible a decade ago. This accomplishment is particularly apparent in the Organisation for Economic Co-operation and Development (OECD) initiative against bribery in international business transactions which culminated in the recommendation and convention of 1997. The path leading to these instruments became something of a high speed track during its evolution with several interesting – and unique – features en route to the final instruments. The first part of this chapter will describe this journey and examine how this convention has developed bite. The second part outlines the latest developments that complement international law with a review of recent initiatives taken by key industries in their efforts to take a proactive stance on the issue of bribery and corruption within their particular spheres of influence.

2. The OECD revised recommendation and convention

The OECD initiative against bribery in international business transactions developed out of the pledge by industrialised nations (representing around 70% of world exports and 90% of foreign direct investment worldwide) to combat the *supply side* of bribery. The approach is aimed at reducing the influx of corrupt payments

Cyrille Fijnaut, Leo Huberts (eds.), *Corruption, Integrity and Law Enforcement*, 349-360
©2002 Kluwer Law International, The Hague. Printed in The Netherlands.

into relevant markets by sanctioning the active bribers and their accomplices as well as by providing for a preventive framework. It is dependent upon other action being taken from the demand side and it is in a sense a narrow approach and unilateral – albeit collectively unilateral. The concepts also apply to the bribery of officials of non-participatory countries. One of the motivational aspects of the OECD approach is the recognition (in the preamble to the convention) that bribery distorts international competitive conditions. The aim of creating a level playing field for commerce backed by tough supervision, may in its turn, wreak a significant change on the situation of a "victim country", obliging it to prosecute the recipients of bribes.

Comprising two main documents, the OECD Revised Recommendation of May 1997 contains a list of agreed preventive and repressive measures that are both criminal and non-criminal in nature.[1] The convention of December 1997 focuses on the criminalisation issue and puts it into legally binding form.[2] The history of these documents is summarised as follows.

In the aftermath of the Watergate scandal, the Carter administration passed legislation to combat "illicit payments in international business transactions".[3] This development was followed a few years later by a United Nations attempt to move the agenda forwards, but these efforts failed due to political problems. In 1989, the catalyst for the preparatory work leading up to the convention was the United States suggestion that the OECD work on an anti-corruption instrument that would tackle the criminalisation of foreign corrupt practices worldwide. Up until that time the private sector in the United States had felt it was at a trade disadvantage and was pressing for change. In addition, the political developments in eastern Europe and galloping globalisation increased the prospects for a successful collective approach which had hitherto eluded other international attempts to combat bribery. The result of the OECD deliberations was embodied in the 1994 Recommendation, a "soft law" document that mapped out the issues for the future.[4]

---

[1] *Revised Recommendation of the Council on Bribery in International Business Trans-actions,* 23 May 1997.

[2] *Convention on Combating Bribery of Foreign Public Officials in International Business Transactions,* 21 November 1997, signed on 19 December 1997, in force since 15 February 1999.

[3] Foreign Corrupt Practices Act 1977, as amended in 1988.

[4] *Recommendation of the Council on Bribery in International Business Transactions,* 27 May 1994.

The ensuing years involved the participants in a detailed examination of the items contained in the recommendation and marked the transition from unilateral to collective action. Once again the result was another "soft law" instrument but this time the growing confidence of the actors was perceptible with language being couched in more prescriptive terms. This revised recommendation of May 1997 provided for a follow-up procedure for monitoring progress in implementing the recommendation by member states. Hard on its heels came the convention itself, signed by ministers in December 1997, and entering into force in February 1999 through ratification by six of the major economic powers. As of October 2001, 34 countries have signed and ratified, and 29 countries have had their implementing legislation evaluated.[5] The rapidity with which the convention has been ratified and implemented is unprecedented in international law.

3. The methodology of "functional equivalence"

This rapid implementation was facilitated by the specific methodology of the convention in its use of "functional equivalence". This principle relates to the measures taken by the parties to sanction bribery of foreign public officials. Functional equivalence is not unlike the directive in European Community law in that it does not require countries to unify their laws but rather seeks harmonisation through defining goals and offering a choice of means tailored to local legal traditions and fundamental concepts. Functional equivalence also draws and expands on a technique developed in comparative law and demands a holistic approach to the examination of a law or legal concept within an individual legal system. In practice this means that the on-site visits – an obligatory part of the monitoring system for all countries that are party to the convention – take on an even greater significance as they present the opportunity for country examiners to get to grips with the nuances of a judicial system through discussions with a broad cross-section of participants on the ground.[6]

---

5   In addition to the 30 OECD members, four non-OECD states are parties to the anti-bribery initiative, namely Argentina, Brazil, Bulgaria and Chile.

6   On "functional equivalence" see *Commentaries on the Convention on Combating Bribery of Foreign Public Officials in International Business Transactions*, 21 November 1997, note 2. *Cf.* also M. Pieth (2000a), pp. 56-58.

Looking at some examples of functional equivalence drawn from the 1997 bribery convention may help to illustrate the flexibility of its application. On the issue of corporate liability the 1997 bribery convention gives parties a degree of latitude on how to deal with sanctions against an offending company. Article 2 requires countries to introduce the "responsibility of legal persons", whilst article 3, para. 2 goes on to say that non-criminal sanctions against a corporation are also acceptable, provided that they include monetary sanctions and that they are, when taken together, "effective, proportionate and dissuasive". The question of criminal as against administrative sanctions is of less relevance here than the more contentious issue of the scope of responsibility as it relates to a corporate entity. The question of strict or vicarious liability is raised – and whether responsibility is attributable to employees or compliance structures. Among the many questions that need to be considered in this context is the adequacy of sanctions and specifically whether forfeiture of profits should be an available sanction.

Article 3, para. 3 of the convention requires parties to take appropriate measures to ensure that bribery and the proceeds of bribes as defined in the Treaty, or their equivalent value, be subject to seizure and confiscation "… or that monetary sanctions of comparable effect are applicable". Following the requirements of the Council of Europe convention on money laundering, search, seizure and confiscation[7] (Eser, Heine & Huber, 1998) and the Vienna convention of 1988[8] on illicit trafficking in drugs, European countries have introduced sweeping confiscation laws, whereas the United States and Korea seek to realise a comparable result through a substantial fine. As confiscation depends on the source of the funds and a fine is related to the gravity of the offence and the culpability of the offender, the two options ostensibly have no correlation in legal terms. However in the context of the OECD both approaches are viable if their effects are comparable, which will be the case if a straightforward, objective proportionality to earnings is used as the criterion. Where judges have a greater margin of discretion in lieu of confiscation, the level of comparability will have to be reviewed. This sort of evaluation may occur in the second phase review of the OECD procedure which is described below.

Whilst "functional equivalence" is an essential tool in the assessment of a country's approach to implementing the recommendation and convention, it is not

---

[7] *Convention on Laundering, Search, Seizure and Confiscation of the Proceeds from Crime,* 8 November 1990.

[8] *United Nations Convention against Illicit Traffic in Narcotic Drugs and Psychotropic Substances,* Vienna, 1998.

without its problems. Its main disadvantage in the monitoring process is, of course, the lack of uniformity of implementing legislation, making a straightforward review or comparison between countries well nigh impossible. Another temptation is a tendency to compare what – superficially at least – appears directly comparable, such as maximum penalties or statutes of limitations. Thus the challenge facing commentators and country examiners is to avoid an oversimplistic application of functional equivalence and instead to demand a holistic perspective of legal systems using an appropriate comparative approach combined with a sensitivity to the legal culture and attitudes to sanctioning in the country they are evaluating (Pieth, 2000b, pp. 477-489).

In addressing the adequacy of laws in a particular country, the level of an applicable standard may also be problematic. The goal cannot be to set minimum levels nor should a law necessarily be considered replete only when it contains the minutiae which some countries take for granted. A balance has to be struck so that the process continues to develop and move forward, with effective implementation as the goal. Overall, functional equivalence is both an inclusive, flexible principle essential to the evaluation process, as well as a pragmatic concession that respects special circumstances, differing legal traditions and constitutions.

4. How peer review works in practice

The country evaluations, already briefly touched upon, are one of the crucial elements of monitoring the implementation of the recommendation and convention. These peer reviews are formal, systematic, detailed appraisals and judgements by the entire membership of the convention (including the non-OECD member states that are parties to the convention) of aspects of each country's policies and their implementation. The OECD Working Group has developed its own procedural rules to apply this technique, drawing on experiences gained through OECD accession procedures and United Nations human rights audits as well as through Financial Action Task Force mutual evaluation procedures in relation to anti-money laundering efforts.

In terms of procedure, the country evaluations are conducted by experts from two different examining countries chosen from a rotational list who in the first phase of monitoring examine the legal implementation of the 1997 recommendation and convention. The examiners use descriptive texts drafted by the OECD secretariat that are based on the countries' answers to a questionnaire as well as on legal materials submitted by the countries. The examiners give the group (namely the participants in the working group) their opinion on the standard of implementation.

Before the actual hearing by the group the procedures ensure a thorough exchange between the examiners and the examined: Written representations by the country evaluated and a pre-meeting of examiners and country experts to answer questions, to clarify misunderstandings and develop a focus for the group's discussion of specific topics takes place. Phase one evaluations of countries that have implemented the international standards completed to date have been published as reports on internet.[9] In a follow up phase, termed "phase one plus", adaptation of laws based on the critique of the group are evaluated and the phase one reports supplemented. (Such amendments have been signalled to the group so far by Bulgaria, Iceland, the Czech Republic, Italy and Japan.)

The second phase of evaluation differs from the first in that it concentrates on the application in practice of the implementing legislation, this involves looking at the structures in place capable of dealing with this type of case, the level of resources deployed, personnel training and so on. Questionnaires are sent out as a preliminary to an on-site visit. Meanwhile in the country itself, the evaluating teams will look at decided cases, meet with industry, trade unions, civil society as well as government officials and practitioners. The aim of the phase two review is to be fact-based and evaluative, identifying potential problems in the effective prevention, detection and prosecution of foreign bribery cases. The examiners may also look at the efficiency of sanctions but this may be difficult at the current stage of developments in this area given the cultural diversity on this issue.

5. The OECD procedures

With regard to both phases of peer review, the OECD working group holds two hearings per country on two consecutive days. In the first, the group discusses questions raised by the examiners and the answers given by the country. During the evening of the first day, the examiners in phase one prepare a draft of a short evaluative text to be attached to the report itself, in phase two they re-examine the suggested conclusions and recommendations. They immediately test the text with the examined country on the same evening. The second hearing, on the following day, concentrates on the parts of the text carrying a value judgement which may be modified if necessary, and then adopted word for word by the group. Whereas the text is adopted unanimously by the group, the country under examination is requested to abstain from voting. To ensure fair treatment, unanimity of the rest of

---

[9]   See http://www.oecd.org.

the group is called for, and the examined country has the right to express a dissenting opinion in the report.

The evaluation in phase one is appended to the descriptive part of the report, which is itself amended on the basis of the discussions, and adopted in a written procedure. The procedure is open to participation by members of civil society who can, and have, contributed written comments. There is an appellate procedure "that gives the ministers of the OECD Council a final decision", which so far has not been resorted to. The publication of the reports is mandatory and they will also be available on the internet.[10]

Finland is the first country to have undergone both phase one and two evaluations. The phase two review was conducted by experts from the Czech Republic and Korea as well as OECD secretariat members. What emerges from the Finland review may well turn up as a phenomenon in other jurisdictions too. Finland has been named by Transparency International (TI) as the least corrupt country out of about 90 countries studied for two years in a row (2000 and 2001), according to the TI Corruption Perceptions Index.[11] This index measures the level of perceived corruption in the public service of each particular country. However, it does not measure the extent to which a country's businesses are prone to bribing foreign public officials. If the review in phase one was to ensure that laws were enacted or amended to conform to the convention, then phase two could be said to ensure that the substance of those laws are also realised.

Thus taking a critical view of how businesses conduct themselves abroad – as oppose to domestically, especially when operating in neighbouring states or other regions where certain environments are known to be corrupt – will require prosecutors to take a fresh look at the behaviour of their highly respected local companies when operating outside their home market. This will involve a reappraisal of investigative techniques, in particular with regard to the collection of evidence from abroad. In addition, governments and industry will have to increase efforts to inform and educate their business communities regarding culpability under new or revised legislation relating to the bribery of foreign officials. At the very least, business will take cognisance of such changes to the law when criminal prosecutions are undertaken by the authorities.

---

[10] See Procedural Order for Phase 1 DAFFE/IME/BR (98)8/REV 1 and Procedural Order for Phase 2 DAFFE/IME/BR (99)33.

[11] See Transparency International, *Global Corruption Report 2001*, pp. 232-236.

6. Other measures to effect change

To continue with Finland as an example, the Finnish authorities have not as yet handled a criminal case concerning the bribery of a foreign public official, and it will clearly take some time for law enforcement practice to make an impact, in Finland as well as everywhere else. However, at this stage of development in the international arena much depends on rapid change taking effect, not least to sustain the credibility of the industrialised countries on this issue in the eyes of their counterparts in the less developed countries of southern and eastern Europe.

Thus the need for additional action within key industry sectors is of paramount importance to sustain and enhance the impetus of change. In practice this will entail the protagonists having to change internally which again will be a development that will occur over time. But for change to be effective and visible, a co-ordinated approach within specific industry sectors is required – especially where competition is fierce.

7. Developing industry standards

The development of the Wolfsberg Principles on Anti-Money Laundering stand out as an example of what can be achieved by major players (in this instance the eleven largest banks in terms of private clients) who are normally rivals in a highly competitive market.[12] These principles were developed by the banks together with civil society over a relatively short period of time. They are continuing to develop the details of best practice and also to respond to unforeseeable challenges such as how to deal with the identification of terrorist funds. Since their implementation by these eleven banks, it is apparent that these principles have also been adopted by banks who are not formally members of the Wolfsberg group and that they are also used for compliance training purposes. Although the Wolfsberg principles do not deal with the issues of bribery and corruption directly, the analogy of what can be achieved through intra-industry co-operation on sensitive issues is patently clear. To take another example, the integrity standards developed by the International Federation of Consulting Engineers (FIDIC) aimed at reducing corruption in aid-funded public procurement from the private sector side are a similarly dynamic set of principles that commit the industry to a standard of behaviour from which there

---

[12] See www.wolfsberg-principles.com.

is no going back.[13]

The concept of industry standards is gradually gaining ground with new efforts discernible in various sectors such as the oil and gas industry and its supply chain industries, the mining industry, contract engineers and companies involved in the defence and armaments industry (Pieth, 2002). All are either contemplating the idea of getting together or are in the process of discussing the issues involved and the consequences of revealing their innermost secrets regarding the issue of bribery as it relates to their international business transactions – dealing, for instance, with such touchy areas as agents contracts, comparing their approaches and possibly even developing a common solution to prevent the use of agents as a conduit for bribery. The motivation for these industries is, on the one hand, the changing international legal framework and, on the other, growing concern about the cost of competitive advantage obtained through corruption and not least the attendant risks to reputation that can arise if a company rides roughshod in its business practices over its customers or the countries in which it conducts business. The prospects for self-regulation through industry standards lend themselves to this risk scenario and will be increasingly deployed by a variety of industries in the future.

8. Methodology of industry standards

The obstacles to bringing together rival companies to address these issues are by no means insignificant. The whole process is very delicate, particularly if there are serious issues of subsisting bribery within the particular industry. In order for industry to make an impact on the problem it is essential that the composition of the group that comes together is of the right balance. This means major companies in the sector in question having a significant world market share, who are active internationally, for whom the importance of a level playing field in competitive terms is of economic significance, and for whom the risk to reputation is of overriding importance. Timing is also of the essence, as bringing the right people together at the right time requires recognising and seizing the moment when an individual company has taken – or is well on the way to taking – the decision to confront the problem of corruption head on.

Once a group of companies wants to tackle the risks facing their business, the way forward is best achieved through a frank and forthright approach. The optimal size of a group of companies to attain the goal of a comprehensive pact is in the

---

[13] See http://www.fidic.org.

region of ten to twelve, each participating company being represented by the top echelons of that company, so that the decision-making capacity of the group is maximised. This lends momentum and weight to the whole process and is of crucial importance to the procedure. The whole process is undoubtedly a novel experience for most of the participants and may be outside their usual business experience. In these circumstances the use of external facilitators playing a positive role in nurturing the process can be invaluable.

In the longer term, the issues of how to control and monitor the implementation of the standards need to be considered, either by adapting the peer review principle in an appropriate fashion or through external agencies. After having achieved an industry standard, the participants might either want to keep the whole process "secret" and monitor each other, or they may want to make their document public and promote its implementation and encourage the participation of others. This alternative may include the involvement of other companies either directly (by "subscription" as was the case in the initial phase of the Wolfberg process) or indirectly via regulators (the current state of the Wolfsberg group). The question of when and how other companies within the industry can join the "club" must also therefore be considered by the group.

The advantages of industry standards are the speed and flexibility with which they can be brought into being and the fact that they can be adapted to address specific aspects of corruption facing any given sector of industry. The acknowledgement by major companies that they are confronting issues related to bribery will, in turn, bolster government efforts to tackle the issues, making it harder for anyone to shy away from their responsibilities, judicial, legislative or legal. The downside of industry standards relates to the question of monitoring and how best to achieve it. So far the Wolfsberg group, for example, have not pursued the option of monitoring each other.

A possible risk in the long term for the participating banks may be a diminishing of their credibility externally. The lack of transparency in the verification of how the banks have actually implemented the principles may negate the public relations effect of the exercise and dilute the prestige of being a founding member of the group. Instead the issue falls to external regulators to pick up with the possibility of developing monitoring mechanisms internally – this variation is currently under examination.[14] The development of industry standards is, of course, subject to all

---

[14] *Cf.* Basle Committee for Banking Supervision and for example, the new "Customer Due Diligence" standard of 4 October 2001, with reference to Wolfsberg.

the advantages and pitfalls of self-regulation. At its best it can act as a dynamic spur to policy makers and achieve a complementary status to existing legislation.

9. How does all this fit together?

Where do international and national laws and industry standards converge? The focal point here must be on companies. Whilst the convention criminalises bribery when committed by a natural person it leaves the issue of criminal liability as it pertains to companies open and only requires that monetary sanctions be "effective, proportionate and dissuasive". Whether the profits of a company can be forfeited is an unresolved question in many jurisdictions and not one that is likely to be determined in a uniform way in the near future.[18] As for non-criminal sanctions against an offending company, there is, for example, the risk of disbarment from public contracts under World Bank regulations.[19]

Criminal law has always been selectively applied and it does not need a large number of cases to promote a deterrent effect. At the same time the drive to change behaviour can also be influenced in the future by the hands-on efforts of companies involved in developing industry standards by taking things a step further and building a grid-like structure of action. This rather abstract notion would in practice entail key industrial sectors coming together to develop an intra-industry standard. This would constitute the horizontal axis (such as oil, defence, pharmaceuticals industries) whilst the vertical axis would comprise the supply chain of each sector and cut across industries and include suppliers, sales agents and joint venture partners. In the longer term this sort of approach may even lead to comprehensive integrity pacts.

Looking at the results so far, it is apparent that change is possible and entrenched behaviour in this area can be altered. Political and economic factors as well as risks to reputation all combine to create a climate of change. It may well be that once 20% of multi-national enterprises are involved in agreements relating to industry standards, a worldwide turnaround could be expected to follow.

---

15 Even though article 3, s. 3 of the 1997 convention does require the confiscation of profits, also with regard to companies.

16 See para. 1.15 of the World Bank's Procurement Guidelines.

References

Eser, A., G. Heine & B. Huber (eds.), *Criminal Responsibiltity of Legal and Collective Entities*, Max Planck Institute of Foreign and International Criminal Law, Freiburg, 1998.

Pieth, M., *No Longer Business as Usual*, OECD, Paris, 2000a.

Pieth, M., "'Funktionale Äquivalenz': Praktische Rechtsvergleichung und internationale Harmonisierung von Wirtschaftsstrafrecht", *Zeitschrift für Schweizerisches Recht*, 2000b.

Pieth, M., "Staatliche Intervention und Selbstregulierung der Wirtschaft", in *Festschrift für Lüderssen*, Nomos, Baden-Baden, 2002 (forthcoming).

CHAPTER 23

The Council of Europe Activities against Corruption

Guy de Vel & Peter Csonka

1. Introduction

Activities of the Council of Europe against corruption are carried out on the basis of a Programme of Action adopted by the Committee of Ministers in November 1996.[1,2] Following the 2nd Summit of Heads of State and Government in October 1997, the Council of Europe Programme of Action against Corruption received considerable political impulse and became one of the first priorities for the Organisation and its 43 member states.[3]

The Council of Europe's approach to the fight against corruption is characterised by its:

- *Multidisciplinarity.* Corruption is a prism with many sides and requires action of different types;

- *Monitoring.* The credibility of instruments against corruption depends upon an appropriate system for evaluating compliance with the obligations arising

---

[1] The views expressed hereafter are personal and do not necessarily reflect those of the Council of Europe.

[2] For information about the Council of Europe, please visit http://www.coe.int or contact the Secretariat General: Directorate General of Legal Affairs, Council of Europe, Palais de l'Europe, F 67075 Strasbourg Cedex, Tel. (33) (0)3 88412125, fax (33) (0)3 88412764.

[3] The member states of the Council of Europe are: Albania, Andorra, Armenia, Austria, Azerbaijan, Belgium, Bulgaria, Croatia, Cyprus, Czech Republic, Denmark, Estonia, Finland, France, Georgia, Germany, Greece, Hungary, Iceland, Ireland, Italy, Latvia, Liechtenstein, Lithuania, Luxembourg, Malta, Moldova, The Netherlands, Norway, Poland, Portugal, Romania, the Russian Federation, San Marino, the Slovak Republic, Slovenia, Spain, Sweden, Switzerland, "the former Yugoslav Republic of Macedonia", Turkey, Ukraine and the United Kingdom.

Cyrille Fijnaut, Leo Huberts (eds.), *Corruption, Integrity and Law Enforcement*, 361-380
©2002 Kluwer Law International, The Hague. Printed in The Netherlands.

therefrom. All Council of Europe instruments are linked to the monitoring mechanism provided by the agreement known as GRECO – Group of States against Corruption;

- *Ambition.* Corruption is a serious and complex problem. The Council of Europe strives, therefore, to tackle all forms of corrupt behaviour, without leaving gaps through which corrupt practices may survive or reappear. The aim of the Council of Europe's action is to raise public life standards, to preserve the integrity and impartiality of public administration and the social fabric;

- *Comprehensiveness.* The Council of Europe is developing an integrated set of instruments of different types, putting at the disposal of its members a full battery of international law measures against corruption. Each instrument complements the others with a view to building up a net of standards that will render corruption more difficult and costly;

- *Flexibility.* Countries are free to sign one or several instrument or to apply soft law as a first step, under appropriate monitoring in all cases. A system of reservations allows for accession to the criminal law convention whilst postponing acceptance of some commitments in order to adapt to new and high standards. Even if there is one single monitoring mechanism, the GRECO, its procedures are also adaptable to the type of provisions being monitored.

2. Achievements

Some of the specific results obtained by the Council of Europe in the implementation of its Programme of Action against Corruption are described below.

2.1. The 20 Guiding Principles for the fight against corruption

Following intensive work to define a common framework for national strategies against corruption, the Committee of Ministers adopted in November 1997 the 20 Guiding Principles for the fight against corruption, identifying the areas in which state action is necessary for a comprehensive and efficient strategy against corruption. The principles deal, *inter alia*, with prevention of corruption, promotion of ethical behaviour, immunities, media freedom, transparency in decision-making, auditing, codes of conduct for elected representatives, financing of political parties and election campaigns and other topical issues.

Although the Guiding Principles are not, as such, a binding legal text, they carry the political weight of their masters since the Heads of State and Government mandated their elaboration. Moreover, the GRECO is entrusted with the task of monitoring their application.

2.2. The Group of States against Corruption – GRECO

In May 1998, six months after the adoption of the Guiding Principles, the Committee of Ministers of the Council of Europe adopted the resolution authorising the setting up of the Group of States against Corruption – GRECO. GRECO aims at improving the capacity of its members to fight corruption by following up, through a dynamic and flexible process of mutual evaluation and peer pressure, compliance with their undertakings in this field and, in particular, with the 20 Guiding Principles for the fight against corruption and the implementation of the Criminal Law Convention and other international legal instruments.

GRECO provides a flexible, dynamic and efficient mechanism to ensure compliance with undertakings in the field of corruption. It defines a master-type procedure, which can be adapted to the different instruments under review. It is opened to the participation of member states and non-member states of the Council of Europe on an equal footing.

Becoming a party to the Criminal Law Convention or other Council of Europe instruments will entail, automatically, the obligation to participate in GRECO, and to accept its monitoring procedures.

The GRECO agreement became operational on 1 May 1999. For the time being, 34 countries have already joined.[4] The first evaluation round started on 1 January 2000. For this evaluation round, GRECO decided to select guiding principles nos. 3, 6 and 7 relating to the functioning of the bodies and institutions in charge of the fight against corruption and the immunities.

Members of GRECO have then been divided in 2 groups : group A (10 countries), to be evaluated in 2000 and group B (the remaining), to be evaluated in 2001.[5] Up

---

[4] The following are member states of GRECO: Albania, Belgium, Bosnia-Herzegovina, Bulgaria, Croatia, Cyprus, the Czech Republic, Denmark, Estonia, Finland, France, Georgia, Germany, Greece, Hungary, Iceland, Ireland, Latvia, Lithuania, Luxembourg, Malta, Moldova, The Netherlands, Norway, Poland, Portugal, Romania, Slovakia, Slovenia, Spain, Sweden, "the former Yugoslav Republic of Macedonia", the United Kingdom, the United States of America.

[5] The first evaluation round was extended until 31 December 2002.

to the end of December 2001, the evaluation reports of 14 member states have been adopted by GRECO.

2.3. The Criminal Law Convention on Corruption

This convention was adopted in November 1998. On the very day of its opening for signature, on 27 January 1999, 21 states signed it. As of today, it already counts 28 signatories not followed by ratifications (including 3 by non-member states) and 13 ratifications. Fourteen ratifications are required for its entry into force.

The convention provides for the criminalisation, on the basis of common elements, of a large range of corruption offences, including active and passive corruption of national, foreign and international or supranational public officials, members of parliaments or assemblies, judges, active and passive bribery in private business transactions, trading in influence, laundering of corruption proceeds and corruption in auditing.

In addition, the convention deals with other substantial or procedural issues, such as jurisdiction, sanctions and measures, liability of legal persons, setting up of specialised authorities for the fight against corruption, co-operation among authorities responsible for law enforcement, protection of witnesses. Finally, it provides for enhanced international co-operation in the prosecution of corruption offences.

For detailed information about the convention see § 4 below.

It is important to note that this is also an instrument open to accession by non-member states. However, as indicated above, becoming a party to the convention entails the automatic acceptance of GRECO's monitoring system.

2.4. The Civil Law Convention on Corruption

In 1997, a feasibility study showed that it was possible to conceive a number of scenarios in which the use of civil law remedies might be useful against given forms of corruption. On this basis, the Council of Europe has elaborated a convention dealing with civil remedies for compensation for damage resulting from acts of corruption. This text deals with substantive and procedural issues including, among others, compensation for damage, evidence, liability, non-pecuniary remedies, validity and effect of contracts, transparency and protection of whistle-blowers.

As is the case with the Criminal Law Convention, the Civil Law Convention is open to accession by non-member states and becoming a party to it implies automatic acceptance of GRECO's monitoring system. The convention was adopted by the Committee of Ministers on 9 September 1999 and was opened for signature on 3-4 November 1999. To date, it counts 25 signatures not followed by ratifications, including one non-member state and 6 ratifications. As with the Criminal Law Convention, ratification by 14 member states is the condition for entry into force.

2.5. The Model Code of Conduct for Public Officials

The purpose of this text is threefold: to define the ethical climate that should prevail in the public service, to spell out standards of ethical conduct expected from public officials and to inform the public of what conduct to expect from public officials when dealing with them. The Model Code of Conduct for Public Officials, both a public document and a message addressed to every individual public official, will reflect and reinforce the basic standards set out in the criminal legislation dealing with dishonesty and corruption; this legislation in turn provides the basis for the code.

The model code is attached to Recommendation No. R (2000) 10 of the Committee of Ministers to the Governments of Member States on Codes of Conduct for Public Officials. This recommendation was adopted at ministerial level in May 2000 (106th session of the Committee of Ministers). The recommendation and the model code attached to it are proving very useful in assisting the member states of the Council of Europe in preparing codes of conducts for their public officials.

3. Complementary initiatives

3.1. The Annual Conferences of Specialised Services in the fight against corruption

The Programme of Action against Corruption stresses the need for exchanges of practical experience among services (e.g. police, prosecutors, senior members of civil service) involved in the fight against corruption, both at national and international level. The Conferences of Specialised Services, organised on an annual basis in co-operation with the authorities of one country, provide a useful opportunity for exchanging up-to-date information on national techniques and experiences among those who are in the front line against corruption.

The First European Conference of Specialised Services in the fight against corruption, organised in Strasbourg in 1996, dealt with the setting up and the functioning of specialised authorities and the special features of the investigation and the prosecution of corruption cases. The second conference, held in Tallinn (Estonia) in 1997 dealt with corruption in public procurement. The third, held in Madrid in October 1998, considered the topic of trading in influence and illegal financing of political parties, a crucial area touching upon the foundations of democracy. The fourth conference was held in Cyprus on 20-22 October 1999 and was devoted to the question of offshore centres and international co-operation against corruption.

The fifth conference took place in Turkey on 15-17 November 2000 on the topic of investigating, prosecuting and adjudicating corruption cases. The issues of the sixth conference in Portoroz (Slovenia) on 26-28 September 2001 were the role of the civil society in corruption and the international community contribution to the prevention of corruption.

These Annual Conferences of Specialised Services led to the adoption of conclusions, which serve as a source of inspiration for future activities.

3.2. Octopus programme against organised crime and corruption

The European Commission and the Council of Europe launched in 1996 a joint initiative entitled the "Octopus project" on the fight against corruption and organised crime in countries in transition. During the first phase of this project (1996-1998) an evaluation was made of the problem and of counter-measures taken by the governments of 16 states concerned.[6] Following expert missions to the participating countries, recommendations and guidelines were addressed to each one of them. Subsequently, a continuation of the Octopus project for the years 1999-2000 (programme Octopus II) fostered the implementation of recommendations addressed in phase I and helped candidate countries of Central and Eastern Europe to prepare for accession to the European Union.

The joint Octopus II programme of the European Commission and the Council of Europe was completed with the final evaluation conference held in Strasbourg in December 2000. Participants from central and eastern European countries as

---

[6] Albania, Bulgaria, Croatia, the Czech Republic, Estonia, Hungary, Latvia, Lithuania, Moldova, Poland, Romania, the Russian Federation, Slovakia, Slovenia, "the former Yugoslav Republic of Macedonia" and Ukraine.

well as from European Union countries and from the European Commission expressed their satisfaction with the organisation and management of the Programme. The meeting concluded that Octopus II achieved its objectives in that it made a significant contribution to the adoption of the relevant acquis of the European Union and the Council of Europe, in that it produced further recommendations for reforms, in that it created a network of professionals and in that it enhanced the skills of those participating in Octopus seminars and study visits (the 18 country reports summarising the recommendations prepared by each country have now been made public). The Octupus II programme has significantly reinforced the capacity of the investigation authorities in the concerned countries in corruption related issues.

The continuation of the programme received broad support at the final conference. The Octopus III programme against corruption and organised crime in Europe should focus on the implementation of Octopus II recommendations through country-specific projects as well as regional activities in support of judicial networking. Several European Union countries expressed their interest in supporting Octopus III. The Octopus III programme is carried out currently with resources provided by the Council of Europe.

3.3. Programme against corruption and organised crime in south-eastern Europe (PACO)

The PACO programme is the contribution of the Council of Europe to support the implementation of the Stability Pact Anti-Corruption Initiative (SPAI) and the Stability Pact Initiative against Organised Crime (SPOC). The SPAI was adopted in February 2000 and the first SPAI Steering Group meeting was held in Strasbourg in December 2000. The SPOC was adopted by the Stability Pact in Sofia in October 2000. The Council of Europe had assumed a crucial role in the elaboration and negotiation of both iniatives and is playing an important role in their implementation.

In 2000, a range of activities was carried out within the framework of the PACO preparatory phase, including planning and assessment missions to Albania, Bosnia and Herzegovina, Kosovo and Moldova, a regional workshop on the efficiency of anti-corruption legislation, and a regional meeting of prosecutors general (both in Bulgaria). The preparatory phase is financed through voluntary contributions by Germany, Norway, Greece, Slovenia and Switzerland.

The preparatory phase is now gradually turning into the implementation phase. A PACO project to support the strengthening of the Anti-Corruption Monitoring Group in Albania started in January 2001 (funded through a voluntary contribution by Sweden). Additional country-specific projects are in preparation. Two regional projects are being designed, one aimed at strengthening capacities for the confiscation of proceeds from crime and a second one aimed at strengthening judicial networking among the countries.

3.4. Other recent developments

A draft recommendation has recently been finalised so as to provide general rules concerning bribery in the field of party financing and the financing of elections. This recommendation shall also be applicable to the individual political candidate.

4. The Criminal Law Convention on Corruption

As already mentioned, the Criminal Law Convention on Corruption is one of the most comprehensive instruments adopted in the framework of the Council of Europe. This comprehensiveness was the result of detailed research in order to describe and define the most common sorts of corruption within all member states. Therefore a first distinction was made between active and passive bribery as well as a distinction between a widespread range of concerned persons and institutions, including persons in the private sector, the officials of international organisations and judges of international courts. Furthermore the convention provides for trading in influence and money laundering. Currently an additional protocol is being elaborated that enlarges the scope of application of the convention to arbitrators and jurors.

The most significant provisions related to the criminalisation of corruption in the convention are described on the following pages.

Article 2 – Active bribery of domestic public officials

Article 2 defines the elements of the active bribery of domestic public officials. It is intended to ensure in particular that public administration functions properly, i.e. in a transparent, fair and impartial manner and in pursuance of public interests, and to protect the confidence of citizens in their administration and the officials themselves from possible manoeuvres against them. The definition of active bribery in article 2 draws its inspiration from national and international definitions of bribery/corruption e.g. the one contained in the protocol to the European Union Convention on the Protection of the European Communities' Financial Interests (article 3). This offence, in current criminal law theory and practice and in the view of the drafters of the convention, is mirrored by passive bribery, though they are considered to be separate offences for which prosecutions can be brought independently. It emerges that the two types of bribery are, in general, two sides of the same phenomenon, one perpetrator offering, promising or giving the advantage and the other perpetrator accepting the offer, promise or gift. Usually, however, the two perpetrators are not punished for complicity in the other one's offence.

The definition provided in article 2 is referred to in subsequent provisions of the convention, e.g. in articles 4, 5, 6, 9 and, through a double reference, in article 10. These provisions do not repeat the substantive elements but extend the criminalisation of the active bribery to further categories of persons.

The offence of active bribery can only be committed intentionally under article 2 and the intent has to cover all other substantive elements of the offence. Intent must relate to a future result: the public official acting or refraining from acting as the briber intends. It is, however, immaterial whether the public official actually acted or refrained from acting as intended.

The briber can be anyone, whatever his capacity (businessman, public official, private individual etc.). If, however, the briber acts for the account or on behalf of a company, corporate liability may also apply in respect of the company in question (article 18). Nevertheless, the liability of the company does not exclude in any manner criminal proceedings against the natural person (para. 3 of article 18). The bribed person must be a public official, as defined under article 1, irrespective of whether the undue advantage is actually for himself or for someone else.

The material components of the offence are promising, offering or giving an undue advantage, directly or indirectly for the official himself or for a third party. The three actions of the briber are slightly different. "Promising" may, for example, cover situations where the briber commits himself to give an undue advantage later (in most cases only once the public official has performed the act requested by the briber) or where there is an agreement between the briber and the bribee that the briber will give the undue advantage later. "Offering" may cover situations where the briber shows his readiness to give the undue advantage at any moment. Finally, "giving" may cover situations where the briber transfers the undue advantage. The undue advantage need not necessarily be given to the public official himself: it can be given also to a third party, such as a relative, an organisation to which the official belongs, the political party of which he is a member. When the offer, promise or gift is addressed to a third party, the public official must at least have knowledge thereof at some point. Irrespective of whether the recipient or the beneficiary of the undue advantage is the public official himself or a third party, the transaction may be performed through intermediaries.

The undue advantages given are usually of an economic nature but may also be of a non-material nature. What is important is that the offender (or any other person, for instance a relative) is placed in a better position than he was before the commission of the offence and that he is not entitled to the benefit. Such advantages may consist in, for instance, money, holidays, loans, food and drink, a case handled within a swifter time, better career prospects, etc.

What constitutes "undue" advantage will be of central importance in the transposition of the convention into national law. "Undue" for the purposes of the convention should be interpreted as something that the recipient is not lawfully entitled to accept or receive. For the drafters of the convention, the adjective "undue" aims at excluding advantages permitted by the law or by administrative rules as well as minimum gifts, gifts of very low value or socially acceptable gifts.

Bribery provisions of certain member states of the Council of Europe make some distinctions as to whether the act, which is solicited, is a part of the official's duty or whether he is going beyond his duties. As far as criminal law is concerned, if an official receives a benefit in return for acting in accordance with his duties, this would already constitute a criminal offence. Should the official act in a manner, which is prohibited or arbitrary, he would be liable for a more serious offence. If he should not have handled the case at all, for instance a licence should not have been given, the official would be liable to having committed a more serious form of bribery which usually carries a heavier penalty. Such an extra-element of "breach of duty" was, however, not considered to be necessary for the purposes of this convention. The drafters of the convention considered that the decisive element of the offence was not whether the official had any discretion to act as requested by the briber, but whether he had been offered, given or promised a bribe in order to obtain something from him. The briber may not even have known whether the official had discretion or not, this element being, for the purpose of this provision, irrelevant. Thus, the convention aims at safeguarding the confidence of citizens in the fairness of public administration which would be severely undermined, even if the official would have acted in the same way without the bribe. In a democratic state public servants are, as a general rule, remunerated from public budgets and not directly by the citizens or by private companies. In addition, the notion of "breach of duty" adds an element of ambiguity that makes more difficult the prosecution of this offence, by requiring to prove that the public official was expected to act against his duties or was expected to exercise his discretion for the benefit of the briber. States that require such an extra-element for bribery would therefore have to ensure that they could implement the definition of bribery under article 2 of this convention without hindering its objective.

Article 3 – Passive bribery of domestic public officials

Article 3 defines passive bribery of public officials. As this offence is closely linked with active bribery, some comments made thereon, e.g. in respect of the mental element and the undue advantage apply accordingly here as well. The "perpetrator" in article 3 can only be a public official. The material elements of his act include requesting or receiving an undue advantage or accepting the offer or the promise thereof.

"Requesting" may for example refer to a unilateral act whereby the public official lets another person know, explicitly or implicitly, that he will have to "pay" to have some official act done or abstained from. It is immaterial whether the request was actually acted upon, the request itself being the core of the offence. Likewise, it does not matter whether the public official requested the undue advantage for himself or for anyone else.

"Receiving" may for example mean the actual taking the benefit, whether by the public official himself or by someone else (spouse, colleague, organisation, political party, etc.) for himself or for someone else. The latter case supposes at least some kind of acceptance by the public official. Again, intermediaries can be involved: the fact that an intermediary is involved, which would extend the scope of passive bribery to include indirect action by the official, necessarily entails identifying the criminal nature of the official's conduct, irrespective of the good or bad faith of the intermediary involved.

If there is a unilateral request or a corrupt pact, it is essential that the act or the omission of acting by the public official takes place after the request or the pact, whereas it is immaterial in such a case at what point in time the undue advantage is actually received. Thus, it is not a criminal offence under the convention to receive a benefit after the act has been performed by the public official, without prior offer, request or acceptance. Moreover, the word "receipt" means keeping the advantage or gift at least for some time so that the official who, having not requested it, immediately returns the gift to the sender would not be committing an offence under article 3.

This provision is not applicable either to benefits unrelated to a specific subsequent act in the exercise of the public official's duties.

Article 4 – Bribery of members of domestic public assemblies

This article extends the scope of the active and passive bribery offences defined in articles 2 and 3 to members of domestic public assemblies, at local, regional and national level, whether elected or appointed. This category of persons is also vulnerable to bribery and recent corruption scandals, sometimes combined with illegal financing of political parties, showed that it was important to make it also criminally liable for bribery. Concerning active bribery, the protected legal interest is the same as that protected by article 2. However, it is different as regards passive bribery, i.e. when a member of a domestic public assembly is bribed: here this provision protects the transparency, the fairness and impartiality of the decision-making process of domestic public assemblies and their members from corrupt manoeuvres. Obviously, the financial support granted to political parties in accordance with national law falls outside the scope of this provision.

Since the definition of "public official" refers to the applicable national definition, it is understood that contracting parties would apply, in a similar manner, their own definition of "members of domestic public assemblies". This category of persons should primarily cover Members of Parliament (where applicable, in both houses), members of local and regional assemblies and members of any other public body whose members are elected or appointed and which "exercise legislative or administrative powers" (article 4, para. 1, *in fine*). This broad notion could cover, in some countries, also mayors, as members of local councils, or ministers, as Members of Parliament. The expression "administrative powers" is aimed at bringing into the scope of this provision members of public assemblies which do not have legislative powers, as it could be the case with regional or provincial assemblies or local councils. Such public assemblies, although not competent to enact legislation, may have considerable powers, for instance in the planning, licensing or regulatory areas.

Apart from the persons who are bribed, i.e. members of domestic public assemblies, the substance of this bribery offence is identical to the one defined under articles 2 and 3.

Article 5 – Bribery of foreign public officials

Corruption not only undermines good governance and destroys public trust in the fairness and impartiality of public administrations but it may also seriously distort competition and endanger economic development when foreign public officials are bribed, e.g. by corporations to obtain business. With the globalisation of economic and financial structures and the integration of domestic markets into the world market, decisions taken on capital movements or investments in one country can and do exert effects in others. Multinational corporations and international investors play a determining role in today's economy and know of no borders. It is in both their interest and the interest of the global economy in general to keep competition rules fair and transparent.

The international community has for long been considering the introduction of a specific criminal offence of bribery of foreign public officials, e.g. to ensure respect of competition rules in international business transactions. The protected legal interest is twofold in the case of this offence: transparency and fairness of the decision-making process of foreign public administrations – this was traditionally considered a domestic affair but the globalisation has made this consideration obsolete – and the protection of fair competition for businesses. The criminalisation of corrupt behaviour occurring outside national territories finds its justification in the common interest of states to protect these interests. The European Union was the first European organisation which succeeded in adopting an international treaty criminalising, *inter alia*, the corruption of foreign public officials: the Convention on the Fight against Corruption Involving Officials of the European Communities or Officials of the Member States of the European Union (adopted on 26 May 1997). After several years, the Organisation for Economic Co-operation and Development (OECD) also concluded, in November 1997 a landmark agreement on criminalising, in a co-ordinated manner, the bribery of foreign public officials, i.e. to bribe such an official in order to obtain or retain business or other improper advantage.

This article goes beyond the European Union convention in that it provides for the criminalisation of bribery of foreign public officials of any foreign country. It also goes beyond the OECD provision in two respects. First, it deals with both the active and passive sides. Of course, the latter, for contracting parties to this convention, will be already covered by article 3. However, the inclusion of passive corruption of foreign officials in article 5 seeks to demonstrate the solidarity of the community of states against corruption, wherever it occurs. The message is clear: corruption is a serious criminal offence that could be prosecuted by all contracting parties and not only by the corrupt official's own state. Secondly, article 5 contains no restriction as to the context in which the bribery of the foreign official occurs. Again, the aim is not only to protect free competition but the confidence of citizens in democratic institutions and the rule of law. As regards the definition of "foreign public official", reference is made to article 1.

Apart from the persons who are bribed, i.e. foreign public officials, the substance of this bribery offence is identical to the one defined under articles 2 and 3.

Article 6 – Bribery of members of foreign public assemblies

This article criminalises the active and passive bribery of members of foreign public assemblies. The reasons and the protected legal interests are identical to those described under article 4, but in a foreign context, "in any other state". It is part of the common effort undertaken by parties to ensure respect for democratic institutions, independently of whether they are national or foreign in character.

Apart from the persons who are bribed, i.e. members of foreign public assemblies, the substance of this bribery offence is identical to the one defined under articles 2 and 3. The notion of "member of a public assembly" is to be interpreted in the light of the domestic law of the foreign state.

Article 7 – Active bribery in the private sector

This article extends criminal responsibility for bribery to the private sector. Corruption in the private sector has, over the last century, been dealt with by civil (e.g. competition), or labour laws or general criminal law provisions. Criminalising private corruption appeared as a pioneering but necessary effort to avoid gaps in a comprehensive strategy to combat corruption. The reasons for introducing criminal law sanctions for corruption in the private sphere are manifold. First of all, because corruption in the private sphere undermines values like trust, confidence or loyalty, which are necessary for the maintenance and development of social and economic relations. Even in the absence of a specific pecuniary damage to the victim, private corruption causes damage to society as a whole. In general, it can be said that there is an increasing tendency towards limiting the differences between the rules applicable to the public and private sectors. This requires redesigning the rules that protect the interests of the private sector and govern its relations with its employees and the public at large. Secondly, criminalisation of private sector corruption was necessary to ensure respect for fair competition. Thirdly, it also has to do with the privatisation process. Over the years important public functions have been privatised (health, transport, telecommunications etc.). The transfer of such public functions to the private sector, often related to a massive privatisation process, entails transfers of substantial budgetary allocations and of regulatory powers. It is therefore logical to protect the public from the damaging effects of corruption in businesses as well, particularly since the financial or other powers concentrated in the private sector, necessary for their new functions, are of great social importance.

In general, the comments made on active bribery of public officials (article 2) apply *mutatis mutandis* here as well, in particular as regards the corrupt acts performed, the mental element and the briber. There are, nevertheless, several important differences between the provisions on public and private sector bribery. First of all, article 7 restricts the scope of private bribery to the domain of "business activity", thus deliberately excluding any non-profit oriented activities carried out by persons or organisations, e.g. by associations or other NGOs. This choice was made to focus on the most vulnerable sector, i.e. the business sector. Of course, this may leave some gaps, which governments may wish to fill: nothing would prevent a signatory state from implementing this provision without the restriction to "in the course of business activities". "Business activity" is to be interpreted in a broad sense: it means any kind of commercial activity, in particular trading in goods and delivering services, including services to the public (transport, telecommunications etc.).

The second important difference concerns the scope of recipient persons in article 7. This provision prohibits bribing any persons who "direct or work for, in any capacity, private sector entities". Again, this is a sweeping notion to be interpreted broadly as it covers the employer-employee relationship but also other types of relationships such as partners, lawyer-and-client and others in which there is no contract of employment. Within private enterprises it should cover not only employees but also the management from the top to the bottom, including members of the board, but not the shareholders. It would also include persons who do not have the status of employee or do not work permanently for the company – for example consultants, commercial agents etc. – but can engage the responsibility of the company. "Private sector entities" refer to companies, enterprises, trusts and other entities, which are entirely or to a determining extent owned by private persons. This of course covers a whole range of entities, notably those engaged "in business activities". They can be corporations but also entities with no legal personality. For the purpose of this provision, the word "entity" should be understood as meaning also, in this context, an individual. Public entities fall therefore outside the scope of this provision.

The third important difference relates to the behaviour of the bribed person in the private sector. If, in the case of public officials, it was immaterial whether there had been a breach of his duties, given the general expectation of transparency, impartiality and loyalty in this regard, a breach of duty is required for private sector persons. Criminalisation of bribery in the private sector seeks to protect the trust, the confidence and the loyalty that are indispensable for private relationships to exist. Rights and obligations related to those relationships are governed by private law and, to a great extent, determined by contracts. The employee, the agent, the lawyer is expected to perform his functions in accordance with his contract, which will include, expressly or implicitly, a general obligation of loyalty towards his principal – a general obligation not to act to the detriment of his interests. Such an obligation can be laid down, for example, in codes of conduct that private companies are increasingly developing. The expression, "in breach of their duties" does not only aim at ensuring respect for specific contractual obligations but rather to guarantee that there will be no breach of the general duty of loyalty in relation to the principal's affairs or business. The employee, partner or managing director who accepts a bribe to act or refrain from acting in a manner that is contrary to his principal's interest, will be betraying the trust placed upon him, the loyalty owed to his principal. This justifies the inclusion of private sector corruption as a criminal offence. The convention, in article 7, retained this philosophy and requires the additional element of "breach of duty" in order to criminalise private sector corruption. The notion of "breach of duty" can also be linked to that of "secrecy", that is the acceptance of the gift to the detriment of the employer or principal and without obtaining his authorisation or approval. It is the secrecy of the benefit rather than the benefit itself that is the essence of the offence. Such a secret behaviour threatens the interests of the private sector entity and makes it dangerous.

Article 8 – Passive bribery in the private sector

The comments made on passive bribery of domestic public officials (article 3) apply accordingly here as far as the corrupt acts and the mental element are concerned. So do the comments on active bribery in the private sector (article 7), as far as the specific context, the persons involved and the extra-condition of "breach of duty" are concerned. The mirror-principle, already referred to in the context of public sector bribery, is also applicable here.

Article 9 – Bribery of officials of international organisations

The necessity of extending the criminalisation of acts of bribery to the international sphere was already highlighted under article 5 (bribery of foreign public officials). Recent initiatives in the framework of the European Union, which led to the adoption on 27 September 1996 (Official Journal of the European Communities No. C 313 of 23 October 1996) of the Protocol (on corruption) to the European Union Convention on the Protection of the European Communities' Financial Interests and that of the Convention on the Fight against Corruption Involving Officials of the European Communities or Officials of the Member States of the European Union (26 May 1997), are evidence that criminal law protection is needed against the corruption of officials of international institutions, which must have the same consequences as the one of national public officials. The need to criminalise bribery is even greater in the case of officials of public international organisations than in the case of foreign public officials, since, as already pointed out above, passive bribery of a foreign public official is already an offence under the official's own domestic legislation, whereas the laws on bribery only exceptionally cover acts committed by their nationals abroad, in particular when they are permanently employed by public international organisations. The protected legal interest in general is the transparency and impartiality of the decision-making process of public international organisations which, according to their specific mandate, carry out activities on behalf or in the interest of their member states. Some of these organisations do handle large quantities of goods and services. Fair competition in their public procurement procedures is also worth protecting by criminal law.

Since this article refers back to articles 2 and 3 for the description of the bribery offences, the comments made thereon apply accordingly. The persons involved as recipients of the bribes are, however, different. It covers the corruption of "any official or other contracted employee within the meaning of the staff regulations, of any public international or supranational organisation or body of which the party is a member, and any person, whether seconded or not, carrying out functions corresponding to those performed by such officials or agents".

Two main categories are therefore involved: first, officials and other contracted employees who, under the staff regulations, can be either permanent or temporary members of the staff, but irrespective of the duration of their employment by the organisation, have identical duties and responsibilities, governed by contract. Secondly, staff members who are seconded (put at the disposal of the organisation by a government or any public or private body), to carry out functions equivalent to those performed by officials or contracted employees.

Article 9 restricts the obligation of signatories to criminalise only those cases of bribery involving the above-mentioned persons employed by international organisations of which they are members. This restriction is necessary for various practical reasons, for example to avoid problems related to immunity.

Article 9 mentions "public international or supranational organisations", which means that they are set up by governments and not individuals or private organisations. It also means that international non-governmental organisations (NGOs) fall outside its scope, although in some cases members of NGOs may be covered by other provisions like articles 7 and 8. There are many regional or global public international organisations, for example the Council of Europe, whereas there's only one supranational, i.e. the European Union.

Article 10 – Bribery of members of international parliamentary assemblies

The comments made on the bribery of members of domestic public assemblies (article 4) apply here as well, as far as the corrupt acts and the mental element are concerned. These assemblies perform legislative, administrative or advisory functions on the basis of the statute of the international organisation which created them. As far as the specific international context and the restriction of membership of the organisation are concerned, the comments on the bribery of officials of international organisations (article 9) apply here as well. The persons involved on the passive side are, however, different: namely, members of parliamentary assemblies of international (e.g. the Parliamentary Assembly of the Council of Europe) or supranational organisations (the European Parliament).

Article 11 – Bribery of judges and officials of international courts

The comments made on the bribery of domestic public officials (articles 2 and 3), whose definition includes "judges", apply here as well, as far as the corrupt acts and the mental element are concerned. Similarly, the above comments on the bribery of officials of international organisations (article 9) should be extended to this provision as far as the specific international context and the restriction of membership of the organisation are concerned. The persons involved are, however, different: "any holders of judicial office or officials of any international court". These persons include not only "judges" in international courts (e.g. at the European Court of Human Rights) but also other officials (for example the prosecutors of the United Nations Tribunal on the former Yugoslavia) or members of the clerk's office. Arbitration courts are in principle not included in the notion of "international courts" because they do not perform judicial functions in respect of states. It will be for each contracting party to determine whether or not it accepts the jurisdiction of the court.

Article 12 – Trading in influence

This offence is somewhat different from the other – bribery-based – offences defined by the convention, though the protected legal interests are the same: transparency and impartiality in the decision-making process of public administrations. Its inclusion in the present convention illustrates the comprehensive approach of the Programme of Action against Corruption, which views corruption, in its various forms, as a threat to the rule of law and the stability of democratic institutions. Criminalising trading in influence seeks to reach the close circle of the official or the political party to which he belongs and to tackle the corrupt behaviour of those persons who are in the neighbourhood of power and try to obtain advantages from their situation, contributing to the atmosphere of corruption. It permits contracting parties to tackle the so-called "background corruption", which undermines the trust placed by citizens on the fairness of public administration. The purpose of the present convention being to improve the battery of criminal law measures against corruption it appeared essential to introduce this offence of trading in influence, which would be relatively new to some states.

This provision criminalises a corrupt trilateral relationship where a person having real or supposed influence on persons referred to in articles 2, 4, 5 and 9-11, trades this influence in exchange for an undue advantage from someone seeking this influence. The difference, therefore, between this offence and bribery is that the influence peddler is not required to "act or refrain from acting" as would a public official. The recipient of the undue advantage assists the person providing the undue advantage by exerting or proposing to exert an improper influence over the third person who may perform (or abstain from performing) the requested act. "Improper" influence must contain a corrupt intent by the influence peddler: acknowledged forms of lobbying do not fall under this notion. Article 12 describes both forms of this corrupt relationship – active and passive trading in influence. "Passive" trading in influence presupposes that a person, taking advantage of real or pretended influence with third persons, requests, receives or accepts the undue advantage, with a view to assisting the person who supplied the undue advantage by exerting the improper influence. "Active" trading in influence presupposes that a person promises, gives or offers an undue advantage to someone who asserts or confirms that he is able to exert an improper influence over third persons.

States might wish to break down the offence into two different parts: the active and the passive trading in influence. The offence on the active side is quite similar to active bribery, as described in article 2, with some differences: a person gives an undue advantage to a another person (the "influence peddler") who claims, by virtue of his professional position or social status, to be able exert an improper influence over the decision-making of domestic or foreign public officials (articles 2 and 5), members of domestic public assemblies (article 4), officials of international organisations, members of international parliamentary assemblies or judges and officials of international courts (articles 9-11). The passive trading in influence side resembles to passive bribery, as described in article 3, but, again the influence peddler is the one who receives the undue advantage, not the public official. What is important to note is the outsider position of the influence peddler: he cannot take decisions himself, but misuses his real or alleged influence on other persons. It is immaterial whether the influence peddler actually exerted his influence on the above persons or not as is whether the influence leads to the intended result.

The comments made on active and passive bribery apply therefore here as well, with the above additions, in particular as regards the corrupt acts and the mental element.

Article 13 – Money laundering of proceeds from corruption offences

This article provides for the criminalisation of the laundering of proceeds deriving from corruption offences defined under articles 12, i.e. all bribery offences and trading in influence. The technique used by this article is to make a cross-reference to another Council of Europe convention, which is the Convention on Laundering,

Search, Seizure and Confiscation of the Proceeds from Crime (November 1990). The offence of laundering is defined in article 6, para. 1 of the latter convention, whereas certain conditions of application are set out in para. 2. The laundering offence, whose objective is to disguise the illicit origin of proceeds, always requires a predicate offence from which the said proceeds originate. For a number of years anti-laundering efforts focused on drug proceeds but recent international instruments, including above all the Council of Europe anti-laundering convention but also the revised 40 recommendations of the Financial Action Task Force, recognise that virtually any offence can generate proceeds which may need to be laundered for subsequent recycling it in legitimate businesses (e.g. fraud, terrorism, trafficking in stolen goods, arms, etc.). In principle, therefore, the convention already applies to the proceeds of any kind of criminal activity, including corruption, unless a party has entered a reservation to article 6 whereby restricting its scope to proceeds form particular offences or categories of offence.

The authors of this convention felt that given the close links that are proved to exist between corruption and money laundering, it was of primary importance that this convention also criminalises the laundering of corruption proceeds. Another reason to include this offence was the possibly different circles of states ratifying the two instruments: some non-member states which have participated in the elaboration of this convention could only ratify the anti-laundering convention with the authorisation of the Committee of Ministers of the Council of Europe, while they can do so with the present convention automatically by virtue of its article 32, para. 1.

This provision lays down the principle that contracting parties are obliged to consider corruption offences as predicate offences for the purpose of anti-money laundering legislation. Exceptions to this principle are only allowed to the extent that the party has made a reservation in relation to the relevant articles of this convention. Moreover, if a country does not consider some of these corruption offences as "serious" ones under its money laundering legislation, it will not be obliged to modify its definition of laundering.

CHAPTER 24

Legal Instruments of the European Union to Combat Corruption

Michael Grotz

1. Two resolutions and a protocol

Although other regional organisations, such as the Organisation of American States (OAS) had already taken action on the basis of the Resolution of the OAS General Assembly on Probity and Public Ethics of 9 June 1995, which led to the adoption and opening for signature of the Inter-American Convention against Corruption on 29 March 1996 in Caracas, the European Parliament did not adopt the Resolution on Combating Corruption in Europe until 15 December 1995.[1] It stated in part that "corruption, particularly in conjunction with organised crime, poses a threat to the functioning of the democratic system and thus destroys public confidence in the integrity of the democratic constitutional state" as well as "that combating corruption nationally and internationally concerns all member states and that the agreements concluded between the member states on this subject are inadequate [and] that legal provisions and stiffer penalties for crimes of corruption are not enough on their own and that success will be achieved primarily through society's resolute condemnation of corruption and the determination of the responsible authorities to combat it ...".

The resolution defines corruption as "the behaviour of persons with public or private responsibilities who fail to fulfil their duties because a financial or other advantage has been granted or directly or indirectly offered to them ...". It also "recommends that member states abolish any tax legislation and other legal provisions or rules which indirectly encourage corruption and make it a punishable offence for national or foreign officials and decisions-makers to be granted or to accept advantages" and calls on "the Commission and the member states to take

---

[1]   Official Journal no. C 17 of 22 January 1996.

Cyrille Fijnaut, Leo Huberts (eds.), *Corruption, Integrity and Law Enforcement*, 381-388
©2002 Kluwer Law International, The Hague. Printed in The Netherlands.

precautionary measures to exclude market operators convicted of and sentenced for corruption from competing for public contracts for given periods of time …".
In addition, it recommends "that the institutions of the European Union and member states administration introduce procedures in particular and generally to make decision-making processes more transparent".

In parallel to the activities of the European Parliament, the European Council in point 7h of its resolution of 6 December 1994 had however already stated that "member states should take effective measures to punish bribery involving officials of the European Communities in relation to the financial interests of the Communities".[2] This point of the resolution was based on the fact that various studies and other projects undertaken in the member states and the Community institutions had highlighted the fact that the legislation of member states contain provisions which can be used to combat fraud and active and passive corruption of national officials.[3] While the specific characteristics of such legislation vary from one member state to another, all have common elements which make it possible to arrive at a common definition. It has also been established that the member states' criminal laws are far from complete in their applicability to the international dimensions of corruption, involving Community officials from other member states, actually or potentially affecting the European Communities' financial interests. The fact that there are these common elements in the national laws points up the need to promote an adequate response at European Union level and to secure greater convergence in the manner in which member states' criminal law apprehend forms of corruption with international ramifications.

In response to this resolution of the European Council, the First Protocol to the Convention on the Protection of the European Communities' Financial Interests[4] was drawn up and adopted on 27 September 1996.[5] This protocol provides for the criminalisation of both active and passive bribery of national and Community officials which damages or is likely to damage the financial interests of the Community. Under this protocol, member states also undertake to criminalise participation and instigation of corruption of officials and to ensure the offences become punishable by effective, proportionate and dissuasive criminal sanctions. The protocol also provides for criminal liability of heads of business for active corruption

---

2   Official Journal no. C 355 of 14 December 1994.

3   *Cf.* Explanatory Report on the Protocol on the Convention on the Protection of the European Communities' Financial Interests (Official Journal no. C 11 of 15 January 1998).

4   Official Journal no. C 316 of 17 November 1995.

5   Official Journal no. 313 of 23 October 1996.

and has provisions providing for extradition and for prosecution of corruption offences.

This protocol, like nearly all legal instruments drawn up on the basis of article K.3 of the Treaty on European Union, has not yet been ratified by all member states of the European Union, so that it has not entered into force pursuant to its article 9. Whereas applicant states are expected to ratify all conventions belonging to the so called *acquis* of the European Union, even if they have not(!), numerous "old" (and not so old), larger member states, which usually put forward bold and innovative proposals for instruments during the negotiations in Brussels, seem to lose all their interest once the instrument is approved (and press interviews are over) and show little readiness to submit them to their national parliaments for approval. This in turn has led to the conviction that legal instruments, which correspond to what is generally understood to be an international convention, are outdated and that any further progress within the European Union can only be achieved through framework decisions. Why there should be high expectations that these will be implemented in future, remains a mystery.

2. The convention on the fight against corruption

The next step of the European Union in its fight against corruption was the negotiation and adoption of the Convention on the Fight against Corruption Involving Officials of the European Communities or Officials of Member States, on 3 December 1998.[6] Its *raison d'être* can be found in the explanatory report, which reads as follows[7]:

"The criminal law in the member states of the European Union, as virtually everywhere in the world, contains provisions to combat the active and passive corruption of national officials. While the definitions of offences of corruption may vary from member state to member state, they have elements in common which make it possible to arrive at a common definition. From an international rather than the national perspective, it has long been recognised that the principal weakness in the fight against corruption with transnational features has been the fact that criminal law in the member states has often failed to address the issue

---

6 Official Journal no. C 195 of 25 June 1997.

7 Official Journal no. C 391 of 15 December 1998.

of the corruption of foreign officials and officials employed by international organisations. Indeed, the definition of 'public officer' or official, for the purpose of applying internal criminal law, is in many member states only applicable to national officials; even if the term is not more narrowly defined, it is often interpreted restrictively. Thus, the criminal law in most member states does not extend to the criminalisation of conduct aimed at corrupting officials of other member states, even where it took place in their own territory or at the instigation of one of their own nationals. Even if the criminal conduct can in certain circumstances be prosecuted using charges other than corruption such as fraud or breach of trust, the chances are that the corruption itself would go unpunished. This situation, which has long been the focus of attention in international forums (in particular the Organisation for Economic Co-operation and Development and the Council of Europe) and the subject of numerous recommendations and resolutions, has become increasingly intolerable in the European Union owing to the tightening links between its member states and their common membership to the European Community, a supranational organisation founded on the rule of law, with its own institutions and a large staff of officials. Quite apart from the question of principle, this state of affairs frequently hampers the process of judicial Cupertino between member states, where the double criminality condition has not been fulfilled."

Contrary to the Protocol to the Convention of 26 July 1995 on the Protection of the European Communities' Financial Interests, which, owing to the subject matter of the parent convention, could only require member states to punish conduct relating to fraud against the financial interests of the European Communities, the corruption convention could (and indeed did) go further and criminalised active and passive corruption of national and Community officials. This was an important development because it showed a recognition that corruption of public officials was in itself regarded as totally unacceptable behaviour. The corruption itself was damage enough, and proof of financial or other damages was not necessary. Once the convention has entered into force – up to now it has only been ratified by eight member states – it will not only have had the important effect of harmonising European penal law in this important sector, but it will also contribute to the proper functioning of the internal market and to the implementation of political guideline no. 13 of the action plan of 28 April 1997 to combat organised crime.[8]

---

[8]   Official Journal no. C 251 of 15 August 1977.

3. Another protocol and a joint action

Further important anti-corruption provisions are contained in the Second Protocol of 19 June 1997 to the Convention on the Protection of the European Communities' Financial Interests.[9] The elaboration of yet another legal instrument goes back to the act of the Council drawing up the "fraud convention" of 26 July 1995. The Council stressed that the convention should be supplemented shortly afterwards by another legal instrument, in such a way as to improve the effectiveness of protection under criminal law of the European Communities' financial interests. The provisions of the protocol include making corruption of officials a predicate offence of money laundering, liability of legal persons for active corruption of officials, sanctioned either by criminal or administrative fines, and confiscation of the proceeds of crime.

Last but not least mention should be made of the Joint Action of 22 December 1998 on corruption in the private sector.[10] It takes account of the fact that the distinction between public and private sector corruption is not perhaps as clear as it might have been some years ago. With growing privatisation, and increasing importance of the operation of international markets to the everyday lives of people, the distinction has become more and more clouded. The Joint Action starts from the premise that active or passive corruption of a person in the course of business activities is a criminal offence. This broad approach is however limited by the imposition of a minimum requirement to criminalise bribery involving distortion of competition, at least within the common market, and which could result in economic damage to others through the improper award or improper execution of a contract.

The Joint Action also contains provisions on the liability of legal persons, again following the different approach member states take, that provides for criminal or administrative sanctions for such acts. On a discretionary basis it provides for such sanctions as exclusion from entitlement to public benefits or aid, temporary or permanent disqualification from the practice of commercial activities, placing under judicial supervision or a judicial winding-up order. The extent to which the Joint Action has been implemented in the domestic law of member states, if at all, is not known. As the Joint Action, abolished by the Treaty of Amsterdam, only obliges governments to submit proposals to parliament, one must be rather sceptical as to

---

[9] Official Journal no. L 221 of 19 July 1997.

[10] Official Journal no. L 358 of 31 December 1998.

whether any action has been taken to fulfil this commitment, especially in the light of non-ratification of conventions or their protocols.

4. Does the European Union policy make sense?

Looking at all the activities of the European Union in the field of corruption – Council Regulation (EC, Euratom) no. 2988/95 of 18 December 1995 on the Protection of the European Communities' Financial Interests[11] and Council Regulation (EC, Euratom) no. 2185/96 of 11 November 1996 concerning On-the-spot checks and Inspections carried out by the Commission in order to protect the European Communities' financial interests against fraud and other irregularities have neither been introduced nor explained here[12] – one does indeed wonder whether such a multitude of legal instruments, which have to a large extent not been ratified by member states and therefore have not entered into force, is an adequate response to the challenge of corruption.

Undoubtedly the European Union has to look for ways and means to protect its financial interests. Corruption, however, is not an issue specifically linked to the European Union, nor is it limited geographically to its territory. Notwithstanding the well known competition between regional organisations, it might and probably would have been wise for the member states of the European Union to combine their efforts to fight corruption in a follow-up to the 19th Conference of the Ministers of Justice of the Council of Europe held in Valetta in 1994 and dedicated to the issue of corruption and which finally led to the adoption of a criminal and a civil law convention against corruption including a permanent peer review mechanism

Having different legal instruments on the same topic in a geographic region does not pose major difficulties insofar as they contain obligations to criminalise certain behaviours, as long as they do not contradict each other. Governments, when signing and ratifying them should be aware of the obligations they have undertaken. Their practical application does however encounter problems when they contain provisions for judicial co-operation in penal matters. For the practitioner in every day casework it is hardly likely to identify which instrument he has to apply. Even if he were aware of the existence of provisions on mutual legal assistance

---

[11] Official Journal no. L 312 of 23 December 1995.

[12] Official Journal no. L 292 of 15 November 1996.

including rules on data protection in specific protocols or conventions of the European Union dedicated to the fight against certain offences, he would hardly be in a position to verify whether they have come into force or not. Even if he should succeed, he would have to resolve the relationship between the numerous conventions and protocols of the Council of Europe and those of the European Union.

Notwithstanding the convention between the member states of the European Communities on double jeopardy of 25 May 1987 (unfortunately – as usual – not ratified by all member states) and the identical provisions in the convention applying the Schengen Agreement of June 1985 between the Governments of the States of the Benelux Economic Union, the Federal Republic of Germany and the French Republic on the gradual abolition of checks at common borders of 19 June 1990 (ratified by all member states with the exception of Ireland and the United Kingdom who nevertheless wish to adhere), the fraud convention contains a corresponding provision on double jeopardy in its article 10. At first glance, the protocol of 27 September 1996, dealing with corruption, does not foresee any provision on the application of the rule of *ne bis in idem*. Under the heading "relation to the convention" one does however discover, that *inter alia* this article also applies to the protocol.

Both the fraud convention and the corruption convention of the European Union contain a provision on "co-operation". It states on the one hand, that in procedures in connection with any offence established under the convention and concerning at least two member states, they shall co-operate effectively in accordance with the relevant legal instruments on mutual legal assistance, extradition, transfer of proceedings or enforcement of sentences. But does this not go without saying? On the other hand the provision stipulates that in cases in which more than one member state has jurisdiction and the possibility of viable prosecution of an offence based on the same facts, the member states involved shall co-operate in deciding which shall prosecute the offence or offenders with a view to centralising the prosecution in a single member state where possible.

The underlying problem in this case is definitely not limited to fraud or corruption. No added value can be seen in such a provision. On the contrary, a formal approach using the *e contrario* argument could come to the conclusion that such co-operation is only limited to cases which involve fraud or corruption, which is something nobody involved with transnational crime would sign up to.

The protocol of 19 June 1997 obliges member states – as pointed out earlier – to make the corruption of officials a predicate offence of money laundering and to foresee the confiscation of the proceeds of crime. Once more, this approach is strange. The member states have long expressed their political determination to apply the sophisticated convention of 8 November 1990 on Laundering, Search,

Seizure and Confiscation of the Proceeds from Crime (drawn up within the Council of Europe) to the widest range possible, relinquishing the former approach of limiting the predicate offences to drug offences. Here again the appropriate solution would have been, as decided later on, for member states to undertake to make all serious offences a predicate offence of money laundering (Joint Action of 3 December 1998 on money laundering, the identification, tracing, freezing, seizing and confiscation of instrumentalities and the proceeds from crime).[13]

The protocol also contains provision on data protection, which are not quite in line with those of the Convention on Mutual Legal Assistance between the Member States of the European Union of 29 May 2000.[14] So which rules apply?

Having encountered all these problems and unsolved questions the practitioner at this stage will probably be convinced, that international co-operation in penal matters is a cumbersome, time-consuming and complicated matter and will decide not to request for mutual assistance in criminal matters, hoping to solve his case without any help from outside.

---

[13] Official Journal no. L 333 of 9 December 1998.

[14] Official Journal no. C 197 of 12 July 2000.

CHAPTER 25

The Organisation of American States and the Fight against Corruption in the Americas

Jorge Garcia-González

1. Introduction

Corruption has been identified as one of the most serious obstacles and threats for the consolidation of democracy and economic and social development in a number of countries in the Americas. The growing conscience on the severity of this problem, led the countries of this region, within the framework of the Organisation of American States (OAS), to being the first to commit themselves not only from a political point of view, but also a legal one, to strengthen co-operation among themselves to prevent and prosecute corruption.

This chapter's purpose is to present the main developments that the countries of the Americas have made, within the OAS framework, for consolidating co-operation for combating corruption. In order to put this issue into context, we will first refer in a concise manner to the OAS and some of the characteristics of its member states. Secondly, we will mention some of the reasons that have led inter-American co-operation in this subject to strengthen. Finally, we will expand on the specific developments made in this field to the present day.

2. The OAS: a community of principles and a variety of realities

The OAS is an international organisation that brings all of the nations from the American Hemisphere together. It is comprised of 35 member states, including the Caribbean nations (although the government of Cuba was excluded from

---

1   The content and opinions expressed in this chapter are the exclusive responsibility of its
    author and do not necessarily reflect those of the OAS.

Cyrille Fijnaut, Leo Huberts (eds.), *Corruption, Integrity and Law Enforcement*, 389-398
©2002 Kluwer Law International, The Hague. Printed in The Netherlands.

participation in 1962). It is, without a doubt, an organisation of a political and juridical nature instead of a financial or economic one. It constitutes the only regional setting in which all the countries of the Americas can come together and debate issues of common interest and reach an accord on them. Many of these debates conclude in legal instruments like conventions or resolutions agreed upon by the OAS General Assembly.

The OAS Charter was signed in 1948 in Bogota, Colombia, and entered into force in 1951, having been amended on several occasions. The unity of the countries within the OAS framework primarily resides in a series of shared principles and values like those that guarantee continental peace and security, preserve, promote and strengthen democracy and the rule of law, and promote respect and defend human rights.

After the Cold War, the OAS garnered high importance and received mandates for strengthening the hemispherical dialogue and action in all the relevant issues on the international agenda (i.e. democracy, human rights, transnational organised crime, sustainable development, and trade).

Although these shared values and community of interest related to the afore-mentioned issues, the member states of the OAS have very different characteristics among them (geography, population, language, legal systems, social and economic development, and the different levels or grades of their political institutions). This variety of characteristics enrich the political and legal debate in the OAS and is frequently expressed in one way or another, in legal instruments that are negotiated and adopted, just like those related to the fight against corruption.

3. Three reasons to fight corruption in the Americas

During the last few years, international interest and concern has risen in regard to the corruption phenomenon. The causes that have incorporated this issue on the international agenda are multiple. Nevertheless, at its origin are the huge trans-formations that have shaken the world during the past years: the end of the Cold War, the demise of the central controlled planned economies, the rise of new values and realities, technology and communication advancement, and changes in the states' role and the role of civil society institutions in issues of common interest.

Assuming the above-mentioned is true, it is convenient to emphasise three reasons for which the fight against corruption is perceived as a collective priority, particularly in Latin America and the Caribbean.

The first reason relates to the impact corruption has on trade, economic growth and sustained development. Numerous studies have empirically proven that when corruption in a country is high, investment and economic growth will decrease. The *Economic and Social Progress Report on Latin America* by the Inter-American Development Bank in 2000 reiterates the point. The report states that more than half the differences in the levels of income between developed countries and the Latin American countries are linked to the deficiencies in the institutions of the latter. And in those cases that have to do with the enforceability of the law and the control of corruption, Latin America finds itself in the lowest category among other groups of countries, except for Africa. It is evident that this is a great challenge to the region.

The second reason has to do with the need of preserving and strengthening of democracy. The Inter-American Development Bank report highlights that only 35% of Latin Americans are satisfied with democracy, that between 85% and 93% consider corruption is getting worse, and many of them consider it the most serious national problem.

Fortunately, the study also reveals that the "low satisfaction rating" with democracy does not necessarily imply weak backing to democratic principles. On the contrary, it demonstrates that Latin Americans prefer democracy to any other alternative form of government. In any case, those low levels of satisfaction and confidence in political institutions, without a doubt, are a sign of high alert.

The third and final reason is intimately linked to the enormous social costs brought on by this problem. In Latin America poverty has not only risen in absolute terms but it has constituted itself in the region with high levels of disproportion between the wealthy and poor. Accordingly, studies have also proven that the principal victims of corruption are the poor and that in countries where poverty flourishes there are unmeasurable and growing acts of corruption. In this sense the fight against corruption is seen as social justice cause.

4. Developments within the OAS framework

4.1. Background

The fight against corruption has been a constant concern of the OAS. The OAS Charter itself states that "representative democracy is an indispensable condition for the stability, peace and development of the region" and member states have recognised corruption constitutes one of the most serious threats to democracy.

That is why the organisation has formulated and reiterated its commitment in fighting corruption and modernising public institutions in, for example, the Santiago

Commitment to Democracy and the Renewal of the Inter-American System and the General Assembly Resolution 1159 in 1992 on Corrupt International Trade Practices; the Declaration of Managua for the Promotion of Democracy and Development; the San Jose Declaration on Human Rights of 1993 and the Belen do Para Declaration of 1994,

Yet the summit process of the Heads of States and of Governments of the Americas has doubtless introduced the vigorous treatment of this issue on a hemispherical level. In fact, the first summit, held in Miami in December 1994, targeted the issue for the first time. On this occasion, the Heads of States and of Governments acknowledged that this problem was of a multilateral nature and, aware of that, they committed themselves to negotiate, within the OAS framework, a hemispherical accord. As a result of this decision and after a process of broad analysis and deliberations, the nations of the Americas adopted in March of 1996 the Inter-American Convention against Corruption.

4.2. The Inter-American Convention against Corruption

The Inter-American Convention against Corruption is, without a doubt, the most important step that has been taken on a hemispherical level in combating this phenomenon. Ultimately, it is regarded as a road map for collective action in the Americas on this subject.

The itinerary designed by the OAS General Assembly for negotiating the convention resulted in a process based on participation that led to an enriched content and concluded in an integral conception on the way corruption must be combated.

First, the two major purposes of the convention express the abovementioned sentiment, namely, to promote and strengthen the development by each of the parties of the mechanisms needed to prevent, detect, punish and eradicate corruption; and to promote, facilitate and regulate co-operation among the parties to ensure the effectiveness of measures and actions to prevent, detect, punish and eradicate corruption in the performance of public functions and acts of corruption specifically related to such performance.

Secondly, the convention expressly recognises, in its preamble and in various articles that this problem cannot be solved with repressive or punishing actions once the evil has emerged. On the contrary, precise decisions of a preventive nature are to be taken also. These are directly linked to the modernisation of institutions and the elimination of its causes or the conditions that facilitate or instigate its use.

Thirdly, the convention conceives the fight against corruption as a process and not as a simple result of pointed actions, isolated and without any connection or co-ordination. On the contrary, a permanent effort is inferred, upon its reading, begun by the countries, which leads to the convention and continues – in a process of "progressive development" – through the negotiation and adoption of additional protocols contributing to the achievement of the above-cited purposes.

Lastly, the convention, without setting aside state responsibility in eradicating corruption, reveals the importance of action taken by all the actors involved. Especially, it recognises the need to strengthen the participation of civil society in preventing and combating corruption and it expresses that states extend to each other broad technical co-operation, exchange experiences and give special attention to the ways and forms citizens participate.

Furthermore, it is worth noting that the convention constitutes the most important inter-American legal instrument for extraditing those who commit crimes of corruption; in co-operation and assistance among the states in obtaining evidence and facilitating necessary procedural acts regarding the investigation or trials of corruption; and for the identification, search, immobilisation, confiscation, and seizure of goods obtained or derived from the commission of the crime of corruption.

In regard to investigating or obtaining information by way of banking or financial institutions, the convention represents an important step towards avoiding bank secrecy being used to aid and abet those who commit corruption.

In relation to the issue of asylum, the convention strikes an equal balance between the values that are protected by asylum and those that combat corruption. During the deliberation process of the project it was attested that the reason for and the essence of asylum could not be weakened, but it may not serve as way of eluding or facilitating the avoidance of legal action against those who commit acts of corruption.

Within this context, the content of article XVII is very important stating the following: the fact that the property obtained or derived from an act of corruption was intended for political purposes, or that it is alleged that an act of corruption was committed for political motives or purposes, shall not suffice in and of itself to qualify the act as a political offence or as a common offence related to a political offence.

Finally, another issue that is touched upon by the convention and worth mentioning has to do with the fight against transnational bribery. Article VIII of the convention not only marked a huge step, but it also placed the American Hemisphere at the forefront of this issue since regulation and the commitment of punishing this illicit practice was established in an obligatory instrument from a legal point of view like a convention. This in complete contrast to the timid steps that have been taken up until then within the frameworks of organisations like the Organisation for Economic Co-operation and Development (OECD), Council of Europe and United Nations. It is worth remembering that until then, developed countries within the OECD framework, systematically refrained from negotiating a legal instrument that would combat this phenomenon, notwithstanding the multiple and solitary efforts and actions displayed by the United States.

4.3. Developments after the adoption of the convention

Once the Inter-American Convention against Corruption was adopted, states realised that the treaty, far from being the final destination, was just the first major step to address this problem collectively. That is why the OAS General Assembly adopted in 1997 an Inter-American Program of Co-operation in Combating Corruption. And the Heads of States and of Governments during the Santiago de Chile Summit held in 1998 committed themselves in providing, in the OAS, an adequate follow-up to the progress made in the convention.

In developing these mandates, the OAS has continued working in this field. Within the framework of the Working Group on Probity and Public Ethics, the states have made great progress. They have taken the recommendations that were adopted in a symposium held in Santiago de Chile in 1998, the results of a special session held by this group with government representatives, international organisations and private sector and civil society representatives. Also, a questionnaire on the adjustments made to national legislations in regard to the convention was distributed, the responses permitting a thorough diagnostic on the areas that still require progress in the American countries.

The states have also begun to consider an important issue: corporate social responsibility in fighting corruption. On this issue, a hemispherical meeting will take place in 2002, in the hope that guidelines and specific plans of action will emerge. The OAS General Secretariat for its part, in developing the mandates of both the Summit of the Americas and the OAS General Assembly, has been supporting the process of ratification of the convention, as well as implementing decisions contained in it or related to it. As a part of this process, in conjunction with the Inter-American Development Bank, support has been given to a number of countries in the region in defining the necessary measures for adjusting their criminal legislation to that expressed in the convention.

Following this same line, a "pilot" program was started in Central America, with the aim of assisting the countries in the region to adjust their legal systems to the preventive measures expressed by the convention. Additionally, an information system on the internet and a network of inter-American institutions and experts against corruption has been created.

Likewise, the OAS General Secretariat is working with the Inter-Parliamentary Forum of the Americas, among others, in all that has to do with the role that corresponds to the legislative bodies in political control matters, as well as in their member ethical norms. It has also been participating in an initiative that emerged from the last Ministers of Justice meeting and backed by the government of Canada, in creating a mutual legal assistance network.

Finally, in conjunction with the Trust of the Americas and other institutions, it co-sponsored a training initiative for investigative reporting.

As a result of this process, the American states have acknowledged the importance of this convention as a road map for their collective action against corruption. An example of this acknowledgement is that, comparatively, this treaty was one of the fastest instruments to be signed and ratified. Today we have 29 states who have signed the convention and 23 have ratified it. The General Secretariat has begun a project to assist in ratifying and implementing the convention those states who have not done so yet. With all the progress made until now, it is possible to imagine that in the near future, this convention shall be enforceable throughout the entire hemisphere.

4.4. The follow-up mechanism for the implementation of the convention

The Inter-American Convention against Corruption had a leading role. In 1996, when it was adopted, many states were still discussing if this was an issue that should be considered within an international treaty. In fact, in the United Nations and the OECD, attempts to negotiate conventions on this issue failed.

If the viability of international treaties in this field were disputable during this time, the possibility of creating monitoring mechanisms or instruments for evaluating compliance of the treaties by the states was practically unthinkable. In fact, no state or non-governmental organisation introduced a formal or informal proposal during the negotiations of the Inter-American convention on the creation of some sort of follow-up mechanism, evaluation or monitoring of compliance of the measures that were to be adopted. The idea simply did not exist, nor was it introduced at the time.

Even though a short time has passed between the adoption of the convention and the present time, the circumstances have changed considerably. Ultimately and for different circumstances, the OECD convention adopted a "monitoring mechanism" for the signatory states to it. Also, the Group of States against Corruption (GRECO) of the Council of Europe adopted a monitoring mechanism regarding its commitment to this field.

This led to the suggestion of creating a follow-up mechanism for the implementation of the Inter-American Convention against Corruption by the parties to it.

The issue itself of monitoring international accords is not something new or strange to the OAS member states. Many countries are part of monitoring mechanisms, for example, in combating money laundering, and some participate in the OECD process of evaluation. Within the OAS framework, states have adopted monitoring instruments in areas of collective interests. Suffice it to cite the activities of the Multilateral Evaluation Mechanism (MEM) in regard to drug abuse and to the activities of the Consultative Committee foreseen in the Inter-American Convention against the Manufacturing of and Trafficking in Firearms, Ammunition, Explosives, and other related Materials.

Taking into account these new circumstances, the OAS General Assembly, in June 2000, requested of the Permanent Council (the body integrated by the Permanent Representatives before the OAS of the member states) that they analyse the existing mechanisms and develop a recommendation on an appropriate model that could be used by the parties.

The Permanent Council, thanks to the efficient and opportune work of the Working Group on Probity and Public Ethics, of a meeting of experts in this field and of the Conference of States Parties held in Buenos Aires, Argentina, in May 2001, completed its task. As a result, within the framework of the ordinary session of the General Assembly held in San Jose, Costa Rica, on 4 June 2001, the parties, through a declaration, approved the Follow-up Mechanism for the Implementation of the Inter-American Convention against Corruption. Of the approved text, the following aspects are worth mentioning.

First, the objectives that have been defined for the follow-up mechanism. They strike an adequate balance between the necessity of following-up the progress made by the states and facilitating co-operation among them as to assure compliance, implementation and application of the convention.

Secondly, the mechanism was developed within the objectives and principles established in the OAS Charter, for example principles like sovereignty, non-intervention and legal equality of states.

Thirdly, characteristics that were defined for the mechanism like impartiality and objectivity in its operation and conclusions, as well as the absence of sanctions.

Fourthly, the search for an adequate balance between confidentiality and transparency in its activities is very important through the publication of the rules and procedures of the Committee of Experts, the selection of issues and methodology, the selection of countries and the final report

Fifthly, even though the mechanism is of an inter-governmental nature, it has foreseen the acceptance of opinions given by civil society and that the committee, in its procedural rules, will regulate their participation.

Finally, the follow-up mechanism incorporates its content within those of the OAS Charter and the guidelines for the participation of civil society in the activities of the organisation, and establishes headquarters for the Committee of Experts and that the functions of secretariat will be offered by the OAS General Secretariat.

Without a doubt, starting this follow-up mechanism marks an important moment at a hemispherical level as to insure the effectiveness of the measures that will be adopted in strengthening inter-American co-operation in combating corruption.

This is, in general terms, the road taken so far within the OAS framework in strengthening co-operation among the nations of the Americas in their fight against corruption. It is clear that the road taken is not complete but is a permanent one, one that starts but never ends and, above all, has no return.

The Heads of States and of Governments of the Americas reiterated in their last Summit meeting, held in Quebec, Canada in April 2001, their commitment in combating corruption, "acknowledging that corruption undermines core democratic values, challenges political stability and economic growth and thus threatens vital interests in our Hemisphere, we pledge to reinvigorate our fight against corruption. We also recognise the need to improve the conditions for human security in the Hemisphere."

PART VIII

INTERNATIONAL INITIATIVES TO COMBAT CORRUPTION

CHAPTER 26

Interpol's Approach to Combating Corruption

Willy Deridder

1. Introduction

Corruption as an issue is not only apparent from the numerous media articles exposing it, but also from the number of governments which have recently collapsed following allegations of high-level corruption. The global impetus towards democratisation has uncovered large-scale abuses of power not only in previously authoritarian regimes, but also in many so-called established democracies. Citizens everywhere are demanding honesty and accountability from their elected representatives. The phenomenon of globalisation and the resulting trade liberalisation bring transparency in domestic and global markets and corruption more quickly to the public eye.

Hence, it can be stated that a remarkable increase in community awareness of the evil of this phenomenon has occurred since the 1st International Anti-Corruption Conference took place in 1983 in Washington, attended by less than 100 delegates. The delegates at the 9th IACC held in 1999 in Durban, South Africa, numbered over 1700. Politicians, policy-makers, bankers, financial managers and other practitioners have been reluctant for a long time to discuss problems related to corruption. Such an attitude can be explained by the fact that nobody wants to raise major problems – like the existence of corruption – that he or she considers internal to his or her jurisdiction. However, as corruption remains prevalent and the involvement of organised crime in this crime area is growing, the subject can no longer be treated, solely within the limits of one jurisdiction. While the will and the actions of governments to address their own problems remain crucial, the understanding is now that corruption needs also to be approached from the angle of international police and judicial co-operation.

The nature of corruption is that it is an "umbrella offence", able to cover a large variety of illegal activities while shielding the actors from detection. In this character is hidden the real threat to the democratic institutions and processes, law enforcement

Cyrille Fijnaut, Leo Huberts (eds.), *Corruption, Integrity and Law Enforcement*, 401-408 agencies included. Law enforcement plays a pivotal role in ensuring respect and preservation of fundamental human rights. It also plays a large role in the conservation of life and property and the protection of the innocent. Corruption can diminish and even destroy the ability of law enforcement to accomplish its mission. Then, the officer or agency involved becomes an obstruction to the pursuit of justice.

Recognising the urgent need in law enforcement circles all over the world for guidance from fellow law enforcement officers, over and above legal and political advice in this sensitive matter, Interpol took initiatives aiming at supporting those who are in the field facing corruption. Before I summarise Interpol's efforts in combating corruption, I would like to share with you briefly what Interpol is.

Interpol is the only truly global police organisation, with a current membership of 178 countries. Its main objective is to facilitate the flow and exchange of information between these members. Interpol has also accepted the responsibility for setting international standards and sharing best practices in priority, serious transnational crime areas. Under its new Secretary General, R. Noble, the organisation is in a modernisation process, both in terms of structure and technical ability. By September of 2002, we will be in a position to offer true international 24/7 police customer service, with special emphasis on a regional approach, with specialisation in high priority crimes, such as corruption.

2. Interpol's Group of Experts on Corruption

In April 1998 Interpol created an International Group of Experts on Corruption (IGEC) as a result of the 1st International Conference on Corruption-related Crime held at the Interpol General Secretariat in Lyons.

The IGEC currently consists of law enforcement officers representing Europe, Asia, Africa and the Americas, and an advisory group consisting of representatives from Transparency International, the United Nations, the World Bank, the Information Co-ordinational Group, the chairman of the organising committee of the International Anti-Corruption Conference, two academics and an internationally renowned judge. The underlying motivation was on the one hand the general belief that law enforcement should combat corruption as a phenomenon holistically, in co-operation with all the major role players and the community at large. On the other hand, the belief is that law enforcement, especially in the field of combating corruption, is viewed somewhat sceptically, and that, if internationally renowned and respected organisations/individuals were involved, this would enhance the status and the products of the IGEC, making these more acceptable to the community at large.

The IGEC continues deliberations on the issue of co-opting additional members, making every effort to extend the principle of equal regional representation; additional members, with the appropriate expertise, are still being sought from especially Eastern Europe and the South American and African continent.

The IGEC advocates that certain principles are fundamental to combating corruption successfully, whether on a national level or internationally:

- First, corruption can only be combated effectively and successfully if a holistic approach is adopted, and is introduced as part of a comprehensive national and international effort. In essence this implies a multi-agency concept dealing with all forms of corruption;

- Further, corruption may be more common in some parts of the world than in others, but we should never confuse bad practice with culture. Interpol does not see corruption as a cultural issue; it is also abundantly clear that corruption is not only a problem faced by developing economies, but one inherent to all societies. However, it is the reaction or response from individual governments to this phenomena that varies considerably and this is probably the greatest distinguishing feature between developed and developing economies;

- Finally, the only acceptable reaction to corruption is the acceptance of a "zero tolerance approach". Any other approach is doomed to failure from the outset.

Apart from these fundamental principles, the IGEC to date has produced the following:

- A mission statement which reflects our holistic approach to combating corruption and reads as follows: "As representatives of international law enforcement we believe in a free and just society. To be truly just, society must be free of corruption and embrace high standards of integrity. To this end we join hands with community to ensure our own ethical standards and accept our responsibility to fight all forms of corruption through effective law enforcement, education and prevention";

- A practical definition of corruption: "Corruption is any agreement between parties to act or refrain from acting in violation of the public trust for profit or gain in either the private or public sector";

- A "declaration of intent" known as the "Seoul Declaration", which was proposed to our 178 members at the occasion of our 68th general assembly session (Seoul, 8-12 November 1999), saying that they adopt the "code of conduct" and the "code of ethics" as proposed by the IGEC as a minimum standard for the conduct and ethical values for a law enforcement officer. We believe that, although this action was long overdue, it has been a step in the right direction to ensure that law enforcement focuses on cleaning up its own shop, thereby creating better service delivery and greater acceptance by, and integration into, the community at large.

This IGEC has also produced an action plan detailing the projects that will set new standards for law enforcement in this millennium:

- It is compiling a "best practices guide" envisaged as an aid to those tasked with the investigation and corresponding management of a corruption investigation. Currently 19 different chapters are envisaged covering topics from anti-corruption structures to recruitment, selection and development of staff to compliance programmes, identifying factors of corruption to training, prevention and education. This guide will be up-dated continuously and be made available to all appropriate law enforcement units;

- It has compiled an "early warning system", consisting of a contact list of agencies, units and other entities involved in combating corruption. This will serve not only to facilitate improved co-operation in corruption investigations, but also serve as a source of information for potentially new investigations;

- The group has decided to create a web site focusing on corruption, which will be linked to the existing Interpol site as well as to the sites of all other anti-corruption organisations or initiatives. Through this site most of its initiatives will be made available to the community at large, except some of the initiatives enumerated in the guide of "best practices". The site will also feature a "calendar of events", to allow law enforcement to focus its resources and to avoid unnecessary duplication and the resultant waste of resources;

- It is in the process of developing a training programme for law enforcement by adopting a project based approach, led by professionals in the field of corruption training;

- Finally and most importantly, the IGEC will this year present to our general assembly a set of standards or norms for the investigation of corruption and the management of corruption investigations.

3. The need for further initiatives

Interpol does not consider these achievements as sufficient to meet future challenges. Its now three-year-old initiative has to be seen as a first step in a process that needs to be deepened and broadened. The reasons therefore are obvious.

A permanent threat is weighing on all law enforcement officers as organised crime has the willingness, the ability and the means to buy services from law enforcement officers. Moreover, organised crime is always strengthening its financial resources and thus its potential to corrupt all kinds of officials who can obstruct the achievements of its objectives. Criminal organisations and networks benefit from globalisation of the society, political instability, economic disparities and growing influence of information and communication technology.

Organised crime is proving to be especially adept at taking advantage of these social factors. There is growing evidence of increased co-operation between criminal networks from different geographical areas and/or ethnic groups. There is also a general trend of criminal organisations to diversify their criminal activities. There is a move towards areas like intellectual property rights violations, fraud and environmental crime, all activities sharing the following characteristics: a relatively low level of law enforcement attention, high potential for profit, significant legal loopholes and low penalties and low risk.

For many years, combating corruption will thus remain a top priority for the law enforcement community, nationally, regionally and globally.

The results of the corruption attempts (success or non-success) will depend on the resistance capability of the law enforcement officials. That capability is weak in some countries, stronger in other, but never firm enough as to state that corruption attempts have no chance to succeed.

Hence, initiatives to improve that capability need to be taken. Legal, organisational, functional, psychological, social and financial provisions have to be made. The challenge for the law enforcement agencies and the responsible political authorities consist of building up that capability as efficiently as possible.

4. Some ideas for the future

The response cannot be given by focusing only on separate aspects. First, an important effort of co-ordination must be made within the law enforcement structures themselves in order to ensure that criminals are targeted from all possible angles. Further, regulatory and law enforcement officials must co-operate. A multi-disciplinary approach consisting of preventive and law enforcement measures, has to be taken due to the multi-faceted aspects of corruption. Finally, as for the other crime areas, it is highly recommended to introduce or develop for combating corruption a proactive approach supplementing the existing reactive measures.

At the national level, strategies and action plans covering all law enforcement agencies and other related agencies and services are needed.

Internationally, co-operation and the broadest possible framework for this purpose need to be created. Mechanisms allowing controlling corruption must be put in place. Interpol and regional law enforcement organisations like Europol are well-positioned to contribute to the improvement of that framework, to make it operational and involve supra-national non-law enforcement bodies when needed.

Can we do more than we do currently?

The initiatives summarised above must be continued. Interpol will seek to complete and refine these initiatives. Others can be developed.

Concerning the measures to be taken at the national level: we can support them by starting up operational projects for which we are collecting information based on ongoing investigations as Interpol already does in other crime areas, analysing that information and putting the analytical products at the disposal of the agencies participating in the project. Interpol can also organise activities like training, working parties or conferences for the benefit of its member countries concerned or involved.

At international level we support the initiative to start the elaboration of an effective international legal instrument against corruption following the decision taken by the General Assembly of the United Nations.

5. By way of conclusion

In conclusion, what Interpol's efforts and these of its GEC boil down to is nothing other than striving to fulfil the purpose for which our organisation was constituted, as set out in article 2 of its constitution. That purpose is:

- "• To ensure and promote the widest possible mutual assistance between all criminal police authorities, within the limits of the laws existing in the different countries and in the spirit of the Universal Declaration of Human Rights;

- • To establish and develop all institutions likely t contribute effectively to the prevention and suppression of ordinary law crimes."

The success in pursuing this purpose will depend on the willingness and/or ability of law enforcement to combat corruption. Interpol must have a monitoring approach, not only serving to identify training and other needs and others within the membership but also permanently assuring the realistic character of its efforts in an area where a lot of lip service to the overarching principles of its approach exist. We are focusing on it.

CHAPTER 27

Combating Corruption in Southern Africa: Towards More Effective Regional and International Law Enforcement Co-operation

Peter Gastrow

1. Introduction: the SADC region

It is generally accepted that corruption is particularly harmful in the developing and the least developed countries. Such countries tend to present more opportunities for corruption, the environment is often a low-risk one, and authorities have meagre resources available to combat it. The debilitating effect of corruption is even more pronounced when poor countries have fragile democracies and are undergoing political and economic transition. In Southern Africa there are a number of states that fall into this category.

The 14 member states of the Southern African Development Community (SADC) cover the larger part of sub-equatorial Africa. The SADC region stretches from Dar-Es-Salaam in Tanzania in the northeast to Cape Town in the South.[1] The member states spread over more than 9 million square kilometres, an area into which Europe's largest country, France, would fit sixteen times. The large geographical areas and long national boundaries and coastlines that many of the SADC states have to police, are factors that need to be taken into account when considering the challenges that law enforcement agencies face. According to the human development index of the UNDP, which measures the country's achievements in terms of life expectancy, educational attainment and adjusted real income, eight of the 14 SADC member countries were categorised as "medium human development" or developing

---

[1] SADC member states are: Angola, Botswana, Democratic Republic of Congo, Lesotho, Malawi, Mauritius, Namibia, Seychelles, South Africa, Swaziland, Tanzania, Zambia, and Zimbabwe.

Cyrille Fijnaut, Leo Huberts (eds.), *Corruption, Integrity and Law Enforcement*, 409-422
©2002 Kluwer Law International, The Hague. Printed in The Netherlands.

countries during 2000. The remaining six were placed into the category of "low human development", or regarded as constituting part of the least developed countries.[2] Four of the SADC member states, namely Tanzania, Angola, Malawi, and Mozambique, form part of the 20 least-developed and poorest countries in the world.

Although South Africa has a good infrastructure and an economy with some well-developed components, it falls significantly short of being ranked as a developed country. It is not in a position to provide any significant material assistance to other SADC countries. The SADC region is therefore poor and under-developed, with meagre resources available to develop regional programmes relating to law enforcement and crime combating. An aggravating factor has been the ongoing conflicts and wars in some of the countries, particularly Angola and the Democratic Republic of the Congo. In the latter there is no functioning national government, and in Angola significant parts of the country are still ungovernable and controlled by rebel forces.

This brief background needs to be borne in mind when exploring possibilities for increased international co-operation with law enforcement agencies of Southern Africa.

2. Regional law enforcement initiatives in the SADC region

At present there are no regional law enforcement agreements in place that specifically aim at combating corruption. It was only in 1998 that SADC member states started to explore possibilities for greater regional co-operation to combat corruption. Their deliberations culminated in a Draft SADC Protocol against Corruption. However, until that protocol has been adopted, attempts to improve regional and international law enforcement co-operation against corruption will have to make use of existing instruments to facilitate multilateral regional co-operation. The following existing regional agreements and initiatives could facilitate such co-operation:

---

2   UNDP Human Development Report Chart, http://www.undp.org/hdi2000/english/ presskit/hdi.pdf (accessed May 2001). Countries falling into the "medium human development" category are Seychelles, Mauritius, South Africa, Swaziland, Namibia, Botswana, Lesotho and Zimbabwe. The least developed countries, or those with a low human development index are Democratic Republic of Congo, Zambia, Tanzania, Angola, Malawi and Mozambique.

1. The Southern African Regional Police Chiefs Co-operation Organisation (SARPCCO agreement);

2. The Interpol Sub-Regional Bureau for Southern Africa;

3. Multi-lateral Agreement in respect of Co-operation and Mutual Assistance in the Field of Crime Combating;

4. SADC Protocol on Combating Illicit Drugs;

5. Draft SADC Protocol against Corruption.

2.1. SARPCCO agreement

No regional law enforcement initiatives were possible during the 1980s. Under apartheid rule, South Africa was a pariah state within a divided region. No official co-operation between law enforcement agencies in Southern Africa was possible. However, by the mid 1990s, after South Africa's integration into the region, cross-border organised crime in Southern Africa reached such proportions that governments were galvanised into developing a regional law enforcement response. It led to the formation of the Southern African Regional Police Chiefs Co-operation Organisation (SARPCCO) in 1995.

SARPCCO was established at the initiative of the chiefs of police from eleven Southern African countries – Angola, Botswana, Mozambique, Namibia, South Africa, Swaziland, Tanzania, Zambia and Zimbabwe. A twelfth country, namely Mauritius, has since joined. The eleven national police chiefs signed an agreement that focused on future police co-operation through SARPCCO. Since then, the agreement has been ratified by the Parliaments of the member countries and significant progress has been made in regional co-operation relating, *inter alia*, to training, joint crime combating strategies, and the exchange of crime information. According to the SARPCCO constitution, its objectives are subject to domestic laws and include the following:

1. To promote, strengthen and perpetuate co-operation and foster joint strategies for the management of all forms of cross-border and related crimes with regional implications;

2. To prepare and disseminate relevant information on criminal activities as may be necessary to benefit members to contain crime in the region;

3. To carry out regular reviews of joint crime management strategies in view of changing national and regional needs and priorities;

4. To ensure efficient operation and management of criminal records and efficient joint monitoring of cross-border crime taking full advantage of the relevant facilities available through Interpol;

5. To make relevant recommendations to governments of member countries in relation to matters affecting effective policing in the Southern African region;

6. To formulate systematic regional training policies and strategies taking into account the needs and performance requirements of the regional police services/forces;

7. To carry out any such relevant and appropriate acts and strategies for purposes of promoting regional police co-operation and collaboration as regional circumstances dictate.

The SARPCCO agreement emphasises cross-border crime and not corruption. During 1995 the former was regarded as a higher priority for Southern African States than corruption. Despite the agreement not specifically focusing on corruption, it can play an important role in generating more effective regional anti-corruption law enforcement steps. It provides the basis for police co-operation across borders and is therefore an instrument through which new regional law enforcement strategies against corruption can be devised.

2.2. Interpol Southern Africa

The Interpol Sub-Regional Bureau in Harare, Zimbabwe, is closely linked to SARPCCO and its operations. The bureau serves as the secretariat for SARPCCO and they share a building complex in Harare. The bureau was established in 1997 and it covers twelve countries that are all members of SARPCCO, namely Angola, Botswana, Lesotho, Malawi, Mauritius, Mozambique, Namibia, South Africa, Swaziland, Tanzania, Zambia and Zimbabwe.

Over and above the general Interpol objectives which the bureau pursues, it has also set itself additional objectives, some of which are:

1. To study and evaluate regional and international crime trends, perceived by the chiefs of police of the region as priority crimes in order to advise police organisations of the region on crime trends and effects thereof so that they may take necessary steps to counter the incidence of crime either as individual countries or jointly as a region through exchange of criminal intelligence, joint operations or joint training exercise;

2. To promote and co-ordinate the initiatives of Interpol in the region in a bid to facilitate regional and international police co-operation on the investigation of criminal matters;

3. To co-ordinate regional training activities in order to assist in bringing up to acceptable standards, as per requirements of the police chiefs of the region, the general performance of specialised police units and to prepare and facilitate any training requirements as may from time to time be required by the general secretary of Interpol.

The role of Interpol in the region is therefore more one of a facilitator than an initiator. Its international links could contribute significantly towards greater international co-operation. Its close link to SARPCCO should provide a door through which access to the region can be gained for the purpose of enhancing international links and co-operation with other law enforcement agencies.

2.3. The SARPCCO Crime Combating Agreement

The Police Chiefs of the SADC region signed this agreement in October 1997. It provides for co-operation and mutual assistance in the field of crime combating and allows, *inter alia*, for police officers from the region to enter into countries of other parties for the purpose of police investigations, seizure of exhibits, and the tracing and questioning of witnesses. The action of seizing exhibits, tracing and questioning witnesses, and arresting suspects, has to be carried out by police officers from the host country. The agreement also allows for the exchange of criminal intelligence to counter organised cross-border crime more effectively.

Police chiefs in the region regard this agreement as having opened a new chapter in policing in Southern Africa. It has broken down barriers between police agencies and during the short period since its inception has led to an increase in the information that is being exchanged for the purpose of combating criminal activities in the region, without too much red tape being involved. Any regional initiatives to combat corruption more effectively will therefore have to place great reliance on the SARPCCO Crime Combating Agreement to facilitate the cross-border activities of law enforcement agencies when pursuing anti-corruption initiatives.

2.4. SADC Protocol on Combating Illicit Drugs

SADC Heads of State signed this regional protocol in August 1996. Its main objective is to address drug trafficking in the Southern African region, but its provisions also focus on law enforcement co-operation and on steps that need to be taken to curb corruption resulting from illicit drug trafficking. In chapter 6 of the protocol, provision is made for co-operation among law enforcement agencies. Amongst the provisions are the following:

1. Establishment of a direct communication system to facilitate free and fast flow of information among the law enforcement agencies in the region;

2. Establishment of an effective infrastructure to enhance effective drug law enforcement, including suitable search and inspection facilities at all designated points of exit and entry.

Chapter 8 of the protocol covers aspects relating to corruption, including the establishment of independent and adequately resourced anti-corruption agencies or units. The protocol also provides for the establishment of administrative and regulatory mechanisms for the prevention of corruption and the abuse of power.

The above provisions have not yet been widely implemented but they do provide the basis for regional police co-operation to investigate corruption relating to drug trafficking.

2.5. Draft SADC Protocol against Corruption

The development of this regional protocol followed three roundtable meetings of senior government officials from the region that were held in 1998, 1999, and 2000. At the roundtable meeting held in August 2000, the Ministers of Justice of the SADC countries agreed to take concrete initiatives to fight corruption in the region by approving a Draft SADC Protocol against Corruption.[3] This draft will be considered for approval by the regional Ministers of Justice in June 2001. If approved, the summit of SADC Heads of State will consider the protocol for adoption in August 2001.

The SADC structure that has the mandate to deal with the development of the SADC Protocol against Corruption is the SADC Legal Sector which is chaired by

---

[3] Since the conference in The Hague in May 2001, the Annual Conference for SADC Heads of State, held in August 2001, approved the SADC Protocol against Corruption.

the Namibian Minister of Justice. The Legal Sector is made up of the Ministers of Justice from SADC countries. Their task is to address regional legislative and institutional issues that would typically form part of the functions of Departments of Justice. A complicating factor for the future, although perhaps only a short-term one, is the recent decision by the SADC Heads of State to completely restructure the SADC and its existing institutions. This is likely to result in the disappearance of the present Legal Sector and in the establishment of a new sub-structure to address the issues presently being dealt with by the Legal Sector.

The draft protocol contains many provisions that one would expect to see in such a protocol. It focuses on corruption in the public and the private sectors; it promotes co-operation against corruption; it urges the harmonisation of policies and legislation in the region; it provides for confiscation and for seizure and for extradition and mutual legal assistance; and it provides for the establishment of a Committee of States Parties to oversee the implementation and operation of the protocol once it is adopted.

This draft protocol constitutes a significant step towards combating corruption in the region more effectively. However, in a region that is made up of developing countries, its effective implementation will depend on whether the political will exists and whether adequate resources are made available by states parties for that purpose. International assistance and co-operation could play an important role in this regard.

Looking to the future, it would seem that the preparatory work that has gone into the Draft SADC Protocol will place SADC countries in a good position to make valuable contributions to the planned United Nations process of negotiating an International Convention against Corruption.

3. The scope for improved international co-operation in anti-corruption law enforcement

From the brief assessment of the five existing regional agreements and initiatives referred to above, it is apparent that the foundation for improved regional and international law enforcement co-operation to combat corruption is already largely in place. A sufficient number of regional agreements and structures provide the basic institutional framework for multilateral co-operation. Once the SADC Protocol against Corruption is adopted, the way will be clear for international co-operation with SADC states to combat corruption more effectively.

In pursuing more effective international co-operation, a number of opportunities and challenges need to be considered. Amongst them are:

1. Strengthening the operational capabilities of police agencies to combat corruption in the region;

2. Supporting SADC governments in countering corruption;

3. Addressing the weak resource base in the region;

4. Addressing the overlap and duplication by the SADC Legal Sector and SARPCCO.

3.1. Strengthening the operational capabilities of police agencies to combat corruption in the region

To date there have not been any co-ordinated regional law enforcement initiatives against corruption specifically. The focus has been on drug trafficking and organised crime. However, discussions have taken place within SARPCCO policing structures about possible joint anti-corruption operations. One option would be to build on the successes of the nine joint operations that have been held against cross-border crime in the region since 1997. Three of the more recent operations were:

- Operation Atlantic (July 1998), covering Botswana, South Africa, and Namibia;

- Operation Sesani (April 1999), covering Botswana, Tanzania, Malawi, South Africa and Zimbabwe;

- Operation Makhulu (July-August 2000), covering Botswana, Lesotho, Mozambique, Namibia, South Africa, Swaziland and Zimbabwe.

Whilst the main focus of the operations was on combating the cross-border movement of stolen motor vehicles, the operations were also designed to gather intelligence on the trafficking of drugs, firearms and diamonds. In exploring how future joint operations could be utilised to also target corruption, consideration is being given to enlarging the scope of such operations by attaching a specialised anti-corruption component to each operation. Such a component would then investigate any indications of corruption where such corruption can be linked to the crimes that are being targeted by the joint operation in question.

The various regional instruments referred to above would certainly allow for such anti-corruption components to be added. If the police chiefs of the region implement this idea, it would constitute a welcome first step towards regional police co-operation in combating corruption. It would constitute a first step only because the investigations would be confined to the corruption that is linked specifically to the targeted organised criminal activities and not to the broader occurrence of corruption in the public and private sectors of the member states. Nevertheless, considerable scope would be provided for greater co-operation amongst regional police agencies in anti-corruption work and other international law enforcement agencies. Such international co-operation would best be channelled through SARPCCO and not merely on a bilateral basis to one or more of the member states.

However, a prerequisite for progress in this area would be a very clear decision by SARPCCO, i.e. the police chiefs of the region, that as a matter of policy, future joint operations will also focus on corruption. To date no such a decision appears to have been taken.

3.2. Strengthening the hand of SADC governments in countering corruption

The intensity with which law enforcement agencies in Southern Africa (and probably elsewhere in the world) target corruption, is often related to the commitment and political will which their governments display in effectively combating it. Police agencies tend to view corruption as a law enforcement issue rather than as a phenomenon that also impacts on governance and economic well-being. It is therefore the responsibility of governments to ensure that the full consequences of corruption for a society are constantly highlighted and that police agencies are given a broad mandate to counter it.

There are governments in the region that have in the past not displayed a strong commitment to addressing corruption. Serious allegations of corruption in government circles and in the business sectors of some states are widespread. Police agencies that do not receive the necessary backing from their governments to fully investigate all serious allegations of corruption are unlikely to do so on their own initiative.

However, there are some indications of a new regional commitment by governments to combat corruption wherever it occurs. The Draft SADC Protocol against Corruption is evidence of this. The test of the political will and the commitment by governments will lie in the determination that they display in implementing the protocol.

The protocol, once approved, will hopefully receive the full backing of the international community. Every effort should be made to assist SADC countries to implement it. The protocol provides a number of entry points for co-operation with international law enforcement agencies that are prepared to assist SADC countries to implement it. The Conference of States Parties will be an important one. This structure will oversee the implementation of the protocol and will have responsibilities such as:

1. Organising training programmes as and when appropriate;

2. Evaluating programmes to be put in place and a programme of co-operation for the implementation of the protocol;

3. Providing any other related assistance to states parties as and when appropriate.

Assistance and co-operation from international law enforcement agencies at an early stage could play a significant role in strengthening the arm of SADC and the Committee of States Parties in implementing the protocol and thereafter combating corruption more effectively.

3.3. Addressing the weak resource base in the region

Reference has already been made to the fact that some SADC countries are amongst the poorest in the world. In countries such as Mozambique and Angola, years of civil war and conflict have exacerbated the general lack of skills and resources that the region presently experiences.

Account must also be taken of the fact that, in comparison with some of the other crime categories, corruption has not been perceived by all the police agencies as a major threat to their state. In a survey conducted with the assistance of nine police agencies in Southern Africa during 2000, it appeared that as far as organised crime was concerned, the following crime categories were perceived by the police agencies to constitute the most serious threat to their respective countries[4]:

*   Motor vehicle theft and high-jacking

*   Robbery

*   Drug trafficking

When prioritising the allocation of scarce resources and the training of investigators, police agencies will have focused on the above priority crimes rather than on

---

[4]   The findings of this survey are published in P. Gastrow, *Organised Crime in the SADC Region: Police Perceptions*, ISS Monograph no. 60, Institute for Security Studies, Pretoria, 2001.

corruption. These policing priorities could partly explain the lack of training, resources and personnel in many of the anti-corruption units of police agencies in the region. International assistance that is provided in this field could vary from country to country but is likely to be required primarily in the field of training and the provision of expertise.

A question that will arise is: should international police assistance to the Southern African region be co-ordinated and multilateral or are bilateral programs preferable? The answer is probably that bilateral as well as co-ordinated multilateral assistance programmes would be appropriate. The needs are so overwhelming that the region is likely to welcome any assistance. Most countries have benefited from ongoing bilateral assistance programmes, although in some cases the assistance packages were clearly more suited to the conditions prevailing in the donor country than in the recipient country. Whilst the benefits of bilateral co-operation programmes cannot be refuted, they sometimes tend to ignore the fact that there are now regional structures such as SARPCCO in place that should in future become part of such programmes. Multilateral regional co-operation arrangements should therefore receive more serious consideration than in the past.

The region as a whole, as distinct from some of the individual countries, is likely to benefit more from well considered and co-ordinated international assistance programmes that are channelled through regional structures such as SARPCCO or the SADC Legal Sector. Such an approach should be informed by a regional assessment of needs that is undertaken by the regional players themselves. The regional actors will therefore have to undertake their own co-ordination and prioritisation in order to facilitate international co-operation. Such an approach is preferable to the one where every member state prepares its own "wish list" for international assistance and co-operation.

If regional structures such as SARPCCO and the SADC Legal Sector were to provide the necessary co-ordination for the recipient states, who would provide the co-ordination for the provider states? In the absence of an international agreement that focuses on law enforcement co-operation in the anti-corruption field, it will be difficult to provide such co-ordination. One possibility could be to explore whether Interpol, with its international reach, could contribute towards such international co-ordination. However, the soon to be negotiated United Nations Convention against Corruption is likely to provide the most comprehensive and effective structures for future international co-operation. Interpol is well placed to undertake some of the responsibilities for international co-operation under such a convention.

3.4. The potential for overlap and duplication by the SADC Legal Sector and SARPCCO

Some homework needs to be done within the Southern African region to facilitate improved international co-operation. At present the regional organisation of police chiefs, namely SARPCCO, has the mandate to promote police co-operation within the SADC region. However, the regional structure that has the mandate to negotiate and then implement the Draft SADC Protocol against Corruption is the SADC Legal Sector. Even though this Sector is likely to disappear soon, as a result of the restructuring of SADC structures, the protocol is likely to continue to be the responsibility of the Ministers of Justice in the region and not the police chiefs or their Ministers.

Those governments or international organisations that plan to provide international law enforcement co-operation to the SADC region in future, will therefore be faced with two regional structures that are active in the anti-corruption field. This could lead to confusion and complicate international efforts to assist. The onus is clearly on SADC countries to address this apparent overlap and to ensure that the current restructuring process produces very clear points of contact for purposes of international co-operation to combat corruption and clear areas of responsibility for the various regional structures.

4. Concluding comments

The need for improved international law enforcement co-operation in combating corruption in the Southern African region is very apparent. Not only does the region have serious resource constraints but it also suffers from a perception that corruption is growing. The annual corruption perception index (CPI) compiled by Transparency International shows that the general trend in Southern Africa is one of higher levels of perceived corruption rather than declining ones.[5]

Improved international co-operation with the law enforcement agencies of Southern African States will strengthen the hand of those who are committed to

---

5   2000 TI Corruption Perceptions Index: http://www.transparency.de/documents/cpi/2000/ cpi2000.html (accessed May 2001). In a ranking system of 1 to 90, the results for Southern Africa are as follows (the 1999 and 1998 rankings respectively appear in brackets): Botswana 26 (24) (23), Namibia 30 (29) (29), South Africa 34 (34) (32), Malawi 43 (45) (45), Zimbabwe 65 (45) (43), Zambia 57 (56) (52), Tanzania 76 (93) (81), Mozambique 81 (–) (–), and Angola 85 (–) (–).

combating corruption more effectively. Such improved co-operation will result in the adoption of international best practises, improved training standards and the provision of some essential resources. The following are some general recommendations about steps that could be taken to achieve these objectives:

1. *Improved co-operation with SARPCCO*:
   The operational anti-corruption components that are to be attached to SARPCCO joint operations should be established by SARPCCO as soon as possible. International law enforcement co-operation with SARPCCO could then commence in earnest with assistance that would lead to the provision of best practice advice, skills training, and the provision of resources such as equipment and experts.

2. *Assistance in implementing the new SADC Protocol against Corruption*:
   A key entry point for future international co-operation against corruption in Southern Africa will be the soon to be approved SADC Protocol against Corruption. International organisations and law enforcement agencies should aim at linking up with the SADC Legal Sector and the Committee of States Parties at an early stage in order to assist in the implementation process of the protocol.

3. *More emphasis on co-ordinated international co-operation*:
   Whilst bilateral anti-corruption assistance programmes often address the needs of the specific country concerned, the Southern African region as a whole would benefit more from international law enforcement co-operation programmes that are well co-ordinated and that are channelled through regional structures such as SARPCCO or the SADC Legal Sector. This would enhance the ability of the region to jointly combat corruption more effectively on a regional level. The proposed United Nations Convention against Corruption could play and important role in facilitating international co-operation between law enforcement agencies in combating corruption.

4. *SADC to provide clear points of regional contact and areas of responsibility*:
   Countries in the Southern African Development Community (SADC) need to address the apparent overlap between SARPCCO and the SADC Legal Sector as regards corruption/law enforcement matters and ensure that clear regional points of contact and areas of responsibility are demarcated to facilitate improved international law enforcement co-operation.

CHAPTER 28

The Repatriation of Embezzled State Funds

Hairat Balogun

1. Introduction

The world has in recent times been plagued by serious offences which require very special and concerted attention because of their devastating effect on the world economy and on image especially. The most devastating of these offences have been drugs and financial crimes, particularly corruption and embezzlement of public funds. It appears that the response the world over has been to fight these crimes with tougher new legislative and institutional measures so sufficiently stringent and intimidating that if properly enforced and monitored, total eradication, or at least significant reduction, would have been achieved.

The effect of corruption on the world economy has been as devastating as the much-dreaded Acquired Immune Deficiency Syndrome (AIDS). It is therefore of utmost importance that the world joins hands in combating corruption. Corruption has no national or geographical barriers. It is not enough for one or two countries to be corrupt-free in the global village that the world has become. At no time has the saying that "no country can be an island" been truer than now. It therefore makes economic sense for the world to join hands in combating corruption. An important element of this is the recovery of embezzled funds, the subject of this chapter.

The greatest cause of political instability in most developing countries, and particularly Nigeria, has been attributed to corrupt practices in public service. It was thus considered most appropriate that, rather than making laws against *coups d'état*, developing countries would successfully stabilise politically if corruption is stamped out of their public service. It has long been established that the major reason for staging *coups* has been either that there has been the desire for the government of the day to be violently changed or it has been corrupt and amassed ill-gotten public funds. Invariably the military government that is often established to replace the corrupt civilian government turns out to be even more corrupt.

Cyrille Fijnaut, Leo Huberts (eds.), *Corruption, Integrity and Law Enforcement*, 423-434
©2002 Kluwer Law International, The Hague. Printed in The Netherlands.

The Nigerian experience could be useful in this respect. In Nigeria the war against corruption has now been given legal and institutional weapons particularly under the present democratic dispensation. In June 2000 the President of the Federal Republic of Nigeria signed the Corrupt Practices and Other Related Offences Act into law, by which the Independent Corrupt Practices and Other Related Offences Commission was established.

2. A short history of corruption and anti-corruption legislation

The Penal Codes dating back to the colonial era contain provisions, dealing with the offence of corruption. These provisions came into existence when corruption was no more a serious offence in its incidence and effects than other petty criminal offences. Even then, the provisions suffered from some defects and inadequacies. They dealt mainly with the straightforward cases of demanding, receiving and offering gratification for some favour and did not encompass modern and sophistic-ated methods of corruption.

The Criminal Code provisions were very technical and compartmentalised resulting in so many loopholes that often persons who were obviously guilty of the offences charged were set free on technical grounds, as in the cases of *R. v. Anyaleme* (1943) 9 WACA 23 and *R. v. Marcellus* (1953) 20 NIR 155.

The problem became so pronounced that in the case of *AMAECHI v. Commis-sioner of Police* (1958) NRNLR 124, the court (at p. 126) observed:

> "We would only add, and repeat what has been said in the past, that the law relating to official Corruption and kindred offences is not easy and that the advice of the law officers should be sought, whenever possible before proceedings are taken."

The Criminal Code and the Penal Code only made provisions for offences by public officers. The private sector was not affected. Again, neither law made provision for any special institutional framework for dealing with offences.

2.1. Improvement

In 1966 an effort was made to improve the Criminal Code provisions on corruption and close some of the loopholes. Consequently sections 98, 100 and 114 to 116 were repealed by the Criminal Justice (Miscellaneous) Act (no. 84) of 1966 and replaced by sections 98, (a), (b), (c) and (d). The 1966 efforts at improving the legal framework on corruption remained defective as they still did not encompass private sector corruption; the offence remained unsimplified with very narrow scope.

After the first *coup* in 1966, the military administration promulgated the Public Officers (Investigation of Assets) Decree (no. 5) of 1966. Under the decree the Head of State could require suspected public officers to declare their assets. Competent persons were appointed to verify the declaration of assets. Thereafter a public officer might appear before a tribunal of inquiry which had the power to investigate; whether a public officer had corruptly or improperly enriched himself or any other person while in office, and the extent of any such enrichment.

The onus of proving that there was no unjust enrichment lay on the public officer and forfeiture of his assets could be ordered. The assets of many public officers considered to have corruptly enriched themselves were consequently forfeited.

Despite these efforts, corruption persisted in succeeding military juntas. Of the twelve governors who served at the time, ten subsequently faced corruption charges. During the short-lived General Murtala Mohammed junta, the government was ardently determined to eradicate corruption. Apart from the retrenchment and retirement of some public officers for various reasons (which included corruption), General Murtala Mohammed had promulgated, as a weapon to fight corruption, the Corrupt Practices Decree (no. 38) of 1975. He unfortunately did not live to implement the said decree. The decree, which is now repealed, created new offences thus widening the narrow scope of earlier legislation. It also established a Corrupt Practices Investigation Bureau to investigate suspected cases of corruption and established tribunals to try offences under the decree. The decree was repealed after the assassination of General Murtala Muhammed in 1976.

2.2. Ups and downs

Corruption reached a high peak during the Alhaji Usman Shehu Shagari Regime (1979-1983). In 1982, after three years in office, President Shagari observed that what worried him most amongst the problems confronting his Government was the:

"… moral decadence in our country. There is the problem of bribery, corruption, lack of dedication to duty, dishonesty, and all such vices."

It should be noted that the 1979 Constitution, which existed when this observation was made, provided for a Code of Conduct for Public Officers, a Code of Conduct

Bureau for enforcing " prescribed behaviours" and a Code of Conduct Tribunal to try offences. The government had also proclaimed an ethical revolution and appointed a Minister for National Guidance. These measures proved futile to cope with the problem. Detection and prosecution of offences by highly placed public officers were never pursued. Many civilian governors, ministers, politicians and public servants brazenly indulged in corruption, and publicly flaunted their ill-gotten wealth. And of course the gains were transferred abroad and invested in landed properties shares or spent their time sitting pretty in Swiss and other banks outside Nigeria.

The Buhari/Idiagbon junta, like Murtala Mohammed junta, was determined to fight corruption. Many civilian governors, ministers, public servants were quickly retired, removed from office or imprisoned for various corrupt practices by special tribunals which were set up to try allegations of diverse improprieties. Among those removed from office were judges, magistrates, university lecturers, civil servants and officials of public corporations. Under this junta, between 1984 and 1985, the prohibition against public officers owning foreign accounts was sternly enforced.

Naturally, in the process of purging the public service, many innocent persons were removed from office. The insecurity of tenure of office which this engendered probably helped to further fuel corruption in the public service. The attitude became that of "making hay while the sun shines".

The War against Indiscipline instituted by the junta (the third phase of which was devoted to public enlightenment against corruption) was manifestly beginning to achieve results when the regime was overthrown in 1985.

The 1985 *coup* ushered in the junta of General Ibrahim Babangida, which was notorious for corruption and other related offences. Governors, ministers and other public officers who had been imprisoned for corrupt practices were released, some were pardoned by the state, rehabilitated and have continued to hold high public office. No effective measures were taken to deal with corrupt officials. However it was under this junta that a National Committee on Corruption and Other Economic Crimes in Nigeria (NCCEC) was set up under the chairmanship of Hon. Justice Kayode Eso, now a retired justice of the Supreme Court.

The terms of reference were:

1. Identification of the causes and possible extent of corruption in Nigeria;

2. Examination of deficiencies in the existing legislation on corruption in Nigeria;

3. Suggestion of remedies which could lead to the curbing of the incidence of corruption, including suggested improvements to the existing legislation.

The committee did a great job. It visited Hong Kong, Zambia and Zimbabwe, which were experiencing similar problems of corruption and drew from the experience of these countries in making recommendations. The report of the committee identified the defects in the existing laws (in general terms), set out the causes of corruption in the country and suggested legislative and non-legislative remedies. One remedy proposed by the committee was a *Compendium of Laws on Corruption and Other Economic Crimes*. It actually included in the Report draft legislation which covered the following:

1. Corruption and economic crimes;

2. Independent Commission against Corruption (ICAC);

3. Private investigations;

4. The Corrupt Practices Court.

The Report was submitted to the President, Ibrahim Babangida, on 5 September 1990. The committee expressed doubts whether the report would see the light of the day because of its far-reaching effects. The pessimism was justified, the report was never seen or acted upon. Quite incredibly the draft decree was printed and circulated to states for comments during the Sanni Abacha junta. But as events turned out, this was a mere facade, as no more was made of it. It was probably window dressing to appease the IMF, the Paris Club or other creditors.

Without doubt, the Sanni Abacha junta presided over the worst era of corruption. It would seem unsurpassable – there is little likelihood of Nigeria ever seeing a worse junta again.

By all accounts, the level and intensity of corruption during that regime, apparently spearheaded by the Head of State himself, was only surpassed by his self-succession bid. Reports later became rife that Abacha's agents physically opened and looted the vaults of Central Bank of foreign currency.

2.3. Assessment of the actual situation

The above account shows:

1. That before June 2000 Nigeria had no satisfactory legal provisions for fighting corruption *per se*;

2. The Heads of State who were minded to deal with corruption had to resort to ad hoc measures which sometimes involved draconian laws;

3. That some corrupt Heads of State helped to compound the problem of corruption in the country.

It is clear that a country cannot fight corruption without a satisfactory legal and institutional framework. It is to fulfil this need that the present democratic administration of Chief Olusegun Obasanjo secured the enactment of the Corrupt Practices and Other Related Offences Act, 2000.

This act has widened the scope and simplified provisions on corrupt practices. It has also created institutions that are saddled with the total war against corruption and other related offences. The need to lead by example has also been institutionalised by the present government.

The present government has put in place the Independent Corrupt Practices and Other Related Offences Commission, under the chairmanship of a retired President of the Court of Appeal, with 12 persons of "proven integrity" as members. By virtue of my position as a member of the commission, I have been able to assess the government's determination to wipe out corruption. I can therefore say that there is the political will to back the legal and institutional framework put in place by the government.

3. Recovery of embezzled state funds

The historical background of efforts which past and present Nigerian administrations have made to eradicate corruption shows that making efforts to curb corruption is not entirely new. That corruption is recognised as an evil and must not be tolerated in any society is also a fact. Of concern however is the question whether the present global efforts will yield the much-desired result. The Nigerian government, taking advantage of this global co-operation to fight corruption has been able to show that, just like the AIDS virus, corruption has no barriers in colour, race, tribe or space.

Nigeria has made encouraging gains in the recovery of embezzled state funds. A couple of examples may demonstrate the seriousness of the government in tackling corruption in our system.

(a) The case of the administrative head of the Ministry of Defence (i.e. a permanent secretary) who along with others embezzled over US$ 400 million. In past regimes, because of the lack of political will to eradicate corruption, this matter would have gone unnoticed and unprosecuted. But the permanent secretary was promptly arrested and is being tried at an Abuja High Court for conspiracy and embezzlement.

The sum of N 120 million has already been recovered. Other very senior officers of the ministry involved are on suspension and are co-operating with the security agents in recovering the balance.

(b) The late Head of State, General Sanni Abacha and his family also reportedly spirited away over US$ 2 billion. The government set up a Special Investigation Panel to determine the amount taken, identify where it is hidden and make suggestions for recovery.

After a series of litigation in the British Courts, over US$ 600 million has been recovered from the Abacha empire alone. Other actions have been filed to recover over US$ 800 million. Over DM 500 million has been recovered from the Ajaokuta Steel Company Limited Debt buy-back scam. In the same transaction, the former Minister of Finance refunded the sum of DM 30 million, whilst his colleague in the Ministry of Power and Steel refunded US$ 5 million.

With the assistance of the Financial Services Authority in England, approximately £1.3 billion has been discovered in 23 foreign accounts. Efforts are being made to recover this. Nigeria possesses legal instruments for forfeiture of this amount.

The mutual legal assistance rendered by countries such as the United States, Britain, Switzerland and Germany in the process of recovery of embezzled public funds will no doubt encourage the government of Nigeria in the war against corruption. Hitherto, public officers lived in the belief that the moment they escape from the Nigerian shores with state funds they cannot be reached. But there is more to be done. We seek and must have the co-operation of developed countries in stemming the flow of our scarce resources abroad. We call on these countries to enact stringent conditions that make it less lucrative or profitable to open foreign bank accounts. Questions must be asked as to the sources of the wealth, and a request that the moneys be certified "clean" before a foreign account is opened.

It is hoped that present and future officers would not find the looting of the public treasury lucrative as the world unites to trace and repatriate such loot.

4. Global legal instruments

4.1. Instruments

Recently, there has been an international movement against corruption. There has taken the form of greater co-operation between nations. However, to a large extent, legal co-operation has remained basically at bilateral and regional levels and most of the bilateral co-operation is on crime in general. Examples of such regional legal instruments are:

1. The Inter-American Convention against Corruption by the Organisation of American States of 1996;

2. The United Nations General Assembly Resolution 51/59 "Action against Corruption" and International Code of Conduct for Public Officials of 1996;

3. The United Nations Declaration against Corruption and Bribery in International Commercial Transactions of 1996;

4. The Convention on the Fight against Corruption Involving Officials of the European Communities or Officials of Member States of the European Union of May 1997;

5. IMF Guidelines Regarding Governance Issues of August 1997;

6. The Lima Declaration against Corruption of September 1997;

7. The OECD Convention on Combating Bribery of Foreign Public Officials in International Business Transactions of November 1997;

8. The Council of Europe Agreement Establishing the Group of States against Corruption – GRECO, Resolution (98) 7;

9. The Criminal Law Convention on Corruption by the European Union of October 1998;

10. World Bank Guidelines: Procurement under IBRD Loans and IDA Credits;

11. The Council of Europe–European Commission Outline of the Octopus II Programme – Second Joint Programme between the European Commission and the Council of Europe on the Fight against Corruption and Organised Crime in States in Transition Octopus (98) 59 Revised 2 (Strasbourg, 26 June 1999);

12. The United Nations Convention against Transnational Organised Crime of December 2000 (not yet in force);

13. The various Mutual Legal Assistance Treaties (MLAT) in criminal matters;

14. The FATF – The 40 recommendations of the Financial Action Task Force;

15. GIABA – The Inter-Governmental Action Group against Money Laundering established by the Summit of the Heads of State of West Africa.

4.2. Nigeria

At the height of our "war against hard drugs" some of the strategies employed were provocative, lacking in respect or at times clearly dehumanising, particularly during body searches. Many prospective travellers thought twice about going outside their own countries for fear of violation. There were extreme measures of detection, some of which paid off – Nigeria is no longer synonymous with drug trafficking. I am not here advocating the extreme but suggesting that the countries which benefit most as receivers of embezzled funds should be "punished" or disgraced. After all in criminal law, if there is no receiver of stolen goods, the thief will be out of business.

4.2.1. Joining hands

Over the years, Nigeria has negotiated and entered into some bilateral international agreements with a view to joining hands with other nations in the fight against crime. Nigeria has a subsisting extradition treaty with the United States of America – the Anglo-American Extradition Treaty of 1931 was adopted in Nigeria by virtue of Legal Notice no. 33 of 1967. Nigeria also has a number of extradition treaties with other countries like the Quadripartite Extradition Treaty between Nigeria, Benin, Togo and Ghana. There is also the Commonwealth Scheme on Extradition, which led to the enactment of the earlier Extradition Act no. 87 of 1966. This was subsequently been repealed by the Extradition Act of 1967 in order to make its application more comprehensive. Nigeria entered into the Mutual Legal Assistance Treaty (MLAT) in criminal matters with the United States in 1989. In 1989, the United States Department of Justice and the Federal Ministry of Justice of Nigeria agreed on procedures for mutual assistance in law enforcement matters. There are similar treaties between Nigeria and Switzerland and a number of other countries, of particular importance is the agreement on mutual legal assistance that Nigeria entered into with the United Kingdom, entitled Agreement Concerning the Investigation and Prosecution of Crime and Proceeds of Crime of 1989. There is also the scheme relating to mutual assistance in criminal matters within the Commonwealth countries.

4.2.2. MLATs

Mutual Legal Assistance Treaties (MLATs) are legally binding obligations to assist one or more countries with documents and evidence. A request under an MLAT is transmitted on an administrative level and does not involve nearly as many steps as the traditional letters rogatory. The advantage of MLATs is that the request goes directly from the attorney general of the requesting country to his counterpart in the Ministry of Justice of the requested or the assisting country, both having been designated as the central authorities.

Furthermore, there is a legal obligation on behalf of both countries to co-operate and provide the information, which is a significant improvement on the traditional letter rogatory.

Virtually, every convention on crime to which Nigeria is a party – such as the United Nations Convention on Illicit Traffic of Narcotic Drugs and Psychotropic Substances of 1988 – has provisions on mutual legal assistance as well as extradition, transfer of convicted offenders, confiscation of proceeds of crime and anti-money laundering. The most significant multilateral instrument in the fight against transnational organised crime and corruption is the recently signed United Nations Convention against Transnational Organised Crime of 2000. The convention provides for the criminalisation of corruption, the confiscation and seizure of proceeds derived from crime, the disposal of confiscated assets, mutual legal assistance, the criminalisation of obstruction of justice as well as the disposal of proceeds of crime.

In spite of the constraints experienced by Nigeria in recovering embezzled state funds offshore, these international instruments have facilitated co-operation in the areas of recovery so far made.

5. Investigation and prosecution

The ease with which national boundaries can be crossed and the extraordinary facilities available for rapid communications and travel today combine to make criminals increasingly mobile. The complex structures of modern societies, coupled with the dynamic growth of international exchange provide greater opportunities for international crime; similarly the ease with which monetary instruments are negotiated makes tracking and tracing a Herculean task.

The International Criminal Police Organisation (Interpol) is directed at combating international crime, including corruption. Interpol provides a platform for international police co-operation, which is increasingly necessary in today's world where criminals are not impeded by national frontiers. Law enforcement agencies must work together in spite of the vast differences in law, customs, judicial systems and law enforcement methods.

The law enforcement officials of most countries co-operate with each other, especially in the areas of information and intelligence. There are situations, however, where joint operations need to be undertaken in order to achieve results in an investigation. This includes tracing and identifying illegal transfers of money from one country to another, which would otherwise be difficult to achieve without joint efforts, as provided for in the MLAT.

For Nigeria, the Ajaokuta Steel Company Limited Debt buy-back scam mentioned earlier and the illegal removal of foreign exchange from the Central Bank by the late Head of State General Abacha and government officials, illustrates how Nigeria has enjoyed the co-operation of most countries in the investigation of the complex system of the bank transfers of money. The National Criminal Intelligence Service (NCIS), which is a special unit dealing with financial crime investigation in the United Kingdom, has been very co-operative in the investigations. Switzerland has been equally co-operative – due to their co-operation, looted money has been traced to various accounts all over the world. At least 60 accounts in countries such as the United Kingdom, Switzerland, United States, Brazil and Liechtenstein have been identified.

Although there have been recent attempts by the United Nations to come up with a multilateral instrument against corruption, these have not yet become concrete. The lack of a multilateral instrument against corruption has unduly limited the scope of investigations.

In crimes with transnational dimensions, as stated earlier, corruption has no boundaries. Corruption has been identified as having links with transnational organised crime. Any initiative to tackle it must be stringent – money embezzled or illicitly obtained needs to be laundered through a network of transfers which only an effective international co-operation can unravel, because bilateral co-operation has its roots in the domestic laws of states. A country may therefore refuse assistance by falling back on its domestic legislation to support such a stance. A multilateral instrument would force countries to review their domestic laws in order to harmonise them with their international obligations.

The international co-operation envisaged in the area of prosecution is catered for by the MLATs in criminal matters and the various extradition treaties. This covers a wide range of co-operation in relation to the taking of evidence of witnesses, obtaining information and evidence specified in a request, service of documents, notifying potential witnesses, tracing and restraining, identifying and immobilising criminally obtained assets, executing searches, seizures and assisting in proceedings related to forfeiture, as well as the execution of the final judgement.

As I have stated earlier, the MLAT operates using the very simple procedure of sending a letter stating clearly the request envisaged and the relevant authority to do so, from an attorney general to his colleague in the requested state Ministry of Justice. Nigeria has enjoyed a measure of co-operation in the area of prosecution involving some central personalities in the past administrations.

Nigeria co-operated with Switzerland in 2000 by allowing the evidence of Mohammed Abacha to be taken in prison by a Swiss law officer, under section 18 of the Extradition Act, which provides:

"The testimony of any witness in Nigeria may be obtained in relation to any criminal matter pending in any court or tribunals in another country. In like manner it may be obtained in relation to any civil matter under any law, for the time being in force in any part of Nigeria as regards the taking of evidence there in relation to civil or commercial matters pending before tribunals in other countries. Provided that this section shall not apply in the case of any criminal matter of a political character."

6. Conclusion

There are countries which clog the wheels of recovery of embezzled state funds in their system, and indeed provide safe havens for criminals leaving one wondering if the criminals were not agents of their host countries in the first place. The international community must come up with resolutions discouraging countries from providing safe havens for criminals hiding under favourable local legislation. The efforts of Transparency International at ensuring the endurance of nascent democracies by its total declaration on corruption should be commended.

It is often said that in international politics "there are no permanent friends but permanent interests". Unless efforts are geared towards ensuring that there are no safe havens for stolen state funds, the academic rhetoric on global fight against corruption will amount to a sheer waste of time and resources. For maximum results, nations should be allowed to enjoy membership of "the global village" by being able to trace and recover looted funds in any part of the world. This will discourage present and future corrupt leaders from looting the public treasury with the hope of later enjoying the gains without harassment. I appeal for legislation to be drafted that can be universally applicable to discourage those who receive looted funds.

In the words of President Olusegun Obasanjo, corruption "does not know tribe, race or colour". Let us all join together to eradicate the virus which defaces and mutilates human values, merit, dignity, development and progress. Let us co-operate and develop stringent measures to expose and punish those who feed on embezzled state funds. It is not only fair and just, it makes solid economic sense.

CHAPTER 29

Restitution of Assets and Corruption

Pascal Gossin

1. Introduction

As with other financial places of major importance, Switzerland had to find an answer to the problem of assets embezzled or stolen abroad and subsequently transferred to its territory. The main problem was to find a way to return such assets quickly to their rightful owner abroad, as well as to take into account any justified claim filed in Switzerland against these funds. In 1983, when the Federal Act on International Mutual Assistance in Criminal Matters (IMAC) entered into force, a provision was enacted to regulate the question (article 74 IMAC). Since then, the Swiss authorities have, on numerous occasions, been able to help foreign countries by returning funds to the victims abroad. This more often concerns funds related with corruption or other offences linked to politically exposed persons.

2. Brief international overview

It is only in recent years that the issue of returning stolen or embezzled assets has been tackled within the field of international co-operation in criminal matters. Most of the time, the rightful owners of such funds were obliged to turn to civil law to recover their property.

There were always doubts whether article 3 of the 1959 European Convention on Mutual Assistance in Criminal Matters (ECMA) covered seizures with a view to compensation (*séquestre conservatoire*) in addition to seizures of evidence (*séquestre probatoire*). The Swiss Supreme Court has ruled that the convention applies only to the transfer of evidence.

The absence of an international rule on the surrender of assets has not been compensated for by the Convention on Laundering and the Search, Seizure and Confiscation of the Proceeds from Crime (hereinafter "money laundering convention",

Cyrille Fijnaut, Leo Huberts (eds.), *Corruption, Integrity and Law Enforcement*, 435-442
©2002 Kluwer Law International, The Hague. Printed in The Netherlands.

or MLC), which regulates support for investigations and the confiscation of criminal moneys, but not their handing over. The basic rule established by the convention is the confiscation of assets in the country where they are located, with a (subsequent) possibility under article 15 to share them with another member country which has helped in the confiscation. But the convention permits extensive reservations in favour of domestic law, thereby often lowering its value in individual cases. An enquiry made by the Council of Europe has shown that the vast majority of members has not frequently applied the MLC in practice.

The return of assets to the victims is now regulated in several recent conventions (not yet in force) or draft conventions.[1]

3. Return of assets under Swiss law

3.1. Legal basis

The new rule on the handing over of assets was one of the main changes in the law amending the IMAC of 4 October 1996. It establishes a clear distinction between handing over for the purpose of giving evidence[2] (normally followed by repatriation to Switzerland) and handing over for the purpose of forfeiture or return to the person entitled abroad.[3]

At this stage, it must be expressly pointed out that the handing over of objects or assets within the framework of an extradition procedure is regulated separately (so-called "extradition of objects and assets").[4]

---

[1] Draft Second Additional Protocol to The European Convention on Mutual Assistance in Criminal Matters (article 8); European Union Convention on Mutual Assistance in Criminal Matters (article 8), United Nations Convention for the Suppression of the Financing of Terrorism; United Nations Convention against Transnational Organised Crime.

[2] Article 74 IMAC.

[3] Article 74a IMAC.

[4] *Cf.* article 59 IMAC; note that such handing over of objects and assets can still be effected if the person is not actually extradited, e.g. in case of the escape or death of the person pursued; article 59, para. 7 IMAC. Under article 74a IMAC, the return of objects and assets is mandatory if the conditions for extradition are met.

The question of the handing over of objects and assets is dealt with in many bilateral agreements.[5]

The requirement of reciprocity plays an important role in the handing over of assets.[6] This requirement is however not absolute, and can be left aside depending on the type of offence or on the necessity of combating certain offences.[7]

3.2. Handing over for the purpose of providing evidence

The handing over of objects, documents (originals) or assets to foreign authorities for the purpose of providing evidence is regulated in article 74 IMAC, as well as in most international agreements.[8] As a rule, third parties that have acquired rights in good faith[9] are protected and the requesting state has an obligation to return.[10] There are also rules in favour of authorities.[11] It is worth mentioning here that, in some cases, valuables used as evidence are not returned because they are restored to the victim within the framework of the foreign proceeding.

In practice, as long as the transport costs remain insignificant, surrender only for the purpose of providing evidence poses few problems.

3.3. Handing over for the purpose of forfeiture or return

Problems of greater significance arise when the assets or objects are to be sent to the foreign authorities for the purpose of forfeiture or return to the person entitled (usually the claimant).

The former provision of the IMAC was not precise enough for the Federal Supreme Court, which subsequently clarified the regulation in two well-known

---

5   An actual obligation to surrender exists with Germany, Austria and France. With the United States, an obligation to surrender exists only for objects and assets belonging to the requesting state or one of its member states or cantons.

6   Article 8 IMAC.

7   Article 8, para. 2 IMAC.

8   For example, article 3 and 6 ECMA.

9   Only property rights remain reserved.

10   Article 74, para. 2 IMAC; article 6, para. 2 ECMA.

11   Also, in particular, the oft-cited fiscal liens (*cf.* article 74, para. 4 and article 60 IMAC), which however are of minor significance in practice.

cases.[12] This was one of the main reasons for amending the IMAC. The present provision of article 74a IMAC broadly follows the solution proposed by the Federal Supreme Court.

At first it should be mentioned that handing over for the purpose of forfeiture or return can be influenced by part three (before the judgement[13]) as well as part five (after the judgement[14]) of the IMAC. If an order for judicial assistance fulfils the condition made in part three of the IMAC that the requesting state must have made a final and enforceable judgement before the handing over is executed, this does not change the nature of the case which remains one of providing assistance in accordance with part three of the IMAC.

The description of the assets or objects to be handed over is regulated in article 74a, para. 2. The list is exhaustive and includes the objects used to commit a punishable offence as well as the profits of the offence and any replacement value.[15]

The handing over is ordered with the usual conclusive decree.[16] However, as a rule, the objects are not handed over until the requesting state presents a final and enforceable decision which settles the question of future ownership (return to the state/return to the person entitled).[17] However, the regulation has a certain degree of flexibility as regards two elements:

1. Instead of a *sentence*, it solely refers to a *ruling*, which implies simpler forms of decree (return decisions, etc.);

---

[12] PEMEX (Mexico) and Marcos (Philippines).

[13] This rule, however, is already ambiguous. In practice, judicial assistance is still permissible for the examination of a plea agreement already accepted by a United States court, i.e. an admission of guilt. The revision of sentences was also considered, *cf.* article 5, para. 2 IMAC.

[14] Article 94 *ff.* IMAC (execution of criminal judgements).

[15] According to article 59, para. 2 Swiss Criminal Code; see also article 7, para. 2 and article 13, para. 3 of the money laundering convention. The return of the replacement value has simplified the matter considerably. Now, it is no longer necessary, e.g. in the case of narcotics dealing, to link each entry made to an account with the corresponding sale of drugs.

[16] Article 80d IMAC; see also article 74a, para. 1 IMAC.

[17] This regulation was particularly disputed on the occasion of the amendment of the IMAC. There was no general acceptance of the objections that handing over should not involve a change of ownership and that the requirement of a judgement would result in a substantive judgement that is otherwise not usual in mutual legal assistance law.

2. The condition is not mandatory, but is to be imposed *only as a rule*, which excludes all clear-cut cases.[18]

Stringent requirements are set not only for the handing over to foreign authorities, but also for the release to an entitled person who has acquired rights in good faith in Switzerland.[19] It is therefore possible that the number of (lengthy) clarification procedures by the Swiss assistance authorities will increase in the future.[20]

3.4. Sharing of returned assets

Presumed drug-trafficking profits are as a rule not surrendered to the requesting state according to article 74 IMAC, but are, after a precautionary freeze in the mutual legal assistance proceeding, forfeited by the respective canton according to article 24 of the Federal Law on Narcotics (SR 812.121). As regards international cases, it has – based on solutions in the United States – become common practice to leave the judgement of the entire case to the judicial system of the other country; the authorities of the other state can thereby also be involved in the sharing of the assets returned. Since 1992, there have been around 50 such sharing cases with an overall value of approximately US$ 200 million, also including (a smaller volume of) confiscations in Switzerland with subsequent sharing in favour of the foreign state.

Article 15 of the money laundering convention has formalised this procedure in a legal disposition.[21] The principle is that the distribution between two states is performed in equal parts. The sharing of confiscated assets is now subject to a draft law in Switzerland which will regulate the question on a national and international level.

By encouraging a successful outcome, the sharing instrument has a positive impact on international co-operation.

---

18 The example given in Parliament was the theft of a famous work of art from a well-known museum. A judgement of the Federal Court , relating to a stolen painting, created an initial positive precedent.

19 Article 74a, para. 4, let. c and para. 5 IMAC.

20 Note also article 33a Decree – IMAC, whereby objects and assets that have been secured can be seized.

21 SR 0.311.53; see also the report from the Federal Council of 19.8.92 (BBI 1992 VI 9).

4. Special issues raised by cases involving politically exposed persons

Based on Switzerland's practical experiences, cases related to politically exposed persons (PEPs), raise the following specific problems:

1. *The long time spent as head of a country*: it is very difficult to trace the proceeds from offences committed during the time when the PEP was governing the country (e.g. Mobutu, Suharto, Duvalier). The evidence needed to confiscate such proceeds is often no longer available;

2. *Immunity of the Head of State*: this can hinder or delay prosecution. The Swiss Supreme Court has ruled that, in relation to bank accounts, the immunity privilege can only be disputed if the link between the account and a foreign state was recognisable (i.e. no immunity is granted to an account opened on behalf of a PEP by a straw man or a shell company);

3. *Political stability, human rights issues (procedural guarantees) in the requesting state*: these factors are often precarious and make a return of funds impossible, or at least risky. Moreover, it is not easy to set conditions for the allocation of funds to a sovereign state.

5. Examples of seizure or transfer

There have been several cases in Geneva and in Zurich of seizure or transfer of stolen or embezzled assets. Mostly these involved corruption or embezzlement cases involving politically exposed persons.

Assets under seizure (1 CHF = 0.6 US$)

Nigeria:	around US$ 660,000,000
Peru:	around CHF 200,000,000
Mexico:	around CHF 200,000,000
Ethiopia:	around US$ 8,000,000
France:	around CHF 1,200,000,000
Democratic Republic of Congo:	CHF 9,000,000

Assets returned to countries of origin (examples of two Swiss cantons)

Geneva

France: CHF 1,600,000

Italy: CHF 15,700,000

Spain: CHF 18,260,000

Ukraine: CHF 14,000,000

Argentina: CHF 7,500,000

Brazil: CHF 4,000,000

Nigeria: US$ 66,000,000

Zurich

Philippines: US$ 700,000,000

Russia: CHF 2,000,000

Germany: CHF 300,000

This chapter is taken in part from the Guideline of the Federal Office of Justice on International Mutual Assistance in Criminal Matters, 8th edition 1998 (2001 revised edition); internet: http://www.ofj.admin.ch/themen/rechtshilfe/wegl-str-e.pdf.

CHAPTER 30

Private Policing and Corruption

Michael Levi

1. Introduction

In the economic and white-collar crime area, there has grown up a considerable area of private policing. This is dominated not just by the forensic services arms of the large accountancy firms – particularly Arthur Andersen, Deloitte & Touche, Ernst & Young, KPMG and PricewaterhouseCoopers – who also carry out broad reviews of corruption and money laundering risk for national aid agencies, but also by some specialist security firms which handle corporate security issues from corruption to kidnapping and product contamination. These security firms are often headed by former intelligence and law enforcement staff: worldwide examples include Kroll, Control Risks and Pinkertons, with other firms – Maxima, Risk Advisory Group, Network Security – having international operations but a less extensive presence in the shape of offices overseas.

The purpose of all these firms is to make profits from trouble-shooting clients' problems, and those profits can be made only from clients with an ability and willingness to pay. Anti-fraud and anti-corruption services overlap, since "grand corruption" is often merely a new label attached to traditional elite fraud or even outright theft. The clients are normally private sector firms, but international agencies and nation states can and do enlist their services, which are not cheap.

Some such firms do play a longer-term operational role, such as running customs services in countries with endemic local corruption problems, usually funded by technical assistance programmes of some kind. Cynics may question whether it is in these firms' interests really to sort out more than rotten apple corruption problems, but quite apart from difficulties that *any* firms may have in creating "islands of integrity" in rotten barrel jurisdictions, technical assistance usually is bound to end, and the more far-sighted firms will want to leave some positive legacy behind, if only to demonstrate to others that they can transform problems into solutions.

Cyrille Fijnaut, Leo Huberts (eds.), *Corruption, Integrity and Law Enforcement*, 443-452
©2002 Kluwer Law International, The Hague. Printed in The Netherlands.

2. Paying for investigation

Some corruption cases have identifiable victims, reducing corporate profits by illicit deals with suppliers or purchasers, for example. In other cases, such as "grand corruption" involving corporate bribery overseas, the nation may suffer revenue loss, sometimes immiserising the entire population where the corruption is long term and structural, as in the former Zaire. As a consequence of regulation and official attitudes (whether or not shared by its domestic public and work force), the bribe-payer may also suffer if exposed, and this means that corporations are stakeholders both in corruption and in its prevention. International companies may have a preference to pay for private policing for fraud and corruption, since they retain control over outcomes. Once a case is handed over to a public sector agency such as the police, the company may find itself unable to decide when to stop, and especially in companies (and governments) that have engaged in some malpractices, this may be a matter for concern. Executives or public officials with something to hide will not want to lose control over the investigation, and bad publicity can create reputational risks both for companies and for governments seeking financial aid.

Furthermore, the existence of better paid jobs and long-term specialist careers with large accounting firms serves as a severe drain on skilled public sector police, especially where investigators expect to be transferred to other areas of policing with fewer later job opportunities and in which they are less interested. In the past, there has always been a drift into bank security and other corporate employment post-retirement but in some parts of Europe and North America there is a growing trend for private firms to buy good fraud and corruption investigators out of their government pension schemes at an early stage in their careers. This is partly because in the new era of reputational risk and regulatory sanctions, international firms can suffer from damage in any of the regions of the world in which they operate, generating a higher premium for private trouble-shooters. Thus, the more concern there is about money laundering and fraud against investors, the more likely it is that firms will be employed to check up on staff, to avoid regulatory penalties (including even de-authorisation from conducting investment/banking business).

This has been accompanied by – and is partly the cause as well as the result of – a decline in public policing of fraud (Doig & Levi, 2001). One should distinguish here (a) corruption in the sense of gaining a private profit from violation of purchasing and allied decisions on behalf of an employer (whether private or public) from (b) corruption in gaining private benefit from failing to do one's public duty in relation to some enforcement function, whether this be criminal investigation, the levying of customs duties, etc. (though not charging customs duties is an economic drain on the Treasury in the way that not arresting drugs traffickers or other "service criminals" is not). A stakeholder analysis of interests in preventing transnational bribery, for example, suggests that the bribe-paying firm itself might have no interest in controlling its corruption of others (though there can be internal "leakage" from slush funds, particularly where deniability by senior management is important) unless they anticipate a genuine risk of discovery by third parties who can impose sanctions. Competitors may employ private agencies to discover corruption by others, and intelligence agencies may encounter electronic and other intercept material which may be difficult to do anything with.

Many bribe-receiving countries may have an interest in reducing corruption but to the extent that they are dominated by direct bribe recipients, no action will be taken and there is no interest in paying private investigators to uncover scandals which might lead to the collapse of the government. On the other hand, new regimes – Pakistan and Nigeria are recent prominent examples – may have an interest in full investigation of their predecessors and, if they are not confident in the competence and integrity of their domestic investigators (who are, in a sense, paid for anyway), they may be willing to incur high marginal costs to recover assets and/or to prove a political point against their adversaries.

3. Investigation, risk management and prevention of corruption

It is inconceivable that corruption and fraud prevention policies will be wholly effective: there will always be a felt need by victims and by people in authority to do something more, whether that something takes a criminal route, a regulatory discipline route, or simply a civil compensation route. Research on crime victims and on what they want from the police indicates, *inter alia*, the need for a sympathetic audience who will take the victim's complaints seriously (see Levi & Pithouse, forthcoming), though nearly all research work relates to *individual* victims, not corporate ones. Most of the individual victims interviewed were broadly satisfied that the police took them seriously – though those whose cases had been turned down as a civil matter were less impressed – but the problem remains: on what acts should criminal justice investigators concentrate and on what acts are they likely, left to their own choices, to concentrate?

The priorities and resources of public policing are connected to the growth of private policing of "commercial fraud", which has flourished as public policing of fraud and non-police corruption arguably has declined, though the causal relationship is not as obvious as that might suggest. Corporations may resort to private police or to their own in-house compliance departments partly because they do not trust or have confidence in the skills of the public police: but they also want to use them to keep control.

Private policing is likely to develop further as businesses become more international and operate in emerging markets such as those of Eastern Europe, where the official police may not have the time or expertise or perceived integrity to investigate fraud allegations. Anywhere in the world, firms may want to know how the suspected fraud or error was committed, who is responsible, and whether they can get their money back. This may be done reactively, in response to a detected event, or proactively, as part of a risk management strategy in dealing with markets known or believed to "problem-prone".

For the most part, what is done to the "offenders" is of very secondary concern. Usually, when they report to the authorities, they will do so (or be encouraged to do so by the police) only after they have first paid for some in-house investigation, conducted – in England and Wales – under the codes that accompany the Police and Criminal Evidence Act 1984 if it involves any interviews with suspects. In the case of transnational corruption risks, private investigations may take place to ensure that the company has not paid bribes, thereby violating the United States Foreign Corrupt Practices Act or legislation elsewhere developed in compliance with the 1997 Organisation for Economic Co-operation and Development corruption convention. This is perhaps not usually a matter of morality as it is a matter of avoiding regulatory fines, reputational damage and the threat of international economic incapacitation by the World Bank and other organisations that refuse to grant contracts to firms with a reputation for bribery.

Thus, as with firms and unions that employ compliance officers, sometimes independent firms, to demonstrate to the American courts that they are taking anti-racketeering policy seriously, this represents an extension of the state's interests to the private sector as a form of governance-at-a-distance.

4. Asset recovery strategies and resources and the public-private policing divide

By contrast with the large forensic services firms, smaller private agencies may be more specialised in their orientation, working (though not exclusively) on trademark infringement and other intellectual property "offences", while others carry out "due diligence" enquiries for financial institutions and professionals who want to ensure that the funds they have been asked to deal with are not proceeds of crime, or (like the Dublin-based Interclaim) specialise in asset recovery on behalf of victims, taking a court-approved contingency fee that varies between three-quarters and one percent of the recoveries on the claim. These agencies employ ex-police and customs investigators and lawyers, and some have computer data recovery services and audio laboratories superior to those of fraud squads or public-sector forensic services laboratories. Typically, substantial or sensitive cases are not reported immediately to the police – partly because this can disrupt the business and slow down civil recovery – but are settled with as small losses as possible, though there may be some formal or informal exchange of intelligence between police and private security firms, and there may be a prosecution if the client wants to take the matter further.

This is important not just in a domestic context but also in an international one, as funds may travel through a complex set of difficult-to-penetrate jurisdictions, which may frustrate public asset-freezing activities by rendering them uneconomic, unless there are mechanisms for compensating police or other agencies for investigation costs (Home Office, 1998; PIU, 2000). This question of who pays for investigation and how this is counted in systems like the United Kingdom that are performance indicator-driven is a problem for poor countries and in wealthier jurisdictions where an absolute shortage of competent investigators and lawyers means inevitably that there is a zero-sum game between "incoming assistance requests" and the investigation of "domestic" crimes. There is an urgent need to consider how broader questions of international responsibilities in a globalised enforcement system can be patched into local and nationally generated performance indicators.

The more that the police withdraw from, or choose not to respond to, frauds against major firms, the greater the role of the private investigative sector will be: the fewer the reports made to the police or official regulators, the more limited will be the public sector database upon which employee or director "dangerousness" judgements can be made. In addition to any more general social inequalities generated by private policing (Loader, 1997), one consequence of the privatisation of enforcement (and of non-reporting of fraud, whether or not investigated privately) is that there is no collective record for "society as a whole" upon which to build a risk profile, whether that profile be of an individual or a sort of commercial activity. This can have major consequences for those jurisdictions such as some Caribbean territories and other offshore finance centres where official governmental sanctions, especially convictions, may be needed to justify the refusal to grant a banking or investment services licence to an individual: someone who has paid millions back to intermediaries acting for victims of previous scams may have no such registered misconduct. Thus, at least outside of areas such as credit card fraud and bad debts, where firms keep quite good data, "actuarial justice" is based on even more deeply flawed white-collar crime than other crime data.

Certainly, however important their role as communicators of risks of street and household crime to *individuals* (Ericson & Haggerty, 1997), European or other public police play a very limited role in communicating corruption and fraud risks to business, government or even individuals: "due diligence" specialists, in-house or external, are supplemented by closed user group networks such as the major alcohol, oil and tobacco companies who share risk information, depending on corporate policies and their mutual trust levels (and on personalities). We thus observe the commercial equivalent of what Ericson and Haggerty felicitously described as "the security quilt": in the case of large corporate victims in the United Kingdom, most of the patchwork is supplied by the private sector, with the public police providing a modest processing contribution to "live" cases and a limited intelligence-led surveillance capability for suspected active fraudsters (Ericson & Haggerty, 1997). Thus, the British police have developed formal memoranda of understanding with the Association of British Insurers, the Association for Payment Clearing Services, the British Bankers' Association, etc. for the communication of information, though the amount of information that can be passed back by the police is very limited. It is important not to get this out of context, however. For small businesses and most private individuals, the public police are the first and the last resort, since they do not have either funds or access to the private security infrastructure.

5. Risk and rationality in policing corruption

Issues such as case screening for investigation and prosecution always arouse controversy, as those who formulated the Metropolitan Police charging guidelines in 1994 were made aware. Discretion may be inevitable but even in countries such as The Netherlands, the United Kingdom and the United States, which espouse the "opportunity model" of prosecution, the media, politicians and many of the public feel uncomfortable with the *formal* elucidation of policies that "allow criminals to get away with it" (despite the fact that since their inception, this discretionary justice has been the constant approach both of the revenue departments to tax fraud and of "business regulatory agencies" dealing with health and safety at work and in food, etc.) (Carson, 1974; Cook, 1989; Croall, 1992). Yet whatever the arguments for increasing the size of fraud squads or for detectives generally dealing with corruption and fraud as a higher priority than they currently do, there will never be sufficient staff to deal rapidly and efficiently with all the economic crime around. *De facto*, though the balance shifts by region and by the temperament of case managers, higher priority is given to "deserving victims", who tend not to be either victims or offenders in corruption in the United Kingdom. As for international enquiries, cases that are serious to less developed countries chasing looted funds which are more appropriately described as proceeds of theft or false accounting than corruption, may have quite a low priority to police managers allocating resources according to governmental or local priorities. Consequently, unless aid agencies are willing to devote a proportion of their aid budget to civil and/or criminal asset recovery/prosecution efforts, often outside the donee country, there may be no alternative to international action by the victims of corruption or fraud, *if they have the funds and political/legal standing to act*. This is one reason why – at least outside an Organisation for Economic Co-operation and Development transnational bribery framework – action tends to occur only when a corrupt regime has fallen.

Consideration of the relative desserts and dangerousness of suspected offenders, where identified (as well as their convictability) is a core component of police work that will be accentuated as forces shift towards the targeting of suspects and away from the "reactive" mode of post-complaint investigations. (If taken to extremes, this policy would have significant consequences for resources for investigating major one-off corruption cases and frauds, and for those persistent nationwide cases whose perpetrators are below the threshold for proactive targeting by the National Crime Squad or those fraud squads who have a proactive orientation.) There are tensions here, for example between the aggravated "badness scores" of spendthrift fraudsters who have "lived high off the misery of their victims" on the one hand, and dealing with offenders "who have salted away their assets" – whose recovery would help victims most – on the other. How are future risks from different categories of fraudster to be assessed?

Because of type-variable but low prosecution risks per crime, the study of federal United States offenders by Weisburd *et al.* is not as helpful as it might be in judging deterrence for any sub-set of white-collar criminals: nor is it clear what proportion of their cases might plausibly be described as "serious corruption or fraud" (Weisburd *et al.*, 2001). It seems clear that one of the first priorities is some refinement in micro-classification of corruption, white-collar and corporate criminals. It is not obvious what constitutes "rationality" in the prioritisation of caseloads – which also is a function of the sort of case mix and overall load the investigators have at the time – but the public and those charged with supervising the *inevitable* use of discretion in taking on cases and deciding how much time is allocated to them (and when) should consider more formally than at present some weighting approach.

In the United States, legions of Federal Bureau of Investigation officials worked a decade later on long-defunct savings and loans corruption/fraud cases, whose victims now are "the government" and taxpayers, since the depositors have been repaid by federal insurance (though by the mid-1990s, the Federal Bureau of Investigation had moved on to prioritise medical care and telemarketing fraud cases). Where the regulatory systems have changed to prevent or reduce the risks and losses, the only purpose other than retribution in such prosecutions lies in the possible incapacitation or deterrence of those who would have switched to new "rackets" and therefore represent a continuing danger to the financial system. Corruption that may have a more abstract effect on public confidence in the economic, legal or administrative system, or frauds against business that may have a serious impact upon employment in an area, may be neglected by default, because no-one has thought through their implications.

However, media and local political campaigns can alter those priorities considerably. Indeed, as with police and prosecution priorities generally, national standardisation may not be desirable, since there may be legitimate local variations in sentiment towards particular crimes, and using simple criteria such as money lost provides too London-centred a focus, as frauds that are very modest by London standards may be enormous in local terms. (Non-British readers may apply this analogy to their own metropolitan/non-metropolitan circumstances.) Sometimes, as in the Belgian Lernout & Hauspie case where there have been allegations of serious inflation of sales of voice-activated electronics, major scandals can occur well away from major metropolitan areas partly because it is precisely there that the need for dynamic employment schemes is most needed and least likely to receive critical scrutiny because of that need. Besides, the notion of "crimes" being in one place is often outmoded: victims, offenders and the location of crime proceeds may be hugely variable.

The issue of "weighting seriousness and complexity" requires sophisticated, time-consuming analysis. But in the absence of particular dedicated funds available from aid budgets, and specific priorities for the police or anti-corruption agencies, private policing is likely to continue to rise to protect businesses from reputational and financial damage, even where corrupt acts are done on behalf of the company (and for the careers and short-term bonuses of sales staff and directors).

6. Concluding remarks

There are arguments for maximising potential offender uncertainty as a counterweight to the desirability of maximising victim certainty and to the unorthodox possibility of deliberately shifting offender choice to areas of criminal (as well as non-criminal) behaviour viewed (though by whom?) as being less harmful. But to improve "criminal market information" so that both potential victims (where corruption has identifiable victims) and potential offenders can make rational choices (given the limited options provided by their circumstances) seems to be a reasonable goal. The devious possible strategy of informing victims without informing offenders seems unlikely to work, partly because they may be the same or similar people/organisations, and partly because information leakage is almost certain to occur in as widespread a range of criminal markets as corruption and fraud represents.

With the growth of both international economic crime and international police and judicial co-operation, there are more minor but still problematic issues such as what priority to give to requests for information from overseas, compared with one's own domestic caseload. Should overseas enquiries be given precisely the same weighting as they would attract if the case was a local one, or should they rank higher or lower than that? Where there is pressure to make policing more local and there are tight budgets, cases are likely to be screened out in favour of frauds with greater local impact that can be investigated more cheaply. In the process, systemic "needs" may be neglected because they are no-one's exclusive concern. However, quite apart from the fact that conventional approaches to "organised crime" normally allocate a subsidiary role to crime by and against business, most fraud and corruption cases are likely to have a national or international component such as will require investigation outside force boundaries, so parochial concerns about the delivery of service to *local* "consumers" will still have a negative effect on resource availability to conduct many investigations.[1]

More profoundly, perhaps, there is also an issue about the extent to which the public police are willing to provide a high level of investigative support for corporate victims in local, national or international cases, or whether they will (or should) prefer to continue with a more populist approach, focusing largely on "traditional" crimes against individuals and the simpler forms of crimes against organisations. It is within this context that I expect the private investigation of corruption to continue in "grand corruption" and internal corporate corruption cases, whether intended to generate business for corporations or not, and whether involving leading politicians or their families or not.

Though the forensic services units of private accountancy firms get more funding and requests from the public sector and police in The Netherlands than elsewhere – from the United Kingdom, for example – the plethora of international initiatives

---

[1] Although the American authorities have a more developed approach to protecting their business interests overseas, and, at least in theory, some emerging market countries see protection of foreign companies as an important part of their effort to attract inward investment by offering a secure operational context.

against corruption in recent times is likely to intensify the demands for assistance in a tight-supply market (Levi & Raphael, 1999). Current proposals to establish an international escrow account in which to place funds recovered from dictators without having to hand them back to possibly corrupt successors represent one element that could cut into private sector involvement in legal recoveries. But the public police will have to improve their motivation, their skills and confidence in them very substantially before they are able to re-appropriate this arena of crime control for the public rather than the private.

References

Carson, W., "Symbolic and instrumental dimensions of early factory legislation", in R. Hood (ed.) *Crime, Criminology, and Public Policy*, Heinemann, London, 1974, pp. 107-138.

Cook, D., *Rich Law, Poor Law*, Open University Press, Milton Keynes, 1989.

Croall, H., *White-Collar Crime*, Open University Press, Milton Keynes, 1992.

Ericson, R. & K. Heggarty, *Policing the Risk Society*, Clarendon Press, Oxford, 1997.

Home Office, *Third Report: Criminal Assets*, Home Office Working Group on Confiscation, 1998.

Loader, I., "Private Security and the Demand for Protection in Contemporary Britain", *Policing and Society*, 7, 1997, pp. 143-162.

Levi, M. & A. Doig, "New Public Management, Old Populism and the Policing of Fraud", *Public Policy and Administration*, 16, 2001, pp. 91-113.

Levi, M. & M. Raphael, "Anti-Corruption – a Signpost for Transactional Lawyers", *Business Law International,* 1, 1999, pp. 80-107.

Levi, M. & A. Pithouse, *White-Collar Crime and its Victims. The Media and Social Construction of Business Fraud*, Clarendon Press, Oxford, forthcoming.

PIU, *Recovering the Proceeds of Crime*, Performance and Innovation Unit, Cabinet Office, London, 2000.

Weisburd, D. & E. Waring, with E. Chayet, *White-Collar Crime and Criminal Careers*, Cambridge University Press, Cambridge, 2001.

About the Authors

Gemma Aiolfi is Programme Officer, OECD Working Group on Bribery in International Business Transactions, Paris, France

Peter Alldridge is Reader in Law at Cardiff Law School, Cardiff, United Kingdom.

Frank Anechiarico is Maynard Knox Professor of Government and Law at Hamilton College in New York, United States.

Hairat Balogun is former Attorney General of Lagos State and Former Chairman of the Body of Benchers and presently Executive Member of the Independent Corrupt Practices and Other Related Offences Commission, Abuja, Nigeria.

Willy Bruggeman is Senior Deputy Director of Europol, The Hague, The Netherlands.

Amy Comstock is Director of the United States Office of Government Ethics, Washington, DC, United States.

Peter Csonka is Principal Administrator at the Economic Crime Division, Directorate General I (Legal Affairs), Council of Europe, Strasbourg Cedex, France.

Benoît Dejemeppe has been Chief Public Prosecutor in Brussels since 1989. He is also part-time teacher at the Facultés universitaires Saint-Louis, Brussels, Belgium.

Willy Deridder is the Executive Director of the International Criminal Police Organisation, Interpol, Lyons, France. Prior to this assignment he held the post of a Lieutenant General in the Belgian Gendarmerie.

Alan Doig is Professor of Public Services Management and Head of the Fraud Management Studies Unit, Teesside Business School, University of Teesside, United Kingdom.

Jan d'Oliveira is Deputy National Director of the National Prosecuting Authority, Pretoria, South Africa.

Cyrille Fijnaut is Professor of Comparative Law at the Faculty of Law, Tilburg University, The Netherlands, Extraordinary Professor of Criminology and Criminal Law at the Faculty of Law of the K.U. Leuven, Belgium, and Visiting Professor of Law at the New York University School of Law, New York City, United States.

Jorge Garcia-Gonzalez is the Director of the Department of Legal Co-operation and Information for the Organisation of American States.

Peter Gastrow is Head of the Organised Crime and Corruption Programme of the Institute for Security Studies in Cape Town. He has practised law, been a parliamentarian, and served as adviser to the South African Minister for Safety and Security.

Pascal Gossin works at the Federal Department for Justice and Police of the Ministry of Justice, Switzerland.

Michael Grotz is Head of the European and Mulitlateral Co-operation in Criminal Matters section at the Federal Ministry of Justice, Germany. In the past years he was head or member of the German delegation to various bodies of the Council of Europe, the European Union and the United Nations.

Barbara Huber is Senior Research Fellow at the Max Planck Institute of Foreign and International Criminal Law, Freiburg, Germany.

Leo Huberts is Professor in Police Studies and Criminal Justice at the Department of Public Administration and Communication Sciences, Vrije Universiteit, Amsterdam, The Netherlands.

James Jacobs is Warren E. Burger Professor of Law at the School of Law at New York University, New York City, United States.

Michael Johnston is Professor of Political Science at Colgate University in Hamilton, New York, United States. He has been a consultant to several international organisations, and is a former director of Colgate's Center for Ethics and World Societies.

Petter Langseth worked on public sector management, governance and anti-corruption with the World Bank for twenty years in Latin America, Africa, Eastern Europe and the Middle East. Since October 1999 he is Programme Manager for the United Nations' Global Programme against Corruption, at the Centre for International Crime Prevention (CICP), located in Vienna, Austria.

Keonjoo Lee is Senior Prosecutor at the Ministry of Justice, Seoul, Korea.

Michael Levi is Professor of Criminology at Cardiff University, United Kingdom.

Robert Mischkowitz is with the Bundeskriminalamt, Wiesbaden, Germany.

Manfred Möhrenschlager is Head of the Combat against Economic, Computer, Environmental and Corruption Criminality by Criminal Law Section in the Federal Ministry of Justice, Berlin, Germany.

Jon Moran is Lecturer in Criminology and Criminal Justice, University of Glamorgan, United Kingdom.

Manfred Nötzel is Head of the Anti-Corruption Department of the Public Prosecutor's Office in Munich, Bavaria, Germany.

Mark Pieth is Professor of Criminal Law and Criminology at the University of Basle, Switzerland, and Chairman of the OECD Working Group on Bribery in International Business Transactions.

Grant Poulton is Executive Director on Corruption Prevention, Education and Research of the New South Wales Independent Commission against Corruption, Sydney, Australia.

Nicolas Queloz is Professor of Criminal Law and Criminology at the University of Fribourg, Switzerland.

Adi Soetjipto is Dean of the University of Trisakti, Faculty of Law, and former chairman of the Joint Investigation Team for Fighting Corruption, Indonesia.

Oliver Stolpe works for the United Nations' Global Programme against Corruption at the Centre for International Crime Prevention, located in Vienna, Austria.

Michael Taylor is Detective Superintendent at the Metropolitan Police Service, London, United Kingdom.

Tom Vander Beken is Professor at the Law Faculty of Ghent University, and Director of the Institute for International Research on Criminal Policy, Belgium.

Guy de Vel is Director General of Legal Affairs at the Council of Europe, Strasbourg Cedex, France.

Index